AUTHORSHIP AND AUTHORITY IN KIERKEGAARD'S WRITINGS

Also Available from Bloomsbury

Blake and Kierkegaard, James Rovira
Kierkegaard, Metaphysics and Political Theory, Alison Assiter
Errant Affirmations, David J. Kangas
Fiction and Art, edited by Ananta Sukla
Beckett's Words, David Kleinberg-Levin
Poetry and Revelation, Kevin Hart
Kierkegaard, Julia Watkin
Kierkegaard's "Fear and Trembling": A Reader's Guide, Clare Carlisle

AUTHORSHIP AND AUTHORITY IN KIERKEGAARD'S WRITINGS

Edited by

Joseph Westfall

BLOOMSBURY ACADEMIC

LONDON • NEW YORK • OXFORD • NEW DELHI • SYDNEY

BLOOMSBURY ACADEMIC
Bloomsbury Publishing Plc
50 Bedford Square, London, WC1B 3DP, UK
1385 Broadway, New York, NY 10018, USA

BLOOMSBURY, BLOOMSBURY ACADEMIC and the
Diana logo are trademarks of Bloomsbury Publishing Plc

First published in Great Britain 2019
Paperback edition published 2020

Cover design: Irene Martinez-Costa
Cover image: Soren Kierkegaard (b/w photo) / © SZ Photo / Bridgeman Images

A catalogue record for this book is available from the British Library.

A catalog record for this book is available from the Library of Congress.

ISBN: HB: 978-1-3500-5595-7
       PB: 978-1-3501-6381-2
       ePDF: 978-1-3500-5596-4
       eBook: 978-1-3500-5597-1

Typeset by Integra Software Services Pvt. Ltd.

To find out more about our authors and books visit www.bloomsbury.com
and sign up for our newsletters.

In Memoriam

Robert L. Perkins
June 23, 1930–March 20, 2018

A True Scholar, Teacher, and Friend

CONTENTS

Contributors   ix
Acknowledgments   xii
A Note on Citations   xiv
Abbreviations   xv

INTRODUCTION: ON KIERKEGAARD'S WORK
AS AN AUTHOR
   Joseph Westfall   1

KIERKEGAARD QUA AUTHOR: "LIKE THE GUADALQUIBIR RIVER"
   Sylvia Walsh   27

RHETORIC AND UNDERSTANDING: AUTHORSHIP
AS CHRISTIAN MISSION
   Robert C. Roberts   41

INSIDE THE ESCRITOIRE: ON KIERKEGAARD'S
EROTIC THEORY OF COMMUNICATION
   Michael Strawser   59

KIERKEGAARD'S SCENE CHANGES: AUTHORSHIP
AS THEATRICAL PRACTICE
   Sophie Wennerscheid   75

KIERKEGAARD THE HUMORIST
   M. G. Piety   91

A DESIRE TO BE UNDERSTOOD: AUTHORSHIP AND
AUTHORITY IN KIERKEGAARD'S WORK
   Daniel Berthold   107

ILLEGIBLE SALVATION: THE AUTHORITY OF
LANGUAGE IN *THE CONCEPT OF ANXIETY*
   Sarah Horton   121

THE VERY TANG OF LIFE: LYRICAL JESTING
IN KIERKEGAARD'S *POSTSCRIPT* TITLE
   Edward F. Mooney   139

"I CAME TO CARTHAGE"; "SO I ARRIVED IN BERLIN":
FLEEING, ESCAPE, AND AUTOBIOGRAPHICAL MEMORY
IN AUGUSTINE'S *CONFESSIONS* AND KIERKEGAARD'S *REPETITION*
    Eric Ziolkowski   153

KIERKEGAARD ON ANDERSEN AND THE ART OF STORYTELLING
    Eleanor Helms   173

ON "S.K.": DECONSTRUCTING SIGNATURE(S)
IN KIERKEGAARD AND SARAH KOFMAN
    Joseph Westfall   193

KIERKEGAARD—WHAT "KIND OF" WRITER? A DIALOGUE
    George Pattison   215

Index   229

CONTRIBUTORS

Daniel Berthold is Chair of the Department of Philosophy at Bard College. He is author of many articles on Kierkegaard, Hegel, Nietzsche, Heidegger, Camus, and topics in environmental ethics. His most recent book is *The Ethics of Authorship: Communication, Seduction, and Death in Hegel and Kierkegaard* (Fordham 2011).

Eleanor Helms received her Ph.D. from Fordham University in 2011 and is Associate Professor of Philosophy at California Polytechnic State University in San Luis Obispo. Her research interests include nineteenth- and twentieth-century Continental philosophy and aesthetics, primarily phenomenology and existentialism, with articles published in *Res Philosophica* (winner of 2013 essay prize) and *Philosophy and Literature,* as well as chapters in *Kafka's Creatures: Animals, Hybrids, and Other Fantastic Beings* (eds. Marc Lucht and Donna Yarri, Lexington Books, 2010) and *Narrative, Identity, and the Kierkegaardian Self* (eds. John Lippitt and Patrick Stokes, Edinburgh University Press, 2015). Her current research examines the role of authorial intent, beliefs, perception, and imagination in literary fiction.

Sarah Horton is a doctoral student in philosophy at Boston College. Her areas of interest include twentieth-century and contemporary French philosophy, desire, ethics, and the philosophy of literature. She is currently working on a phenomenology of friendship.

Edward F. Mooney is author of several Kierkegaard books, including *Selves in Discord and Resolve* (1996), *On Søren Kierkegaard* (2007), *Excursions with Kierkegaard* (2012), and *Knights of Faith and Resignation* (1991). He is also author of *Lost Intimacy in American Thought* (2009) and *Excursions with Thoreau* (2015). He is Emeritus professor in Philosophy and Religion, Syracuse University, and has taught at Hebrew University and Tel Aviv University.

George Pattison is 1640 Professor of Divinity in the University of Glasgow, having previously taught in the universities of Cambridge, Aarhus, and Oxford. He has published extensively on Kierkegaard, including *Kierkegaard and the Quest for Unambiguous Life* (2013) and *Kierkegaard and the Theology of the Nineteenth Century* (2012). He is also coeditor of the *Oxford Handbook of Kierkegaard* (2013).

M. G. Piety is Associate Professor of Philosophy at Drexel University. She has published numerous scholarly articles in professional journals and books, as well as popular articles and essays. Her translations of Søren Kierkegaard's *Repetition* *and Philosophical Crumbs* for Oxford University Press appeared in 2009, and her book *Ways of Knowing: Kierkegaard's Pluralist Epistemology was published by Baylor* University Press in 2010. Piety is a frequent contributor to the online political journal *CounterPunch*, and she is currently working on a book for Gegensatz Press entitled *Fear and Dissembling: The Copenhagen Kierkegaard Controversy*.

Robert C. Roberts writes on the thought of Kierkegaard and the moral psychology of emotions, virtues, and vices. He is the author of *Faith, Reason, and History: Rethinking Kierkegaard's Philosophical Fragments* (Mercer University Press, 1986), *Emotions: An Essay in Aid of Moral Psychology* (Cambridge University Press, 2003), *Spiritual Emotions* (Eerdmans, 2007), *Emotions in the Moral Life* (Cambridge University Press, 2013), and coauthor with W. Jay Wood of *Intellectual Virtues: An Essay in Regulative Epistemology* (Oxford University Press, 2007). He is currently editing, with Daniel Telech, *The Moral Psychology of Gratitude* (Rowman and Littlefield) and writing a book tentatively titled *Kierkegaard's Psychology of Character* (Eerdmans). He has also published numerous articles on Kierkegaard's thought, emotions, and virtues and vices. He has taught philosophy at Western Kentucky University, Wheaton College, and Baylor University. He retired in 2015 from the Baylor philosophy department.

Michael Strawser is Chair of the Department of Philosophy and Associate Professor of Philosophy at the University of Central Florida. His primary philosophical interests and research areas are the philosophy of love, ethics, and the history of modern and contemporary philosophy with emphasis on Søren Kierkegaard, Baruch Spinoza, and the Continental tradition. He has previously published *Both/ And: Reading Kierkegaard from Irony to Edification* (Fordham University Press, 1997), *Asking Good Questions: Case Studies in Ethics and Critical Thinking* (with Nancy Stanlick, Hackett Publishing, 2015), and *Kierkegaard and the Philosophy of Love* (Lexington Books, 2015).

Sylvia Walsh is currently Scholar in Residence at Stetson University, and she has been an adjunct professor and visiting associate professor in philosophy at Stetson University in DeLand, Florida, since 1989. Previously she taught religious studies at Clark College and Emory University in Atlanta, GA. She holds an A.B. degree from Oberlin College, M.A. in Religion from Yale University, and Ph.D. from Emory University. She is the author of *Kierkegaard: Thinking Christianly in an Existential Mode* (Oxford, 2009), *Living Christianly: Kierkegaard's Dialectic of Christian Existence* (Penn State, 2005), and *Living Poetically: Kierkegaard's Existential Aesthetics* (Penn State, 1994); coeditor and translator of *Kierkegaard's Fear and Trembling* (Cambridge, 2006); editor and translator of *Kierkegaard's Discourses at the Communion on Fridays* (Indiana University Press, 2011); and coeditor of *Feminist Interpretations of Søren Kierkegaard* (Penn State, 1997). She has presented numerous scholarly papers at regional, national, and international meetings and has published many articles and reviews in academic journals and books. In 1985, she was selected to direct the first National Endowment for the Humanities

Summer Seminar for College Teachers on Kierkegaard. She has served twice as president of the Søren Kierkegaard Society in the United States and has been a member of the advisory board of the *International Kierkegaard Commentary*, as well as co-chair of the Kierkegaard, Religion, and Culture Group in the American Academy of Religion. In retirement, she is active in political activities and continues to do research and writing on Kierkegaard.

Sophie Wennerscheid is Professor in Scandinavian Literature at Ghent University, Belgium. She is the author of the books *Das Begehren nach der Wunde. Religion und Erotik im Schreiben Kierkegaards* (Desire for the Wound. Religion and Eroticism in Kierkegaard's Writing, 2008) and *"Close Your Eyes". Phantasma, Kraft und Dunkelheit in der skandinavischen Literatur* ("Close Your Eyes". Phantasm, Force and Darkness in Scandinavian Literature, 2014). Together with Armen Avanessian, she edited the book *Kierkegaard and Political Theory. Religion, Aesthetics, Politics and the Intervention of the Single Individual* (2014). Other research interests include studies on sexuality and technology, science fiction film and literature, and minority and migrant literature.

Joseph Westfall is Associate Professor of Philosophy at the University of Houston-Downtown. He is the author of *The Kierkegaardian Author: Authorship and Performance in Kierkegaard's Literary and Dramatic Criticism* (Walter de Gruyter, 2007), as well as numerous articles on Kierkegaard, Nietzsche, twentieth-century Continental philosophy, aesthetics, and the philosophy of the arts. He is the editor of *The Continental Philosophy of Film Reader* (Bloomsbury, 2018) and coeditor of *Foucault and Nietzsche: A Critical Encounter* (Bloomsbury, 2018). He also serves on the editorial board of the journal *Evental Aesthetics* and is a member of the steering committee of the Kierkegaard, Religion, and Culture Group of the American Academy of Religion.

Eric Ziolkowski, H. P. Manson Professor of Bible, and Head of the Department of Religious Studies at Lafayette College, is author of numerous books, essays, and articles in religion and literature. His two most recent books are both edited volumes: *The Bible in Folklore Worldwide*, vol. 1: *A Handbook of Biblical Reception in Jewish, European Christian, and Islamic Folklores* (Berlin: De Gruyter, 2017) and *Kierkegaard, Literature, and the Arts* (Evanston, IL: Northwestern University Press, 2018), a sequel to his monograph with the same press, *The Literary Kierkegaard* (2011). He has lectured widely in North America, Great Britain, and Western Europe, as well as Poland, Australia, and China (Beijing, Shanghai, Suzhou, and Hong Kong). Having served for eight years (2004-2012) as North American Senior Editor of *Literature and Theology: An International Journal of Religion, Theory and Culture* (Oxford), he is also main editor of "reception" for the prospective thirty-volume *Encyclopedia of the Bible and Its Reception* (Berlin: De Gruyter, 2009–; fifteen volumes published to date) and coedits two book series: Studies in Religion and the Arts (Leiden: Brill) and Studies of the Bible and Its Reception (Berlin: De Gruyter).

ACKNOWLEDGMENTS

I would like to thank all those persons and institutions who have made this work—a long time coming—possible. Many thanks are due to my home institution, the University of Houston-Downtown (UHD), for the frequent support (both material and otherwise) they have given me over the course of editing this book. Specifically, I am grateful for an Organized Research and Creative Activities Grant, which was awarded in 2017 and which funded a course release in Spring 2018, giving me much-needed time to complete the project. I also thank my colleagues in philosophy at UHD, Sharin Elkholy, Jeffrey Jackson, Andrew Pavelich, and Norman Whitman, for the buoying power of our occasional dialogues. I owe much as well to the staff of UHD's W. I. Dykes Library—especially the Interlibrary Loan Office.

I would like to thank everyone at Bloomsbury Publishing for everything they have done in support of this book. In particular (as always), I'd like to mention Frankie Mace, whose patience seems to know no bounds.

Scholars, colleagues, and friends who have helped me—and helped this book— in one way or another include Niels Jørgen Cappelørn, Joakim Garff, Marius Timmann Mjaaland, and Vanessa Rumble. Most sincere thanks to you all.

For bringing the possibility of a collaborative book on Kierkegaard's work as an author to my attention, as well as having joined me for the first steps along the way, I am extremely thankful to Mark Tietjen. His willingness to work with me, across many philosophical disagreements and divides, in pursuit of interests and goals we have had in common—even if our methods differ—is and will long be a model for me of the best that collaborative scholarship can make possible. You should read his book(s).

And, finally, I offer my deepest gratitude and highest praise to the eleven extraordinary writers, scholars, thinkers, and—*dare I say it?*—authors whose work also appears in these pages. They are among the very best readers Kierkegaard has these days, and we are all quite fortunate that they're sharing their readings with us here.

* * *

As the manuscript for this book was in the final stages of preparation, we received word of the passing of Robert L. Perkins, one of the most significant scholars of Kierkegaard in the United States. Bob's authorial and editorial contributions are numerous, and his work—as a colleague, a scholar, a teacher, and an editor—has touched all of us in the field. On a personal note, however, Bob served as a scholarly friend and mentor at a time in my life when I sorely needed one, and appropriately enough, he was my first great role model in the thorny work of editorship. Whatever I have done right in editing this book, it owes a great deal to his example—and whatever I have done right as a scholar certainly owes a great deal to his encouragement and friendship. It is, thus, to him and his memory that this book is dedicated.

J. W.
Houston, Texas, USA
March 2018

A NOTE ON CITATIONS

References to works written by Søren Kierkegaard will follow a standardized format throughout the text. In accord with the customary practice in Kierkegaard scholarship, references to Kierkegaard will be made both to the English translation in question and the most recent Danish edition of Kierkegaard's writings, *Søren Kierkegaards Skrifter* (SKS). References to English translations of Kierkegaard's works are, in the case of published and most unpublished books and articles, most often to *Kierkegaard's Writings* (Princeton University Press; general editor, Howard V. Hong), although occasionally to older or newer translations by others as the contributors have deemed it necessary. (In most such cases, a parallel reference to the cited passage in *Kierkegaard's Writings* has also been provided.) In the case of Kierkegaard's voluminous unpublished journals, notebooks, and miscellaneous other writings, reference is made to *Kierkegaard's Journals and Notebooks* (KJN), an English translation of the relevant volumes of SKS. References to KJN and SKS are to volume number followed by page number; following the page number in references to KJN or the unpublished journals, notebooks, and papers in SKS, the specific journals, notebook, or loose page is noted in parentheses. In some cases, references are made to *Søren Kierkegaard's Journals and Papers* (JP); in those cases, citations are to volume number followed by the entry numbers (specific to JP) rather than page numbers.

ABBREVIATIONS

Danish

ASKB   *Auktionsprotokol over Søren Kierkegaards Bogsamling*, ed. H. P. Rohde (Copenhagen: Det Kongelige Bibliotek, 1955).

B&A   *Breve og Aktstykker vedrørende Søren Kierkegaard*, ed. Niels Thulstrup, vols. I–II (Copenhagen: Munksgaard, 1953–1954).

Pap.   *Søren Kierkegaards Papirer*, ed. P. A. Heiberg, V. Kuhr, and E. Torsting, vols. I–XI-3 (Copenhagen: Gyldendal, 1909–1948).

SKS   *Søren Kierkegaards Skrifter*, ed. Niels Jørgen Cappelørn, Joakim Garff, Jette Knudsen, and Johnny Kondrup, vols. 1–28, K1-K28 (Copenhagen: Gads Forlag, 1997–2013).

English

AN   *Armed Neutrality*, in *The Point of View: On My Work as an Author; The Point of View for My Work as an Author; Armed Neutrality*, edited and translated by Howard V. Hong and Edna H. Hong, Kierkegaard's Writings, vol. XXII (Princeton: Princeton University Press, 1998).

ANI   *Armed Neutrality*, edited and translated by Howard V. Hong and Edna H. Hong (Bloomington: Indiana University Press, 1968).

BA   *The Book on Adler*, edited and translated by Howard V. Hong and Edna H. Hong, Kierkegaard's Writings, vol. XXIV (Princeton: Princeton University Press, 1998).

C   *The Crisis and a Crisis in the Life of an Actress*, in *Christian Discourses; The Crisis and a Crisis in the Life of an Actress*, edited and translated by Howard V. Hong and Edna H. Hong, Kierkegaard's Writings, vol. XVII (Princeton: Princeton University Press, 1997).

CA   *The Concept of Anxiety: A Simple Psychologically Orienting Deliberation on the Dogmatic Issue of Hereditary Sin*, edited and translated by Reidar Thomte, in collaboration with Albert B. Anderson, Kierkegaard's Writings, vol. VIII (Princeton: Princeton University Press, 1980).

CD   *Christian Discourses*, in *Christian Discourses; The Crisis and a Crisis in the Life of an Actress*, edited and translated by Howard V. Hong and Edna H. Hong, Kierkegaard's Writings, vol. XVII (Princeton: Princeton University Press, 1997).

CI   *The Concept of Irony, with Continual Reference to Socrates; Notes of Schelling's Berlin Lectures*, edited and translated by Howard V. Hong and

	Edna H. Hong, Kierkegaard's Writings, vol. II (Princeton: Princeton University Press, 1989).
CIC	*The Concept of Irony*, translated by Lee M. Capel (London: Collins, 1966).
COR	*The Corsair Affair and Articles Related to the Writings*, edited and translated by Howard V. Hong and Edna H. Hong, Kierkegaard's Writings, vol. XIII (Princeton: Princeton University Press, 1982).
CUP1	*Concluding Unscientific Postscript to Philosophical Fragments, Volume I: Text*, edited and translated by Howard V. Hong and Edna H. Hong, Kierkegaard's Writings, vol. XII:1 (Princeton: Princeton University Press, 1992).
CUPH	*Concluding Unscientific Postscript to the Philosophical Crumbs*, edited and translated by Alastair Hannay (Cambridge: Cambridge University Press, 2009).
CUPSL	*Concluding Unscientific Postscript*, translated by David F. Swenson, completed after his death by Walter Lowrie (Princeton: Princeton University Press, 1941).
DCF	*Discourses at the Communion on Fridays*, translated by Sylvia Walsh (Bloomington: Indiana University Press, 2011).
EO1	*Either/Or, Part I*, edited and translated by Howard V. Hong and Edna H. Hong, Kierkegaard's Writings, vol. III (Princeton: Princeton University Press, 1987).
EO2	*Either/Or, Part II*, edited and translated by Howard V. Hong and Edna H. Hong, Kierkegaard's Writings, vol. IV (Princeton: Princeton University Press, 1987).
EOFL	*Either/Or: A Fragment of Life*, abridged and ed. Alastair Hannay (New York: Penguin, 1992).
EOS1	*Either/Or, Volume I*, translated by David F. Swenson and Lillian Marvin Swenson, revised by Howard A. Johnson (Princeton: Princeton University Press, 1959).
EUD	*Eighteen Upbuilding Discourses*, edited and translated by Howard V. Hong and Edna H. Hong, Kierkegaard's Writings, vol. V (Princeton: Princeton University Press, 1990).
FPOSL	*From the Papers of One Still Living*, in *Early Polemical Writings*, edited and translated by Julia Watkin, Kierkegaard's Writings, vol. I (Princeton: Princeton University Press, 1990).
FSE	*For Self-examination*, in *For Self-examination; Judge for Yourself!*, edited and translated by Howard V. Hong and Edna H. Hong, Kierkegaard's Writings, vol. XXI (Princeton: Princeton University Press, 1990).
FT	*Fear and Trembling*, in *Fear and Trembling; Repetition*, edited and translated by Howard V. Hong and Edna H. Hong, Kierkegaard's Writings, vol. VI (Princeton: Princeton University Press, 1983).
FTL	*Fear and Trembling*, in *Fear and Trembling and The Sickness unto Death*, translated by Walter Lowrie (Garden City, NY: Doubleday, 1941).
JCC	*Johannes Climacus, or: A Life of Doubt*, translated by T. H. Croxall (London: Serpent's Tail, 2001).

JFY   *Judge for Yourself!*, in *For Self-examination; Judge for Yourself!*, edited
           and translated by Howard V. Hong and Edna H. Hong, Kierkegaard's
           Writings, vol. XXI (Princeton: Princeton University Press, 1990).

JP   *Søren Kierkegaard's Journals and Papers*, edited and translated by Howard
           V. Hong and Edna H. Hong, assisted by Gregor Malantschuk, vols. I–VI
           (Bloomington: Indiana University Press, 1967–1978).

JSK   *The Journals of Søren Kierkegaard*, selected, edited, and translated by
           Alexander Dru (London: Oxford University Press, 1938).

KJN   *Kierkegaard's Journals and Notebooks*, ed. Niels Jørgen Cappelørn,
           Alastair Hannay, David Kangas, Bruce H. Kirmmse, George Pattison,
           Vanessa Rumble, and K. Brian Söderquist, vols. I–XI (Princeton:
           Princeton University Press, 2007ff.).

OMWA   *On My Work as an Author*, in *The Point of View: On My Work as an
           Author; The Point of View for My Work as an Author; Armed Neutrality*,
           edited and translated by Howard V. Hong and Edna H. Hong,
           Kierkegaard's Writings, vol. XXII (Princeton: Princeton University Press,
           1998).

PC   *Practice in Christianity*, edited and translated by Howard V. Hong and
           Edna H. Hong, Kierkegaard's Writings, vol. XX (Princeton: Princeton
           University Press, 1991).

PF   *Philosophical Fragments*, in *Philosophical Fragments; Johannes Climacus*,
           edited and translated by Howard V. Hong and Edna H. Hong,
           Kierkegaard's Writings, vol. VII (Princeton: Princeton University Press,
           1985).

PV   *The Point of View for My Work as an Author*, in *The Point of View: On My
           Work as an Author; The Point of View for My Work as an Author; Armed
           Neutrality*, edited and translated by Howard V. Hong and Edna H. Hong,
           Kierkegaard's Writings, vol. XXII (Princeton: Princeton University Press,
           1998).

PVL   *The Point of View for My Work as an Author: A Report to History, and
           Related Writings*, translated by Walter Lowrie (New York: Harper, 1962).

R   *Repetition*, in *Fear and Trembling; Repetition*, edited and translated by
           Howard V. Hong and Edna H. Hong, Kierkegaard's Writings, vol. VI
           (Princeton: Princeton University Press, 1983).

RPC   *Repetition and Philosophical Crumbs*, translated by M. G. Piety (Oxford:
           Oxford University Press, 2009).

SLW   *Stages on Life's Way*, edited and translated by Howard V. Hong and Edna
           H. Hong, Kierkegaard's Writings, vol. XI (Princeton: Princeton University
           Press, 1988).

SUD   *The Sickness unto Death: A Christian Psychological Exposition for
           Upbuilding and Awakening*, edited and translated by Howard V. Hong and
           Edna H. Hong, Kierkegaard's Writings, vol. XIX (Princeton: Princeton
           University Press, 1980).

SUDH   *The Sickness unto Death: A Christian Psychological Exposition for
           Edification and Awakening*, translated by Alastair Hannay (New York:
           Penguin, 1989).

TA   *Two Ages: The Age of Revolution and the Present Age*, edited and translated
            by Howard V. Hong and Edna H. Hong, Kierkegaard's Writings, vol. XIV
            (Princeton: Princeton University Press, 1978).

TC   *Training in Christianity and the Edifying Discourse Which "Accompanied"
            It*, translated by Walter Lowrie (Princeton: Princeton University Press,
            1967).

TDIO   *Three Discourses on Imagined Occasions*, edited and translated by Howard
            V. Hong and Edna H. Hong, Kierkegaard's Writings, vol. X (Princeton:
            Princeton University Press, 1993).

TM   *The Moment and Late Writings*, edited and translated by Howard V.
            Hong and Edna H. Hong, Kierkegaard's Writings, vol. XXIII (Princeton:
            Princeton University Press, 1998).

TSI   *The Single Individual: Two Notes Concerning My Work as an Author*, in
            *The Point of View: On My Work as an Author; The Point of View for My
            Work as an Author; Armed Neutrality*, edited and translated by Howard V.
            Hong and Edna H. Hong, Kierkegaard's Writings, vol. XXII (Princeton:
            Princeton University Press, 1998).

UDVS   *Upbuilding Discourses in Various Spirits*, edited and translated by Howard
            V. Hong and Edna H. Hong, Kierkegaard's Writings, vol. XV (Princeton:
            Princeton University Press, 1993).

WA   *Without Authority: The Lily in the Field and the Bird of the Air; Two
            Ethical-Religious Essays; Three Discourses at the Communion on Fridays;
            An Upbuilding Discourse; Two Discourses at the Communion on
            Fridays*, edited and translated by Howard V. Hong and Edna H. Hong,
            Kierkegaard's Writings, vol. XVIII (Princeton: Princeton University Press,
            1997).

WL   *Works of Love*, edited and translated by Howard V. Hong and Edna H.
            Hong, Kierkegaard's Writings, vol. XVI (Princeton: Princeton University
            Press, 1995).

INTRODUCTION: ON KIERKEGAARD'S WORK AS AN AUTHOR

Joseph Westfall

Authorship has long been recognized as an important issue in studies of the work of the nineteenth-century Danish philosopher, theologian, and litterateur Søren Kierkegaard, and issues of authorship—from the use of multiple pseudonyms and anonyms, to contributions in a variety of media and genres (journalism, religious discourses, diaries, short fictions and dramatic works, philosophical and theological treatises, etc.)—abound. Readings of Kierkegaard in the scholarly literature often make some effort to address these issues, but focused, book-length examinations of the issue are uncommon, to say the least. Recently, however, a number of scholars in a variety of academic disciplines and with different theoretical and methodological commitments have begun to concentrate their attention on these issues, and the result is something of a renaissance in studies of Kierkegaard as an author.

While it might seem useful to attempt to divide approaches to Kierkegaard's work as an author into a few camps or categories ("deconstructive," "intentionalist," "anti-intentionalist," etc.), the reality is somewhat more complicated. Some scholarly readers take a more or less straightforwardly deconstructive and anti-intentionalist approach to Kierkegaardian authorship (such as Louis Mackey[1] and Roger Poole[2]); some ask us to take Kierkegaard's intentions and conclusions about his own authorship, as expressed in his published and unpublished writings, quite seriously (Niels Jørgen Cappelørn[3] and Mark Tietjen,[4] for example). But one might also suggest that respecting Kierkegaard's intentions about his work as an author requires us to read him at least somewhat deconstructively; others

1. Louis Mackey, *Points of View: Readings of Kierkegaard* (Tallahassee: Florida State University Press, 1986).

2. Roger Poole, *Kierkegaard: The Indirect Communication* (Charlottesville: University Press of Virginia, 1993).

3. Niels Jørgen Cappelørn, "The Retrospective Understanding of Kierkegaard's Total Production," in *Kierkegaard: Resources and Results*, ed. Alastair McKinnon (Waterloo, Canada: Wilfrid Laurier Press, 1982), pp. 18–38.

4. Mark Tietjen, *Kierkegaard, Communication, and Virtue: Authorship as Edification* (Bloomington: Indiana University Press, 2013).

might suggest that Kierkegaard's insights into the human psyche should inform our understanding of his authorial practice; still others that, in the context of the literary world of Kierkegaard's Copenhagen, what seem like authorial excesses and idiosyncrasies today would have been much more ordinary and thus do not demand special attention.

Unlike other divisive and divided issues in Kierkegaard research, however, the issue of authorship—of how and why Kierkegaard wrote in the ways he did, and what readers of Kierkegaard should make of the authorship he ultimately produced thereby—resonates throughout every other aspect of the study of Kierkegaard. Before one can rightly assess the nature and feasibility of Kierkegaard's thoughts on the matters for which he is justifiably famous (such as faith or anxiety or love, or the relationship between what he called "the aesthetic," "the ethical," and "the religious"), one must, I think, first address the problems that accompany how best to approach the written works in which those thoughts are expressed. For example, given the multiply authored nature of those works, how does one establish some means by way of which to relate the various elements of the authorship to one another? Can one find a definitively Kierkegaardian view—a view that is definitively Kierkegaard's own—across readings of the pseudonymous and non-pseudonymous writings? Can entries in his voluminous unpublished journals and notebooks serve as evidence of what Kierkegaard himself thought— and as such, be used to undergird or undermine interpretations of the published writings? When inconsistencies (or potential contradictions) appear between two differently named authors within the Kierkegaardian authorship, on what basis might a contemporary reader adjudicate or even simply understand the conflict? Without at least tentative answers to these questions, it seems fewer of the other pressing questions about Kierkegaard's works can even begin to approach resolution. One simply cannot make definitive claims about Kierkegaard's work as a thinker without taking up or assuming some point of view on Kierkegaard's work as an author (even if only implicitly or unconsciously).

The Kierkegaardian Record

This seems to be a point Kierkegaard himself recognized, given his many attempts to explain himself, perhaps most notably in his posthumously published *The Point of View for My Work as an Author*. But *The Point of View* is by no means the first appearance of serious critical self-reflection on questions of authorship in Kierkegaard's writings. In addition to *The Point of View*, Kierkegaard wrote and published his *On My Work as an Author* in 1851, a much shorter and somewhat more ambiguous account of his work as a self-declared religious author. Before that, in 1846, Kierkegaard appended "A First and Last Explanation," an effort to account for his pseudonymous writings since *Either/Or*, to the otherwise pseudonymous *Concluding Unscientific Postscript to Philosophical Fragments*. That work stands as what may be Kierkegaard's most direct attempt to differentiate between his own work as an author and that of the pseudonyms he created.

But even before that work, there are brief, sometimes tentative attempts at self-explanation, all in the form of newspaper articles: "Public Confession" (1842), "Who Is the Author of *Either/Or*?" (published pseudonymously, as "A. F. ....", 1843), "A Little Explanation" (1843), and "An Explanation and a Little More" (1845). Significantly, in each of these four early articles on his own work as an author, Kierkegaard (thrice in his own name, and once not) denies authorship of one or more pseudonymous works ascribed to him—despite the fact that, in every case, he did write them. All of these articles try to maintain a distance between the pseudonymous writings and the writings Kierkegaard published under his own name; one of them ("Who Is the Author of *Either/Or*?") argues that the "real" authorship of the pseudonymous *Either/Or* ought to be a matter of indifference to readers; and one of them ("An Explanation and a Little More") argues that, if Kierkegaard were the "real" author of the pseudonymous books, only he would have the authority to say so publicly. Although the Kierkegaardian authorship's bifurcation between pseudonymous and signed works predates these articles, it is nevertheless a significant point that Kierkegaard's first efforts at addressing his uniquely complicated authorial situation are all attempts to maintain an absolute distance and difference between Kierkegaard "himself" and the Kierkegaardian pseudonymous authors.

Kierkegaard takes a somewhat different tack in the later "A First and Last Explanation," although not one that abandons the earlier strategy of distance and difference altogether. In this sort-of-postscript to the *Postscript*, set in a different type and without page numbers, Kierkegaard articulates for the first time and in his own name a version of his authorial relationship to the pseudonymous writings. Gone are the denials and evasions of "Public Confession" and "An Explanation and a Little More." "I am, as is said," Kierkegaard confesses, "the author of *Either/ Or* (Victor Eremita), Copenhagen, February 1843; *Fear and Trembling* (Johannes de silentio), 1843," and so on, up through the *Postscript* and two pseudonymous newspaper articles from 1846.[5] A straightforward enough statement of his authorial accountability—but, then again, not. He adds, significantly for all readings of Kierkegaard, "in the pseudonymous books there is not a single word by me."[6] But then, also, "on the other hand I am very literally and directly the author of, for example, the upbuilding discourses and of every word in them."[7] And then, again, finally (for now): "My role is the joint role of being the secretary and, quite ironically, the dialectically reduplicated author of the author or the authors."[8] Kierkegaard is not simply trying to explain the pseudonymous writings in their pseudonymity, as he did in an admittedly different way in the earlier newspaper articles. He is doing that, to be sure, but he is in addition trying to explain the situation of the pseudonymous writings in the context of an authorship that has

5. CUP1, 625 / SKS 7, 569.
6. CUP1, 625–626 / SKS 7, 569–570.
7. CUP1, 627 / SKS 7, 571.
8. Ibid.

both pseudonymous and non-pseudonymous ("veronymous" or "signed") parts. In this regard, in 1846, Kierkegaard does not get very far; his explanation lacks any sense of project or purpose. He tells us *that* the pseudonymous authors ought to be read as absolutely distinct authorial personae, solely responsible for their own writings and essentially different from their own author, "the author of the authors," Søren Kierkegaard—but he does not tell us *why*. He claims to lack the authority to decide what the books authored by the pseudonyms mean (just as he claimed, elsewhere, that no one else had the authority to ascribe authorship of those works to him[9]), but he also does not tell us what it means for there to be pseudonymous writings at all. Leaving us with a wish and a prayer and an ambiguous reference to the dialectical hands of an ordinary seaman,[10] he leaves us on our own.

At least, that is, until 1851. In that year, in the very short book—a pamphlet, really—*On My Work as an Author*, Kierkegaard addresses publicly[11] for the first and last time the meaning and significance of his simultaneously pseudonymous and signed authorship, and of the simultaneity. He casts himself this time not as just one (metaphysically privileged) voice among many, but as somehow also author of absolutely everything in the Kierkegaardian authorship, signed *and* pseudonymous, although these two differently. He suggests that his work as an author has had a plan, or a design, from the very beginning, but he admits that he, personally, was not always aware of the fact or nature of that plan or design, as he notes: "This is how I *now* understand the whole. From the beginning I could not quite see what has indeed also been my own development."[12] This, of course, raises the question of the ultimate identity of the planner or designer (or Planner or Designer), a question which Kierkegaard himself does not or cannot answer in *On My Work as an Author*. Fortunately for proponents of this view, Kierkegaard left among his unpublished papers the draft of a book arguing for the identification of the author of the overarching, lifelong plan of Kierkegaard's meticulously crafted authorship with Kierkegaard's own author: God, or as he styles it in *The Point of View for My Work as an Author*, Governance.

As readers of Kierkegaard know, Kierkegaard seems to have struggled a great deal with the question of whether to publish *The Point of View* at all, and if so, whether he should publish it pseudonymously or under his own name. For readers today, this latter question can seem a bit perplexing, seeing as the real gift promised by the book is a window into Kierkegaard's own thoughts on his authorship—the point of view on *his* work as an author. Had the volume been published under a pseudonym (alternatively, A—O or Johannes *de silentio*, according to Kierkegaard's

---

9. "An Explanation and a Little More," in COR, 24–27 / SKS 14, 65–66.
10. CUP1, 630 / SKS 7, 573.
11. Privately, in his unpublished journals, notebooks, and papers, Kierkegaard often wrestles with questions about the authorship of his authorship—and, specifically, with the question whether he has the authority to answer that question once and for all.
12. PV, 12 / SKS 13, 18.

journals[13]), its significance for interpretations of Kierkegaard would be difficult to assess, at best. That said, some of that difficulty—and its resolution—is embedded in the argument of *The Point of View*, where Kierkegaard maintains that an author's declarations are not sufficient grounds for a reader to believe that the author's perspective on his or her authorship is the most accurate one. Kierkegaard asserts that, when discussing their own writings, authors must provide readers with arguments—good, rigorously reasoned arguments that rest on the writings themselves rather than any personal knowledge or beliefs about them that those authors might possess. In essence, Kierkegaard suggests that an author lacks the authority that would be necessary to dictate any reader's interpretation. The association of authorship with authority here is not unusual for Kierkegaard, whether in his writings on his own writings or those dealing with other authors (Orla Lehmann, Hans Christian Andersen, Thomasine Gyllembourg, etc.). In fact, in many ways, for Kierkegaard, the question of the proper authority of an author—in what he or she writes, and what he or she writes about what he or she writes—is the central question for (and about) an author. Does an author have the authority to make the claims made in his or her authorship? Clearly, in his own case, Kierkegaard wants to say both yes and no: yes, the authorship was coauthored with Governance; but also no, Kierkegaard himself could never say this directly, authoritatively, publicly, in print. As such, in *The Point of View* as in "A First and Last Explanation," Kierkegaard claims that he comes to his authorship (in this self-interpretative regard, at least) only as a reader—which is to say, only with the authority over interpretation that any reader might possess.[14]

What *On My Work as an Author* and *The Point of View* do both claim, however, is that Kierkegaard's authorship is a religious one "from the very beginning"[15] and that Kierkegaard is a religious author, through and through. Given the explicitly religious content of so very much of the Kierkegaardian authorship, this is on the face of it not an outrageous claim—although what it means, exactly, for readings of Kierkegaard's works is not entirely clear. The claim is complicated by Kierkegaard's efforts to organize his taxonomy of authors in such a way that Kierkegaard himself—the author within the Kierkegaardian authorship who writes under the name, "Kierkegaard"—is not the highest, not the closest to revealed, Christian truth: that's Anti-Climacus, a pseudonym.[16] This admission would seem to situate Kierkegaard's point of view on an admittedly limited vista, such that Kierkegaard's

13. PV, 222–223 / SKS 22, 347 (NB14: 8); JP 6, 6327 / SKS 21, 250 (NB9: 78).

14. CUP1, 626 / SKS 7, 570; PV, 33 / SKS 16, 18.

15. This is a somewhat contentious claim, considering that Kierkegaard omits a number of his own works from his accounts of his authorship. See Joakim Garff, "The Eyes of Argus: *The Point of View* and Points of View on Kierkegaard's Work as an Author," trans. Jane Chamberlain and Belinda Ioni Rasmussen, in *Kierkegaard: A Critical Reader*, ed. Jonathan Rée and Jane Chamberlain (Oxford: Blackwell, 1998), pp. 77–82.

16. In *Journal NB11*: "The pseudonym is Johannes Anticlimacus in contrast to Climacus, who said he was not a Christian. Anticlimacus is the opposite extreme: A Christian on an extraordinary level—but I myself manage to be only a very simple Christian" (JP 6, 6431 /

point of view (*the* point of view communicated in *The Point of View*) might not be the most accurate, might not be presented so that we, as readers, *believe* it (much as many argue Johannes *de silentio*'s view on faith in *Fear and Trembling* is not the final or most accurate view presented in the Kierkegaardian authorship, as evidenced in part by Silentio's admission that, although he knows what faith is, he himself does not possess it). Here, then, we start to see reminiscences of the argument in "A First and Last Explanation," for keeping the pseudonyms apart—from each other, and from Kierkegaard himself, as an author. And this is, in another sense, further support for the basic claims made in those early newspaper articles that Kierkegaard is Kierkegaard and the pseudonyms are the pseudonyms, and no reader has the authority to claim otherwise in anything even remotely like a definitive way.

It is something like this idea that captures the imagination of Peter Christian Kierkegaard, Søren's older brother and a bishop in the Danish church, who authorizes the posthumous publication of *The Point of View* but who also says, "One could indeed almost come to imagine the possibility that even that which appeared with the signature 'Søren Kierkegaard', might not unconditionally be his last word (but a point of view)."[17] While this was certainly a minority opinion even then—it seems unlikely that Kierkegaard would have gone so long and so actively disregarded in Danish theological circles had the dominant interpretation been that what he had to say about the Danish Lutheran Church, in his own name in *The Moment* and some of the later books, was just one possible (and possibly *fictional*) point of view among many—it *is* an intriguing one. And although the intentions of different interpreters certainly differ, it's a view that springs up again and again in the Kierkegaard literature, as we can see in the late work of Louis Mackey,[18] as well as in my own work.[19]

SKS 22, 127–8 [NB11: 204]). Also, discussing Anti-Climacus in *On My Work as an Author*: "All the previous pseudonymity is lower than 'the upbuilding author'; the new pseudonym is a higher pseudonymity" (PV 6 / SKS 13, 12).

17. Peter Christian Kierkegaard in *Encounters with Kierkegaard: A Life as Seen by His Contemporaries*, ed. Bruce H. Kirmmse (Princeton: Princeton University Press, 1996), pp. 148–149.

18. Louis Mackey, "Points of View for His Work as an Author: A Report from History," in *Points of View: Readings of Kierkegaard* (Tallahassee: Florida State University Press, 1986), p. 188. Mackey notes: "When a man fabricates as many masks to hide behind as Kierkegaard does, one cannot trust his (purportedly) direct asseverations. And when he signs his own name, it no longer has the effects of the signature. Søren Kierkegaard was one of his own pseudonyms. Or perhaps all of them are God's pseudonyms. That's what Søren would have us believe."

19. See Joseph Westfall, *The Kierkegaardian Author: Authorship in Kierkegaard's Literary and Dramatic Criticism* (Berlin: Walter de Gruyter, 2007); and "Who Is the Author of *The Point of View*? Issues of Authorship in the Posthumous Kierkegaard," *Philosophy and Social Criticism* 38: 6 (2012), pp. 569–589.

After Kierkegaard: A Review

As Kierkegaard scholarship has developed, from at least the early twentieth century into the present, it has become increasingly specialized—by academic discipline, of course, but also within disciplines by theoretical and methodological commitments. The earliest Kierkegaard scholars seem largely uninterested in issues of authorship, taking for granted that Kierkegaard himself is expressed in each of his works. This has led to widespread mistaken views on Kierkegaard based on things said in the pseudonymous works (such as that Kierkegaard believed Mozart's *Don Giovanni* was the greatest musical work ever produced—a view properly attributed to *Either/Or*'s aesthetic anonym, A—or that faith is both reliant upon "the absurd" and a nonrational "leap"—views espoused not by Kierkegaard but by his pseudonym, Johannes *de silentio*), and to some extent this is as it likely had to be: one does not produce an authorship such as Kierkegaard produced without necessarily sowing some confusion along the way. Of course, such confusion is not reserved for Kierkegaard's novice and student readers alone; in fact, some of the most infamous and egregious errors associated with Kierkegaard's practice as an author appear in the works of major figures in the histories of philosophy and theology. Theodor Adorno, Martin Buber, Albert Camus, Alasdair MacIntyre, and Jacques Derrida, to take but five prominent examples, all offer (admittedly sometimes otherwise brilliant) misreadings of Kierkegaard rooted in their treatment of his writings as all issuing from a single, simple authorial perspective. Not only do they and likeminded readers ignore the problems posed by the authorship's polyvocality, but they read Kierkegaard without an ear for irony or an awareness of differences in genre or rhetorical purpose or mood. Such readers read Kierkegaard to tease out "the lesson," the argument or assertion they will claim as *Kierkegaard's*, but ignorant of the possibility that they are themselves the ones being teased. They treat Kierkegaard like a schoolmaster communicating his truths more or less directly to his pupils, but whatever Kierkegaard might have been, he was no author of textbooks.

Setting aside for the moment, however, all those readings which ignore or deny the significance of the polyvocality and multiplicity of styles for interpretations—even philosophical or theological interpretations—of Kierkegaard's work, we are still left with a number of different perspectives on just what that significance is. These differing perspectives sometimes anchor themselves in one or more elements of Kierkegaard's own self-interpretation, and sometimes, they are guided by prior methodological commitments. In one sense, those readings criticized above that read every word written by Søren Kierkegaard as if it were voiced by the same author, that is, as if every book and article constituting the Kierkegaardian authorship were authored by and articulating the same point of view, fall into this last camp: they are (whether they state it explicitly or even consciously realize it, or not) committed to a bio-historical authorial literalism, according to which writers—nonfiction, philosophical/theological writers, at any rate—are to be read without any openness to or awareness of possible literary aspects of their writings. Whatever can be said for such a perspective on authorship, it seems indisputable that Kierkegaard, at least, does not share it—and thus that one will have to ignore rather than account for a number of formal, stylistic, and perspectival elements at work in the foundations of the Kierkegaardian authorship. Someone who agreed with Alasdair MacIntyre about how to read Kierkegaard would not write like Kierkegaard.

Although approaches to authorship in the field of literary theory abound, fewer of them have made their way across the disciplinary divides into readings of Kierkegaard. Theories of Kierkegaardian authorship, or methods for reading Kierkegaard, tend to adhere more closely to Kierkegaard's own accounts of his authorship than the more general theories of authorship typically do. (One notable exception to this rule, however, is deconstruction—about which I will have something to say below.) Thus, instead of organizing themselves around the classic literary theoretical questions about authorial intentions, textual implications, and reader response, the gamut of Kierkegaardian approaches to Kierkegaard's authorship runs from (a) those readers, like Buber, MacIntyre, and Derrida (discussed above), who ignore questions of authorship—including authorial identity and intent, genre, style, and so on—such that Kierkegaard is taken to mean whatever literally is said on the page of any of the books ultimately ascribable to him, to (b) those for whom *Kierkegaard* is not really saying anything in his writings, whether (b-i) because the nature of language itself prevents such texts from amounting to anything more than nonsense or (b-ii) because the division between Kierkegaard and the pseudonymous authors is absolute, such that there really is nothing that could be brought together in any way to constitute Kierkegaard's writings (at least as "Kierkegaard" has typically been understood, to indicate whichever author is responsible for both the signed and pseudonymous works).[20] In between these two extremes,[21] as it were, are situated (c) those readers who take Kierkegaard's own self-interpretation seriously enough to do their very best, as Kierkegaard requests in *The Point of View*, independently to verify and ultimately to justify what Kierkegaard has to say for himself. Finally, there are (d) those whose points of view on Kierkegaard's work as an author rest to some extent or another upon aspects or elements of the writings of Kierkegaard

20. These two positions, which I have called (a) and (b), map more or less exactly onto the first two approaches identified by Genia Schönbaumsfeld in the introduction to her book, *A Confusion of the Spheres*. Schönbaumsfeld calls them "the literal-minded reading" and "the purely literary reading," respectively. See Schönbaumsfeld, *A Confusion of the Spheres: Kierkegaard and Wittgenstein on Philosophy and Religion* (Oxford: Oxford University Press, 2007), p. 5.

21. In describing this spectrum of interpretative possibilities as limited on either side by "extreme" views, I mean only to indicate something of the nature of the spectrum of possibilities itself—not in any way to claim that those views, or those who hold those views, are "extremist" in any way. All of the views presented in this section from this point forward are ones with which I have some degree of sympathy, and which I think any thoughtful reader of Kierkegaard must be able to understand and appreciate—if not espouse.

(or his pseudonyms), but for whom Kierkegaard's self-interpretation is ultimately unpersuasive. Among these views, we find the greatest diversity of interpretative standpoints, whether we call the view (d-i) "moderate" or "philosophical," (d-ii) "Socratic" or "maieutic," (d-iii) "poetic," (d-iv) "staged" or "dramatic," (d-v) "deceptive," (d-vi) "deconstructive," or something else.

Before proceeding, let me say that the summary accounts of each of these perspectives on Kierkegaard's work as an author are my own—not those of the authors themselves and certainly not those of the other contributors to this volume (although there is some overlap between those two groups). I admit freely that complete stock of no one of these theories of Kierkegaardian authorship can be or is taken here, that my taxonomy is largely limited to the English-language literature, and that each approach discussed here is deserving of much more complete and careful treatment than I can provide. This wide range of perspectives and interpretative methods forms an explicit or implicit basis for much of the discussion of Kierkegaard's work as an author in this book, and as such it is (to varying degrees, depending upon the chapter) useful background information for reading the essays collected here as part of an ongoing project. I offer what follows, then, as both a brief summary reference for those unfamiliar with the literature on Kierkegaard's authorial practices and as a gesture of appreciation on my part for the challenging and thoughtful contributions each of these thinkers has provided to the ongoing conversation about Kierkegaard's work as an author.

As already noted, (a) has already been discussed, admittedly rather minimally, in the earlier part of this section. At this point, I wish only to add that it is of course, from a certain point of a view, a natural position to take on reading not only Kierkegaard's writings but anything written to take for granted, as it were, without feeling a need for methodological argument, explanation, or justification, that when an author commits words to the page, that author really means what s/he says. The seeming naturalness of the positions stems at least in part, certainly, from the relatively naive way in which most of us who do occasionally commit words to pages do so: without any thoughts of deceiving, manipulating, or otherwise interfering in the reader's attempt to understand what we have written. This is why this problem is relatively rarely raised in the reading of most writers. But to treat the written word as a more or less direct conduit to its author's true thoughts is in fact to have a hermeneutic methodology—and a rather complex and problematic one, psychologically speaking—without knowing it. Kierkegaard is the sort of author who challenges such easy assumptions about the relationships between readers, books, and authors, and for this reason, if no other, questions of authorship come more frequently to the surface both in readings and the contents of his works. So many difficult and interesting decisions have so clearly been made in the Kierkegaardian writings, about tone and mood and style and genre, about authorial persona and authorial authority, even about grammar, punctuation, and typesetting, that to hold the position that *none* of it matters for interpretations of those writings seems foolish, at best. Despite the pretense of deep philosophical seriousness, this approach certainly does not demonstrate an earnestness about even the (perhaps impossible) project such readers have set out upon: to uncover what Kierkegaard really meant. Among other things, Kierkegaard really meant for Johannes *de silentio*'s name to appear on the title page of *Fear and Trembling*, not his own.

(b-i) James Conant offers a different sort of reading of Kierkegaard, one which takes extraordinarily seriously at least one important instance of Kierkegaardian pseudonymity, Johannes Climacus's *Concluding Unscientific Postscript*. Conant is not talking about pseudonymity per se, although the pseudonymity of the book is relevant to his reading: in any case, the phenomenon he wishes to describe in the *Postscript* is also at work, he argues, in the *Tractatus Logico-Philosophicus* of Ludwig Wittgenstein. In three essays comparing Kierkegaard and Wittgenstein as philosophical authors,[22] Conant works through the idea that they both delineate a contrast between sense and nonsense (that is, non-sense), and between speech and silence, so as to revert ultimately themselves to silence and nonsense on philosophical grounds. Conant—following the early Wittgenstein, and relying heavily upon both Wittgenstein's and Kierkegaard/Climacus's uses of revocation in these particular works—argues that language, as an instrument for the communication of objective concepts, cannot accommodate meaningful (i.e., "sensical") discussion of those aspects of human existence capable of being approached or apprehended only subjectively, such as faith or morality. Because subjective moods and passions cannot be objectively communicated, and because language is a medium suited only to the communication of objectivity, all language about things like faith and morality ultimately must be shipwrecked on silence, whether by ceasing communication altogether (as in the famous final line of the *Tractatus*) or in nonsense (as, Conant argues, in Climacus's "objective" account of faith or of truth "as subjectivity").

(b-ii) The most forceful and influential proponent of the view that the pseudonymous authors must be accorded absolute independence and autonomy from Kierkegaard is set forth by Roger Poole.[23] Poole's view rests in large part on a single-mindedly literal reading of Kierkegaard's assertion in "A First and Last Explanation" that there is not a single word ascribable to him in any of the pseudonymous books and thus that readers should be careful only ever to ascribe the views espoused in the pseudonymous writings to the appropriate pseudonymous authors rather than to Kierkegaard. The structure of Kierkegaard's authorial project, according to Poole, maintains an absolute distance between all of the authorial personae—Kierkegaard's own included—such that there is no legitimate means by which to make anything like an "authorship" cohere. The

22. James Conant, "Must We Show What We Cannot Say?" in *The Senses of Stanley Cavell*, ed. Richard Fleming and Michael Payne (Lewisburg, PA: Bucknell University Press, 1989), pp. 242–283; "Kierkegaard, Wittgenstein, and Nonsense," in *Pursuits of Reason: Essays in Honor of Stanley Cavell*, ed. Ted Cohen, Paul Guyer, and Hilary Putnam (Lubbock: Texas Tech University Press, 1993), pp. 195–224; and "Putting Two and Two Together: Kierkegaard, Wittgenstein and the Point of View for Their Work as Authors," in *Philosophy and the Grammar of Religious Belief*, ed. Timothy Tessin and Mario von der Ruhr (New York: St. Martin's Press, 1995), pp. 248–331.

23. Poole, *Kierkegaard: The Indirect Communication*.

different works of the authorship, and the different authors at work therein, wind around each other so intricately and completely that the possibility of unraveling them so as to make any determination as to the overall meaning or purpose of the work as a whole is eliminated. Kierkegaard becomes a near-total mystery thereby; as Poole concludes, "the mystery is impenetrable to the end, and that is because Kierkegaard's writing has made all solutions impossible."[24]

(c) In between the view that Kierkegaard's work as an author is ultimately best understood in light of the cultural, philosophical, and literary world in which he actually historically operated, and the view that Kierkegaard's work as an author can only be understood as inherently unable to be understood, there is a third possibility: that Kierkegaard's work as an author means, or can be understood to mean, precisely what Kierkegaard said it did. This acknowledges the historicity and historical actuality of Kierkegaard's authorship, while at the same time refusing to subordinate the authorship to history. The chief proponent of this view—other than Kierkegaard himself, of course—is Niels Jørgen Cappelørn, in a brief essay from 1982, "The Retrospective Understanding of Kierkegaard's Total Production."[25] There, Cappelørn argues for treating Kierkegaard's unpublished papers as a full-fledged component of the Kierkegaardian authorship, and in so doing, for understanding the significance and purpose of the authorship retrospectively— that is, in reflection, looking from its end back toward its beginning. This is, as we have seen, precisely the approach Kierkegaard takes in *On My Work as an Author* and *The Point of View*: from the vantage point of the (nearly) finished authorship, looking back and uncovering that, "from the very beginning," it has been a religious work in collaboration with Governance. Following Kierkegaard's own advice, that we should not take as decisive the declarations of authors, Cappelørn tries to show that the retrospective approach is the most appropriate one for Kierkegaard's authorship, and that, on the basis of that approach, it can be seen that Kierkegaard's self-understanding in his self-interpretative works is a reasonable one. All things being equal, Cappelørn suggests, in the absence of conclusively contradictory evidence, we should trust Kierkegaard about Kierkegaard.[26]

Another author who centralizes the importance of understanding and defending Kierkegaard's own self-interpretation in *The Point of View* is Eleanor D. Helms.[27] Unlike Cappelørn or Tietjen, Helms approaches Kierkegaard neither theologically

---

24. Ibid., p. 1.

25. Cappelørn, "The Retrospective Understanding of Kierkegaard's Total Production," pp. 18–38.

26. According to David R. Law, we ought to include Michael Theunissen and Wilfried Greve in this camp, as well. See Law, "A Cacophony of Voices: The Multiple Authors and Readers of Kierkegaard's *The Point of View for My Work as an Author*," in *International Kierkegaard Commentary, Volume 22: The Point of View*, ed. Robert L. Perkins (Macon, GA: Mercer University Press, 2010), pp. 12–13.

27. Eleanor D. Helms, "Can Kierkegaard Be Serious? A Phenomenological Point of View for Kierkegaard's Authorship," in *International Kierkegaard Commentary, Volume 22: The Point of View*, ed. Robert L. Perkins (Macon, GA: Mercer University Press, 2010), pp. 238–267.

nor in terms of virtue ethics, but instead phenomenologically. Writing in response to postmodern, poststructuralist, or deconstructive readings of Kierkegaard, especially that of Joakim Garff,[28] Helms argues that the differences in authorial perspective throughout the authorship are best understood not as differing authorial personae, per se, but as artful disguises and self-transformations; the right approach to the authorship is thus not one of fragmentation (as in some deconstructive readings) but to identify and follow the thread that runs throughout the writings, the authorial essence of the authorship, as it were, which, on Helms's reading as on Kierkegaard's (and Cappelørn's), is intentionally religious.

More recently, but in a related vein, is the work of Mark Tietjen. In one of those few books devoted exclusively to the question of authorship in Kierkegaard, Tietjen's *Kierkegaard, Communication, and Virtue*[29] argues forcefully against the "hermeneutic of suspicion" at the heart of many deconstructive interpretations of Kierkegaard's work as an author.[30] To trust Kierkegaard as we read him—as a hermeneutical strategy, in fact, and in direct opposition to those literary theoretical methods that counsel detachment and distance from the author when reading their work—is to open oneself not only to being educated by whatever objective conclusions he or she might reach in writing but also, and infinitely more importantly, to being subjectively edified by the experience. Such openness and edification are, according to Tietjen, best understood in terms of virtue ethics, with reading Kierkegaard then becoming an edifying opportunity for the reformation of the reader's self. Tietjen suggests that this not only dovetails nicely with what Kierkegaard has to say about his work as a religious author intent on presenting his readers with the opportunity/challenge of Christianity, but it makes taking Kierkegaard seriously in the written accounts of his own authorship—again, *On My Work as an Author* and *The Point of View*, especially—absolutely essential.

(d-i) Near the beginning of *The Point of View*, Kierkegaard writes of the "duplexity" of his authorship as a whole, that is, the appearance of alternately religious and aesthetic or poetic works, the former largely identified with the *Upbuilding Discourses* and *Christian Discourses*, the latter with the pseudonymous authorship. Of this duplexity, Kierkegaard claims that it should be apparent to anyone who reads all the works carefully that the aesthetic works are "the incognito," whereas the religious works are the true heart of the authorship, supporting his overarching claim in *The Point of View* (and *On My Work as an Author*) that he has been, from the beginning, a religious author.[31] He suggests that, were someone to read the authorship in this way, and then to misunderstand one of the aesthetic

---

28. See section (d-vi), below.

29. Tietjen, *Kierkegaard, Communication, and Virtue: Authorship as Edification*. See also Mark Tietjen, "To Believe or Not to Believe: Toward a Hermeneutic of Trust," in *International Kierkegaard Commentary, Volume 22: The Point of View*, ed. Robert L. Perkins (Macon, GA: Mercer University Press, 2010), pp. 78–103.

30. Such as those of Roger Poole (discussed in [b-ii], above) and Joakim Garff (discussed in [d-vi], below).

31. PV, 23–26 / SKS 16, 11–14.

works, this would be "incidental"; but were one to thoroughly understand one of the aesthetic—that is, pseudonymous—works but not see the larger Christian character of the authorship, this would be a total misunderstanding of Kierkegaard.[32] Although others have also engaged in this effort, Louis Mackey stands at the head of a way of reading Kierkegaard which challenges Kierkegaard precisely on this point: he reads Kierkegaard as "a kind of poet," and the Kierkegaardian authorship as essentially aesthetic and poetic in nature, rather than offering the more customary acknowledgment of the truth of Kierkegaard's own assertions about its religiousness.[33] Mackey does not deny the duplexity but instead suggests that one could just as legitimately—and just as easily—read in the opposite of the way Kierkegaard himself recommends. Rather than deciding the point once and for all, Mackey's work reopens an interpretative door that some had thought was closed, raising the possibility of reading Kierkegaard in a way of which Kierkegaard might disapprove. Mackey seems to suggest that the undecidability of even this most basic question about Kierkegaard's work as an author, whether it is or is not a religious project overall, makes reading Kierkegaard all the more productive a task for the reader—leaving us all, as it were, in an either/or every time we begin to read any of Kierkegaard's writings.[34]

(d-ii) Situating himself in a mediating relationship between those views we have encountered in (c) and (d-i), above, Michael Strawser takes an intermediary approach to Kierkegaard's writings which he calls "philosophical."[35] For Strawser, altogether too much work on the question of how to read Kierkegaard has taken for granted that either the aesthetic or the religious aspects of the authorship ought, in the final account, to be privileged over the other. Thus, in readings such as those of Louis Mackey, the aesthetic qualities of the authorship—irony, pseudonymity, and the like—take precedence over Kierkegaard's own stated religious motivations. And in readings such as those of Niels Jørgen Cappelørn, Kierkegaard's late claims to being from the very beginning a religious author take precedence over any apparently contradictory aesthetic elements or motives. Strawser, reading *The Point of View* not as a commentary upon the authorship but as one piece of it, suggests that there is a way to read Kierkegaard—reading his works chronologically and openly, without agenda or prior methodological commitment—which unifies

---

32. PV, 24 / SKS 16, 12.

33. Louis Mackey, *Kierkegaard: A Kind of Poet* (Philadelphia: University of Pennsylvania Press, 1971). This question in particular is also the subject of Mackey's later essay, "Points of View for His Work as an Author: A Report from History," although the essay (and the volume in which it appears) is better considered, I think, a foundational work in the deconstructive Kierkegaardian tradition; see the treatment of Mackey in (d-vi), below.

34. With this in mind, we can see how the reading of Kierkegaard as a kind of poet might intersect the reading of Kierkegaard as a Socratic or maieutic figure in an interesting way; see (d-iii), below.

35. Michael Strawser, *Both/And: Reading Kierkegaard from Irony to Edification* (New York: Fordham University Press, 1996).

the aesthetic and the religious in pursuit of a common authorial goal. Ultimately, for Strawser, this brings one to the (non-)conclusion that the ultimate character of Kierkegaard's authorship—aesthetic, religious, or otherwise—is undecidable. While this approach certainly lacks the radicality of some other methodologies, it enables Strawser to offer a grounded and interesting reading of Kierkegaard that neither requires a commitment to any specific literary theory nor automatically alienates some readers by way of its theoretical orientation. In this, Strawser's "philosophical" approach to Kierkegaard's work as an author anticipates much of the "moderate" position staked out later by Genia Schönbaumsfeld.

In the introduction to her book on Kierkegaard and Wittgenstein, Schönbaumsfeld offers an overview of the various methodological approaches to reading Kierkegaard similar to the one I have provided here.[36] Schönbaumsfeld divides the field into four basic approaches to reading Kierkegaard: the "literal-minded reading," the "purely literary reading," the "killjoy reading," and the opposite of the killjoy reading (to which she does not give a name). These four approaches consist of two pairs of opposed ways of reading, the first pair of which, as noted above, line up nicely with the two approaches to the Kierkegaardian authorship which I have labeled (a) and (b)—(a) corresponding to Schönbaumsfeld's literalists and (b) corresponding to her "purely literary" readers. The remaining two, the killjoy and its opposite, represent views which recognize that pseudonymity is an important aspect of Kierkegaard's authorship, but which always prioritize either the signed works over the pseudonymous (in the killjoy's case) or the pseudonymous works over the signed (an approach which Schönbaumsfeld includes for the sake of logical completeness but for which she has found no actual proponent).[37] Schönbaumsfeld herself espouses none of these positions, opting instead for a view she refers to as "moderate," and which amounts to privileging Kierkegaard's published writings over the unpublished ones, and acknowledging that Kierkegaard put pseudonymity and other literary strategies to philosophical purpose, such that one cannot give the same sort of credence to every view expressed in Kierkegaard's writings. That said, Schönbaumsfeld treats the Kierkegaardian authorship as the work ultimately of a single author (although, importantly, not a single authorial perspective), such that meaningful correspondences can be found between works and across the pseudonymous-signed divide. Rather than seeking to privilege Kierkegaard's voice

---

36. Schönbaumsfeld, *A Confusion of the Spheres.*

37. On some readings of his work—although not my own—Joakim Garff might serve as a candidate for this open position in Schönbaumsfeld's taxonomy. Arguments in favor of classifying his work in this way might include Garff's open suspicion of anything Kierkegaard said in his own name about his own work, as exemplified in his essay, "The Eyes of Argus: *The Point of View* and Points of View on Kierkegaard's Work as an Author," as well as Garff's apparent view that more genuine knowledge of Kierkegaard can be gained from readings of his more overtly poetic and pseudonymous works than can be gained in readings of the signed and explicitly self-referential writings, a view put into practice in Garff's biography of Kierkegaard. See Garff, *Søren Kierkegaard: A Biography*, trans. Bruce Kirmmse (Princeton: Princeton University Press, 2005).

(that is, the authorial voice of the signed works) over the pseudonyms or vice versa, she tries to read all of the aspects, elements, and authorial personae at work in the authorship as cooperating in the authorship's production and thus as pursuing a common end even if by differing means. While this is in some ways very close to (c), inasmuch as Kierkegaard also presents his authorship (at least at the end of his authorship) as a single work in pursuit of a single end, Schönbaumsfeld's "moderate" view seems to deny Kierkegaard the ultimate authority over the authorship which he seems to presume in *The Point of View*.

One final entrant in this category is the work of Kierkegaard scholar Jon Stewart, and in particular, in an essay of his on the interpretative problems posed by pseudonymity.[38] Stewart's approach is both historically and philologically minded, and he maintains that, although we ought not ignore the pseudonyms altogether (contrasting his view with that of the infamously insensitive readings noted above), there is no reason to believe that understanding the literary consequences of Kierkegaardian pseudonymity is the be-all and end-all of Kierkegaard interpretation (contrasting his view with that of someone like Poole, or as we'll see in (d-vi), below, some of the other deconstructionists). He notes both that anonymity and pseudonymity were common literary ploys in Kierkegaard's time (and especially, it seems, in literary and journalistic Copenhagen) but that this fact alone does not explain Kierkegaard's sometimes quite subtle use of alternative authorial personae. Thus, in very much the same manner as Strawser and Schönbaumsfeld, Stewart opens a space in Kierkegaard interpretation for readings that attend both to the form and content of Kierkegaard's writings—granting neither authority over the other in advance of reading.

(d-iii) The next possible understanding of Kierkegaard's work as an author is less fully identified with the work of a single scholar or interpreter, although significant and singular contributions to this approach have been made. Following on claims made by the pseudonyms (especially Johannes Climacus), as well as Kierkegaard's published (especially *On the Concept of Irony*) and unpublished works in his own name, some readers have found in Kierkegaard a nineteenth-century Danish Socrates: a maieutician, or philosophical midwife, in the Socratic tradition. With specific reference to the work of Johannes Climacus, in both *Philosophical Fragments* and its *Postscript*, both Jacob Howland and Paul Muench have made some headway in showing how Climacus's (pseudonymous) philosophical perspective is essentially Socratic[39]; Muench, following the early

38. Jon Stewart, "Søren Kierkegaard and the Problem of Pseudonymity," *Graduate Faculty Philosophy Journal* 32: 2 (2012), pp. 407–434.

39. Jacob Howland, *Kierkegaard and Socrates: A Study in Philosophy and Faith* (Cambridge: Cambridge University Press, 2006); Paul Muench, "The Socratic Method of Kierkegaard's Pseudonym Johannes Climacus: Indirect Communication and the Art of 'Taking Away,'" in *Søren Kierkegaard and the Word(s)*, ed. Poul Houe and Gordon Marino (Copenhagen: C. A. Reitzel, 2003), pp. 139–150; and Muench, "Kierkegaard's Socratic Pseudonym: A Profile of Johannes Climacus," in *Kierkegaard's Concluding Unscientific Postscript: A Critical Guide*, ed. Rick Anthony Furtak (Cambridge: Cambridge University Press, 2010), pp. 25–44.

lead of Mark C. Taylor, has also done some work extending the analysis to show that Kierkegaard himself was a Socratic figure, as well.[40] In addition, Benjamin Daise has written another of the few books devoted entirely to the question of Kierkegaard's authorial work, *Kierkegaard's Socratic Art*, in which he argues for a maieutic-existentialist interpretation of Kierkegaard's work overall on the basis of a close reading and comparison of Plato's *Meno* and Climacus's *Fragments*.[41] What all of these interpretations have in common, in addition to the comparison of Kierkegaard to Socrates, is a reading of Socrates as primarily a midwife—that is, as espousing no (or very few) philosophical views of his own but working to occasion thought, self-reflection, and self-reform in others. There is certainly much of Socrates in Kierkegaard, from his dissertation, *On the Concept of Irony with Continual Reference to Socrates*, to the Socratic hue of Victor Eremita's challenge to the reader in *Either/Or*, to the discussions of the Socratic in its relation to the Christian in the works of Johannes Climacus, but of greatest significance, I think, to considerations of Kierkegaard's work as an author is his claim, in *The Moment* 10, that "The only analogy I have before me is Socrates; my task is a Socratic task, to audit the definition of what it is to be a Christian—I do not call myself a Christian (keeping the ideal free), but I can make it manifest that the others are that even less."[42]

(d-iv) Although Kierkegaard expressed interest in many of the arts, the theater does seem to have played a special role in his authorship: not only as the subject of much of his aesthetic thought but also, some of his readers have argued, as a sort of model for his authorship itself. One notable contribution is that of George Pattison, who has offered a reading of Kierkegaard's *Repetition* (ascribed to the pseudonym, Constantin Constantius) along dramatic lines.[43] Pattison sees the theater and the theatrical in *Repetition* on a variety of levels: there is, as is well known to readers, an extended theory of theatrical farce at the center of the book, and Pattison situates this theory in the context of the book's dramatic storyline overall and discusses both in the context of the world of the Danish theater in Copenhagen in the 1830s

40. Mark C. Taylor, *Kierkegaard's Pseudonymous Authorship: A Study of Time and the Self* (Princeton: Princeton University Press, 1975), pp. 51–62; and Paul Muench, "Kierkegaard's Socratic Point of View," in *A Companion to Socrates*, ed. Sara Ahbel-Rappe and Rachana Kamtekar (Oxford: Blackwell, 2006), pp. 389–405. In a similar vein, although in a different context, see my "Ironic Midwives: Socratic Maieutics in Nietzsche and Kierkegaard," *Philosophy and Social Criticism* 35: 6 (2009), pp. 627–648.

41. Benjamin Daise, *Kierkegaard's Socratic Art* (Macon, GA: Mercer University Press, 1999).

42. TM, 341 / SKS 13, 405.

43. George Pattison, "Play It Again: Kierkegaard's *Repetition* as Philosophy and Drama," in *Theatrical Theology: Explorations in Performing the Faith*, ed. Wesley Vander Lugt and Trevor Hart (Eugene, OR: Cascade Books, 2014), pp. 113–125. For work in a similar vein, see Martijn Boven, "A Theater of Ideas: Performance and Performativity in Kierkegaard's *Repetition*," in *Kierkegaard, Literature, and the Arts*, ed. Eric Ziolkowski (Evanston, IL: Northwestern University Press, 2018), pp. 115–130.

and 1840s.[44] In contrast to Pattison's reading of Kierkegaard's relationship to (and appropriation of) the theater, Martin Beck Matuštík reads the Kierkegaardian authorship taken as a whole as a dramatic work, with "stage directions" provided in (as Matuštík reads it) *The Point of View*.[45] Ultimately, on Matuštík's reading, the Kierkegaardian theater begins in maieutics (as with the Socratic readings of Kierkegaard, discussed in [d-ii] above) but ends in edification: specifically, the realization that everyone is the neighbor whom we are commanded to love.

Finally, perhaps the most significant contribution in this area—and certainly the most sophisticated, in its intertwining of the work of the author and the reader—is the theological approach taken by Carl S. Hughes.[46] Although one might think that reading the authorship as (modeled on) a work of literature or drama is a fairly straightforward affair, especially when thinking of the many "characters," the pseudonyms as well as those in Kierkegaard's many allusions, anecdotes, reminiscences, and stories,[47] Hughes suggests that we read the Kierkegaardian authorship in terms of deliberately established stage settings. Thus, Hughes moves us through various settings as they are either established literarily within the Kierkegaardian authorship or as they existed in the Denmark of Kierkegaard's time and were relied upon by him in his writings (Vor Frue Kirke, the church which Kierkegaard attended with some regularity, figures prominently). Hughes argues that Kierkegaard establishes these settings for the reader, inviting him or her to inhabit them (imaginatively) as a means of entering the authorship and of entering into the imaginative performance of the different and developmental stages of desire. The ultimate goal of this series of theatrical settings seems, to Hughes, to be a progression toward the realization of an infinite desire for God—a

---

44. Some of what Pattison says about the theatrical in here relates back to what he says about the carnivalesque in Kierkegaard elsewhere. See George Pattison, "Bakhtin's Category of Carnival in the Interpretation of the Writings of Søren Kierkegaard," *Kierkegaard Studies Yearbook* (2006), pp. 100–128.

45. Martin Beck Matuštík, "Reading 'Kierkegaard' as a Drama," in *International Kierkegaard Commentary, Volume 22: The Point of View*, ed. Robert L. Perkins (Macon, GA: Mercer University Press, 2010), pp. 411–430. Another reader who interprets Kierkegaard as writing dramatically, although on a smaller scale, is Howard Pickett. See Pickett, "Beyond the Mask: Kierkegaard's *Postscript* as Antitheatrical, Anti-Hegelian Drama," in *Kierkegaard, Literature, and the Arts*, ed. Eric Ziolkowski (Evanston, IL: Northwestern University Press, 2018), pp. 99–114.

46. Carl S. Hughes, *Kierkegaard and the Staging of Desire: Rhetoric and Performance in a Theology of Eros* (New York: Fordham University Press, 2014).

47. Two excellent contributions reading Kierkegaard's work as an author on the model of literature or stories are Marcia C. Robinson, "Kierkegaard's Existential Play: Storytelling and the Development of the Religious Imagination in the Authorship," and Joakim Garff, "Kierkegaard's Christian Bildungsroman," both in *Kierkegaard, Literature, and the Arts*, ed. Eric Ziolkowski (Evanston, IL: Northwestern University Press, 2018), pp. 71–84 and 85–96, respectively.

desire which, as in the theater, is always only accessible by way of a simultaneous relationship to (and desire for) the material world of our fellow human beings. Like Pattison, Matuštík, and others, then, Hughes suggests that Kierkegaard's work as an author is very much the work of a playwright, with his writings themselves as the play, wherein the reader plays alternatively the role of spectator in the theater or character on the stage.

(d-v) Kierkegaard's work as an author is manifold and diverse, and many of the readings of the Kierkegaardian authorship privilege one or more elements over the others—if only as a means of finding some foothold within the writings so as to come to a point of view on them. We have already seen in James Conant an interpretative point of view suggesting that the works (at least the works of Johannes Climacus) are nonsense, and another in Roger Poole, arguing that no meaningful connection can be forged between the pseudonymous and signed works to constitute a single authorship at all. Both of these approaches dismiss the incorporation of (at least some of) the pseudonymous works into whatever it is we mean when we say "Kierkegaard." There is, however, a third entry in this list of dismissive readings of at least some of the writings: the view that a careful reader will see that, at least in some instances, Kierkegaard is outright and intentionally deceiving us, presenting us with falsehoods as if they were truths. There are two chief proponents of (admittedly different versions of) this view, and neither is suggesting that we abandon Kierkegaard altogether: just that we acknowledge that some parts of the authorship are "truer" than others.

The first of these is the Danish scholar, Henning Fenger, who, in his influential collection of essays, *Kierkegaard, the Myths and Their Origins*, argues for a number of somewhat controversial—if not groundbreaking—views on Kierkegaard's writings.[48] In the first of the essays collected there, "Kierkegaard as a Falsifier of History," Fenger argues that Kierkegaard used his unpublished journals, his ironic works, the pseudonyms, and what amounts effectively to the whole of the Kierkegaardian authorship consciously and intentionally to deceive anyone who might consult them about the nature of Kierkegaard's life and works. Fenger argues that Kierkegaard does this primarily to "make literature out of his life. Or to make literature with his life."[49] And the notion that one's life could (or should) be understood as a work of art, literary or otherwise, is not foreign to students of nineteenth- and twentieth-century European thought and letters. Fenger lays the groundwork, then, for approaching Kierkegaard's writings with a certain degree of suspicion—ever aware of the possibility that what Kierkegaard is telling us in any given moment is untrue and meant to be untrue as a snare for the unwary or thoughtless reader—and claims that it is not Kierkegaard's fault if some of his readers "have taken him at his word."[50] This is an admittedly extreme view on

---

48. Henning Fenger, *Kierkegaard, the Myths and Their Origins: Studies in the Kierkegaardian Papers and Letters*, trans. George C. Schoolfield (New Haven, CT: Yale University Press, 1980).

49. Ibid., p. 31.

50. Ibid.

Kierkegaard's work as an author, although perhaps not as extreme as Conant or Poole.[51] In any case, it makes the work of reading Kierkegaard infinitely more difficult—and highly individualized, from reader to reader.

The second interpretative approach to reading Kierkegaard as deceptive that I wish to mention here is that of M. Holmes Hartshorne. Hartshorne, in his book, *Kierkegaard, Godly Deceiver*,[52] suggests that the pseudonymous writings are all intentionally produced so as to present and espouse untenable positions. Ultimately, Hartshorne argues, the point of such a deception is to move readers existentially toward the truth—that is, for Hartshorne as for Kierkegaard, Christianity—by helping them to see the flaws and failings in their own (and the pseudonyms') points of view. Hartshorne's view is thus much like Fenger's, in that both assert that Kierkegaard intentionally attempts to deceive us—although for Hartshorne, in contrast to Fenger, that deception has a specific purpose that can be known. In this, Hartshorne compares Kierkegaard's deceptiveness to the irony of Socrates, which he also takes to have had a specific, existential purpose in mind (ethical, in the case of Socrates, rather than religious) for the edification of the reader. Fenger and Hartshorne are akin, however, in their recommendation that we read Kierkegaard very much aware of the possibility that, in at least some of what he writes, he is lying to us.

(d-vi) The last of the many different approaches to understanding Kierkegaard as an author that I will discuss here is perhaps the most controversial and is one to which many of the approaches and scholars already discussed have been responding: deconstruction. As a general philosophy of reading and an influence on literary theory, deconstruction has its origins in the work of Jacques Derrida beginning in the 1960s, but deconstruction comes to Kierkegaard studies only really in the 1980s and 1990s.[53] One of the most frequently cited deconstructive readings of Kierkegaard is that of Roger Poole, already discussed in (b-ii) above. Poole's brand of deconstruction results in a fascinating reading of Kierkegaard, which succeeds in keeping the pseudonyms and Kierkegaard at an absolute distance from one another, but which also leaves the reader with very little sense of why it is Kierkegaard might have produced an authorship of this peculiar sort. As such, one might argue that, on Poole's reading, Kierkegaard's work as an author becomes a sort of curiosity, an idiosyncratic but trivial entry in Danish and world

---

51. Fenger's distrustful approach to Kierkegaard's writings, and especially Kierkegaard's writings about himself, anticipates (and influences) some of the foundational elements of the deconstructive approach taken by Joakim Garff; see (d-vi), below.

52. M. Holmes Hartshorne, *Kierkegaard, Godly Deceiver: The Nature and Meaning of His Pseudonymous Writings* (New York: Columbia University Press, 1990).

53. Derrida himself writes a book on the biblical story of Abraham's intended sacrifice of Isaac, which deals centrally with Kierkegaard's *Fear and Trembling*. However deconstructive Derrida's approach to biblical ethics is, however, the book is not a deconstructive reading of Kierkegaard. See Jacques Derrida, *The Gift of Death*, trans. David Wills (Chicago: University of Chicago Press, 1995).

literature. A great deal of the negative response to deconstruction had by some readers of Kierkegaard seems to stem from deconstructive readings in the manner of Poole's.

A full decade before the appearance of Poole's *Kierkegaard: The Indirect Communication*, however, a different sort of deconstruction of Kierkegaard was undertaken in a short essay by the British philosopher and literary theorist, Christopher Norris.[54] Like those who approach Kierkegaard by way of his own statements about his work as an author, in (c) above, Norris takes seriously Kierkegaard's explanation of his apparently fragmented, alternatively pseudonymous and signed, authorial method. And like those views taken in (d-v), above, Norris takes Kierkegaard to admit to using the pseudonymous authorship to deceive his readers. This is so far in accord with Norris's understanding of deconstruction as a process of "textual demystification," by way of which the inner workings of a text undermine its explicit (and assumed) intent.[55] Yet, as Norris notes, Kierkegaard intentionally employs strategies of authorship anticipatory of deconstruction to a purpose deconstruction could not set for itself: Kierkegaard does not simply try to deceive us but to deceive us *into the truth*. Thus, Norris thinks Kierkegaard's work as an author sits between more conventional readership and interpretation, on the one hand, and deconstruction, on the other. Kierkegaard's authorship presupposes the possibility of using deconstructive (or pre-deconstructive) techniques in pursuit of a higher truth—a religious, or divine, or providential truth—which is a presupposition totally foreign to (early) Derridean deconstruction. Norris does not resolve this discrepancy in either the Kierkegaardians' or the Derrideans' favor. Instead, he notes simply that Kierkegaard presents "the highest and most resourceful" deconstructive challenge to the practices and presuppositions of deconstruction.[56]

A second (or first, depending upon how we date its publication) deconstructive possibility in examinations of Kierkegaard as an author comes in the form of Louis Mackey's second Kierkegaard book, *Points of View*.[57] As we saw (in [d-iii], above), Mackey's initial approach to Kierkegaard's work as an author is an aesthetic one: he first reads Kierkegaard as "a kind of poet." This is an understanding of the Kierkegaardian authorship for which there are rather conventional resources within the authorship itself. By the early 1980s, however, Mackey had reconsidered his point of view on authorship and textuality, having been deeply influenced by the introduction of deconstruction (and postmodernism, generally) into Kierkegaard scholarship during that time. While Norris offers us a Kierkegaard who writes to pose an either/or challenge to deconstruction itself, Mackey moves one step further along the deconstructive line. The late Mackey disagrees with Norris—

54. Christopher Norris, "Fictions of Authority: Narrative and Viewpoint in Kierkegaard's Writing," *Criticism* 25: 2 (1983), pp. 87–107.

55. Ibid., p. 106.

56. Ibid.

57. Mackey, *Points of View: Readings of Kierkegaard*.

and the early Mackey—that Kierkegaard presents a stable position (or presents his position as if it were stable) in the face of the textual-authorial fragmentation posed by deconstruction. Although the essays in *Points of View* represent many stages along Mackey's way—from the 1960s through the 1980s—in the latest of them, on Kierkegaard's *The Point of View*, Mackey has adopted a position that looks forward to Poole's. For this Mackey, Kierkegaard so thoroughly disguises himself that the "real" Kierkegaard is no longer visible to readers, and as such, readers are justified in taking whatever stance on Kierkegaard as an author—explicitly including reading the signed works as if they were written by just another pseudonym, named "Kierkegaard"—they choose. In this way, we can see that Mackey comes as close to the open reading of Poole, or the nonsense reading of Conant, as any of the deconstructive interpreters of Kierkegaard does.

Finally, one of the most influential of the deconstructive readings of Kierkegaard is that of the Danish scholar, Joakim Garff. There are certainly significant correspondences between Garff's approach to Kierkegaard's authorial enterprise and the approaches of other Kierkegaard deconstructionists, such as Norris, Mackey, and Poole, but unique to Garff's work, I think, is a concern not simply for the relationship between authorial identity and written text (a traditionally deconstructive concern) but additionally between the deconstructed text and the biography of Søren Kierkegaard—the actual human being, as opposed to the authorial persona.[58] Garff (following Fenger) reads Kierkegaard as presenting a fictionalized version of himself and his life in his own writings, such that one must read both the signed and pseudonymous works in order to get the clearest possible picture of Kierkegaard himself—almost in the manner of a psychoanalyst, distrusting (although not always disbelieving) Kierkegaard's self-explanations while remaining ever on the lookout for those ways in which he unintentionally or unconsciously reveals himself. Garff characterizes this process as reading "Kierkegaard with Kierkegaard against Kierkegaard," an approach he suggests offers the most *Kierkegaardian* sort of reading of Kierkegaard possible.[59] In taking this approach, and despite his characterization by some anti-deconstructionist readers as espousing an extremist position, we find Garff somewhere on the spectrum of those interpretations of and methodologies for reading Kierkegaard as an author in between the absolute literalist and the nonsense or "anything goes" readings discussed in (a) and (b), above. And in this, we might begin to see an unexpected kinship between the methods of interpretations in (c), like those of Cappelørn,

---

58. See Garff, "The Eyes of Argus: *The Point of View* and Points of View on Kierkegaard's Work as an Author," pp. 75–102; *Den Søvnløse: Kierkegaard læst æstestisk/biografisk* (Copenhagen: C.A. Reitzel, 1995); "'What Did I Find? Not My I': On Kierkegaard's Journals and the Pseudonymous Autobiography," trans. K. Brian Söderquist, *Kierkegaard Studies Yearbook* (2003), pp. 110–123; and "The Esthetic Is above All My Element," trans. Stacey E. Ake, in *The New Kierkegaard*, ed. Elsebet Jegstrup (Bloomington: Indiana University Press, 2004), pp. 59–70.

59. Garff, "The Eyes of Argus," p. 77.

Helms, and Tietjen, and Garff's more distrustful, deconstructive view—methods that are otherwise diametrically opposed to one another.

***

A diverse array of both rising and established contemporary Kierkegaard scholars has contributed to this volume. Each of these authors has staked out a perspective on the thorny issues of authorship and authority, and each chapter presents its author's take (sometimes in general, sometimes in a more focused way, and sometimes by way of comparison with other important figures) on the nature, function, purpose, or value of Kierkegaard's work as an author. Although there have been monographs and journal articles dealing with authorial issues in the Kierkegaardian corpus, there are only a few resources available for interested readers of Kierkegaard to find a range of differing views on authorship in Kierkegaard in a single place.[60] This book is meant in part to correct this discrepancy in the scholarly literature. In addition, the writings gathered here are—like Kierkegaard's own—written from a variety of perspectives, and in a variety of genres and styles. Given the significance of the question of authorship for readings of Kierkegaard, the renewed interest of the Kierkegaard community in questions of authorship, and the usefulness of examinations of this sort beyond the bounds of Kierkegaard scholarship—in the philosophy of literature, aesthetics, the history of art, art theory, and literary studies, for example—I do not think the contributions of these authors could be more valuable or more timely. And given the diversity of modes of expression and points of view, I do not think any collection of this sort could be more Kierkegaardian.

In Chapter 1, "Kierkegaard qua Author: 'Like the Guadalquibir River,'" Sylvia Walsh explores Kierkegaard's references to the Guadalquibir River in Spain as a simile to his activity as an author. Just as the Guadalquibir plunges underground and reemerges along its course to the sea, so, Walsh argues, Kierkegaard sees his own activity as an author doing the same, winding its way in and out of pseudonymity to a final reemergence in the *Discourses at the Communion on Fridays*: the telos and resting point for the writings penned in his own name as well as for the authorship as a whole. For Walsh, the communion discourses thus constitute key writings for understanding Kierkegaard as an author in two respects: both as poet and penitent, and for awakening the reader to the religious element which in his view characterizes the authorship in its totality.

In Chapter 2, "Rhetoric and Understanding: Authorship as Christian Mission," Robert C. Roberts thinks through the concepts of knowledge and understanding in light of Kierkegaard's revival of a Socratic-Platonic understanding of understanding and of knowledge. On Roberts's view, the revived concept of knowledge is crucial

---

60. Two of the most useful are Robert L. Perkins, ed., *International Kierkegaard Commentary, Volume 22: The Point of View* (Macon, GA: Mercer University Press, 2010), and Eric Ziolkowski, ed., *Kierkegaard, Literature, and the Arts* (Evanston, IL: Northwestern University Press, 2018).

to Kierkegaard's conception of his divine calling to reintroduce Christianity to Christendom—and, thus, his work as a religious author. Roberts notes that Kierkegaard conceives his task as requiring both poetics and dialectics, in combination, and thus Roberts explains how this integration of communicative disciplines in Kierkegaard's writings has the potential to achieve Kierkegaard's Christian, missionary goal.

In Chapter 3, "Inside the Escritoire: On Kierkegaard's Erotic Theory of Communication," Michael Strawser begins with Kierkegaard's assertion in *The Point of View* that "*the issue*"—"the total thought"—of his entire authorship is centered on the task of becoming a Christian. Rather than interpreting this with a theological focus on *what* it means to become a Christian, Strawser asks us to consider that Kierkegaard is focused rather on *how* one becomes a lover. Thus, on Strawser's view, Kierkegaard should be read as first and foremost a philosopher of love whose work centers on the question "How does one communicate and enable love in writing?" If we sincerely ask this question of Kierkegaard, Strawser suggests, we can find concealed a theory of communication that informs his understanding of the practical aspects of both reading and writing—a theory of communication driven by and focused on love, and with important resonances with the work of Jean-Luc Marion.

In Chapter 4, "Kierkegaard's Scene Changes: Authorship as Theatrical Practice," Sophie Wennerscheid draws on Gilles Deleuze's characterization of Kierkegaard as a philosopher of the theater who affects the reader's mind "outside of all representation." Wennerscheid examines Kierkegaard's use of theatrical means in his writings, such as role playing, dialogue, and the complexity of points of view and voices. She contends that, by writing in this way, Kierkegaard can make the reader part of his work. Wennerscheid reads Kierkegaard's texts, published and unpublished, pseudonymous or not, as a single, dramaturgically shaped, complete work of art in which the individual texts play different roles dependent on the reader—who thus has to take the role of director him- or herself.

In Chapter 5, "Kierkegaard the Humorist," M. G. Piety notes that something doesn't add up in the popular perception of Kierkegaard. Although his works seem at first glance to be both dark and impenetrable, Kierkegaard remains one of the most widely read and beloved of philosophers among the general public. Piety suggests that the explanation of this seeming paradox is that Kierkegaard is one of Denmark's greatest humorists. She traces the path of Kierkegaard's humor from his earliest published works through some of his most famous later ones, arguing ultimately that humor is one of the aspects of Kierkegaard's writings that gives them such a broad and enduring appeal.

In Chapter 6, "A Desire to Be Understood: Authorship and Authority in Kierkegaard's Work," Daniel Berthold explores Kierkegaard's ethics of authorship. Berthold suggests that the directness and tidiness of Kierkegaard's own explanation of his authorial work is suspiciously straightforward and that the unity of Kierkegaard's authorship is more a unity of recurring preoccupations and themes rather than of authorial personalities. One such theme, Berthold notes, is certainly that of faith and the religious—but, he argues, the "aesthetic works" are neither simply wrong turns on the way to faith nor merely deceptive texts that, if decoded correctly, harbor a hidden invitation to the religious life. They are projects in a larger preoccupation on Kierkegaard's part with the disinstallment of his own authority as author, or in a word, with his commitment to the death of the author. Berthold argues that a recognition of the author's lack of authority is central to his ethics of authorship: as Roland Barthes will argue a century later, for Kierkegaard, Berthold suggests, the author must vanish so that the reader can find her own path.

In Chapter 7, "Illegible Salvation: The Authority of Language in *The Concept of Anxiety*," Sarah Horton examines the analysis of language in *The Concept of Anxiety* and argues that language ultimately reveals itself as both dangerous and salvific. Vigilius Haufniensis, the pseudonymous author of the text, is suspicious of language because it divides the individual from him- or herself and thereby makes possible the self-forgetfulness of objective chatter. Horton acknowledges the validity of the warning but also notes that Haufniensis fails to grasp that, by rendering the self other than itself, language constitutes the self: the individual's very existence depends on language. Moreover, Horton suggests, the attempt to establish oneself as absolutely self-identical is precisely sin, for Kierkegaard. Ultimately, salvation can come only if we renounce the attempt to establish distinctions that are beyond our power. Horton argues that, by employing a pseudonymous figure who views language with suspicion, Kierkegaard shows that language is dangerous—even deadly—but it is also the condition of possibility for salvation.

In Chapter 8, "The Very Tang of Life: Lyrical Jesting in Kierkegaard's *Postscript* Title," Edward F. Mooney argues that, in addition to the many philosophical, psychological, even religious gifts Kierkegaard's writings bestow upon readers, there is also—and just as importantly—a dramatic unfolding of both Kierkegaard's and the reader's selves that is performed in any reading open to what the text does in addition to what it says. By way of demonstration, Mooney works through the lengthy and seemingly self-contradictory title of one of Kierkegaard's most important pseudonymous books, the *Concluding Unscientific Postscript* of Johannes Climacus, showing us that, read in a lyrical or musical way, even just the title of the book can give readers the much more personal gift of an openness to those moments that cut to the heart of the human experience.

In Chapter 9, "'I Came to Carthage'; 'So I Arrived in Berlin': Fleeing, Escape, and Autobiographical Memory in Augustine's *Confessions* and Kierkegaard's *Repetition*," Eric Ziolkowski brings the writings of two of Western history's greatest Christian thinkers into dialogue on the recurring theme (across religions, East and West) of escape. Both Augustine and Kierkegaard's pseudonym, Constantin Constantius, flee their homes in moments of apparent religious abandonment, and for both, these moments become critical turning points in their lives. Through a close comparative analysis of the two statements in his title and the passages surrounding them, as well as of Augustine's and Kierkegaard's actual lives, Ziolkowski reveals a remarkable kinship between these two moments—at Carthage and Berlin—that transcend the various obvious but largely superficial differences by way, at least in part, of the narrative techniques and strategies by which the two authors relate these moments to their understanding of autobiographical memory and of the existential workings of providence and repetition.

In Chapter 10, "Kierkegaard on Andersen and the Art of Storytelling," Eleanor Helms examines Kierkegaard's early literary review of Hans Christian Andersen's novel, *Only a Fiddler*. By way of her careful analysis, Helms shows that Kierkegaard—echoing Aristotle and Kant—finds unity and continuity to be essential features of storytelling. She argues that the continuity of a story is necessary to sustain the believability of a story's events for the reader and draws a useful comparison to some elements of J. R. R. Tolkien's *On Fairy-Stories* as further support for Kierkegaard's account of what makes stories believable. On Tolkien's view, a story needs some amount of dissolution to avoid feeling contrived, but the plot, characters, and themes must ultimately converge toward a unified ending. Sustaining a reader's belief in this ending is the primary art of storytelling, according to Tolkien. According to Helms, Kierkegaard likewise thinks that the reader's belief depends on the relation of each part of the literary work to its whole—the crux of Andersen's failing as a storyteller.

In Chapter 11, "'On S.K.': Deconstructing Signature(s) in Kierkegaard and Sarah Kofman," I offer an analysis of the concept and practice of literary signature, both as it is presented in Kierkegaard's signed writings and in the deconstructive writings of Jacques Derrida and Sarah Kofman. I argue that, of the French deconstructionists, Kofman is far more attuned to the work of Kierkegaard, and I show this by way of her writings on Derrida and signature, her writings on her own name, and her analysis of Kierkegaard's discussion of Socrates in *On the Concept of Irony*. On the basis of the comparison between Kofman, Kierkegaard, and Socrates, I suggest that signature is, for Kierkegaard, an approach to authorship with far deeper and more dangerous roots in an undecidable, ambiguous, unmastered irony than is pseudonymity.

Finally, in Chapter 12, "Kierkegaard—What 'Kind' of Writer?: A Dialogue," George Pattison brilliantly broaches the question of Kierkegaard's work as an author by way of a dramatic dialogue focused on the idea that Kierkegaard was "a kind of poet" or "a poet of the religious." Inquiring into the meaning of such a claim, Pattison shows how it leads naturally to other, related authorial questions: how does Kierkegaard's claim to be a poet square with his self-description in *The Point of View* as an "author" and his frequent complaints that, qua author, he had not received the financial rewards he would have received in any other European country? Are we then to read him as a nineteenth-century man of letters, a professional prose writer whose work covers the typical gamut of the period, from criticism, to philosophy, to fiction, to religious polemics or as, indeed, a poet, compelled to write by a divine vocation? Pattison addresses these questions, deepening and elucidating the value of the inquiry itself—if not answering them conclusively—in the form of a conversation between a critic, a poet, a German philosopher, and an Analytic theologian, all out for a beer together during a break from a Kierkegaard conference in Copenhagen.

Chapter 1

KIERKEGAARD QUA AUTHOR: "LIKE THE GUADALQUIBIR RIVER"

Sylvia Walsh

A metaphor that appealed to Kierkegaard very much as a simile for his activity as an author was the Guadalquibir River, one of the longest rivers in Southern Spain, which he mistakenly confused with the Guadiana River in describing it as plunging underground at one point and later resurfacing along its course.[1] Kierkegaard refers to this river five times in his journals and once in his writings, comparing it to himself in the journals and to Socrates in *The Concept of Irony*.[2] These references thus provide a metaphor by which to understand how Kierkegaard saw himself as an author in relation to his pseudonymous and signed writings and how he wished to be understood as an author by his readers as well. While Kierkegaard claimed that his authorship was religious from beginning to end, he also recognized with regard to his writings as a whole that "in a certain sense it is a question posed to the times in the form of a choice: one must choose either to make the esthetic element into the idea behind it all, and then explain everything in that way, or the religious element. Precisely therein lies what is awakening."[3]

1. According to the *Encyclopedia Britannica* online at www.britannica.com, the Guadalquivir River, as it is usually spelled today, flows westward from the mountains of Jaén province through a narrow valley and reservoir to the cities of Córdoba and Seville before meandering through a coastal plain and swamps and emptying into the Atlantic Ocean at the Gulf of Cádiz. Both Kierkegaard and the new English translation of his journals are inconsistent with regard to the spelling of this river, sometimes spelling it as Guadalquivir and other times as Guadalquibir. I shall refer to it as spelled in the English translations, even though the original Danish text may spell it differently. On Kierkegaard's confusion of the Guadalquivir River with the Guadiana River, see Eric Ziolkowski, "Guadalquivir: Kierkegaard's Subterranean Fluvial Pseudonymity," in *Kierkegaard's Literary Figures and Motifs*, Tome I, ed. Jon Stewart and Katalin Nun (Burlington, VT: Ashgate, 2014), pp. 279–297.

2. JP 5, 5397 / SKS 18, 46 (EE: 128); JP 6, 6416 / SKS 22, 70 (NB11: 123); JP 6, 6431 / SKS 22, 127 (NB11: 204); JP 6, 6445 / SKS 22, 149 (NB12: 7); JP 6, 6461; CI, 198 / SKS 22, 169 (NB12: 52).

3. JP 6, 6520 / SKS 22, 323 (NB13: 81). On the interpretation of Kierkegaard as an esthetic or religious author, see Henning Fenger, *Kierkegaard, the Myths and Their Origins*:

In Kierkegaard's view, however, the key writings for understanding him qua author and for awakening the reader to the religious element that characterizes the authorship as a whole are his *Discourses at the Communion on Fridays*.[4] Just as the Guadalquibir plunges underground and reemerges along its course to the sea, so Kierkegaard sees his own activity as an author doing the same, winding its way in and out of pseudonymity to a final reemergence in the communion discourses as the telos and resting point for the writings penned in his own name as well as for the authorship as a whole. The communion discourses are therefore important for understanding Kierkegaard qua author in two respects, both as poet and penitent.[5]

Kierkegaard first makes reference to the Guadalquibir River in his journal from 1839 at a time when he was getting ready to prepare for his comprehensive examination for the *Candidatus Theologiae* degree, which he passed on July 3, 1840. Approximately a year prior to that date, he announced in his journal: "I shall now, for a season, for some miles in time, plunge *underground* like the Guadalquivir—to be sure, I shall come up again!"[6] Having already published his first book, *From the Papers of One Still Living*, a literary critique of Hans Christian Andersen as a novelist, Kierkegaard suggests in this entry that he not only intends to suspend any more writing for the time being but also definitely plans to resume it when the exam is over.

The first writing to appear after emerging from underground was his dissertation for the Magister (Doctoral) degree, which he defended on September 29, 1841.[7] It

Studies in Kierkegaardian Papers and Letters, trans. George C. Schoolfield (New Haven: Yale University Press); Joakim Garff, "The Eyes of Argus: *The Point of View* and Points of View with Respect to Kierkegaard's 'Activity as an Author,'" trans. Bruce Kirmmse, *Kierkegaardiana* 15 (1991), pp. 29–54; Sylvia Walsh, "Reading Kierkegaard with Kierkegaard Against Garff," *Kierkegaard Newsletter* 38 (July, 1999), pp. 4–8, and Garff's reply, "Rereading Oneself," in the same volume, pp. 9–14; Joseph Westfall, *The Kierkegaardian Author: Authorship and Performance in Kierkegaard's Literary and Dramatic Criticism* (Berlin: Walter de Gruyter, 2007), pp. 223–240; and *International Kierkegaard Commentary, Volume 22: The Point of View*, ed. Robert L. Perkins (Macon, GA: Mercer University Press, 2010), especially the essays by David Law, Mark A. Tietjen, Carl S. Hughes, Eleanor D. Helms, David Cain, John E. Whitmire, Jr., and W. Glen Kirkconnell.

4. See Søren Kierkegaard, *Discourses at the Communion on Fridays*, trans. Sylvia Walsh (Bloomington: Indiana University Press, 2011), referred to in this essay in parentheses with the siglum DCF, followed by the corresponding reference in the Hong translations.

5. DCF, 125 / WA, 165 / SKS 12, 281; JP 6, 6418 / SKS 22, 75 (NB11: 125); JP 6, 6461 / SKS 22, 238 (NB12: 52); JP 6, 6487 / SKS 22, 223 (NB12: 133); JP 6, 6519 / SKS 22, 322 (NB13: 79).

6. JP 5, 5397 / SKS 18, 46 (EE 128).

7. For a detailed account of Kierkegaard's defense of his dissertation, see Bruce H. Kirmmse, "Socrates in the Fast Lane: Kierkegaard's *The Concept of Irony* on the University's Velocifère," *International Kierkegaard Commentary, Volume 2: The Concept of Irony*, ed. Robert L. Perkins (Macon, GA: Mercer University Press, 2001), pp. 17–99.

is in this work that the second reference to the Guadalquivir River appears, this time as a simile to the life of Socrates:

> For the observer, Socrates' life is like a magnificent pause in the course of history: we do not hear him at all; a profound stillness prevails—until it is broken by the noisy attempts of the many and very different schools of followers to trace their origin in this hidden and cryptic source. With Socrates the stream of historical narrative, just like the river Guadalquivir, drops underground for some distance, only to rush out again with renewed power. He is like a dash in world history, and the ignorance about him, due to the lack of opportunity for direct observation, is an invitation not so much to bypass him as to conjure him forth with the aid of the idea, to make him become visible in his ideal form—in other words, to become conscious of the idea that is the meaning of his existence in the world, of the phase in the development of the world spirit that is symbolically indicated by the singularity of his existence in history.[8]

Given Kierkegaard's close association of his own maieutic task as a writer to that of Socrates, especially with regard to the use of dialectic, irony, and indirect communication in seeking to communicate ethical-religious truth to others, this reference is important not only for understanding Kierkegaard's view of Socrates but also his view of himself. According to Kierkegaard, it was the "profound stillness" or silence of Socrates in contrast to the "noisy attempts" of his followers to trace their origins back to him as the "hidden and cryptic source" of their own views that distinguished him as an ironist and made him an enigma to the observer. Like the Guadalquivir River, Socrates, or the historical narrative of his life, "drops underground" in the sense that no one knows where he stands, one of the characteristics of irony being that it cancels itself or does not mean what it says, with the result that the observer does not know whether the ironist speaks earnestly or in jest.[9] As an ironist, then, Socrates's life is like "a magnificent pause" or "a dash in world history," inaccessible for direct observation or immediate apprehension by others, keeping them ignorant of who he really was yet inviting them "to conjure him forth" in ideal form by becoming "conscious of the idea that is the meaning of his existence in the world," namely infinite absolute negativity or irony.[10] It is in this sense that Kierkegaard sees the historical narrative of Socrates's life as "rushing out again with renewed power."[11] His significance in the development of world history was to provide a turning point for it through a negation of the established order or given actuality of the time in the introduction of the principle of subjectivity or inwardness in the single individual. In Kierkegaard's view, however, Socrates himself did not manifest subjectivity in its positive fullness as a

8. CI, 198 / SKS 1, 244.
9. CI, 248 / SKS 1, 286–287.
10. CI, 198 / SKS 1, 244.
11. Ibid.

concrete personality but only negatively or abstractly as a possibility in opposition to the family and state.[12]

Kierkegaard did not embrace Socratic irony as such, claiming that "in the end irony overwhelmed him [Socrates]; he became dizzy, and everything lost its reality."[13] Yet the freshly minted Magister did find Socratic irony to be "world-historically justified" in its negation of the given actuality by virtue of "a higher something that still is not."[14] He also recognized the validity of irony as a controlled element in the personal life of an individual, maintaining that "no genuinely human life is possible without irony."[15] It remains to be seen, however, to what extent Kierkegaard plunged into the underground of irony himself, employing it as a controlled element in the development of his own life as well as a tool of communication to others in his writings.

All the remaining references to the Guadalquibir River occur in the journals of 1849, ten years after the first journal reference to it, and all of them liken it to Kierkegaard as an author. A perusal of the entries from this year in the new chronological edition of Kierkegaard's journals and notebooks (one of the advantages of this edition over the Hongs's topical arrangement of selected entries) reveals that this was a year in which Kierkegaard engaged in a good deal of reflection on his activity as an author, particularly in the second half of that year as a result of having concocted the new pseudonym Anti-Climacus to present what it means to be a Christian in the strictest sense. All of the references to the Guadalquibir River in the journals of this year were penned in the latter half of the year during the period of May through September.

The first (or third chronologically) reference likens the pathway of the river to plunging into and out of pseudonymity on the part of Kierkegaard himself: "So, just as the river Guadalquibir plunges underground at one point and then emerges later, I must now plunge into pseudonymity; but I have now also understood where I will emerge again in my own name."[16] Of course, this was not the first time Kierkegaard had plunged into pseudonymity inasmuch as most of his early aesthetic writings were published pseudonymously, accompanied

---

12. CI, 165, 178, 185 / SKS 1, 214, 225, 232–233. On Socrates as an ironist in *The Concept of Irony*, see Carl S. Hughes, *Kierkegaard and the Staging of Desire: Rhetoric and Performance in a Theology of Eros* (New York: Fordham University Press, 2014), pp. 9–45; K. Brian Söderquist, *The Isolated Self: Truth and Untruth in Søren Kierkegaard's "On the Concept of Irony"* (Copenhagen: Museum Tusculanum Press, 2013); Sylvia Walsh, "An Amorist Interpretation of Socratic Eros," in *International Kierkegaard Commentary, Volume 2: The Concept of Irony*, ed. Robert L. Perkins (Macon, GA: Mercer University Press, 2001), pp. 123–140; and John Lippitt, *Humour and Irony in Kierkegaard's Thought* (London: Macmillan, 2000).

13. CI, 264 / SKS 1, 302.

14. CI, 261, 263–264 / SKS 1, 298, 301–302.

15. CI, 326 / SKS 1, 355.

16. JP 6, 6416 / SKS 22, 70 (NB11: 123).

by a series of upbuilding or edifying discourses issued under his own name. Unlike his first plunge, therefore, he did not cease writing altogether nor in his own name during this plunge. Moreover, by 1849, he had already published a number of Christian discourses under his own name, including Part Three of *Upbuilding Discourses in Various Spirits* (1847), *Works of Love* (1847), and *Christian Discourses* (1848), but in a milder tone than the two Christian pseudonymous works already completed but not yet published in 1849, namely *The Sickness unto Death*, intended "for edification and awakening," and *Practice in Christianity*, the first part of which is designated "for awakening and inward deepening."[17] It is with reference to these two works that Kierkegaard now contemplates plunging again into pseudonymity, but for a different reason than before, inasmuch as "all this productivity … has the tension and contraction of the dialectical in relation to the doctrine of sin and redemption," which could not be presented in his own name, or if it were, he suggests it would have to be "in character, as a finale to all my striving," meaning that he would personally have to exemplify the Christian ideal so rigorously put forward in them.[18] That, however, would create "a monstrously stressful problem" for him, he writes, in wanting "neither untruthfully to hold myself back nor untruthfully to go too far, but truthfully to understand myself, to remain true to myself" in relation to the authorship.[19] After plunging into pseudonymity this time, therefore, Kierkegaard now professes to understand "where I will emerge again in my own name," namely with "a simple, edifying discourse," which had been his category as an author from the very beginning.[20] Assuming the equality of all persons before God, an edifying or upbuilding discourse takes its point of departure in the universally human or that which applies to every human being regardless of individual differences with respect to sex, class, age, education, or spiritual cultivation.[21] It thus seeks to build up the reader as a single individual, which in Kierkegaard's view every person is or can be "in the expression of true fear of God, true love to one's neighbor, true humanity, and true human equality."[22] The goal of edifying or upbuilding writing is to build up the individual spiritually "from the ground up" in love, which for Kierkegaard is "the source of everything" and "the deepest ground of the spiritual life."[23] Presupposing knowledge of the qualifying concepts under discussion, edifying discourses are thus ethical-

---

17. SUD, 1 / SKS 11, 115; PC, 5 / SKS 12, 9.
18. JP 6, 6416 / SKS 22, 70 (NB11: 123).
19. Ibid.
20. Ibid.
21. EUD, 239–240 / SKS 5, 238–240; EUD, 473–474 / SKS 27, 453–455.
22. JP 2, 2033 / Pap. X-5 B 117; JP 5, 5975 / KJN 4, 89–91 (NB: 129) / SKS 20, 90–91. On the category of upbuilding, see also Sylvia Walsh, "Comparing Genres: The Woman Who Was a Sinner in Kierkegaard's *Three Discourses at the Communion on Fridays* and *An Upbuilding Discourse*," in *Kierkegaard Studies Yearbook* (2010), pp. 73–76.
23. WL, 211, 215 / SKS 9, 214, 218.

religious or universally religious in nature, seeking to win and move the reader
to engage in self-examination and self-activity in relation to the eternal.[24] That is
what Kierkegaard understood himself to be doing or seeking to do as an edifying
author.

The next journal reference to the Guadalquibir River takes up where the previous
one leaves off, again raising the question of Kierkegaard's personal existence, but
this time with respect to whether he is a Christian or "a purely poetical existence
with even an element of something demonic" in him.[25] Kierkegaard wonders
whether he dares to measure himself against the "colossal standard" of Christianity,
which would put him in a situation where he could really become a Christian. But
he is dubious about doing it "in such a dramatic way that the Christendom of an
entire country becomes involved," asking: "Is there not something dubious about
all this, about treacherously setting a fire in order to throw oneself into the arms
of God—perhaps, because it might turn out that I didn't become Christian after
all."[26] For this reason, he decides that nothing he has written pertaining to his
own "authorial persona," namely "On My Work as An Author" and "The Point
of View for My Work as An Author," can be used, partly because it would make
him more deeply immersed in "the interesting," which he is loathe to do except
for retaining an element of it by putting an end to being an author altogether,
a step he now resolves to take. "Up to this point," he declares, "I am a poet and
absolutely nothing more than a poet, and it's a desperate struggle to try to go
beyond my limits."[27] That is why he cannot directly take authorial responsibility
for *Practice in Christianity*, which he thinks would make him "a phenomenon in
the world" rather than someone who stands to benefit from it by getting serious
about becoming a Christian. Noting that *The Sickness unto Death*, which at that
time was in the process of being published with his name as editor, is labeled "for
edification," Kierkegaard observes that this designation "is beyond my category,
the poet's category: edifying."[28]

It is at this point that the reference to the Guadalquibir River appears in this
entry: "Like the River Guadalquibir … which plunges underground, so also is
there a stretch, the edifying, that carries my name. There is something lower
(the aesthetic) and something higher, which is also pseudonymous because my
personality doesn't correspond to it."[29] Here the simile of the Guadalquibir River
is associated not with a temporary cessation of writing as in the first reference,
nor with Socratic silence or irony as in the second, nor with pseudonymity as in
the third, but with the group of edifying works which Kierkegaard claims as his
own and which designate his limit as an author. He nevertheless ends this journal
entry with the following statement: "In general, I must now move in completely

24. JP 1, 641 / SKS 20, 211 (NB2: 176).
25. JP 6, 6431 / SKS 22, 127 (NB11: 204).
26. Ibid.
27. Ibid.
28. Ibid.
29. Ibid.

different directions. I must dare believe that through Christ I can be saved from the grip of melancholia in which I've lived; and I must dare to try to be more economical."[30]

In the next comparison to the Guadalquibir River, Kierkegaard first thanks God that he did not publish the works about his work as an author or "in any way … force myself to be more than I am," namely an edifying author.[31] Satisfied that *The Sickness unto Death*, already in print, and *Practice in Christianity*, soon to be printed, are pseudonymous, he states: "The point of the whole thing is that there is an ethically rigorous, highest point of Christianity that must be heard. But no more than that. It must be left to every individual's conscience to decide whether he is capable of building his tower so high."[32] Because the whole of Christendom, including the clergy, "not only lives in worldly shrewdness" but also "in shameless defiance," declaring "Christ's life to be fantasy," he insists that "the alternative must be heard," but "no more than that."[33] Having reached this point in his self-understanding as an author after much suffering over matters that were clear to him early on but had to be learned a second time before understanding himself so completely as he does now, Kierkegaard suggests: "Were I now to continue to be an author, 'sin' and 'atonement' would have to be my topic in such a way that I now in an edifying discourse made use of the fact that the pseudonym had properly jacked up the price."[34] Noting that "pseudonyms are continually used for this purpose," he contends that "It was a sound idea to stop my literary production by once again using a pseudonym. Like the river Guadalquibir—that image appeals to me so much. And so not one word about myself in relation to the entire authorship."[35] With this statement, Kierkegaard comes full circle, plunging underground once again in the cessation of writing, silence, and pseudonymity in analogy to the Guadalquibir River. But he also envisions in this entry the possibility of emerging to write again in his own name, which he in fact does with the production of *An Edifying Discourse* (1850), *Two Discourses at the Communion on Fridays* (1851), *For Self-Examination* (1851), *Judge for Yourself!* (written in 1851–52 and published posthumously in 1876), and the late writings that make up *The Moment* (1854/55). Except for the first two writings listed above, Kierkegaard also takes advantage of the rigorous portrayal of Christian existence presented by his Christian pseudonym Anti-Climacus, applying it now under his own name. In *For Self-Examination*, he emphasizes the need for self-examination in the form of earnestness or an "honest distrust of oneself" in looking at oneself in the mirror of the Word and the difficult requirement of "dying to" selfishness and worldliness in order to receive new life in the gifts of faith, hope, and love from the Holy Spirit.[36] In *Judge for Yourself!* he

30. Ibid.
31. JP 6, 6445 / SKS 22, 149 (NB12: 7).
32. Ibid.
33. Ibid.
34. Ibid. Translation modified.
35. Ibid.
36. FSE, 20–21, 76–77, 81–87 / SKS 13, 48–49, 98, 102–108.

recommends the acquisition of self-knowledge by "becoming sober" in coming to oneself in "sheer transparency" as nothing before God and in suffering for the doctrine through acts of true self-denial in the imitation of Christ as the prototype of humanity and what it means to be a Christian.[37] This reemergence, however, is followed by another plunge into the underground for a period of three years of silence before unleashing a scathing critique of the established church in the collection of late writings entitled *The Moment*. It is notable, however, that in one of the newspaper articles in this collection, Kierkegaard states with respect to the (unaltered) second edition of *Practice in Christianity*:

> If it were to come out now, now when both pious consideration for the late bishop [Mynster] has lapsed and I have convinced myself also by having this book come out the first time, that Christianly the established order is indefensible, it would be altered as follows: *it would not be by a pseudonym but by me*, and the thrice-repeated preface would be dropped and, of course, the Moral to No. 1, where the pseudonym turns the matter in a way I personally agreed to in the preface.[38]

In other words, Kierkegaard now believes that the established order no longer has any right to resort to grace at all, neither in relation to salvation nor with respect to the striving to be like Christ that should follow it, making his understanding of Christianity at this final stage more rigorous than that of Anti-Climacus as well as his own more lenient presentations of it in his earlier signed writings.[39] It is significant, however, that on his deathbed, Kierkegaard continued to voice his trust in God's grace in Christ, ultimately affirming Christianity's leniency, not its rigor, as forming the very heart of the gospel.

Before that happens, however, in his last journal reference to the Guadalquibir River, Kierkegaard envisions putting an end to his literary production altogether after the publication of *Practice in Christianity*. With regard to what is entirely his own, namely those works issued under his name rather than pseudonymously, he suggests that "essentially" it has already come to an end or a "halt" with the publication of his "Friday Discourses" or "Discourses at the Communion on Fridays," seven of which had already been published in 1848 as Part Four of *Christian Discourses* and three more in a separate publication titled *Three Discourses at the Communion on Fridays: The High Priest—The Tax Collector—The Woman Who Was a Sinner* in 1849, with one more to come as the first Christian exposition in No. 3 of *Practice in Christianity* in 1850, and two more in a separate publication in 1851.[40]

37. JFY, 89, 104–106, 203–209 / SKS 16, 147, 161–163, 249–254.

38. TM, 69 / SKS 14, 213 (emphasis added).

39. For an excellent discussion of Kierkegaard's progressive intensification of the rigor of Christianity in relation to its grace and leniency, see David D. Possen, "The Voice of Rigor," in *International Kierkegaard Commentary, Volume 20: Practice in Christianity*, ed. Robert L. Perkins (Macon, GA: Mercer University Press, 2004), pp. 161–185.

40. JP 6, 6461 / SKS 22, 169 (NB12: 52).

"*Qua* author," he states, "I am like the river Guadalquibir, which at one point plunges underground: there is a stretch that is mine, the edifying; behind it and ahead of it lie the lower and the higher pseudonymity; the [']edifying['] is mine, not the aesthetic, nor that which is written [']for edification['] and even less that which is written [']for awakening[']."[41] It is not entirely clear in this statement whether it is his edifying works or the pseudonymous works that constitute the underground writings, but it would appear that he is referring to his own writings, in line with his previous reference to the Guadalquibir River, whereas earlier he saw himself as going underground in relation to the publication of the pseudonymous works.

In another journal entry later that year, Kierkegaard goes on to state that he "must find a point of rest," which cannot be a pseudonym or the pseudonymous discourses since they represent a position that is higher than his own.[42] He thus decides that "the position of *Discourses at the Communion on Fridays* is once and for all designated as the point of rest for my works"—a decision about which he never changed his mind.[43] On the contrary, it is reiterated several times in the journals.[44] In *On My Work as an Author*, written in 1849 but not published until 1851, the communion discourses are further designated as constituting not only the final resting point for the authorship as a whole but also its ultimate telos: "The movement the authorship describes is: *from* 'the poet,' from the esthetic— *from* 'the philosopher,' from the speculative—*to* the indication of the most inward qualification of the essentially Christian: **from** the *pseudonymous Either/ Or*, **through** *Concluding Postscript*, with my name as *editor*, **to** *Discourses at the Communion on Fridays*, of which two were delivered in Frue Church."[45] And in the Preface to *Two Discourses at the Communion on Fridays* (1851), written in order not to end the authorship with the polemical character of Part Three, "From on High," of *Practice in Christianity*, Kierkegaard states:

> A gradually advancing author-activity that began with *Either/Or* seeks here its decisive point of rest at the foot of the altar, where the author, personally most conscious of his own imperfection and guilt, by no means calls himself a truth-witness but only a singular kind of poet and thinker who, "without authority," has had nothing new to bring but "has wanted to read through once again, if possible in a more inward way, the original text of the individual human

---

41. Ibid.
42. JP 6, 6519 / SKS 22, 322 (NB13: 79).
43. Ibid. Translation modified.
44. JP 6, 6407 / SKS 22, 36–37 (NB11: 53); JP 6, 6418 / SKS 22, 75 (NB11: 125); JP 6, 6487 / SKS 22, 223 (NB12: 133). See also DCF, 125 / WA, 165 / SKS 12, 281; OMWA, 5–6 / SKS 13, 12, and my essay "At the Foot of the Altar: Kierkegaard's Communion Discourses as the Resting Point of His Authorship," in *The Theologically Formed Heart: Essays in Honor of David J. Gouwens*, ed. Warner M. Bailey, Lee C. Barrett III, and James O. Duke with a foreword by D. Newell Williams (Eugene, OR: Pickwick Publications, 2014), pp. 241–263.
45. OMWA, 5–6 / SKS 13, 12.

existence relationships, the old, familiar text handed down from the fathers" (see my postscript to *Concluding Unscientific Postscript*).[46]

As the decisive resting point and telos for Kierkegaard's signed writings as well as for the authorship as a whole, the communion discourses thus play a crucial role in the authorship, providing the key (from Kierkegaard's point of view at least) not only for understanding and responding to the authorship as a whole but also for understanding his own existential position in relation to the authorship and to Christianity qua author. As indicated in the quotation above, the purpose and direction of the authorship in its totality, as Kierkegaard sees it, is to bring the reader *to the foot of the altar*, where those who are heavy-laden with the consciousness of sin are invited by Christ to receive rest for their weary souls and reconciliation with God through the forgiveness of sin wrought by Christ's sacrificial death and atonement.

The communion discourses, of which there are thirteen in all, are intended to give the reader pause on the way to the altar for the expression of heartfelt longing and the need for forgiveness, reconciliation, and the establishment or renewal of communion with Christ.[47] Although technically sermons (and sometimes even referred to as such in the journals), in Kierkegaard's view they lack the authority of a sermon and thus are called discourses rather than sermons in conformity with his claim that he speaks and writes without authority.[48] As discourses rather than sermons, they fall under the category of the edifying or upbuilding, which Kierkegaard claimed as "his" category. Within that category, they belong to the subcategory of specifically Christian discourses that make up most of the second authorship. Written specifically for the communion service on Fridays, Kierkegaard's favorite time to take communion, they may also be distinguished from confession discourses, which were delivered at separate services for the confession of sin prior to taking communion in the main sanctuary of the Church of Our Lady where Kierkegaard communed.[49] But the communion discourses

---

46. DCF, 125 / WA, 165 / SKS 12, 281; see CUP1, 629–630 / SKS 7, 572–573.

47. In addition to the series of seven, three, and two communion discourses published either in *Christian Discourses* or separately, the first Christian exposition of No. III of *Practice in Christianity* was originally delivered by Kierkegaard as a communion discourse at a Friday communion service in 1848, thus bringing the total number to thirteen. All of the expositions in No. III were originally intended to be communion discourses but had to be renamed when Kierkegaard decided to publish the work pseudonymously and therefore impersonally in contrast to the personal character of a communion discourse (see JP 6, 6245 / SKS 21, 77 [NB7: 4]; JP 6, 6487 / SKS 22, 223 [NB12: 133]).

48. On the classification of the communion discourses, see Niels Jørgen Cappelørn, "Søren Kierkegaard at Friday Communion in the Church of Our Lady," trans. K Brian Söderquist, in *International Kierkegaard Commentary, Volume 18: Without Authority*, ed. Robert L. Perkins (Macon, GA: Mercer University Press, 2006), pp. 255–294.

49. Ibid., pp. 278–283.

do presuppose and require both the consciousness of sin and the confession of sin on the part of the prospective communicant as prerequisites for receiving the forgiveness of sin. Noting that the depth of sin in human beings is so great that a revelation from God was needed in order for them to become aware of their sinful condition, Kierkegaard impresses the consciousness of sin upon his readers by reminding them of the many atrocities committed by humans against each other as well as against Christ, whose death in his view is not a past event "over and done with" but a present event in which every human being is not merely a spectator but an accomplice inasmuch as it is the whole human race, to which all of us belong, that is responsible for his crucifixion.[50] To remind us of our sinfulness, there dwells within the inner recesses of every human heart a "privy preacher" or conscience that accompanies us wherever we go and "speaks simply and solely about you, to you, within you," making it impossible for us to hide our sins from God or from ourselves.[51] The biblical figures of the tax collector and the woman who was a sinner from the Gospel of Luke serve as models or prototypes of the appropriate penitential posture at communion for Kierkegaard, illustrating the type of consciousness of sin required for forgiveness, namely an anguished conscience or contrite heart that condemns itself and sorrows over sin and a strong sense of shame or self-hatred signifying inversely that one loves Christ much, for which one's sins are forgiven.

For Kierkegaard, however, what is most essential at the altar is to hear Christ's voice there, without which one goes to communion in vain. Affirming the Lutheran doctrine of the real presence of Christ not only in the elements themselves but also in the oral invitation and administration of the elements by the priest, Kierkegaard suggests that hearing Christ's voice at the altar is what determines whether one is really at the altar or not, for where Christ is, there the altar is, spiritually speaking. Inasmuch as Christ accompanies those who belong to and follow him, the task of his followers is to remain at the altar upon leaving it, making the Christian life one of participation in "divine service every day."[52] Although Kierkegaard by his own admission stresses the imitation of Christ as the prototype for Christian striving in the specifically Christian writings of his second authorship, he nevertheless maintains that "the Atonement and grace are and remain definitive" as well as "unconditionally needed" to prevent our striving from being transformed into an "agonizing anxiety" and to atone for the continuation of sin in our lives.[53] As he sees it, therefore, the imitation of Christ and the atonement of Christ stand in a complementary dialectical relation to one another, each presupposing and necessitating the other. It is notable, however, that the communion discourses constitute "the only place in Kierkegaard's writings where the significance of the atonement for the single individual is actually spelled out."[54] That alone seals their importance in the authorship as a whole. Inasmuch

---

50. DCF, 65 / CD, 278 / SKS 10, 298.
51. DCF, 138–139 / WA, 182–183 / SKS 12, 296–297.
52. DCF, 60 / CD, 274 / SKS 10, 292.
53. JP 2, 1909 / SKS 24, 483–484 (NB25: 67).
54. "Introduction" to DCF, p. 26.

as Kierkegaard views his authorship as constituting his own religious upbringing and development in what it means to be a Christian, the communion discourses also give expression to his own existential situation and thus are crucial for understanding his personal relation to Christianity. In a journal entry from 1849, he declares: "An understanding of the totality of my literary activity, its maieutic purpose, etc. requires also an understanding of my personal existence as an author, what I qua auth[or] have done with my personal existence to support it, illuminate it, conceal it, give it direction, etc."[55] Observing in this entry "that Socrates himself was a part of his own teaching, that the conclusion of his teaching pointed to his own person, that he himself was his own teaching, that, artistically, he was what he taught in his actual context," Kierkegaard indirectly agrees with that conclusion in another journal entry attributed to a potential pseudonym called A-O, who states that "an author's body of work ... requires for its definitive completion that the author himself be included in the conclusion" but "this is really impossible for Mag. Kierkegaard himself to do, for by doing it himself he would dialectically explode the dialectical structure of the entire body of work by the author."[56] The idea of explaining his work as an author by way of a pseudonym, however, never came to fruition, nor could he see his way to publishing it himself or to speak publically of his own personal relationship to God. Painfully conscious of his own shortcomings in actualizing the Christian ideals portrayed in the specifically Christian writings that make up the second period of his authorship, both those penned in his own name and those by Anti-Climacus, Kierkegaard repeatedly describes himself as a "penitent" in his own personal religious life, maintaining in one journal entry that "as an author I am a penitent" and in another that "this is what explains me at the deepest level."[57] It was precisely because he was a penitent that he could not speak directly, and it was for this reason too that he described himself as being essentially a poet qua author.[58] To the question, "What is it to be a poet?" Kierkegaard replies: "It is to have one's own personal life, one's actuality, in quite other categories than those of the poetic production; it is to relate oneself to the ideal only in imagination, so that one's personal existence is more or less a satire on the poetic and on oneself."[59] In another journal entry from 1849, he defines it this way: "to poetize means mendaciously to remove some

---

55. JP 6, 6360 / SKS 21, 293 (NB10: 68).
56. KJN 6, 351 (NB14: 8) / SKS 22, 347.
57. JP 6, 6177 / SKS 20, 412–413 (NB5: 96); JP 6, 6195 / SKS 20, 427 (NB5: 146); JP 6, 6206 / SKS 21, 20 (NB6: 21b); JP 6, 6261 / SKS 21, 101 (NB7: 53); JP 6, 6317 / SKS 21, 232–233 (NB9: 56); JP 6, 6325 / SKS 21, 244–246 (NB9: 74); JP 6, 6327 / SKS 21, 248–251 (NB9: 78); JP 6, 6335 / SKS 21, 262 (NB10: 14); JP 6, 6364 / SKS 21, 298 (NB10: 78); JP 6, 6383 / SKS 21, 340–341 (NB10: 169); JP 6, 6389 / SKS 21, 356–359 (NB10: 191); JP 6, 6395 / SKS 22, 20–21 (NB11: 25); JP 6, 6396 / SKS 22, 23 (NB11: 27); JP 6, 6426 / SKS 22, 115–116 (NB11: 192); JP 6, 6522 / SKS 22, 332 (NB13: 88a).
58. JP 6, 6327 / SKS 21, 248–251 (NB9: 78); JP 6, 6383 / SKS 21, 340–341 (NB10: 169).
59. JP 6, 6300 / SKS 21, 204–205 (NB9: 11).

extra something; in becoming poetry, it becomes one key lower than actuality."[60] Consequently, he claims that his writings "are separated from me by the yawning gulf of indirect communication: they are not mine, they belong to something higher."[61] Kierkegaard therefore calls himself a "poet of the religious," although not in such a way that his life expresses the opposite; "no," he says, "I am striving, but my being a 'poet' expresses that I do not confuse myself with the ideal."[62] In his view, such a poet differs from the usual poet in several respects but chiefly by the fact that he "is ethically aware that the task is not to poetize the ideal but to be like it" by personally striving toward it.[63] Identifying himself more specifically in another journal entry as "a Christian poet and thinker," Kierkegaard sees his task as casting Christianity into reflection in such a way as "to present the entire ideal poetically, fervently, in accordance with the most ideal criterion and then always to end with: I am not it, but I am striving. If this latter does not suffice, if it isn't the truth within me, then everything has been transposed into intellectuality and has failed."[64] In presenting this ideal, Kierkegaard clearly understands that:

> The one who presents this ideal must be the very first one to humble himself under it, and even though he himself is striving within himself to approach the ideal, he must confess that he is very far from being it. He must confess that he is related only poetically to this ideal picture *qua* poet to the *presentation* of this picture, while he (and here he differs from the ordinary conception of a poet) personally and Christianly is related to the *presented* picture, and that only as a poet presenting the picture is he out in front.[65]

Perhaps the best way to describe and understand Kierkegaard qua author, both as poet and penitent, then, is captured in a lovely phrase from a revision to an unpublished polemical writing on Bishop Mynster and the established order, namely that he is "a poet who flies to grace."[66] Like the Guadalquivir River, after plunging underground into and out of pseudonymity, he emerges at last as both poet and penitent at the foot of the altar, where it is hoped that he found the forgiveness and reconciliation with God and Christ that is promised there.

60. KJN 6, 352 / SKS 22, 348 (NB14: 8).
61. Ibid.
62. JP 6, 6511 / SKS 22, 298 (NB13: 37).
63. JP 6, 6528 / SKS 22, 354 (NB14: 19); JP 6, 6632 / SKS 23, 322 (NB18: 100). For a more extensive discussion of Kierkegaard as religious poet, see Sylvia Walsh, *Living Poetically: Kierkegaard's Existential Aesthetics* (University Park, PA: The Pennsylvania State University Press, 1994), pp. 223–242.
64. JP 6, 6391 / SKS 21, 367–368 (NB10: 200); JP 6, 6511 / SKS 22, 298 (NB13: 37).
65. ANI, 37 / AN, 133 / SKS 16, 115.
66. Pap. X-6 B 215, pp. 340–341.

Chapter 2

RHETORIC AND UNDERSTANDING: AUTHORSHIP AS CHRISTIAN MISSION

Robert C. Roberts

Introduction

Inevitably, Christian missionary work centers on communication—on a presentation of the Christian message in such a *way* that it is taken up, grasped, and appropriated by those to whom the missionary is sent. This appropriation is called "belief," and so the missionary aims, in presenting the message in the special *way*, to engender belief in his or her hearers. But in the Christian context, "belief" has special depth. In ordinary English, a person may be said to believe a statement merely on the grounds that he sincerely assents to it and has a minimal understanding of it. The minimal understanding is crucial, even if this is not often recognized. If the one who affirms the belief has no understanding *at all*—say, the statement is in a language he doesn't understand, and he assents to it only on the authority of a trustworthy speaker of that language—then I don't think it makes sense to say that *he* believes the *statement*. He identifies the statement in a way (it's *that* one, whatever it was, that was just uttered in Russian), he thinks it's true and may even have a good reason for thinking so, but he doesn't believe it. After all, he has no acquaintance whatsoever with the content of the belief. Belief is a relation of a person to a content (something believed), namely the relation of assenting, either dispositionally or episodically, *to that content*, and that relation is not achieved if the person has no personal intimacy or contact at all with that content. The intimacy I speak of comes by way of personally grasping or understanding what the belief is about. Such understanding doesn't have to be very profound or extensive, but the person must have some, on pain of not believing.

By the standard of ordinary English, a person might be said to believe that Jesus is his savior if only he understands Jesus to be somebody very important and powerful and has some vague notion of what it is to be saved. But the Christian missionary will aim at a deeper understanding, a deeper belief (let's call it faith) that involves a formation or transformation of the individual's entire attitude toward God, the world, and himself, a transformation of his joys and griefs, of his aims and hopes and loves. Ultimately, to believe, and thus to understand, that

Jesus is one's savior, is to have been shaped in this very personal way. The shape of character is required for the firmer grasp (now we might call it an embrace) that the Christian message calls for. A grasping tool must be shaped to accommodate the shape and character of what it grasps. Pliers, for example, typically have little ridges on the pinching faces that dig just a bit into whatever is being held to make the holding more secure; if the faces were very smooth, they wouldn't hold on as well. Similarly, the human mind must be shaped to embrace the gospel of Jesus Christ. Thus, the missionary's task of communication is not just to get the hearers to believe in a minimal sense but to shape their personal understanding by facilitating a transformation of their character.

It is well known that Søren Kierkegaard conceived his writing career, from beginning to end, as an endeavor in Christian missions. And so we find throughout his writings reflections on the nature of his authorship and on the nature of the kind of understanding that authorship will foster if successful. In a journal entry from 1845, he says, "A new science must be introduced: the Christian art of speaking, to be constructed *admodum* [after the manner of] Aristotle's *Rhetoric*. Dogmatics as a whole is a misunderstanding, especially as it now has been developed."[1] That is, the form of discourse that is known as dogmatics (we would perhaps call it systematic theology) is such as not to encourage the kind of understanding that is required for faith and even has potential to undermine or corrupt such understanding. Let us take a closer look at the concepts of knowledge and understanding in ordinary life and in Kierkegaard's thought, as a preliminary to appreciating his thought about rhetoric and his practice of communication.

Knowledge and Understanding

Knowledge and understanding are sometimes contrasted as follows: knowledge is justified true belief plus some condition that guarantees that the justification connects with the truth in the right way. The "right way" condition is meant to rule out "Gettier" cases, cases in which, despite the believer's being justified in believing the statement and the statement's being true, the belief doesn't amount to knowledge. One of Edmund Gettier's original cases was that of *Smith Owns a Ford or Brown is in Barcelona.*[2] Smith, who is generally trustworthy, tells you that he owns a Ford, and on the strength of his testimony you come to believe, somehow, that *Either Smith owns a Ford or Brown is in Barcelona*, though you have no reason to think that Brown is in Barcelona and never find out whether he is. It turns out that Smith was pulling your leg. He doesn't own a Ford, but it just happens that Brown *is* in Barcelona. So the proposition you believe—that either Smith owns a Ford or Brown is in Barcelona—is true. You have a justified true belief. Is it

---

1. JP 1, 627 / SKS 18, 236 (JJ: 305).
2. See Edmund Gettier, "Is Justified True Belief Knowledge?" *Analysis* 23 (1963), pp. 121–123.

knowledge? Most people feel that, despite your being justified in believing the proposition, and its being true, you still don't *know* that either Smith owns a Ford or Brown is in Barcelona. The justification doesn't hook up with the truth in the right way: you're justified in believing the disjunction because you are justified in believing the *first* disjunct, but the proposition turns out to be true in virtue of the *second* disjunct's being true. So knowledge has to be something more than justified true belief. It turns out to be very difficult to specify this fourth condition, and a great deal of epistemology in the late twentieth century was devoted to figuring it out—without much success, some might think.

My point in mentioning this case is not the importance of the controversy over the nature of justification but just to illustrate one kind of knowledge, which is indeed the kind that overwhelmingly occupied the talents of the best epistemologists of the late twentieth century. In ordinary discourse, we often use "know" in this way: "Did you know that Lincoln was the first Republican president?" "Everybody knows that water is H_2O." In such cases, the content of knowledge is individual propositions that are true and believed in a sense that requires only minimal understanding. For example, you might know that Lincoln was the first Republican president without having any understanding of what being a Republican meant in the context of mid-nineteenth-century American politics. Furthermore, this kind of knowledge is thought to be on-off rather than graded. That is, for any individual proposition, you either know it or you don't; there's no in-between state, and further thought or inquiry will not increase or deepen your knowing of it. It may deepen your justification for believing the proposition, but if you reach the minimum of justification required for knowing it, you know it, and if you're under that threshold by a hair, you don't. Admittedly, it may be hard to locate that threshold precisely, so it may be hard in some cases to decide whether somebody knows something in this sense.

Understanding, in contrast with knowledge, comes in degrees. For relatively complex or subtle things that you understand, it is almost always possible that you—or somebody else—could understand them better. How shall we explain this difference? One explanation turns on the fact that knowledge (supposedly) can be of individual propositions. By contrast, understanding is often achieved by making *connections* between propositions—say, explaining one proposition by reference to another. Jackson made that cutting remark *because* he took your remark as an insult. The explanation is an expression of understanding—seeing how one fact or proposition bears on another. You wondered why Jackson made that cutting remark, but now you "see," because you have an explanation. By virtue of seeing what "caused" Jackson's remark, you not only know that he made it; you understand it. We also speak here of the *significance* or *meaning* or *point* of Jackson's remark, as though the remark points to its cause. These are all relational, connecting terms. Knowing why something is the case would appear to be a kind of understanding.

But not all understanding is about causes. We began with the apparently very simple example of someone understanding a sentence and said that if you have no understanding at all of the sentence, you can't even believe it. But understanding a sentence is not a matter of seeing *causal* connections between its parts but other kinds of connections—grammatical ones and conceptual (logical, semantic) ones. When we hear a sentence that we understand, "You have mud on your face," we instantaneously *assemble* the concepts *you, mud, have, face, on*, in a grammatically ordered, sense-making way and we "grasp" what the interlocutor is saying. We see how mud is being claimed to relate to you and face, namely it's *your* face and the mud is *on* it. We make a whole out of the sentence-parts and so grasp it. Similarly, understanding a piece of music is not a matter of making causal connections among the parts but of making other kinds of connections—hearing this passage as an inversion of the opening theme, hearing this cadence as a resting point before departure in a new direction, and so on.

When the prophet Nathan tells King David the story (2 Samuel 12:1–4) about the rich man with many flocks who took his poor neighbor's only lamb, his cherished pet, and served it up to the rich man's guest, David immediately understands the rich man's action as monstrous and loathsome and responds with appropriate indignation. He puts together the elements of Nathan's narrative in such a way as to make a coherent story, a story with striking moral import, and the story's import contacts David's heart and arouses anger against the rich man, and a call for his punishment. So David grasps a lot of connections in the story. He understands it. But as we know, he doesn't yet make *the* connection that Nathan has in mind; he doesn't grasp the meaning of the story *for him*; he doesn't get the "point." He needs to understand the story *better*. Nathan helps David make that connection: "You are the man." Whereupon David has what a philosopher might call an *insight*: he is struck again, this time not with indignation but with remorse. Those four words have the effect of connecting, by the relation of analogy, Nathan's story with actions of *David's* recent biography. David undergoes a powerful moral impression of himself and the situation.

Nathan is an astute rhetorician and philosopher of understanding. He knows that if he simply goes to David and denounces him, saying, "What you did with Uriah and his wife is reprehensible," he may not induce in David a very deep appreciation of his crime. By contrast, the story he tells creates a vivid concrete image of arrogant injustice and of the suffering of its victim, an image fraught with pathos and, since David doesn't make the application to himself right away, the story sneaks past his defenses and powerfully seizes his moral sensibilities.

The fact that it seizes those sensibilities by way of *emotion* is crucial for David's understanding. In one sense, a person might understand Nathan's story "disinterestedly." Such a person (imagine an intelligent psychopath) would correctly connect the poor man with the lamb and the rich man with the visit of the guest and with the action of butchering the poor man's lamb for his guest's dinner, and be able to pass an exam that asks him to make narrative connections like these. Perhaps he even sees the story's connection to his recent adultery and murder. But if he makes all these connections and so understands the story, but in a purely disinterested, unemotional way, then his understanding of the story will be morally deficient, because he will fail to grasp the outrageous injustice of the situation that the story depicts. He'll miss the "meaning" of the story. Deep and morally appropriate understanding here requires a sense for the moral import of the rich man's action, and that cannot be had without emotion. The connection involved in this deeper, moral kind of understanding is with the *import* of the rich man's action, its significance, its bearing on what is important. In the case of Nathan's story, the rich man's action bears on justice, on the rights and well-being of the poor man. David's indignation connects that action to those values by touching David's concern for justice and for the well-being of the poor man. The story wakens David's concerns. If David lacked these latent concerns (if they were not an aspect of his character), the story couldn't touch him as it does, and he would be import-blind with respect to it even if, as in the case of the psychopath taking the school exam, he were master of the narrative. So Nathan's rhetorical skill as a character-growth facilitator involves moral-psychological wisdom about his hearer's preexisting moral sensibilities. This is one way that Kierkegaard's rhetoric is after the manner of Aristotle's.

As Nathan has calculated, David responds to the story with indignation, thus appreciating its moral import. But as I say, he doesn't yet get *Nathan's* point. He doesn't make the connection to *himself*. When David does make the application, it occasions a deep understanding of his crime. In a phrase with which Kierkegaard describes some of his own moral and spiritual efforts at rhetorical induction of understanding, Nathan's story is "a thought that wounds from behind, for edification."[3]

Socrates on Moral Knowledge

I said that late twentieth-century analytic epistemology took knowledge, roughly, to be justified true belief, where the object of belief was individual propositions whose content was grasped in some minimal sense. At the end of that century, as virtue epistemology was coming into its own, epistemologists began to take an interest in understanding, conceived as quite different from knowledge, not directed at individual propositions but at connections among things (including propositions). But I think the divide between knowledge and understanding, even where these are conceived as contemporary epistemology conceives them, is hard to maintain. Whatever plausibility it has depends on commitment to a rather thin and artificial conception of knowledge. I've already pointed out that even the simplest cases of propositional knowledge require that the subject understand the proposition in question, so it seems that no knowledge is entirely without understanding. Even the simplest knowledge is structured, and epistemic access to a structure requires grasping the relations among its parts. Conversely, it would be very odd for someone to understand something without knowing anything about what he understood. You have to know *that* some things are the case to know *why*

---

3. See Part III of *Christian Discourses*, ed. and trans. Howard V. and Edna H. Hong (Princeton: Princeton University Press, 1997).

something is the case (notice the second use of "know" here for "understand"). Furthermore, if a person's knowing something requires that he be justified in believing it, then on at least an internalist understanding of justification, the knower must understand the connection between the proposition that he knows and the consideration that justifies him in believing it. For example, if I know that I have mud on my face by my friend's testimony, I have to "see" the connection between my friend's telling me so and its being so. Or if I know it by looking in the mirror, I have to understand the relevance of the mirror image to my belief that I have mud on my face. In cases like these, then, I can't know without understanding. Understanding comes into knowledge in at least two ways—in relation to the content of the belief and in relation to its justification.

So knowledge implies understanding; understanding is a part of knowledge. Furthermore, when we say that a scholar "knows a lot about" something— say, the way traits depend on genes, or the history of the universe, or climate change—we don't just mean that she knows a lot of individual facts within her field; we are claiming that she knows how those facts bear on one another, that she can explain them, and that she has a systematic mastery of the elements in the field. In other words, when we say she knows a lot, we are claiming that she understands a lot. And when we say, "Alfred knows what he believes in believing X," we are saying that he understands the content of his belief; he has the cognitive intimacy with it that I mentioned earlier. This kind of knowledge is compatible with saying that Alfred does not know X but only believes it. He believes X without knowing X, but he knows what he believes in believing X.

What is true of knowledge in general seems even more obviously true of moral knowledge—that it is not so much a matter of knowing discrete facts, as of seeing their significance. The person who has only a school exam understanding of Nathan's story doesn't get its moral point because he fails to construe the rich man's action in moral terms.

Socrates famously held that people never knowingly do evil or fail to do what they know to be good; when they do evil, it is always from ignorance of the good.[4] This thesis has come to be known as a "Socratic paradox." It is said to be paradoxical because we have all experienced what is called "weakness of will" or *akrasia*. My action is "akratic" when, knowing perfectly well that I ought to stop what I am so enjoyably doing and do something else that is morally demanding but perfectly within my power, I just keep on doing what I am so enjoyably doing; or knowing that the greater good would be served by my doing X than by my doing Y, I do Y— because I'm in the habit, or because I prefer doing Y. We have all, supposedly, had this experience, so Socrates must be wrong to think that if I knew what was best to do, I would do it. Right?

Well, that depends on what you mean by "know." If you think that "Socrates knows it's better for him to do X than Y" entails Socrates's *understanding*[5] why it's

---

4. *Protagoras* 358c.
5. See Julius Moravscik, "Understanding and Knowledge in Plato's Philosophy," *Neue Hefte für Philosophie* 15/16 (1979), pp. 53–69.

better for him to do X than Y, where "understand" includes an emotional grasp of the reasons that X is better for him to do than Y, where that emotional grasp of the moral truth is like the understanding that King David had when he heard Nathan's narrative and made the connection of that narrative to himself clear by way of Nathan's "you are the man"—then it will seem much less paradoxical to think that if Socrates knows it's better for him to do X than Y, and it's within his power to do X rather than Y, he will do X. In other words, if "know" means *fully appreciate*, then Socrates's thesis is not a paradox. We, like Socrates's contemporaries, use "know" in more casual and less demanding ways than Socrates does, and the appearance of paradox results from this less rigorous usage.

Understanding as Intrinsic to Virtues

So far, I have discussed ethical knowledge in connection with actions to perform or not perform. But this is only a simplifying expository tactic on my part. Kierkegaard's writings seldom address particular actions. The overall aim of Kierkegaard's authorship is to reintroduce Christianity to Christendom, and this means ultimately to "edify" or build up his readers, that is, to facilitate their growth in such Christian character traits as faith, love, hope, patience, humility, bold confidence, purity of heart, dispositional joy, earnestness, meekness, forgiveness, obedience, conscientiousness, contrition, and honesty, to mention those that are perhaps the most prominent. In some cases, a trait that is called by one of these names is found in outlooks other than Christianity, and so the word can be ambiguous. The most notable example is love, which can be found in the aesthetic and the ethical spheres, as well as in Christianity, and in each of these contexts, it has a different meaning, a different psychological or characterological configuration. Love is expounded at length in both volumes of *Either/Or*, as well as in *Works of Love* and elsewhere, and in each of these places, it has such different conceptual-psychological characteristics that it might well be thought of as three different traits. A major purpose of Kierkegaard's notion of the existence spheres is to show the differences among traits that may go by the same name, yet belong to different spheres. His ultimate purpose in inviting comparison of worldviews and the corresponding possible shapes of human character is to clarify the distinctively Christian life, that is, to inculcate the understanding of self and world that belongs to the Christian virtues, to provide, through writing, something like an upbringing in Christianity.

Aristotle describes a number of virtues in his *Nicomachean Ethics*, but he thinks that one virtue, which he calls practical wisdom (*phronêsis*), pervades all the others. Each of the other virtues—justice, courage, temperance, gentleness, and so forth— partakes of an aspect of practical wisdom. For example, the virtue of justice partakes of the aspect having to do with the distribution of goods (honors, material goods) and evils (opprobrium and penalties). But the part of practical wisdom that belongs to justice is not separable from the part that belongs to courage and temperance but links to those other parts in such a way as to constitute a consistent overall system of potential judgments about the practical good in human life, judgments that take into consideration the appeals of other virtues as situations demand. Thus, for Aristotle, practical wisdom is the overall evaluative understanding of human life. For him, as for Kierkegaard, real understanding of the human good intrinsically involves caring about, or personally aiming at, the human good. If caring and aiming were not psychologically involved (if practical "wisdom" were just used to spin theories about what is good for human beings), its deliberations wouldn't result in choices and actions, as they are meant to do. Aristotle's understanding of the demands of practical wisdom differs at least as much from Kierkegaard's Christian understanding of understanding as Christianity differs from the "ethical" sphere that Kierkegaard's pseudonyms present. They are different wisdoms with different virtues and different understandings of human nature. Nevertheless, Kierkegaard's understanding of understanding *parallels* Aristotle's understanding of practical wisdom in that each of the Christian virtues occupies its own space of Christian thought about self, God, world, and others, that space being connected to the other parts of the larger space of Christian thought about the human good.

An aspect of understanding that comes out more forcefully in Kierkegaard and Plato than in Aristotle's ethics is imagination—the arena, we might think, of the poet. Plato's dialogues that focus on virtues are dialectical, with Socrates asking for definitions of concepts and then relentlessly sifting and resifting by logical criticism what is offered, in search of the perfect formula, which he and his interlocutors often fail to attain. But these conceptual refinements are often interspersed and supplemented with myths and stories to arouse and cultivate the emotional imagination. In Plato's *Seventh Letter*, he describes philosophical success in the following terms:

> There is no writing of mine about these matters, nor will there ever be one. For this knowledge is not something that can be put into words like other sciences; but after long-continued intercourse between teacher and pupil, in joint pursuit of the subject, suddenly, like light flashing forth when a fire is kindled, it is born in the soul and straightway nourishes itself.[6]

This is a strong statement of the idea of understanding as "insight." As my earlier discussion suggests, ordinary English for understanding often makes use of the idea of seeing. The idea is that understanding is sometimes not just an ability to manipulate the concepts, an ability, as Wittgenstein might say, to "go on," but is a disposition to be *impressed*, to have an inescapable impression of the rightness of a connection or an application of a word or idea. Such is often achieved by a story, a metaphor, a simile, an analogy, an example, an appeal to the reader's imagination, skillfully integrated into a conceptual discussion. An insight achieved on such a literary occasion can arguably lodge in a person's consciousness (unconscious)

---

6. Plato, *Seventh Letter*, trans. by Glenn R. Morrow, in *Plato: Complete Works*, ed. John M. Cooper and D. S. Hutchinson (Indianapolis: Hackett Publishing Company, 1997), p. 341c.

and so become a dimension of the appreciation that belongs to some of the virtues. Note also that if "this knowledge is not something that can be put into words," then the definitions that Socrates so doggedly pursues cannot be the final aim of dialectic. For Plato, as for Kierkegaard, its goal is a formation of the soul.

Because the Christian virtues, like the Aristotelian ones, integrate thought (conceptual clarity properly salted with imagination) and concern, the person who is eminently equipped to present, not Christian doctrine (dogmatics, systematic theology), but a fully truthful ideal picture of what it is *to exist as a Christian*, will need to combine the skills of a psychologist-logician and a poet. Kierkegaard describes his vocation as that of a poet-dialectician and the training in Christianity that he is called to supply for Christendom a pathetic-dialectical one. The dialectic of the psychologist-logician is neither the "speculative" dialectic that Hegel practiced nor what our contemporaries call logic; it is rather a discipline that, following Wittgenstein, we might call the grammar of the virtues (and the vices and related concepts such as choice and the various emotions). It is a study of the conceptual structure of the virtues, that is, an account of the thought that shapes the actions, emotions, and perceptions of the person who exemplifies the virtues. Such an account will make use of contrasting comparison of the "grammar" of, say, the Christian virtue of love, with some analogous non-Christian virtue (say, that of the aesthete's romantic love or of secular friendship). But since the universal task of humanity, every human being's calling to become fully human, is the proper object of fundamental passion, of seeking, aiming, striving, this psychological logic will need to be couched, for maximal effectiveness, in humanly fetching and warning terms.

It will not do for the mood of the discourse to be cold, scientific, disinterested, and academic, because such discourse would deny with its mood what it says with its concepts. The beings to whom the discourse is addressed are not emotionless robotic calculators, even if what they are calculating is the psychological logic of the virtues. They have to be in the mood to think profitably about their lives in connection with the Christian ideal, and discourse that is properly edifying will assist them into the mood. This requires the empathic-imaginative powers of a "poet."

Kierkegaard's Rhetoric

All discourse, even the most pedestrian record keeping, is meant to bring about changes in people's minds—to inform, to remind, to convince, to enlighten, to amuse. Rhetorical discourse, however, aims to change *attitudes*, judgments, and understanding about matters of value and practice. Edifying or upbuilding rhetorical discourse has the even more strenuous aim of bringing about deep and lasting change in the character of the reader or hearer. And for Kierkegaard, as for the classical tradition in ethics, character, with the understanding that is essential to it, is intimately tied up with passions and emotions. His task, then, in writing for edification, is to inculcate in his reader, as far as is possible through writing, deep dispositions of emotional understanding shaped by the conceptual framework of apostolic Christianity.

To examine Kierkegaard's rhetoric, I'll focus on the seventh discourse in the third part of *Upbuilding Discourses in Various Spirits*, "The Gospel of Sufferings." The theme of the series of seven discourses is the joy that can be felt in the midst of sufferings; in each discourse, Kierkegaard explores a thought that can make the suffering an occasion of joy. The seventh discourse is about the virtue of "bold confidence" (*Frimodighed*) and this virtue's power to mediate joy in persecution, and thus for a certain kind of joy to be a mark of bold confidence. Kierkegaard's text is Acts 5:41 in which, after having been flogged by the authorities in Jerusalem for openly confessing Christ, the disciples go on their way "rejoicing that they were counted worthy to suffer dishonor for the name [of Christ]." As an upbuilding discourse, it is designed to help the reader actually become boldly confident and so to experience joy in suffering for his convictions. In the terms of the earlier parts of this paper, Kierkegaard aims to facilitate a deep understanding—something approaching the knowledge with which Socrates thinks it impossible not to do what is right—of the aspect of Christianity under discussion. I'll proceed by identifying aspects of the writing that constitute its rhetorical character. These aspects are of course artfully woven together into a single fabric in Kierkegaard's writing; I separate them only for the purpose of discussion.

The focus of Kierkegaard's upbuilding discourses is itself a rhetorical element, inasmuch as rhetorical discourse aims to affect the reader's emotions and values, and discussion of emotions (provided it's in the right mood) tends to engage the reader's emotions. Throughout Kierkegaard's writings about emotions and virtues, he assumes and says that emotions are structured by thought (they are not irrational or nonrational by nature). For example, the theme of the discourse that precedes the one I'm discussing here is about the joy *in the thought* "that the happiness of eternity still outweighs even the heaviest temporal sufferings."[7] Furthermore, we respond emotionally to the names and descriptions of virtues and vices (**vices**: "presumption,"[8] "lightmindedness," "thoughtlessness," "hypocrisy," "zeal without wisdom,"[9] "arrogance,"[10] "the spreading infection of the envious and pusillanimous small-mindedness of incessant comparison," "small-minded fear of people,"[11] "brazenness,"[12] "timorous sagacity"[13]; **virtues**: "faith,"[14] "calmness," "self-control,"[15] "bold confidence,"[16] "pride," "earnestness," "humility," "thankfulness"[17])[18] and are

---

7. UDVS, 308 / SKS 8, 401.
8. UDVS, 321 / SKS 8, 413.
9. UDVS, 323 / SKS 8, 415.
10. UDVS, 325 / SKS 8, 417.
11. UDVS, 326 / SKS 8, 417.
12. UDVS, 329 / SKS 8, 420.
13. UDVS, 333 / SKS 8, 424.
14. UDVS, 322 / SKS 8, 414.
15. UDVS, 323 / SKS 8, 414.
16. UDVS, 326 and *passim* / SKS 8, 417.
17. UDVS, 336 / SKS 8, 422.
18. In this list, I have changed some adjectives and adverbs into nouns for the sake of consistency.

thus repelled by the vices and attracted by the virtues. It is true that virtues and emotions can be discussed in a "scientific" mood that saps them of their natural power to commandeer our moral attention. So the mood[19] or tone of the discourse needs to be personal, serious, earnest, ethically "primitive." Kierkegaard achieves this mood by speaking directly as one ethically involved agent to another (his reader). Compare Aristotle's *Nicomachean Ethics*, which is also about virtues and emotions but is composed much less in conversational tones of one ethical pilgrim to another.

Many of the above-mentioned references are brief, little more than passing. But it is fairly typical that Kierkegaard centers an edifying discourse on a single virtue concept, walking leisurely around it so as to give a rich sampling of its various aspects to induce synoptic understanding. In our seventh discourse, that concept is *bold confidence* (*Frimodighed*). Like the New Testament word *parrhêsia* (openness, frankness, boldness, confidence, assurance), *Frimodighed* embodies the notion of freedom from inhibition, especially inhibition by social pressure to conform to a standard alien from one's own.[20] Thus, it fits nicely with Kierkegaard's positive notion of *the single individual* in complementarity with the negative notion of *the crowd*. A *frimodig* person is free from the oppressive "leveling" influence of the unspoken expectations of the social environment. The virtue could perhaps be thought of as a kind of pride. Bold confidence is a self-assurance and independence of mind in action and feeling: a kind of security in one's own agency (patiency), not as independent of God, but precisely *in* one's dependency on God, yet very much in *in*dependence from forces in the world that would induce a compromise of one's integrity and God-relationship. Relative to those forces it is a kind of "pride" that is premised on a deep humility before God.[21] Kierkegaard notes the relation between pride and humility in Christian character in the following characterization of the apostles' sense of their own independent agency: "Never has a human being lifted his head as proudly (*stolt*) in elevation over the world as did the first Christians in humility before God! ... No, proud as they were in their humility before God, they said, 'It is not for us to hang back and dawdle along the way; we do not stop—until eternity.'"[22] But *Frimodighed* also laps over the virtue of courage, insofar as the inhibiting factor from which bold confidence is a freedom is fear of people. We can see, I think, how independence of mind serves courage, especially where courage faces up to the personal intimidations of other people.

The "poetic" element of the discourse is represented by parables, similes, metaphors, analogies, and narrative sketches. I will organize the rest of this

---

19. For a discussion of moods in discourse, see Reidar Thomte's introduction to CA, vii–xviii.

20. Kierkegaard does not explicitly connect *Frimodighed* with *parrhêsia*, as far as I can tell, and Paul doesn't include it in lists of Christian virtues such as we find in Galatians 5 and Colossians 3.

21. See UDVS, 336 / SKS 8, 426.

22. FSE, 87 / SKS 13, 107.

discussion around seven instances of such devices in our discourse: the parable of the *priceless dish*,[23] the *metaphor of the evil spirit*,[24] the parable of the *youth who knew the truth*,[25] the similes of the *sleep walker*,[26] the *joy of a girl on the day of her betrothal*,[27] and of *dangerously strong medicine*,[28] and the parable of the *burning house*.[29] Within the framework of these devices, I'll discuss Kierkegaard's conceptual dialectic.

As a way of introducing the virtue of bold confidence, Kierkegaard begins the discourse by talking about confessing Christ in a pagan context, where the deterrent to doing so is a fear of people. Early Christians were treated as a sort of criminals. But a person with real faith would surmount that deterrent because the inwardness of his faith would be so strong that he couldn't do otherwise than give voice to it. Thus, bold confidence would be an aspect of his faith, as it was of the apostles Peter and John, whose boldness (*parrhêsia*) in testifying to Christ made the members of the high priestly family wonder, because Peter and John "were common, uneducated men."[30] And the church was aware of the importance of this virtue, for when the authorities had released Peter and John and they had reported their experience to the church, the church prayed, "And now, Lord, look upon their threats, and grant to thy servants to speak thy word with all boldness."[31]

But the situation in Kierkegaard's Denmark is very different, because the overt opposition has disappeared through the Christianization of the society. It's now the non-Christians who are the oddballs, as far as appearances go. It's the appearance of Christianity, and its apparent falsity, that presents the new situation in which confession of Christ must take place. To give a strong impression of the situation that most people show no sign of recognizing, Kierkegaard offers his somewhat comical parable of the priceless dish.

Imagine someone for whom a certain food is so wonderful that he feels a strong urge to tell others about its loveliness and to defend it against any detractors. (Think of lutefisk or haggis.) But then he notices that everybody around him is saying the same things that he feels an urge to say, except that when it comes to *eating* this food that they all praise to the skies, they avoid it in favor of other foods (maybe cheeseburgers and fries). If he now joined the chorus and testified to the wonderfulness of the food, he would just sound like everybody else, and his testimony would be pointless, inasmuch as no one disagrees with him and he convinces no one—but also, nobody seems to share his enthusiasm.

---

23. UDVS, 323–324 / SKS 8, 415–416.
24. UDVS, 327 / SKS 8, 418.
25. UDVS, 328–330 / SKS 8, 419–421.
26. UDVS, 332 / SKS 8, 423.
27. UDVS, 337 / SKS 8, 427.
28. UDVS, 340 / SKS 8, 430.
29. UDVS, 341 / SKS 8, 431.
30. Acts 4:13.
31. Acts 4:29

This is an image of the situation of a person in Christendom who has something approaching a Socratic knowledge of the value of Christianity. Everyone is ready to praise Christianity, but most of these praisers don't seem to grasp its excellence. They speak without the virtues and the understanding that they entail. What will such a person's testimony look like? Well, for one thing, he might tell such a parable as this one about the priceless dish to raise consciousness of the situation. That would promote at least a beginning of some understanding. It conveys this beginning by its vivid ridiculousness, by the image-producing potency of the analogy.

In connection with the parable, Kierkegaard makes the more purely dialectical or conceptual point that confession, as the concept occurs in the New Testament and early Christian literature, presupposes opposition. Confession of Christ ceases to make sense where all are Christians, and it raises difficult questions about mission strategy where the missionary suspects that there are far fewer Christians in Christendom than appears. He also makes the conceptual point that confession is properly from the heart, out of love for the one confessed, and is decidedly not properly made out of a selfish interest in currying favor with the one confessed, as though that one required adulation to shore up a tyrannical ego.

But the topic of this discourse is not the confession of Christ but the virtue of bold confidence, and Kierkegaard is interested in its more general application: "we call to mind the supreme example of fighting for a conviction, so that from the highest we might learn for the lesser."[32] The virtue of bold confidence needs to be called to people's attention because people in the current culture are subjected to an insidious "evil spirit":

> The small-minded fear of people in relation to equals and the tyranny of the equal, this evil spirit, which we ourselves conjure up and which does not reside in any individual and is not any individual person but covertly sneaks around and seeks its prey, insinuates itself into the relation among individuals—this evil spirit, which essentially wants to do away with every individual's relation to God.[33]

We ourselves have "conjured up" this evil spirit that saps our sense of human dignity, our self-confidence, and self-respect:

> Gradually with the spreading of a certain superficial culture and with the proliferating of peoples' various reciprocal interests, gradually with the spreading infection of the envious and pusillanimous small-mindedness of incessant comparison, it unfortunately seems as if everything is aimed at stifling people's bold confidence. At the same time that there are struggles to overthrow dominions and regimes, there seems to be a supreme effort to develop more and more the most dangerous slavery: the small-minded fear of people who are one's equals.[34]

32. UDVS, 325 / SKS 8, 417.
33. UDVS, 327 / SKS 8, 418.
34. UDVS, 326 / SKS 8, 417–418.

In ringing the alarm that this "evil spirit" is in our midst and in offering exorcism through bold confidence, Kierkegaard is calling for a Godly magnanimity or greatness of soul that befits and completes a creature made in the image of God. Instead of "comparing" ourselves "enviously" with one another—a policy that only ends in our fearing one another—we ought to be measuring ourselves with God and thus be above and beyond that craven fear. The metaphor of the evil spirit for the sociopsychological fact of this corrupting, dehumanizing influence is rhetorically apt both because it is vividly alarming and because it captures the intensely spiritual character of the threat.

So much for the introduction to the discourse, which occupies its first third. Kierkegaard begins the actual exposition of the biblical text (Acts 5:41) with his parable of the youth who knew the truth. This parable is about knowledge or understanding and represents a distinction that Kierkegaard often alludes to, the conceptual distinction between "understanding and understanding"—that is, between knowing with a minimal grasp and a knowing of moral and spiritual truth that approaches more nearly the kind we have been calling "Socratic." This kind of knowledge or understanding will be crucial to the virtue of bold confidence.

Kierkegaard imagines "a youth who has been well instructed in the truth" (let's say he has been well catechized in Christianity), "but he is ignorant of and without experience of the conditions of actuality." He lacks a life context in relation to which to *appreciate* the *bearing* of the truth that he knows so well. But he creates one for himself: "his immature but beautiful imagination then creates for him a picture that he calls the world, where what he has learned now unfolds before him as on a stage."[35] Kierkegaard briefly mentions two important insights that confront the youth as he becomes more intimately acquainted with the actual world: "the defectiveness and mediocrity and instability and small-mindedness" of people, and that "he himself is also beset with frailty."[36] But Kierkegaard's particular interest here is in "a reverseness that may be called *brazenness (Frækhed)*."[37] The well-instructed youth is horrified to find out about people who not only perform shameful actions but actually "glory in their shame."[38] Shameful actions are to be ashamed of, and right objects of pride and glory are deeds of virtue; so to find, after his excellent upbringing, that some people "reverse the concepts,"[39] priding themselves on their vicious actions and lifestyle, is to be pretty shaken in one's moral mind.

If brazenness is the deplorable reverseness, a sublime reverse analogy of brazenness is the disciples' reaction to their being flogged for the name of Christ—for they too glory in their shame. The conceptual difference between these two ways to glory in one's shame is vast, but the unspoiled youth finds the Christian reverseness almost as upsetting as the other: actions for the good like proclaiming

35. UDVS, 328 / SKS 8, 420.
36. Hebrews 5:2.
37. UDVS, 329 / SKS 8, 420.
38. Philippians 3:19.
39. UDVS, 329 / SKS 8, 420.

the savior deserve praise and gratitude, not anger and rejection and punishment. So what are the disciples doing *glorying* in their shame? Shouldn't they be lamenting that the good name of Jesus should provoke such vindictiveness? Well, they don't glory in the pagans' perverse actions but in their own suffering. *Their* shame is their *suffering*,[40] their being treated shamefully; the pagans' shame is their actions (such as treating others shamefully). In treating their mistreatment as something to glory in, they are displaying the very positive, proud virtue of bold confidence. They are actively taking it upon themselves to own their suffering in its resemblance to Christ's. You might say they are taking pride in their being despitefully used. Using the parable of the youth who knew the truth, Kierkegaard gives the reader an impression, through the unaccustomed horror-stricken eyes of the youth, of the extraordinary *activeness* of the disciples in reversing by God's grace the axiological order of the world—turning their shame into glory.

The simile of the sleepwalker treading "with assurance over the abyss, yet in an incomprehensible way" works similarly. We "shudder" at such a sight, as we do at "this apostolic assurance, which, at the height of madness, speaks in tongues with bold confidence,"[41] saying that their bleeding stripes are joyous tokens of God's blessing. Apostles differ from ordinary enthusiasts in that they are not just willing to give up something good (money, reputation) for the sake of their favored cause, but count wealth, honor, and esteem as *loss* (Philippians 3:8) in comparison with the glory for which they fight. The bold confidence with which they rejoice in persecution "stamps the concepts [of gain and loss]" with the mark of the divine.[42] The mark of the divine is the reversal of worldly values. The same mark can be seen on the apostolic concepts of *honor* and *danger*, where the apostle may wonder "whether it would not be too great an honor to be crucified"[43] and where danger is the possibility of forsaking the crucified one for comforts and longevity.[44]

Kierkegaard impresses on the reader the character of an apostle by inviting him or her to contemplate the irony of an apostle living the life of a prominent nineteenth-century Danish clergyman.

> Try it, imagine that he who was to proclaim to the world this message about the Holy One's being crucified as a criminal between two robbers, that this man was dressed in purple and glory, that this man possessed all the world's goods, this man who was to proclaim a crucified one's teaching that the kingdom was not of this world—try it, if you can just bear the attempt, if it is not out of the question because the mere thought of anything like this has the ring of a presumptuous mockery of an apostle.[45]

40. UDVS, 334 / SKS 8, 425.
41. UDVS, 332 / SKS 8, 423.
42. UDVS, 333 / SKS 8, 424.
43. UDVS, 338 / SKS 8, 428.
44. UDVS, 338–339 / SKS 8, 428–429.
45. UDVS, 338 / SKS 8, 428.

Three times on pages 338–339, Kierkegaard invites the reader to imagine such ironic scenarios involving an apostle.

To impress the reader that this apostolic joy, so strange to the ways of the world, is real joy, Kierkegaard likens it to a paradigm case of human gladness: "no girl has ever been more joyful on her betrothal day than the apostles were on the day of whipping and on every such day which for them was a day of betrothal with God."[46] But he also warns the reader that one must take this joy with full seriousness and bold confidence, ready "to become in dead earnest what an apostle became, 'scum in the world, a spectacle to the world'"[47]: "This joyful thought is not like a so-called harmless remedy that can be used in any way without danger and can be used for a light cold, but it is like a strong medicine, the use of which involves some danger, but rightly used also delivers from a sickness unto death."[48]

The last of the imagination-rousing and -sharpening devices in this discourse that I'll mention is the parable of the burning house. The last two pages in the English translation conclude the discourse, and Kierkegaard there reminds the reader that he is speaking of a broader application of the virtue of bold confidence than the apostolic context of confessing Christ. Anyone who suffers for a conviction can and should do so with bold confidence, in the pride of honoring God, not depending on support from fellow human beings.

> A conviction is not something one should rush to bring out in the world. Alas, much confusion has been created and great harm done because an immature person has brought out an immature conviction. No, just allow the conviction to grow quietly, but let it grow together with bold confidence before God.[49]

Then, with the case of a house fire, he illustrates the overwhelming power of fully flowered bold confidence:

> A spark in some wood shavings is put out with a glass of water, but when a fire has had time to spread slowly through the whole house and then with a deep sigh .... bursts into flames all at once—then the firemen say: There is nothing to be done here; here the fire is victorious. It is indeed sad when the firemen say that the fire is victorious, but it is joyful when it is the fire of conviction that is victorious and the enemies say: There is nothing to be done here.[50]

Again, the likening of bold confidence to the indomitable power of a house fire well underway fires the imagination with a kind of perceptual understanding that is more likely than merely conceptual discourse to be embraced by virtue formed in the reader.

46. UDVS, 337 / SKS 8, 427.
47. UDVS, 334 / SKS 8, 425.
48. UDVS, 340 / SKS 8, 430.
49. UDVS, 341 / SKS 8, 431.
50. Ibid.

Conclusion

I've attempted to describe Kierkegaard's recovery of a Socratic understanding of knowledge and understanding against a background of contemporary epistemological concepts and to illustrate some of his strategies for inculcating such understanding—or better, an approximation to it—among his readers in Christendom as an aspect of Christian virtues. Kierkegaard's missionary calling was writing, which, though perhaps essential to missionary work in the modern world, requires great artfulness and is not the most promising of missionary strategies. Kierkegaard's concept of understanding integrates conceptual rigor with vitality of imagination and intensity of passion. As a "poet-dialectician," he exploits the power of bold conceptual contrasts in combination with richly described narrative sketches that speak to primitive human concerns. By his enormous creativity and penetration in these regards, he seeks to "edify," to build up—or better, contribute to the building up—of his reader's character.[51]

51. This chapter was made possible through the support of a grant from the Templeton Religion Trust. The opinions expressed in it are those of the author and do not necessarily reflect the views of Templeton Religion Trust.

Chapter 3

INSIDE THE ESCRITOIRE: ON KIERKEGAARD'S EROTIC THEORY OF COMMUNICATION

Michael Strawser

Introduction

If we accept that Søren Kierkegaard is first and foremost a philosopher of love, then a central question arises: how does he communicate and enable love in writing? In my recent work, *Kierkegaard and the Philosophy of Love*, I have argued for reading Kierkegaard as a philosopher of love, or instead, one whose works can be read not only as dealing with the question of becoming a Christian[1] but more broadly with the more inclusive question concerning how one best becomes a lover. Such an approach shifts from a narrow theological focus on what it means to become a Christian to a phenomenological focus on how one becomes a lover. In contrast to Kant, for whom the central philosophical question is "How is understanding possible?" Kierkegaard's writings are pervaded by the question "How is love possible?" Such a view is already (ironically) present in Kierkegaard's magisterial dissertation, *The Concept of Irony with Continual Reference to Socrates* (1841), where the longing for the actualization of "a sound and healthy love [*en sund Kjærlighed*] ... through action"[2] is the goal of the only life worth living.[3] Kierkegaard's actuality—ironically and in contrast to Socrates—acquires its validity through the action of writing.

In this contribution, I shall argue that throughout Kierkegaard's activity as an author, he is writing in order to make love, and thus we should be able to detect an at least implicit erotic theory of communication that informs his understanding of the practical aspects of both reading and writing. Following Magister Kierkegaard's call to master irony and actualize love, when we turn to *Either/Or*, the privileged

---

1. Thus, I am extending the view put forth in *The Point of View for My Work as an Author* to understand "the issue" (PV, 31 / SKS 16, 17)—"the total thought" (PV, 41 / SKS 16, 23)— of Kierkegaard's entire authorship as centered on the task of becoming a lover, a perspective that has the benefit of providing a more inclusive appeal appropriate to the goal.

2. CI, 328–329 / SKS 1, 357.

3. This refers to the last of the fifteen theses appended to Kierkegaard's magisterial dissertation. See CI, 6 / SKS 1, 65.

beginning of the authorship for Kierkegaard, we find our author of authors thoroughly engaged in the process of courting desire and attempting to bring forth love. Kierkegaard's central exercise in this early pseudonymous work is to invoke an erotic maieutics, but this practice is no less prevalent in his later signed writings. Even the supposedly direct deliberations in *Works of Love* are conditioned upon certain theoretical insights regarding writing and love, which has led Pat Bigelow to suggest in *Kierkegaard and the Problem of Writing* that "surely there is some hidden connection between the maieutic practice of *Works of Love* and the feat or fact of writing."[4] Bigelow even goes further by claiming that "a unique theory of writing" is "intimated on every page of *Works of Love*."[5] What could this possibly mean? Here I shall explore this hidden connection with a focus on *Either/Or* and *Works of Love* in an effort to understand the theory of writing intimated by Kierkegaard. I intend to show how the acts of reading and writing perform the love of the neighbor as oneself through an interpretation of the neighbor as reader and the writer as the self that renounces itself. Along the way, we shall find it necessary to account for the irony of love (in short, that it is not directly what it is in writing, reading, and thinking), the indirection of veronymous writing,[6] and the goal of edification. Furthermore, I shall also consider how Kierkegaard's theory can be read in light of the "free eroticization"—writing to make love—which Jean-Luc Marion describes in *The Erotic Phenomenon* and suggest that Kierkegaard's erotic theory of communication is ultimately derived from his phenomenology of love.

Courting Desire

From beginning to end, the central theme in *Either/Or* is love. This has not been the common view, which instead reads *Either/Or* as an essential work in existential philosophy and focuses on the stages or spheres of existence. But the spheres of existence presuppose the foundational focus on love, for they only become manifest and are differentiated through the pursuit and expression of love. Whether they are fully successful or not, all of the sub-authors in *Either/Or* are essentially marked as lovers. This includes "A," Johannes, Judge William, and the unnamed parson from Jutland. This is easily seen at a glance by considering the following: (1) the first sustained essay by "A," titled "The Immediate Erotic Stages or the Musical Erotic," focuses on exposing the origin of desire, (2) Johannes writes in his diary of seduction that he is an eroticist, not a seducer, who loves with love,[7] (3) William takes up "The Aesthetic Validity of Marriage," understanding

4. Pat Bigelow, *Kierkegaard and the Problem of Writing* (Tallahassee: The Florida State University Press, 1987), p. 65.

5. Ibid.

6. See Michael Strawser, "The Indirectness of Kierkegaard's Signed Writings," *International Journal of Philosophical Studies* 3: 1 (March 1995), pp. 73–90.

7. Johannes writes: "Such a person is and remains a bungler, a seducer, which I can by no means be called. I am an esthete, an eroticist, who has grasped the nature and the point

that the essence of marriage is love and intimating that love is the central free choice that solidifies the personality, and finally (4) the parson's edifying sermon expresses the exponential deepening of love that creates a literary merger of all the prior directions of love.

What is perhaps less obvious at first glance is that the pseudonymous editor, Viktor Eremita, who is also an author—at least of prefaces, but perhaps of so much more—is essentially a lover. It is actually in the writing of Viktor Eremita that Kierkegaard sets the stage for an exposition of love not only in this text but in his authorship proper. Consider Eremita's initial encounter and subsequent courting of the attractive escritoire he views in a shop. Without understanding why or how, Eremita experiences the arousal of desire at the first sight of the escritoire. He is captivated and can neither express nor explain how he feels, and yet he acknowledges that "most people have experienced something similar in their lives."[8] As each day passes, Eremita has to see the escritoire, such that it "acquire(s) a history" for him. Since Eremita does not need such a piece of furniture, there is no practical or sufficient reason for his desire, which leads him to go out of his way in order to be in the presence of his beloved and to cast his "loving eyes"[9] upon it. Finally, he succumbs and purchases the escritoire and a new life begins.

Of course, readers of *Either/Or* are well aware of the secret contents of the escritoire that become exposed after a blow with a hatchet. These contents appear to readily make up the substance of this work, for they are the work itself, but the central subject matter has already been revealed prior to the discovery of the papers, for it is the curious desire that inexplicably arises and leads one to change one's life and go out of one's way on behalf of another. The source of this desire remains hidden, and this inwardness cannot ever be adequately expressed outwardly. Not only is the thesis that the inward is not the outward stated from the start of the text in Viktor Eremita's preface to his "dear reader," but it is already illustrated through the courtship with the escritoire, even before it is progressively deepened through a reading of the escritoire's contents.

What does this signify? What is Kierkegaard after? Is it not the attempt to exhibit through writing the hidden origin of desire that marks the birth of love? Thus, the initial point that emerges is that in order to work to write to express this curious desire known as love, one cannot proceed straightforwardly but instead must use extraordinary measures to awaken readers to the extraordinary immediacy of the erotic phenomenon. What has come to be known as Kierkegaard's method of indirect communication is thus founded on the desire of desire, love seeking love, such that this theory is essentially erotic. This is no less present in Kierkegaard's signed writings, the most important of which is *Works of Love*.

of love [*Kjærlighedens Væsen og Pointet*], who believes in love [*Kjærligheden*] and knows it from the ground up." (EO1, 368 / SKS 2, 356), and "everything I do I do with love, and so I also love with love" (EO1, 337 / SKS 2, 326).

8. EOFL, 28 / EO1, 4 / SKS 2, 12.
9. EOFL, 28–29 / EO1, 5 / SKS 2, 13.

In the second to last diapsalm, Kierkegaard's anonymous author writes: "What is youth? A dream. What is love? The dream's content."[10] With this, we can understand that love is the unifying source of the meaning of experience. It is the content, the life-view that transubstantiates reality making it a meaningful whole. Already in "Kjerkegaard's"[11] first publication, *From the Papers of One Still Living* (1838), the goal of finding a life-view is expressed as a requirement to truly exist as a human being. "For a life-view is more than a quintessence or a sum of propositions maintained in its early abstract neutrality; it is more than experience, which as such is always fragmentary. It is, namely, the transubstantiation of experience; it is an unshakable certainty in oneself won from all experience."[12] This shows how Kierkegaard is fundamentally concerned with an investigation of human experience (i.e., the study of phenomenology) and to find a way to transubstantiate this experience so that one can become a lover.

By acknowledging that the inward is not the outward, one must also acknowledge that one cannot outwardly transubstantiate the inward experience of a person. Thus, one cannot directly call forth one's inward transformation into a sound and healthy lover. Instead, one must engage with language in a way that searchingly attempts to provide an opportunity for an individual to come to effect the transubstantiation through "him- or herself," while noting that this will still be dependent upon the mysterious hidden source (the deeper self? the God self?) that lies within and is yet beyond us.

Such is the irony of love that Kierkegaard's writings expose. The phenomenon of love is an active experience, not a passive concept. Thus, language, which deals with concepts, cannot itself touch the experience of love, and herein lies the irony, which we understand as the rupture, the disconnection, between concept and phenomenon. The irony of love thus presents a paradox for the writer who would hope to make love manifest in the experience of the reader. How does one move the other?

The writing then that will attempt to address this rupture must be aware of its own limits and will thus wander the valley between philosophy and literature. It will involve the author bringing his reader as close as possible and yet realizing the distance between them. Wanting to write about this remarkable experience of love that enflames his soul, Kierkegaard's anonym knows the impossibility that he faces, but this does not prevent him from expressing himself.

In "The Immediate Erotic Stages or the Musical Erotic," the ostensible goal of the author is to demonstrate that Mozart is the greatest artist who has ever lived, but the subgoal is to unravel the experience of love, the immediacy of desire, and its stages. Kierkegaard's anonym writes: "The immediate task of this exploration is to show the significance of the musical-erotic and to that end in turn to indicate the various stages, which, since they are all characterized by the immediate erotic,

10. EOFL, 57 / EO1, 42 / SKS 2, 51.
11. This is the alternative spelling of Kierkegaard's name that appears on the title page of his first publication.
12. FPOSL, 76 / SKS 1, 32.

also harmonize in this, that essentially they are all musical."[13] Toward this end, "A" makes conceptual distinctions between the dreaming desire, the seeking desire, and the immediacy of desire, but he knows full well that the conceptual distinctions that he is making ultimately fail to touch the unified phenomenon of love and the hidden origin of desire. Thus, in writing with this knowledge, he is writing toward an end that cannot be directly achieved in writing. Consider:

> Of course, the difficulties always encountered when one considers music aesthetically are not to be avoided here either. The difficulty in the foregoing lay chiefly in the fact that while I wanted to prove through a process of thought that sensual genius is the proper object of music, really this can only be proved with music, just as it is only through music itself that I myself have come to an appreciation of music. The difficulty the following must contend with is really that since what the music under discussion expresses is essentially music's proper object, this music expresses it far more perfectly than does language, which makes a very poor showing in comparison. Of course, if I had been concerned with different levels of consciousness, the advantage would be on my side and that of language, but that is not the case here. So what remains to be explained can only have meaning for the person who has listened and who continues constantly to listen. For him it may perhaps contain a suggestion or two that may move him to listen once more.[14]

The parallel to love should be clear, for let us not forget that what Kierkegaard's anonym is ultimately after is to give expression to the sheer phenomenon of love,[15] and toward this goal, Kierkegaard frequently calls on his readers to read aloud and to listen carefully. The proper object of experience is love, and consequently love can only be truly understood experientially (i.e., phenomenologically), thus leaving the actions of the writer who is also a lover forever in question. From one perspective, the difficulty is no doubt profound, and yet from another, one finds that the difficulty may not be as great as one might think. For as one can only grasp the meaning of music through listening to it, one can only appreciate the meaning of love through loving. Consequently, Kierkegaard is here and elsewhere writing to readers as if they are lovers and suggesting that they continue to love with love.

13. EO1, 59 / SKS 2, 66. These stages, as well as the stages of existence, ought not to be considered as separate and fixed categories without interpenetration. For further clarification of this point regarding the so-called theory of stages, see Michael Strawser, *Both/And: Reading Kierkegaard from Irony to Edification* (New York: Fordham University Press, 1997), pp. 136–137.

14. EOFL, 84 / EO1, 74–75 / SKS 2, 80–81.

15. For a reading of this text that offers a unifying view of the sensual erotic as the sheer phenomenon of love, see Pia Søltoft, "Kierkegaard and the Sheer Phenomenon of Love," *Kierkegaard Studies Yearbook* (2013), pp. 289–306.

Writing to Make Love

One of the many interesting intersections to explore between Kierkegaard's philosophy of love and Jean-Luc Marion's phenomenology of love is the question of how to write about love. Marion addresses the question of language and the erotic phenomenon in "Words for Saying Nothing," the final section of the chapter "Concerning the Flesh, and Its Arousal." Here, after describing the experience of the flesh, how the other gives my flesh to me, and that my flesh is ultimately limited by eroticization's finitude, Marion considers the meaning and force of erotic language.

> The phenomenon of eroticization leaves me in fact no memory, or at least an abstract memory—that of the most perfect consciousness, but a consciousness of nothing; a perfectly clear idea, but absolutely not distinct—a flash of lightning, but not definable or recognizable, without a sign to recognize it by, which thus becomes confused with every other void; so, unable to describe or name it, one can only repeat it.[16]

From within the experience of the immediacy of love, or eroticization, everything is perfect and clear, and yet this experience cannot be maintained infinitely as we inevitably succumb to the automation of the flesh. In love, however, we are as if struck by a bolt of lightning and charged to give expression to our love in infinite repetition.

Marion continues:

> It is not a matter of a saturated phenomenon, where the excess of intuition would call for an excess of conceptual hermeneutics and description. Rather, it is a matter of an erased phenomenon, where the excess of intuition over the concept does indeed invade all of the horizon of manifestation, but withdraws itself and disappears immediately, so that nothing, upon this beach without waves, remains to explain, to comprehend, and to put into evidence. Of eroticization, this erased phenomenon, one can say nothing, even to oneself, even from lover to lover. The words are lacking.[17]

Thus, if there are no words to express the love that is inexpressible, does this mean that one must remain silent? As Marion asks, "Where there is nothing to say, since there is nothing to describe, is it necessary to keep quiet?"[18] As Kierkegaard shows throughout his writings, the inability to communicate the essential (i.e., love) does not result in a suspension of language and writing, and instead it is for him the

---

16. Jean-Luc Marion, *The Erotic Phenomenon*, trans. Stephen E. Lewis (Chicago: University of Chicago Press, 2007), p. 144.

17. Ibid.

18. Ibid.

beginning of writing, an authorship that cannot be self-contained and cannot be closed, notwithstanding Kierkegaard's (ironic?) attempt at closure through the composition of *The Point of View*.[19] What role, then, does the act of communication play within the limits of erotic language?

Marion's writing focuses on the erased phenomenon of the climax, which is brought about through the crossing of the flesh, and as he explains, unlike other seemingly ineffable singular experiences of immediacy (and isn't every experience in some aspect one of immediacy?), the experience of love is unique in that it calls forth language, even though language will not be able to succeed in expressing its inexhaustible ineffability or describe its indescribability. But love is unlike other first person experiences of, for example, suffering, for love requires that "I turn to the other and address myself to her, and thus address her with speech and await her response."[20] Of faith, one may perhaps remain silent, but not of love, for love is only possible through a relation to the other.

In my loving relation to the other, who is no-thing of the world, I must speak, even though I lack the words to speak of the love we share. "Precisely by virtue of that of which I cannot speak, I must speak to the other," Marion writes. "Thus the erotic reduction redefines the rules of language."[21] By virtue of the absurd, Kierkegaard knows that he cannot write to express the hidden desire to love that he so ardently desires, and yet this does not lead to silence but to a redefining of the way his philosophy of love is expressed. This leads to what Bigelow calls "the Kierkegaardian gambit: to say by unsaying and unsay by saying."[22] Bigelow elucidates further:

> But: what *is* the gambit?
>
> It is hard to say: to say what the gambit is *about* requires learning to unsay the saying that says that every saying is always a saying-*about*. Though all saying is inwardly involved with this gambit, though all saying testifies to this gambit and is cryptic and decrepit documentation of this gambit, no saying could ever say what this gambit is *about*—for *that* there is this gambit means that there is a way of saying that is not *about* anything.
>
> Yet it is irresistible to try to insist that this way of saying is nonetheless about something, about, perhaps, what takes place both before and after thinking, both before and after saying. ... And this is the force of the Kierkegaardian gambit: to

---

19. Kierkegaard's posthumously published *The Point of View for My Work as an Author* is a so-called direct report that was nevertheless conceived as a potentially indirect work and may be seen as successfully establishing the dialectical structure of his authorship. This "ending," this supposed final word and explanation, has, however, an altogether different effect, for as I have shown previously, it contributes to the higher dialectical structure of Kierkegaard's writings, which constitutes the both/and and leaves in place the whirlwind of writing—which like Aristophanes's clouds and Marion's erased phenomenon manifest the void.

20. Marion, *The Erotic Phenomenon*, p. 144.

21. Ibid., p. 145.

22. Bigelow, *Kierkegaard and the Problem of Writing*, p. 3.

offer a little uplifting story in order to get us to want to say this unsayable saying before we are even aware that something new and uncanny has suddenly started upon us, suddenly startled upon us.[23]

What Bigelow appropriately left unsaid and I cannot resist now unsaying by saying is that the Kierkegaardian gambit is all about love.

The context of our examination of Marion's writing on erotic language is related to the climax, but it is not necessary to understand climactic enjoyment in a sexual way but rather as the moment when lovers recognize themselves as lovers through giving themselves to the other. I do not think that Marion would object to this reading, for after all, "love is said and is given in only one, strictly univocal way. As soon as one multiplies it into subtle and differentiated acceptations, to the point of equivocality, one ceases to analyze it better."[24]

From within the erotic reduction, language is "no longer a matter of predicates or of subjects, but instead of you and me," and we speak "in order to arouse ourselves."[25] This arousal not only pertains to my flesh, although that is central to it, but it serves a performative function as well. The language of love is not categorical, cognitive, or descriptive; it does not directly communicate anything but instead makes love through the saying. Because of this, as Marion tells us, erotic language "stages the oath."[26]

> A love begins when each speaks to the other of the other him- or herself, alone and of nothing else. … Lovers speak to one another solely in order to provoke one another to eroticization; alone in the world, or more precisely alone outside of the world, they only use words in order to arouse one another, and never in order to know or to describe anything. … Lovers thus speak without saying anything in order to accomplish thoroughly the erotic reduction.[27]

This analysis helps illuminate "the Kierkegaardian gambit," which, as "explained" above, is "to say by unsaying and unsay by saying. In writing."[28] It is important to see that for Marion, "erotic speech thus provokes a transgressive language—because it transgresses objectivity, transports us out of the world,"[29] and this provides an insightful way of analyzing the writing of Kierkegaard, which is clearly focused on "the single individual" beyond the world or worldliness.

In the love relationship that involves a crossing of the flesh, one succumbs to suspension and automation, and these make it possible for involuntary darker experiences to occur in which the personhood of the other may be lost. How might

23. Ibid., pp. 4–5, 8.
24. Marion, *The Erotic Phenomenon*, p. 217.
25. Ibid., 146.
26. Ibid., p. 147.
27. Ibid., pp. 147–148.
28. Bigelow, *Kierkegaard and the Problem of Writing*, p. 3.
29. Marion, *The Erotic Phenomenon*, p. 148.

we prevent this from happening? How would it be possible to eroticize the other freely in a way that her personhood remains in focus and not the things of the world? As Marion attempts to show, such a possibility can occur through "free eroticization," through which one reaches the other flesh without contact. As Marion explains:

> And, just as it is not enough to enter into contact to make love, in order to make love I do not always, or first of all, or necessarily, need to enter into contact with the other; I can just as well give her her flesh, and thus have her experience my nonresistance, by speaking to her. I make love *first* by speaking.[30]

The question then involves what manner of speech, or more generally, language usage, needs to be employed to make love happen. Here Marion refers to what he previously discussed as performative language that transgresses objectivity and speaks only "to the other of the other him- or herself, in the other's own right, as an unsubstitutable person, first and last."[31] Does this not clearly characterize the central focus of Kierkegaard's writing on the individual and his or her subjectivity? Does Kierkegaard not repeatedly write in a manner that is without authority and thus nonresistantly opens itself to the other?

According to Marion, "thus there opens before free eroticization an immense field of activity—it allows one to give (and to receive) an eroticized flesh there where sexuality does not reach. From parent to child, from friend to friend, from man to God."[32] What I wish to suggest is that what Kierkegaard does in his writings is precisely to embark onto this immense field of activity in order to arouse and make love (happen) (to/with the other). For Kierkegaard, writings express key points of free eroticization. They aim "to touch [the] heart and give [the other] her flesh in its completeness."[33] Each act of writing is given freely; it expresses the responsibility the author takes upon himself to touch the other (without contact) through speaking (or writing) in order to give the other herself. This, for Marion, amounts to "mak[ing] love to the other *in person*,"[34] but he also recognizes, as Kierkegaard most clearly does, that, this particular kind of language of free eroticization is ultimately about love expressing itself—about love making love. Thus, little by little, "my speech will no longer speak to the other only of herself, but, little by little, of the interval between the other and me, of what is between us, of this non-thing, unreal and invisible, wherein we stay with one another, live, and breathe."[35] Thus, ultimately the language of love leads both myself and the other to experience the relation between us,[36] in which case love makes love.

30. Ibid., pp. 181–182.
31. Ibid., p. 182.
32. Ibid., p. 183.
33. Ibid., 182.
34. Ibid.
35. Ibid.
36. In *Works of Love*, Kierkegaard speaks of love under the name of God, that third between us that makes manifest love, and this helps in characterizing Kierkegaard's erotic theory of communication in light of Marion's work. According to Marion, there are three

From a draft of *The Point of View*, Kierkegaard explains that "the subject of the single individual appears in every book by the pseudonymous writers [and] ... every one of my upbuilding books," and a look at all these works will easily confirm this claim.[37] Thus, that Kierkegaard is writing to the other alone is clear. Furthermore, in "The Single Individual: Two Notes Concerning My Work as an Author,"[38] Kierkegaard calls his reader to be a lover of the other in perfect equality, which is only possible when *worldliness* is "completely eradicated."[39] Thus, Kierkegaard knows that in order to arouse his single reader to love, he must work against "the public" and "the crowd," writing in a way that transgresses objectivity and the world in the hope of upbuilding the other in the truth that is subjectivity, which is ultimately the "how" of love. In a draft "For the Dedication to 'That Single Individual,'" Kierkegaard writes:

> Dear Reader,
>   Please accept this dedication .... you are my hope, my joy, my pride ....
>   It comforts me, dear reader, that you have this opportunity, the opportunity for which I know I have honestly worked. If it were feasible, that reading what I write came to be common practice, or at least pretending to have read it in hopes of getting ahead in the world, this would not be the opportune time for *my* reader .... No, if reading what I write becomes a dubious good, or still better, if it becomes foolish and ludicrous to read my writings, or even better, if it becomes a contemptible matter so that no one dares to acknowledge it, that is the opportune time for my reader; then he seeks stillness, then he does not read for my sake or for the world's sake.[40]

Consequently, the inwardness that Kierkegaard seeks to establish through his writings could not be more pronounced. As far away from our author as from the world, the goal is to allow love, God's love, to transform the reader into a lover.

lexicons for expressing the erotic phenomenon—obscene, puerile, and mystical theological language—but surprisingly none of these account for Marion's own phenomenological lexicon, and it is hard to see how Kierkegaard's language fits here. Fortunately, in *The Erotic Phenomenon* Marion also mentions poetry, which is "in league" with the erotic reduction (p. 148), and this provides us with a way of understanding Kierkegaard's writings. Fittingly, Kierkegaard's lexicon is entirely unique, but it may be characterized as the activity of a "poet" whose language approaches "the language of spiritual union of man with God" (*The Erotic Phenomenon*, p. 149), although this may be better expressed, since his actual work as an author quite clearly expresses the spiritual union of the author with the reader in which case "love"/"God" is the middle term.

37. PV, 276 / Pap. VIII-2 B 192.
38. In the *Kierkegaard's Writings* series, this material is published in "The Supplement" to *The Point of View*.
39. TSI, 104 / SKS 16, 84.
40. PV, 151–152 / SKS 20, 54–55 (NB: 64).

Perhaps, however, someone will object to this reading on the grounds that Marion's analysis involves describing the climactic enjoyment of the crossing of flesh (i.e., the experience of orgasm), which is surely a foreign concept for what Kierkegaard is doing. First, it is important to see that Marion defines the climax, the pinnacle of love, as "unit[ing] oneself with the other for the other herself,"[41] so it is clearly meant to be understood beyond the sexual context. Second, this union of oneself with the other is easily seen as an act of friendship, and it is interesting, while perhaps also surprising, how this definition is aligned with Spinoza's definition of love/nobility: "endeavor[ing] to help others and join them in friendship."[42] For Marion, "love is only told in one way,"[43] and while friendship involves a shortcut avoiding climactic enjoyment, it still "unquestionably, straightforwardly, and without any ambiguity takes the very path of the erotic reduction," one that can even be seen as a "more accomplished figure of the erotic reduction."[44] Throughout his writings, Kierkegaard repeatedly and intimately addresses his reader, but what has not been commonly recognized is that Kierkegaard's *dear* reader is a friend in the truest sense. Kierkegaard's writings, I maintain, thus express a notion of friendship derived from a philosophy of love, but this other who is the friend is not a friend in the preferential sense, for as Marion explains, "such a figure of friendship, which interprets it as the reciprocal enjoyment of a worldly third party, introduces no equivocality at all into the concept of love, simply because it in no way derives from it."[45] Kierkegaard was thus right to separate preferential friendship from the notion of true love in *Works of Love*, but what he failed to make plain is that the other who is one's equal in the love of the neighbor, the other who is his hope, joy, and pride, the other who is an unknown but favorable one addressed throughout his writings (free eroticization) is a *friend*. Therefore, Kierkegaard's erotic theory of communication is structured on the phenomenological view that his reader is essentially a *friend*.

Praising Love's Hidden Life

The Point of View for My Work as an Author: A Direct Communication, Report to History is an interesting yet problematic work, for it raises the issue of whether Kierkegaard can directly reveal his inwardness as an author to the reader. Furthermore, it seems to conflict with Kierkegaard's erotic theory of communication, for self-denial is a key aspect of Kierkegaard's theory, and yet *The Point of View*, while still speaking of self-denial, can nevertheless be read, at least on the surface and in a straightforward manner, as a work of self-affirmation. Undoubtedly, Kierkegaard struggled with these issues, which is why he considered

41. Marion, *The Erotic Phenomenon*, p. 144.
42. See Spinoza's *Ethics* 3P59S.
43. Marion, *The Erotic Phenomenon*, p. 3.
44. Ibid., p. 219.
45. Ibid., p. 218.

publishing the work under a pseudonym—"the poet Johannes de Silentio"[46]—and finally decided not to publish the writing at all. Fortunately, the work appeared posthumously, and the theoretical value of this work, as I have argued elsewhere, is that while it clarifies the dialectical structure of Kierkegaard's authorship, it also serves to constitute the higher dialectical structure that makes the total thought of Kierkegaard ultimately undecidable.[47]

Given the context and aim of the present essay, we must ask ourselves whether Kierkegaard's avowed "point of view" is also a work of erotic communication expressing a philosophy of love. Unsurprisingly, this question can be answered affirmatively.

In a telling passage from *On My Work as an Author*, Kierkegaard closes the opening section of "The Accounting" with this expression of his faith:

> And this is my faith, that however much confusion and evil and contemptibleness there can be in human beings as soon as they become the irresponsible and repentant "public," "crowd," etc.—there is just as much truth and goodness and lovableness in them when one can get them as single individuals. Oh, to what degree human beings would become—human and lovable beings—if they would become single individuals before God![48]

This passage is particularly significant for several reasons. First, it emphasizes the focus on "the single individual," which as shown above structures Kierkegaard's erotic theory of communication. Second, we find Kierkegaard expressing here his faith in love. Not only does he presuppose the lovableness of human beings—and we do well to remind ourselves that seeing others as lovable is a work of love and lies at the root of edification[49]—but he also clarifies that the goal of the focus on single individuals is to build them up as lovers. Thus, it should not be surprising for us to read an unused supplement to *The Point of View* where Kierkegaard writes: "I honestly know that I have loved every person."[50]

Kierkegaard's activity as an author, as I have been arguing, is an exercise in erotic maieutics centered soundly on the singular other who is both neighbor and friend. As Kierkegaard recognizes, however, "the maieutic actually hides the fact that God is the one who moves the whole thing."[51] "God," of course, *is love*, so we are once again left to ponder the hidden source inside the escritoire.

It is interesting to see the parallel that exists between the opening pages of *Either/Or* and *Works of Love*. As we have seen, *Either/Or* opens by attuning

---

46. PV, 176 / KJN 5, 261 (NB9: 78) / SKS 21, 250.

47. See Strawser, *Both/And: Reading Kierkegaard from Irony to Edification*, pp. 237–242.

48. OMWA, 10–11 / SKS 13, 17.

49. See "Love Builds Up" in Kierkegaard's *Works of Love*, where he develops the central claim that "to build up" and "to be loving means: to presuppose love in others" (WL, 224 / SKS 9, 226).

50. PV, 170 / KJN 5, 101 (NB7: 41) / SKS 21, 97.

51. PV, 166 / KJN 5, 63 (NB6: 81a) / SKS 21, 62.

readers to the thesis that the inner is not the outer and referring them to the non-conceptualization of the hidden and mysterious origin of desire. *Works of Love* opens by (non-)identifying love as *"essentially* indescribable" and *"essentially* inexhaustible"[52] and begins by discoursing on the hidden life of love, the origin of which lies deeply hidden like the secret source of an overflowing lake.

> Love's hidden life is in the innermost being, unfathomable, and then in turn is in an unfathomable connectedness with all existence. Just as the quiet lake originates deep down in hidden springs no eye has seen, so also does a person's love originate even more deeply in God's love. … Just as the quiet lake originates darkly in the deep spring, so a human being's love originates mysteriously in God's love. Just as the quiet lake invites you to contemplate it but by the reflected image of darkness prevents you from seeing through it, so also the mysterious origin of love in God's love prevents you from seeing its ground. When you think that you see it, you are deceived by a reflected image, as if that which only hides the deeper ground were the ground. Just as the lid of a clever secret compartment, for the very purpose of completely hiding the compartment, looks as if it were the bottom, so also that which only covers what is even deeper deceptively appears to be the depths of the ground.[53]

We can say, then, that Kierkegaard's activity as a writer and the erotic maieutics he practices are an attempt to confront this deeply hidden inner love of love. Kierkegaard's theory of indirect communication is aimed at the communication of love, where the emphasis lies on "love's hidden life" and that which cannot be communicated directly. Kierkegaard's "writing itself sustains"[54] an "unfathomable connectedness with all existence," a relationship that Bigelow explains as follows:

> To say what the relationship between writing and a written discourse on love is is to elaborate a unique theory of writing, a theory intimated on every page of *Works of Love*. But such is this theory that it can only be intimated; it cannot be explicated directly, for it is the secret about which "indirect communication" is *indirect* communication.
>
> Yet we can learn to develop a sensitivity toward this secret; we can learn to heighten our sensibilities about what is involved in writing—both in the activity of writing and the written word.[55]

---

52. WL, 3 / SKS 9, 11.
53. WL, 9–10 / SKS 9, 17–18.
54. Bigelow, *Kierkegaard and the Problem of Writing*, p. 65.
55. Ibid. Given this significance of *Works of Love* for understanding Kierkegaard as a writer, it is surprising that *Works of Love* does not figure prominently in Eric Ziolkowski's *The Literary Kierkegaard*, which emphasizes the "essentially literary" aspects of Kierkegaard's writings. See Ziolkowski, *The Literary Kierkegaard* (Evanston, IL: Northwestern University Press, 2011), p. 4.

And we can also learn to praise love. For in the final discourse of *Works of Love*, we can find a discourse that provides the culminating point of view for reading Kierkegaard as an author devoted to writing about love. In "The Work of Love in Praising Love," Kierkegaard again seeks to efface himself as an author, as he writes:

> But with regards to love, it is neither partially nor totally true that the art is to say it, or that to be able to say it is in any way essentially conditioned by the accident of talent. For just that reason it is very upbuilding to speak about love, because one must continually bear in mind and say to oneself, "This is something everyone can do or everyone ought to be able to do"—whereas it would be strange to say that everyone is or could be a poet. Love, which overcomes all dissimilarities, which dissolves all bonds in order to bind all in the bonds of love, must of course lovingly watch out lest a special kind of dissimilarity assert itself divisively here.[56]

In such a way, after our author has distinguished himself in discoursing on the profound aspects of love, he denies any special talent when it comes to praising love. He thus invites all his readers to realize that they too are included as lovers, praisers of love, who can also do the good work of upbuilding others in love. Since love is the common watermark[57] that marks all human beings, writing to praise love is no distinguishing art. It is a work that each of us can perform, but it can only be performed through self-denial, and "to love the neighbor is, of course, self-denial."[58]

> Therefore, in order to be able to praise love, self-denial is required *inwardly* and self-sacrificing unselfishness *outwardly*. If, then, someone undertakes to praise love and is asked whether it is actually out of love on his part that he does it, the answer must be: "No one else can decide this for certain; it is possible that it is vanity, pride—in short, something bad, but it is also possible that it is love."[59]

Consequently, even if we affirm the interpretation that Kierkegaard is first and foremost a philosopher of love whose authorship is written to both make and praise love, we nevertheless do not revoke the irony of love and the undecidability thesis that I defended in *Both/And: Reading Kierkegaard from Irony to Edification*. In *Both/And*, I explain the higher dialectical structure of Kierkegaard's writings, and I show how this leads to the ultimately undecidable nature of Kierkegaard's methodology as an author.[60] While in this earlier work I may seem to place more emphasis on the opposition between the aesthetic and the religious and the corresponding methods of irony and edification, it is still nevertheless the case that the point of view of the higher dialectical structure of Kierkegaard's writings offers a more

56. WL, 359 / SKS 9, 353.
57. See WL, 89 / SKS 9, 94.
58. TSI, 111 / SKS 16, 91.
59. WL, 374 / SKS 9, 367.
60. See Strawser, *Both/And*, pp. 237–242.

unifying perspective, and it is this perspective that I have attempted to develop in my most recent work, *Kierkegaard and the Philosophy of Love.*[61] When we realize that Kierkegaard's anonym and Johannes the so-called seducer are best viewed as lovers, we will be less inclined to judge them as erroneous and perditious,[62] and we must likewise realize, as Kierkegaard does, that the religious writer who praises God or praises love might be something bad. Given the uncrossable distance between the inward and the outward—something Kierkegaard acknowledges from the outset of his authorship proper in *Either/Or* and something that is again expressed in *Works of Love*—we cannot dogmatically decide that Kierkegaard's writings actually do express love. The voices of believers, cynics, and lovers will thus continue, as the possibilities lie in the hands of Kierkegaard's readers. This, of course, is exactly how it should be.

61. See Michael Strawser, *Kierkegaard and the Philosophy of Love* (Lanham, MD: Lexington Books, 2015).

62. For such a reading, see Mark Tietjen, *Kierkegaard, Communication, and Virtue: Authorship as Edification* (Bloomington: Indiana University Press, 2013). While Tietjen somewhat reluctantly accepts that "'undecidability' is an appropriate concept to apply here," he argues for a weaker sense of undecidibility and cites Johannes Climacus to support a strong condemnatory judgment of aesthetic existence (Tietjen, *Kierkegaard, Communication, and Virtue*, p. 28). The contrast to reading Kierkegaard as a philosopher of love should be clear, and the last passage cited above shows that even in his direct, signed, and so-called religious writings, Kierkegaard still maintains a strong sense of undecidability.

Chapter 4

KIERKEGAARD'S SCENE CHANGES: AUTHORSHIP AS THEATRICAL PRACTICE

Sophie Wennerscheid

One of the preeminent thinkers of the twentieth century, the French philosopher and literary theorist Gilles Deleuze, in his work *Difference and Repetition*, brought Søren Kierkegaard to the fore as a pioneer of theatrical philosophy. Opposed to Hegel's dialectical thought, which aims at the reconciliation of opposites in a higher unity, Deleuze recognizes in Kierkegaard a thinker whose work remains in the mode of permanent tension, movement, and transformation. This is the case, according to Deleuze, not so much owing to the content of Kierkegaardian thought as to its style. Deleuze credits Kierkegaard with bringing "new means of expression" to philosophy and thereby with overcoming the Hegelian understanding of philosophy as an "abstract logical movement of 'mediation.'"[1] Deleuze sees Kierkegaard alongside Nietzsche as putting metaphysics into action.

> They want to make it act, and make it carry out immediate acts. It is not enough therefore, for them to propose a new representation of movement; representation is already mediation. Rather, it is a question of producing within the work a movement capable of affecting the mind outside representation; it is a question of making movement itself a work, without interposition; of substituting direct signs for mediate representations; of inventing vibration, rotations, whirlings, gravitations, dances or leaps which directly touch the mind.[2]

In relation to the dynamism of Kierkegaardian thought, Deleuze accords central importance to the concept of repetition, which he himself also uses for elaborating his theory of duplication and deferment. Rather than expounding argumentatively on the relevance of the concept of repetition, for Kierkegaard, it is a matter of giving, by the stylistic process of repetition, a performative—as it were, eventful—quality to language, into whose movement the reader should be taken. This is not,

---

1. Gilles Deleuze, *Difference and Repetition*, trans. Paul Patton (London: Bloomsbury, 2014), p. 10.
2. Ibid.

however, to reach a certain goal but conversely to hold the reader open for that which eventuates in the repetition as "forward movement," ever anew and, above all, unexpectedly.

Furthermore, according to Deleuze, Kierkegaard's linguistic detours, loops, and leaps do circumvent not only the idea of a straight-line development but also the idea of a fixed center. His language decentralizes the center and offers "a Cogito for a dissolved self."[3] Just as the self is said to have no center, so too is none featured by the text; it has no fixed reference point and consequently no longer any authoritative speaker. Repetition shatters the idea of an origin and introduces the idea of a simulacrum as a copy "which overturns all copies by also overturning the models."[4] As an example of such a literary procedure, Deleuze names, alongside Kierkegaard, the Spanish author Jorge L. Borges who, in his short story, "Pierre Menard, Author of the Quixote," wrote a narrative about a fictive author who has rewritten Cervantes's *Don Quixote* in a completely identical manner, but which due to its mimicry is much more complex than the "original." Deleuze wants to follow the example of this form of multiplication for literary and philosophical writing in general, claiming: "It should be possible to recount a real book of past philosophy as if it were an imaginary and feigned book."[5]

Reference to similar play with an author figure who is duplicated repeatedly, and in whose duplication is himself unraveled as a fixed unit, is also found at the end of the first volume of Kierkegaard's *Concluding Unscientific Postscript to Philosophical Fragments*. Under the heading "A Glance at a Contemporary Effort in Danish Literature,"[6] the writing's pseudonymous author, Johannes Climacus, is astonished by some remarkable literary historical coincidences. Always at the moment in which he wishes to begin a new book, exactly this book appears. Others become the author and he himself the reader of texts whose author he would have liked to become. Initially, Johannes Climacus is unhappy in view of this state of affairs, but then he reconciles himself to them, since "the cause I had resolved to take up is advancing, but not through me."[7] What's more, with each of the writings that appears, Johannes Climacus realizes more clearly what he himself really wanted. Withdrawing to his role as reader makes him realize at once that he cannot of course know if his interpretation of the texts conforms to the intention of the respective authors, because, smart as they are, they refrained from making comments on their authorial intentions.

It's this play with authorships that I would like to take up as regards the question in which way Kierkegaard as author, according to Deleuze, indeed not only reflects upon particular types of (intellectual) movement but also, as Klaus Müller-Wille describes it elsewhere, realizes these movements directly performatively through

---

3. Ibid., p. xvii.
4. Ibid.
5. Ibid., p. vxiii.
6. CUP1, 251 / SKS 7, 228.
7. Ibid.

the specific dynamics of his texts.[8] Müller-Wille demonstrates how Kierkegaard, following Lessing in the contradictory form of his own texts' presentation and the resulting "difference between the expressive instance and the message,"[9] inhibits the reader's immediate intellectual understanding and in this way "compels" him or her to independently appropriate that which has been read. Müller-Wille sees this kind of indirect praxis for communicating by Kierkegaard, which has been frequently examined, as a manifestation of Kierkegaard's dramaturgical thinking.

I would like to go a step beyond this equation of indirect communication with dramaturgical practice by examining more precisely three formal strategies of Kierkegaard, which I consider genuinely theatrical First, I would like to present the concept of theatrical thought as a play between actor and spectator in changing roles. Subsequently, I will go into greater detail about the concept of "scene change." Thirdly, I seek to analyze Kierkegaard's frequent reference to the (thought-)experiment as a form of intellectual performance. And in steps four and five, by way of conclusion, I will carefully explain how the seemingly disparate themes of theater, marriage, and belief are closely interwoven.

Scenes of the Self

In the posthumously published *Adventures of a Danish Student*, a novella by Poul Martin Møller (a Danish professor of philosophy held in high esteem by Kierkegaard), there is a short passage in which the concept of dramatic thinking is invoked, and crucially for Kierkegaard's thought, linked to the question concerning the relationship between scene and self. The passage is interesting insofar as it touches upon the necessity to disclose oneself, instead of indulging oneself in "scheming secrecy." Mention is made of how the figure of the socially neurotic Claudius explains to his cousin why he conceals from him, a family member, his sorrows and worries. He doesn't understand it himself, Claudius concedes at first, deeming it "a remarkable psychological problem."[10] He then gives a further account:

> I am feeling like a mortally ill patient who has not even the courage to reveal himself to his own doctor. In this way man divides himself on various occasions into two persons of which the one or the other makes an attempt at deception, while a third, who is in fact identical with both of the others, is rather astonished by this confusion. In short, thinking becomes dramatic and plays in all quietness

---

8. Klaus Müller-Wille, "Lessings Theaterlogik und Kierkegaards dramaturgisches Denken," in *Kierkegaard und das Theater*, ed. Klaus Müller-Wille and Sophie Wennerscheid (Tübingen: Narr Francke Attempto Verlag, forthcoming 2018).

9. Ibid.

10. Poul Martin Møller, *En dansk students eventyr og Lægdsgaarden i Ølsebye-Magle* (Copenhagen: Gyldendal, 1964), p. 45. All translations from this text are my own.

with itself and for itself the most entangled intrigues; and the spectator becomes actor ever anew.[11]

The dissociation of the individual into different figures who, as thematized by Møller, assume the roles of actor and audience in alternating fashion, can be identified as a figure of thought in which theatricality is defined as an anthropological category, and theater is regarded as a stage, as a scene of the self. The scholar of theater studies Erika Fischer-Lichte characterizes this kind of theatrical self-reflection with reference to Helmut Plessner's concept of "eccentric positionality" as a *conditio humana*. She explains:

> When with Plessner one comprehends the conditio humana as man's distantiality from himself, as his eccentric position, the thesis then appears plausible that with the conditio humana the possibility and necessity of staging is set: Man steps forward vis-à-vis himself or another, to conceive and to bring to light an image of himself as another, which he has perceived through the eyes of another or seen reflected in the eyes of another.[12]

Constantin Constantius, in *Repetition: A Venture in Experimenting Psychology*, interprets one such form of self-doubling, that is, of exteriorization of the subject in his or her alter ego, as an existence of an "audible shadow."[13] The stage upon which such shadow figures are found would be Kierkegaard's work in its entirety. Here, he allows his numerous dramatized authors, narrators, and story characters to assume positions in which they mutually mirror and comment on each other.

The possibility of creating an image of oneself in theatrical self-reflection is, however, viewed by Møller as well as by Kierkegaard as a problematical process. Provided that the two Danish thinkers of the early nineteenth century are in accord with Plessner and Fischer-Lichte's stance, to the extent that theater is to be viewed as an existential hall of mirrors, this kind of self-mirroring stands opposed to the Enlightenment motto, often cited by Kierkegaard, "*Gnothi se auton.*" In the end, according to Kierkegaard, rather than leading to one's own self-recognition, theater leads away from oneself.

The misgiving about losing oneself in the multiplicity of mirrored existences or becoming entangled in intricate intrigues is expressed above all in the reflections of Constantin Constantius. On the one hand, he explains how important the theater is for the development of the subject who has been "enthralled by the magic of the theater and wished to be swept along into that artificial actuality in order like a double to see and hear himself and to split himself up into every

---

11. Ibid.
12. Erika Fischer-Lichte, "Inszenierung und Theatralität," in *Inszenierungsgesellschaft: Ein einführendes Handbuch*, ed. Herbert Willems and Martin Jurga (Wiesbaden: Springer VS, 1998), p. 87. My translation.
13. R, 155 / SKS 4, 31.

possible variation of himself."[14] On the other hand, Constantin airs a pedagogical point of view, cautioning that the possibility of self-imaging in (dramatic) play can only be play for youth and emphasizing that shadow existences need be subsumed under the one "true" existence so that "every variation is once more himself."[15] This means that the individual has to step outside the shadowy realm of fantasy, gather oneself, and be revealed. George Pattison aptly concludes: "There comes a time when we must leave the theatre behind, the shadows of the stage flee away, and we are faced with the cold light of everyday, bourgeois reality in which we must learn to be who we are."[16]

Scene Changes

The collecting of oneself toward the decisive moment is concretized in other texts of Kierkegaard as a decision for existence as a husband. In the text already mentioned, "A Glance at a Contemporary Effort in Danish Literature," Johannes Climacus emphasizes that the figure of the ethicist from *Either/Or* has overcome the position of the aesthete veiled from himself, by having gathered himself toward marriage; in fact, marriage is "the most profound form of life's disclosure."[17] Interestingly, in this passage, Climacus describes the shift of focus from the aesthetic to the ethical explicitly as a change of scene, during which it comes to a decisive transformation of the individual. Climacus explains: "This is the change of scenery, or, more correctly, now the scene is there; instead of a world of possibility, animated by imagination and dialectically arranged, an individual has come into existence."[18] Only there, where the world of possibilities and thereby the world of the theater (or, rather, theatrically realized shadow and fantasy existence) have been left behind, does man really become man; that is, does he take the stage of action as a self. He's become manifest because he has gathered himself toward himself, because he has decided—namely, *for* marriage.

With this way of thinking, Kierkegaard follows Hegel's position, as postulated apodictically in his *Elements of the Philosophy of Right*: "The objective determination, thus the moral obligation, is to enter into the state of matrimony."[19] Echoing Hegel, Kierkegaard lets Judge Wilhelm argue in *Either/Or*: "When the person who loves ethically marries, he actualizes the universal."[20] Wilhelm also points out that,

---

14. R, 154 / SKS 4, 30.

15. Ibid.

16. George Pattison, "Play It Again: Kierkegaard's *Repetition* as Philosophy and Drama," in *Theatrical Theology: Explorations in Performing the Faith*, ed. Wesley Vander Lugt and Eugene Trevor Hart (Eugene, OR: Cascade Books, 2014), p. 70.

17. CUP1, 254 / SKS 7, 230.

18. CUP1, 254 / SKS 7, 231.

19. Georg Wilhelm Friedrich Hegel, *Grundlinien der Philosophie des Rechts*, in *Werke*, vol. 7 (Frankfurt am Main: Reclam, 1986), p. 240. My translation.

20. EO2, 256 / SKS 3, 244.

for this act of realization, one thing is needed above all else: willpower, courage, manliness. Thus, the married man becomes for him the epitome of true manliness. Only the "husband" [*Ægtemand*], the "married man," is the "real man" [*ægte Mand*].[21]

This position does not stand in Kierkegaard's work, as is generally known, without contradiction. The argument is made from both the aesthetic and religious sides against the general validity of marriage. Interestingly, different arguments are certainly ascribed to different figures, but these figures never speak with one another directly. In Kierkegaard's work, there are practically no directly reproduced dialogues. Instead, each figure expresses himself in a self-contained text of his own. Pattison quite rightly observes that Kierkegaard does indeed create certain figures in order thereby to embody certain ideas, but it never comes to a mutual interaction and development of these figures or ideas. Kierkegaard "treats each idea as somehow complete and finished in itself; although his characters and ideas interact or, at least, get juxtaposed, they do not essentially develop through this interaction and their scope is strictly defined from the start."[22]

Although Kierkegaard's texts cannot be characterized in a strictly literary sense as dramatic texts in which the figures' speech is directly presented and stage directions are merely added to clarify the setting of the figures, they stand out nonetheless in a singular way through the change of diverse scenes—and as a consequence bring Kierkegaard as author into proximity with dramatic authorship and theater arts. But exactly what kinds of scenes are involved? When with drama theory we define a scene as a textually evoked spatiotemporal entity in which neither the setting nor the number of figures changes, we can first of all establish that, as described above, oftentimes indeed only one figure appears or different figures appear successively and give their "speeches" in turn, as is the case for instance in the text, inspired by Plato's *Symposium*, "In Vino Veritas," in which these figures do not speak in an undefined space but are rather very concretely situated. Characteristically, such texts are frequently preceded by another shorter text, which can be regarded as a kind of introductory scene.

A good example is the short text by the figure Frater Taciturnus under the title "Notice: Owner sought," which precedes the text "'Guilty?'/'Non Guilty?' A Story of Suffering: A Psychological Experiment by Frater Taciturnus." "'Guilty?'/'Non Guilty?'" is the third part of *Stages on Life's Way: Studies by Various Persons, Compiled, Forwarded to the Press, and Published by Hilarius Bookbinder*. In the foregoing "Notice," Frater Taciturnus describes how he and a friend rowed out to the hidden "Søborg Lake" one day where they, altogether unexpectedly, pulled out from the depth of the lake a sealed treasure chest containing the diary entries of a young man. This is precisely that text that he then later published as "A Story of Suffering."

21. EO2, 125 / SKS 3, 125.
22. Pattison, "Play It Again," p. 71.

What makes this scene typical for Kierkegaard's complete oeuvre is, for one thing, the fictional publisher created here, the likes of which we also find in *Either/ Or*. Moreover, this publisher releases a text in which he tells of a young man who tarries with the question, to what extent a love affair is realizable or repeatable in a marriage. This constellation of problems surfaces in different variations time and again in Kierkegaard's work and can be understood to that extent as the primary form of a scenic repetition, in which the problem presented is restaged from an ever slightly shifted perspective.

In this linguistic process of repetition as a dynamic process, something becomes visible, which as such defies again and again conceptual representation, that is, being defined and determined, and in this way continues the movement of thought, which does not come to a conclusion. Something genuinely passionate and playful belongs to this movement, as illustrated for example by the humoristic text, "The Rotation of Crops: A Venture in the Theory of Social Prudence," by the aesthete "A" from *Either/Or*. However, the movement can also, as many of Kierkegaard's texts attest, contain something torturous and self-demoralizing. The passionate consists in one being able to play randomly with past experiences and, owing to the never-ending approach and the ever new perspectives it affords, in one's never being bored. That holds true especially for the realm of love. When one breaks off a relationship in a timely manner and properly, namely "poetically" or "aesthetically," recalls this, then "an inexhaustible variation of combinations can be achieved."[23]

By contrast, this process is agonizing when one ethically recalls and repeatedly asks anew whether the break in the relationship was right or not. Many of the pseudonymously published texts report this agony, as do many of the letters and diary entries in which Kierkegaard grapples with having broken off his engagement with Regine Olsen. Thus, we read in *Notebook* 8 that breaking off the engagement produces "a terrible consequence,"[24] which has left behind "such a deep wound"[25] and frequently leads to frightful unrest, raising the question, "whether returning to her wouldn't be but possible."[26] Kierkegaard is well aware of the ambivalence of the situation and summarizes: "The thing is simply decided and yet I am not able to be done with it."[27]

Just what scenic quality this question possesses becomes in turn quite clear in a letter of Kierkegaard to his friend Emil Boesen, shortly after the engagement to Regine Olsen had been broken off. Responding to Boesen's belief that Kierkegaard was being plagued by an inner restlessness owing to the decision he made to break with his fiancée, Kierkegaard presents himself as deeply indignant. In doing so, he renders his indignation in direct speech to begin with and then comments on his own appearance.

---

23. EO1, 298 / SKS 2, 287.
24. KJN 3, 228 (Not8: 26) / SKS 19, 233.
25. KJN 3, 226 (Not8: 20) / SKS 19, 230.
26. Ibid.
27. KJN 3, 229 (Not8: 32) / SKS 19, 235.

"Death and Pestilence, does he wish to be my guardian, to incapacitate me …?" You can well imagine the rhythm of this lecture which was held in my room with unusual energy and this all the more, as I went this day with thin soles and so more easily with that highly tragical gait, both light and powerful at once.[28]

Kierkegaard is composing here a scene in which he plays the main role, taking himself into view at one and the same time as the author and as the actor of this very scene. The question emerges: which role is he playing? What is he showing? What is he seeking to show himself and his reader? And to what extent does the scene allow itself to be compared with a kind of experimental stage upon which a certain experimental arrangement, like going with thin soles, should bring about a certain effect?

Psychological Experiments

In the 1847 draft lecture on his theory of indirect communication, Kierkegaard compares the lecture with "a physical presentation at which experiments are being performed simultaneously."[29] With the concept of experiment, Kierkegaard aims at an experimental setup, about which the experimenter wishes to explain nothing but rather to show the observer. The observer alone can and must infer the significance of the experiment. It is up to him or her to get the presentation independently.

In his pseudonymous works, Kierkegaard takes up the experimental character of his thinking by linking it with the concept of psychological inquiry. Thus, he characterizes his writing *Repetition* as *A Venture in Experimenting Psychology*. And he gives to the third part of *Stages on Life's Way*, headed "Guilty?"/"Not Guilty?," the aforementioned subheading, "A Psychological Experiment by Frater Taciturnus." Both texts show, much like the above-cited scene from the letter to Boesen, a restless young man who is driven by the question of how he should conduct himself in relation to a young woman whom he loves. Indeed, the narration about both men suggests that it deals with "true human beings." This is suggested by, among other things, the reproduction of supposedly authentic material like letters or diary entries. It is nonetheless clear that with the main narrators, Constantin Constantius and Frater Taciturnus, we are dealing with *literary* figures about whom what is narrated is narrated in order to elucidate a certain problem, namely that of marriage, and more precisely, in order to illustrate this problem with the staging of both young men. Frater Taciturnus notes this in his "Letter to the Reader" rather directly: as regards the text authored by himself, with its literary representation of an "imaginary construction of thought"[30] by the figure of his creation, we are dealing with "a character in an imaginary construction."[31]

28. B&A 1, 73–74. My translation.
29. SKS 27, 425. My translation.
30. SLW, 403 / SKS 6, 374.
31. SLW, 400 / SKS 6, 371.

In ascertaining the importance of the experiment for Kierkegaard's dramatic, or better still, theatrical technique, it seems to me worth noting that, in the Danish original, reference by Kierkegaard is always made to *eksperiment*; however, the rather free translation by Edna and Howard Hong as "imaginary construction" seems to be even more suitable, as Kierkegaard's technique deals as a matter of fact with an illustration or perhaps better still with a visualization of a specific movement. The reader should see, at least before his or her inner eye, how the respective figure moves (mentally) back and forth, and how it doubts, weighs out, reiterates, and varies. The reader should be able to visualize the movement and to fathom it imagined as such. He or she should see what he or she cannot understand and should feel affected and exposed, sensually engaged, not only intellectually inspired, by that which he or she imagines. As in an experiment or indeed in a theater performance, it does not have to do with the conveyance of propositional content but rather with a procedural cognition, a sensual appropriation. In his postscript, Frater Taciturnus addresses his reader directly when remarking that the figure presented by him speaks in a manner "so that you can see him (loquere ut videam),"[32] and Climacus, in the *Concluding Unscientific Postscript*, aptly describes the experiment as "the conscious and teasing withdrawal of communication."[33]

For the reader, this means that that which has been made visible needs interpreting independently, even where many of Kierkegaard's fictional publishers still attempt to guide the reader, at least a step of the way, toward a "correct understanding." In his unpublished work, "The Book on Adler," Kierkegaard elaborates more carefully on this double movement where referring to the text "'Guilty?'/'Not Guilty?'" On the one hand, the text is said to be written in such a way that the reader comes very close to the event, but this dangerous closeness is then undone by making the whole thing transparent as an experiment. Kierkegaard illustrates this strategy with the help of the following comparison.

> If the imaginary construction has made any impression, it might be like that which happens when wing strokes of the wild bird, in being heard overhead by the tame birds …. prompt these to beat their wings, because those wing strokes simultaneously are unsettling and yet have something that fascinates. But now comes what is reassuring, that the whole thing is an imaginary construction, and that the imaginary constructor stands by.[34]

The assistance provided by the experimenter appears according to Kierkegaard in the following manner: "He points interpretively to the imaginatively constructed character in order to indicate how he makes the movements according to the drawing of the strings."[35] Yet that which Frater Taciturnus allows to follow

32. SLW, 398 / SKS 6, 369.
33. CUP1, 263 / SKS 7, 239.
34. SLW, xii / BA, 16 / SKS 15, 101–102.
35. Ibid.

as commentary in connection with this elucidation possesses no definitively determined character. The literary configuration of the young man's diary leaves the reader sufficient breathing space for making an appropriation self-dependently.

Interesting in this connection, for example, is that the fictitious protagonist, the diary-writing young man, conducts an experiment himself about a month after becoming engaged to the young woman to see whether she, too, really loves him or whether she instead merely enjoys being loved by him. In retrospect, the narrator reports:

> What happens? In the most candid way of the world, indeed, with an unbecoming intensity bordering on bad temper, she declares that she does not care for me at all, that she had accepted me out of sympathy and could not at all understand what I wanted with her. In short, a little improvisation *ad modum* Beatrice in *Viel Lärmen um Nichts*.[36]

How exactly the young man devised his experiment is not disclosed to the reader. But the result is altogether clear. "The exploration became an explosion, and I received the full force of it right in my face."[37] While the young man wants, despite all the difficulties, to hold on to his bond with the young girl, it appears that she loves too immediately and thereby too indiscriminately, too erratically and too impermanently. What she lacks is the break with immediacy, the will for repetition— and thereby for the ideality of marriage. The woman has, as made evident by the experiment, hindered a marriage because she did not believe in matrimony.

Kierkegaard's Text-Theater as Mirror of Self-Recognition?

Kierkegaard explains that women, in matters of love, can hardly (if at all) be relied upon through his figure of the aesthete in another text, "The First Love," in which the author works through the importance of the French playwright, Eugène Scribe. As regards the question about Kierkegaard as a dramatic thinker and producer of repetition, this text is important, for one thing, because it once more repeats the above-sketched experiment of the young man. For another thing, the scene in which the actor becomes his own audience/spectator is staged anew. This occurs as the aesthete thinks himself back into the role of the immediate spectator as well as into the role of the immediately smitten young man. Hence, he plays himself, as he once was, and cites himself in direct speech to make clear those feelings with which he ran back then to the theater to see Scribe's play: "The poetic power of this play will prompt the love in my breast to spring forth, its flower to open with a snap as the passion flower does."[38] At the same time, however, the narrator also assumes

---

36. SLW, 267 / SKS 6, 249.
37. SLW, 268 / SKS 6, 249.
38. EO1, 241 / SKS 2, 235.

the position of the mature man who, shaking his head, takes account of himself in his former naivety: "Ah, I was very young at the time! I scarcely understood what I said, and yet I found it stated well."[39]

Yet what happens during the visit to the theater and what occurs upon later reflection? Apparently it has come to a disillusionment, to a disenchantment in a double sense of the word: a sad realization on the one hand and a soothing liberation from false notions on the other. It comes to a disillusionment, since in his theater piece Scribe shows first love not as splendidness but much to the contrary as the expression of phantasmic-theatrical illusion. By comedic means, it's shown that the notion of a first and therefore everlasting love is a farce—and indeed especially, then, where women are speaking of their first and only love.

The heroine of the piece does exactly that: Emmeline fell in love as a child with her cousin Charles and then, upon reuniting with him many years later, keeps hold of this (supposed) first love. Diverse machinations and complications result in Emmeline, as she means after so many years to finally meet up again with her Charles, not standing face to face with him but rather with Rinville. Since she really blindly *believes* in her first love, she is unable to recognize in Rinville anyone other than Charles. "A" comments on the absurdity of this scene: "The scene is a recognition scene. The situation is just as lunatic as would be the comment from a man who had never seen his own image and then saw it in a mirror for the first time: I recognize myself right away."[40]

Scribe presents Emmeline and the others as figures who misunderstand themselves in presumed self-awareness but without his thematizing that explicitly. Similarly to what Kierkegaard elsewhere claimed for his theory of indirect communication, Scribe makes something apparent accordingly without thereby having to resort to a narrator's commentary or other program statements. The theater critic "A" explains these scenographic practices with the following words: "The effusions of the monologue are made superfluous; the substance and the dramatic action are commensurate with the situation; the novelistic details are made superfluous; and the dialogue finally becomes audible in the transparency of the situation."[41]

With Emmeline's replies and actions, it becomes evident that love as an expression of ostensibly immediate feelings is something totally random, or worse still, a clear case of self-deception. And the explosion, from which "A" had hoped that the flower of love would have opened, laid bare nothing further than a great ironic nothing: "The curtain falls; the play is over. Nothing remains but the large outline in which the fantastic *Schattenspiel* [shadow-play] of the situation, directed by irony, discloses itself and remains afterward for contemplation."[42]

39. EO1, 241 / SKS 2, 235.
40. EO1, 268 / SKS 2, 260.
41. EO1, 247 / SKS 2, 241.
42. EO1, 277 / SKS 2, 268.

Repetition as a Break with Immediacy, or Marriage
as a Drama of Self-deception

The concept of repetition, albeit coded so multifacetedly in Kierkegaard's work, invariably possesses a transformational quality. Repetition is the movement of return to an original and immediate position after a break with this has occurred. Repetition, as Kierkegaard says of metamorphosis in his later text, "The Crisis and a Crisis in the Life of an Actress," is "the return to a first,"[43] thus to an origin, to the so-called first immediacy, which however, now, in the movement of repetition has become a "second immediacy." Constantin Constantius and Judge Wilhelm can in this sense see marriage and repetition as one or rather understand marriage as the paradigm of a successful repetition. In marriage as a movement of reflection, the return or even turnaround occurs as the "transfiguration"[44] of the immediate erotic. Transfiguration means here idealization. The erotic is negated as real (and thereby also as a concrete physical-sensual entity) but preserved as idea. And thus idealized, according to Wilhelm, love first attains its constancy.

To what extent this thought is closely interwoven with Kierkegaard's considerations of performance is illustrated by the aforementioned text about the crisis of an actress. In this text, the authorial figure "Inter et Inter" explains that the "mature" actress Johanne Louise Heiberg can much better perform the role of the youthful Juliet (from Shakespeare's *Romeo and Juliet*) than the youthful actress Johanne Louise Heiberg ever could. And this is because she is no longer immediately what she enacts but henceforth relates to the "idea" of youthfulness. The author clarifies that the immediate is the accidental; the accidental, however, is the contingent. Only the relation to the idea, indeed the one explicitly *serving*, hence the relation to the idea functionally subordinate to the idea itself, is "the eternal and essential."[45]

How such a relation to the idea implies a religious dimension becomes clear, in turn, with a view to the explanations of the husband in *Stages on Life's Way*— yet in doing so without actually losing ambivalence. On the contrary. In his text, "Some Reflections on Marriage in Answer to Objections by a Married Man," Kierkegaard's figure of the husband rises to top theatrical form and presents his effusive dithyramb to the institution of marriage, which is at one and the same time a dithyramb to (self-)deception. This text, which after "In Vino Veritas" comprises the second part of *Stages on Life's Way*, is preceded by the following motto: "The deceived is wiser than the one not deceived."[46] This sentence has to do with a saying found in Plutarch's writings which is said to stem from the sophist Gorgias regarding the theater audience. The nameless narrator of the text, simply introduced as a "married man,"[47] suitably elaborates on this motto that there is

43. C, 322 / SKS 14, 105.
44. EO2, 94 / SKS 3, 96.
45. C, 320 / SKS 14, 105.
46. SLW, 88 / SKS 6, 86.
47. SLW, 87 / SKS 6, 85.

nothing worse than a husband who does *not* believe in matrimony. He is, according to Kierkegaard's narrator, like a spectator at showings from the realm of so-called natural magic, who holds what has been seen, merely because he or she does not understand the underlying context, for a magic act. Just like such disbelievers, the marriage disbeliever holds the "genuineness" of marriage in doubt. Kierkegaard's figure of the husband protests in indignation:

> But a believer one must be, and a married man who is not a believer is a tiresome character, a real household pest. There is nothing more fatal when one goes out in the company of others to enjoy demonstrations and ventures in natural magic than to have a killjoy along who continually disbelieves even though he cannot explain the feats.[48]

A husband who behaves like such a killjoy has earned his punishment and "ought to be put in a sack like a patricide and thrown into the water."[49] The vehemence with which Kierkegaard's married man calls for punishing all doubters of marriage like patricides suggests that what he says does not correspond with what he really thinks. He resembles rather the Møllerian figure of Claudius cited at the outset, who keeps his suffering a secret to himself, by vehemently assuring a dissociated part of himself that he is completely healthy. Doubts about this statement seem thus more than justified. These doubts are reinforced where the husband later emphasizes once more that matrimony has to do with a—blessed— deception. Analogous to the Gorgias citation above in which it is asserted that the deceived are wiser than those not deceived, the husband also declares that precisely *the* husband who is enthusiastic for marriage and who thereby remains committed to the world of illusion is especially wise. "It is indeed true that it takes a quite different kind of wisdom to remain in the blessed deception of ardor and of mystery and of erotic love and of illusion and of the wonder than to run away from house and home split naked, half sappy from sheer sapience."[50] Significant in this context is that Kierkegaard found the quote from Gorgias in the then widely distributed textbook for acting by the renowned drama theorist Heinrich Theodor Rötscher, *Die Kunst der dramatischen Darstellung*.[51] In *Journal JJ*, Kierkegaard remarks in a note from the year 1844 that Rötscher cites this quote in the context of his thought "that the dramatic art of acting is and wants to be deception."[52]

Rötscher sets the Gorgias quote in a discussion of the relation between "ideality and natural truth,"[53] two qualities that in the theater, in his view, need to come

---

48. SLW, 90 / SKS 6, 88.
49. Ibid.
50. SLW, 119 / SKS 6, 113.
51. Heinrich Theodor Rötscher, *Die Kunst der dramatischen Darstellung* (Berlin: Reiß Verlag, 1919). All translations from this text are my own.
52. SKS 18, 227 (JJ: 272). My translation.
53. Rötscher, *Die Kunst der dramatischen Darstellung*, p. 11.

through and as such constitute "the absolute law of dramatic representation."[54] Under "ideality," Rötscher understands the timeless form of beauty: under "natural truth," on the other hand, the immediacy of life with all its privations and in all its transience. Only where both permeate one another does it come according to Rötscher to "true art." Rötscher uses the Gorgias quote to justify as artistic form the supposedly deceptive ideality. The real spectator is for him in this context he or she who in art does not seek immediate nature but rather who is capable of an artistically broken standpoint, who accordingly experiences art as art or even as deception. "Evidently he is arguing here in this paradoxical manner for the higher position both of the tragic poet as well as the real spectator in contrast to a standpoint which is for this reason incapable of being deceived, because it brings with it a prosaic sense governed by the truth of nature."[55]

Rötscher's emphatic defense of drama as an art form in contrast to the "prosaic sense of reality" finds more explicit expression in his introductory chapter, which offers a number of interesting suggestions as to the extent to which Kierkegaard, too, idealizes marriage as drama in this sense. Rötscher underscores that "the dramatic representation conjures up before us a world of fantasy as a world of sensual reality" and so elevates us "from the last into the free and impeccable domain of the first."[56] If applied to the "drama of marriage" that Kierkegaard evidently enacts here with his figure of the husband, this simply means that this play leads beyond the prosaic-real relationship and into a world of the beautiful marriage fantasy.

For that to succeed, as elucidated by Rötscher and with him, then, Kierkegaard as well, the ethical dimension of this drama needs to be taken seriously. The actor has the responsibility, stressed by Rötscher, to conceal the "true identity" of his own personality—and not, say, because such a mask amuses him or because he is a dubious character but rather because "the idea" demands it. Rötscher accentuates this point: the actor is obliged "to enshroud before the world his real nature and to appear at all times as another."[57] He transforms himself into an "ideal personality,"[58] thus sacrificing himself for the idea of art and thereby for the ideality of the world. The gesture of the ideational self-denial that Rötscher pushes here strongly, in order to defend the frequently questioned moral integrity of the actor, is also ascribed by Kierkegaard to himself. Time and again he highlights in his texts that he has for Regine's sake donned a mask and hidden his "true feelings." In 1844, again in *Journal JJ*, he expounds on that with reference to Rötscher in the following:

> Prompted by that which I read from Rötscher about the ethical accent, it occurs to me that I have also properly availed myself of him as poet and as declaimer in my personal life, as I have said with view to my relationship with Regine and

54. Ibid.
55. Ibid., p. 13.
56. Ibid., p. 3.
57. Ibid., p. 5.
58. Ibid., p. 6.

to the breaking off of the engagement, and its certain death: she chooses the scream, I the grief.[59]

What these "true feelings" are can never be definitively revealed to the reader. What is scream, and what is grief, what will be forgotten and what remembered, shifts anew with each scene change. Where figures, positions, and scenes permanently repeat, comment on, complement, and question themselves, there can be no unambiguousness. In fact, as the aesthete "A" puts it, they set the reflection ever anew "into motion."[60]

59. SKS 18, 228 (JJ: 279). My translation.
60. EO1, 263 / SKS 2, 256.

Chapter 5

KIERKEGAARD THE HUMORIST

M. G. Piety

Introduction

Something doesn't add up in the popular perception of Kierkegaard. His writings are often considered dark and impenetrable, yet he is also one of the most widely read and beloved of philosophers among the general public. How can that be? The answer is not simply that Kierkegaard is one of the greatest Danish prose stylists, but that, contrary to his reputation for gloominess, he is one of the country's greatest humorists as well. "There can scarcely be an experienced reader of Kierkegaard," observes Danish scholar Helge Hultberg, "who is unaware that Kierkegaard is the funniest man in Denmark."[1] Hultberg was not a contemporary of Kierkegaard. His essay is from 1988, so what he is actually saying is that Kierkegaard is the funniest man in Danish history, funnier even than that famous Danish humorist, Victor Borge.

Many Kierkegaard scholars are aware of the importance of the concept of humor in Kierkegaard's thought. The first comprehensive study of this was Julius Schousboe's *Om Begrebet Humor Hos Søren Kierkegaard* (on Kierkegaard's concept of humor) from 1925.[2] Since that time there have been several dissertations on the topic,[3] a dozen or so articles,[4] and most recently a study entitled *Humor and the Good Life in Modern Philosophy: Shaftesbury, Hamann, Kierkegaard*, by Lydia B.

1. Helge Hultberg, "Kierkegaard som Humorist," *Kierkegaardiana* 14 (1988), pp. 49–56. My translation.
2. Julius Schousboe, *Om Begrebet Humor Hos Søren Kierkegaard* (Copenhagen: Arnold Busk, 1925).
3. Annelise Daab, "Ironie und Humor bei Kierkegaard," diss., Heidelberg Universität, 1926; Lloyd Ellison Parrill, "The Concept of Humor in the Pseudonymous Works of Søren Kierkegaard," diss., Drew University, 1975, and Lowell Allen Nissen, "Kierkegaard on Humor," M.A. thesis, University of Minnesota, 1958.
4. There are too many articles on the concept of humor (and/or comedy) in Kierkegaard's thought to list here. A comprehensive bibliography of these articles can be found at the end of Thomas C. Oden's *The Humor of Kierkegaard: An Anthology* (Princeton: Princeton University Press, 2004).

Amir.[5] But while there are two articles in Danish with the titles "Kierkegaard som humorist" (Kierkegaard as humorist),[6] fewer scholars outside Denmark seem aware that Kierkegaard is himself a humorist. This chapter looks first at how Kierkegaard came to be viewed as dark and depressing. It then looks briefly at his concept of humor, or of the comic, before tracing the path of humor in his authorship from his earliest published works through some of his most famous later ones. This chapter is not intended to be an exhaustive account of humor in Kierkegaard but merely a demonstration that humor is one of the aspects of Kierkegaard's writings that give them such a broad and enduring appeal with the general reading public.

The Origin of the Image of Kierkegaard as a "Melancholy Dane"

Danish Kierkegaard scholar Tonny Aalgaard Olesen asserts that "Kierkegaard scholarship for the past 150 years has had a tendency to invoke Kierkegaard in the shape of the melancholy Dane, particularly disposed to the tragic and whose religious philosophy expressed a passionate gloominess."[7] *Kierkegaard, The Melancholy Dane* was, in fact, the title of one of the first scholarly works on Kierkegaard in English.[8] This view of Kierkegaard may be partly the result of the fact that Kierkegaard was a Christian thinker. There are those who would argue that Christianity is itself a gloomy interpretation of human existence, at least to the extent that it would appear to emphasize sin. How could Kierkegaard's thought be anything but dark and depressing? Indeed, W.H. Auden, in his essay "A Knight of Doleful Countenance," describes Kierkegaard as a melancholy author, an author who could hear only "one theme in the New Testament, ... the theme of suffering and self-sacrifice."[9]

Kierkegaard does sometimes seem to depict Christian existence as one of unrelenting suffering. One might be tempted to conclude from this, as so many less-experienced readers of Kierkegaard clearly have, that he was a fundamentally negative thinker. But to do this is to forget that Kierkegaard saw much of his

---

5. Lydia B. Amir, *Humor and the Good Life in Modern Philosophy: Shaftesbury, Hamann, Kierkegaard* (Albany: State University of New York Press, 2014). John Lippitt's, *Humor and Irony in Kierkegaard's Thought* (London/New York: MacMillan Press/St. Martin's Press, 2000) could perhaps be added to this list, but Lippitt looks at both irony and humor rather than at humor alone.

6. Edvard Lehmann, "Kierkegaard som Humorist," *Gads Danske Magasin*, 8 (1913), pp. 292–301, and Hultberg, "Kierkegaard som Humorist."

7. Tonny Aalgaard Olesen, "The Painless Contradiction: A Note on the Reception of the Theory of the Comic in *Postscript*," trans. Paul A. Bauer, *Kierkegaard Studies Yearbook* (2005), pp. 339–350.

8. H. V. Martin, *Kierkegaard: The Melancholy Dane* (London: Epworth Press, 1950).

9. W.H. Auden, "A Knight of Doleful Countenance," *The New Yorker* (May 25, 1968), p. 151.

literary output as serving an essentially "corrective" function.[10] That is, his occasional association of Christianity with suffering was a "corrective" directed against a bourgeois Christianity that associated Christianity with material prosperity. Kierkegaard knew that the picture he presented of Christianity was sometimes too harsh,[11] but he felt that such exaggeration, if one may call it that, was necessary to shake bourgeois Christianity out of a comfortable complacency in which salvation was viewed as a "done deal" and in which Grace, consequently, was an anachronism.[12]

Kierkegaard's objective in, as he describes it himself, "reintroducing Christianity into Christendom"[13] was not to replace bourgeois complacency with relentless suffering but to replace a superficial kind of contentment with a deeper, more genuine kind of contentment, a kind of contentment that could be had, he believed, only by relating oneself properly to transcendent truth.

One would be hard-pressed to find any essentially negative messages in Kierkegaard's works—even those with the apparently negative titles such as *Fear and Trembling* and *The Sickness unto Death*. Take, for example, *The Sickness unto Death*, Kierkegaard's meditation on despair as an expression, or more correctly, as *the* definitive expression, of sin. Most of what Kierkegaard qualifies as despair in *The Sickness unto Death* is not actually experienced by the individual as such. Despair in Kierkegaard's technical sense can even take the form of happiness,[14] so *The Sickness unto Death* does not present a phenomenology of human experience as bleak and depressing. The objective of that work is to make clear that even when despair *is* experienced as such, this is actually a positive step in an individual's development, a step forward in the direction of the complete eradication of despair in both its technical and ordinary senses.

10. See, for example, SKS 22, 194, 208, and SKS 24, 56. See also the chapter entitled "Authorship/Corrective" in Frederick Sontag's *A Kierkegaard Handbook* (Atlanta: John Knox Press, 1979), pp. 23–31.

11. Emil Boesen, a close friend of Kierkegaard, visited him in the hospital just before his death. Boesen asked Kierkegaard whether he would like to modify any of the statements he had made in his attack on the Danish Lutheran church. "They don't correspond to actuality," Boesen explained. "They are too harsh." "And so they must be," replied Kierkegaard, "or they won't help." This statement corresponds with Kierkegaard's description of his picture of Christianity as a "corrective." See note 10 above.

12. That is, Kierkegaard's harsh portrayals of Christianity would appear to be an expression of Aristotle's dictum in the *Nicomachean Ethics* that when one is aware of a certain tendency in oneself to err in a particular direction away from the truth, one needs to aim to overshoot the truth in the opposite direction. Only in that way, Aristotle explained, could one be confident of hitting the mark.

13. See, for example, SKS 12, 49; SKS 13, 25; SKS 16, 24 and 103; SKS 20, 261; SKS 21, 152 and 289; SKS 22, 314; SKS 23, 18; SKS 24, 56 and 74; SKS 25, 155.

14. See, for example, SUD, 25 / SKS 11, 141.

Unfortunately, the earliest interpreters of Kierkegaard were Danish theologians who appear to have felt obliged to defend the Danish Lutheran Church, and the Danish people, against Kierkegaard's attacks.[15] That was much easier to do, of course, if Kierkegaard's harsh portrayals of Christianity were taken literally rather than as the corrective he had intended them to be.

Another probable origin of Kierkegaard's reputation as a melancholy thinker comes from his own references in his journals and papers to his purported struggles with melancholy and depression.[16] It is well known, however, that as Kierkegaard puts it, "the melancholy have the best sense of the comic," so the fact that Kierkegaard appears to have struggled privately with depression should not obscure how humorous are many of his published works.[17]

So much for the reasons Kierkegaard is often thought to be a dark, melancholy thinker. That he is not more widely appreciated as a humorist is certainly due, at least in part, to the pervasiveness of this picture of him, but it is likely also due to the fact that philosophers tend to look down on humor[18] and not to have much of a sense for it themselves. Philosophical works are generally written in a very straightforward and humorless way, not unlike the operating manuals that come with many household appliances.[19]

Such a direct manner of communication was appropriate, according to Kierkegaard, when the truth one was attempting to communicate to the reader was not essentially related to his or her individual existence as such. Direct communication was completely ineffective, he believed, however, when the truth in question *was* essentially related to the existence of the reader. Take, for example, what is known in the philosophy of mind as "raw feels," which is to say subjective experiences as such. There is no way to communicate directly in language what it is like to have a particular experience such as that of eating an ice cream cone, or to take examples more apposite to Kierkegaard's authorship, the experiences of shame, guilt, joy, anxiety, and love.

Kierkegaard's preferred method of communication is indirect. Humor, as we will see below, is particularly suited to this type of communication. Humor is, in fact, a means, according to Kierkegaard, by which religiousness can conceal itself. That is, humor, in the wording of the most explicitly humorous of Kierkegaard's many

---

15. See, for example, Aage Kabell, *Kierkegaard Studiet in Norden* (Copenhagen: H. Hagerup, 1948), especially Chapter II, "Studiets Begyndelse," pp. 91–134.

16. See, for example, SKS 20, 97 (NB: 141), as well as SKS 19, 213 (Not7: 28), and 443 (Not15: 14). Many more references to Kierkegaard's struggles with depression can be found by doing a search under *Tungsind* (melancholy or depression) in the online version of *Søren Kierkegaards Skrifter*: http://www.sks.dk/forside/indhold.asp.

17. SKS 19, 212 (Not7: 26). This sad fact was brought home most recently with the suicide of the comedian Robin Williams in 2014.

18. See John Morreall, "Philosophy of Humor," *The Stanford Encyclopedia of Philosophy* (Spring 2013 Edition), ed. Edward N. Zalta, <http://plato.stanford.edu/archives/spr2013/entries/humor/>.

19. And yet, they are, in general, considerably less helpful than such manuals.

pseudonyms, Johannes Climacus, can serve as an "incognito of the religious."[20] Hence, one ought to expect to find a lot of humor in works Kierkegaard published under that pseudonym.

Kierkegaard's Concept of Humor

Before we look at Kierkegaard's use of humor, we need to look at his theory of it, or more specifically, at his theory of what he calls "the comic." Kierkegaard's theory of the comic is referred to by philosophers as "the incongruity theory."[21] It is essentially continuous with the theories of Kant and Schopenhauer and, in fact, continues to be "the dominant theory of humor in philosophy and psychology."[22] According to the incongruity theory, what makes something funny is its incongruity with, or opposition to, the expectations generated by what preceded it. One of my favorite examples of this principle in action is comedian Joe Wong's joke about his impending marriage. "It is a very important step," he explains, "and I'm really stressed out about it. I keep thinking: Fifty per cent of marriages—last FOREVER!"[23] What makes the joke so funny, of course, is that we expect him to say: "end in divorce."

There is more to humor for Kierkegaard, however, than there is for most other adherents of the incongruity theory. Humor provides what one could call a kind of existential dynamic that helps the individual to progress toward the truth and becomes, in the words of Lydia Amir, "the main positive indicator of the individual's relation to the truth."[24] The fullest presentation of this theory is put forward by Kierkegaard's pseudonym Johannes Climacus in the *Concluding Unscientific Postscript to the Philosophical Crumbs*.[25] The theory itself appears

20. See CUPH, 419, 424–6, 436, 445n. / CUP1, 500, 504–509, 521, 531-532n. / SKS 7, 453, 457–460, 473, 483n.

21. See Morreall, "Philosophy of Humor."

22. Ibid.

23. I heard Joe Wong deliver this joke at the famous Comedy Studio on Harvard Square in Cambridge, Massachusetts, in 2010. I have had to rely on my memory in reconstructing the joke, so what I have here, with the exception of the last line, is merely a paraphrase of the original.

24. The strong association Kierkegaard makes of humor with Christianity owes much to the views on humor of Johann Georg Hamann. It is hence something of an exaggeration to say, as Tonny Aagaard Olesen does, that Kierkegaard's theory of the comic as presented in his *Concluding Unscientific Postscript* is "entirely unique" (Olesen, "The Painless Contradiction").

25. Some readers may be more familiar with the title *Concluding Unscientific Postscript to the Philosophical Fragments*. The titles *Philosophical Fragments* and *Philosophical Crumbs* refer to the same work (*Philosophiske Smuler*). *Fragments* was the first translation of the Danish term *Smuler*, but *crumbs* is actually a more accurate translation. See RPC, 181.

in what Hultberg refers to as *"verdenslitteraturens længst fodnote"* (the longest footnote in literary history).[26]

"The comic is present," explains Climacus,

> wherever there is a contradiction .... When a peasant knocks at the door of a man who is a German, and talks with him to find out whether there is someone in the house whose name the peasant has forgotten but who has ordered a load of peat, and the German, impatient at being unable to understand what the peasant is talking about, says: "Das ist doch wunderlich [That's strange]," to the great joy of the peasant, who says, "That's right, Wunderlich, that was the man's name," then the contradiction is that the German and the peasant cannot talk together because the language is an obstacle, yet the peasant nevertheless .... gets the information through the language.[27]

Or to take another example from this same footnote:

> If a soldier stands in the street and gazes at the wonderful window display of a fancy-goods store, and comes closer to take a better look, with glowing countenance and eyes fixed only on the window display failing to see the basement yard coming unduly near, and just as he is about to have a really good look, he disappears into the basement, then the contradiction is in the movement, the direction upward of the gaze, and the direction down, infernally, into the basement. Had he not been gazing upwards it would not have been so ridiculous. So it is more comic for a man who walks about gazing at the stars to fall into a hole in the ground than when it happens to someone not thus elevated above the earthly [as famously happened to the Greek and pre-Socratic philosopher Thales].[28]

Another example from this same note, which shows Kierkegaard's sense of humor extends even to ethical and religious subjects, involves a German priest with a poor understanding of Danish, who confusedly declares from the pulpit, "The word became pork (*Fleisch*) [John 1:14]."[29] The comedy, explains Climacus,

---

26. Hultberg, "Kierkegaard som Humorist," p. 49.

27. CUPH, 432n. / CUP1, 516n. / SKS 7, 466n. Hannay actually interpolates "thinks he" where I have the second ellipsis so that the translation reads "the contradiction is that the German and the peasant cannot talk together because the language is an obstacle, yet the peasant nevertheless [thinks he] gets the information through the language." No such qualification appears, however, in the original text. The contradiction would thus appear to be that the peasant gets the information when reason, or logic, tells us he should not.

28. CUPH, 432-433n. / CUP1, 516n. / SKS 7, 466n.

29. The Danish cognate of the German *Fleisch* is *flæsk*, but while *Fleisch* means both meat and flesh, the Danish *flæsk* means pork. The Danish term that is used at John 1:14 is *kød*, which, like the German *Fleisch*, means both meat and flesh.

lies here not only in the ordinary contradiction arising when someone speaks in a foreign language unfamiliar to them and the effect produced by their words differs from the one wanted; the contradiction is made more acute by its being a priest and that he is preaching, since speech in the context of a priest's address is used only in a rather special way, and the least that can be taken for granted is that he can speak the language. Furthermore, the contradiction verges on the ethical domain; that one can make oneself guilty of blasphemy innocently.[30]

But if the comic is present wherever there is contradiction, then human existence is essentially comical in that human beings, according to Kierkegaard, are composed of contradictions. That is, human beings are syntheses of temporality and eternality, of finitude and infinitude, of possibility and necessity, of body and soul.[31] Hence, Gregor Malantschuk, one of Kierkegaard's most distinguished interpreters, observes that "in humor," according to Kierkegaard, "a person discovers the disparity between the eternal qualifications of his essence and his phenomenal actuality, and this misrelation is deepened further when he sees the difficulty of fulfilling the ethical requirement."[32]

Kierkegaard, like many other thinkers of the same period, believes that existence can be divided into different stages. The aesthetic stage is the first, the stage of what Kierkegaard calls "immediacy." After that comes the ethical stage, and finally the religious stage. Irony constitutes a sort of boundary, according to Kierkegaard, between the aesthetic and ethical stages, and humor a boundary between the ethical and the religious stages. Humor, according to Climacus, "is the last stage of existence inwardness before faith." In fact, it is, for Kierkegaard, what Malantschuk refers to as "the boundary for the human understanding of life."[33] "Humor," explains Climacus, "is not faith but is prior to faith; it is not after faith or a development of faith. Understood in the Christian way, there is no going beyond faith, because faith is the highest."[34]

And yet there is a sense in which humor *is* "after faith," for Kierkegaard. It is not after faith in the Hegelian sense of succeeding faith as a development from it, but it comes after faith, or perhaps it is more correct to say it *remains* after faith as what Climacus calls "the incognito" of faith.[35] "In his innermost

---

30. CUPH, 433-434n. / CUP1, 518n. / SKS 7, 466n.

31. See SUDH, 43 / SUD, 13 / SKS 11, 129; and UDVS, 307 / SKS 8, 400.

32. Gregor Malantschuk, *Kierkegaard's Thought*, ed. and trans. Howard V. Hong and Edna H. Hong (Princeton: Princeton University Press, 1971), p. 202. Malantschuk directs his readers to an entry in Kierkegaard's papers (i.e., *Papirer*), which he asserts provides an account of the difference between irony and humor, but the reference he gives, Pap. III B 19, must be erroneous because it is not an account of the difference between irony and humor. An extended account of the difference between irony and humor can be found, however, in KJN 1, 216–217 (DD: 18) / SKS 17, 225–226.

33. Malantschuk, *Kierkegaard's Thought*, p. 216.

34. CUPH, 244 / CUP1, 291 / SKS 7, 265–266.

35. CUPH, 423–426 / CUP1, 504–509 / SKS 7, 457–461.

being," writes Climacus, "the religious one is anything but a humorist, on the contrary, he is absolutely occupied with his God relationship."[36] Humor is how the religious, or more specifically, the Christianly religious person, expresses himself *outwardly.* The Christian humorist, explains Kierkegaard in an early entry in his journals, "is like a plant of which only the roots are visible, [because it] blooms in the light of a higher sun."[37] The Christian uses humor in his relations to others not, Climacus continues, in order to make them look "ridiculous, or to laugh at them."[38] The humor of the Christian has a very different sort of objective.

Kierkegaard uses humor to communicate indirectly truths that cannot be communicated directly. All of what Kierkegaard calls "essential truth," or truth that relates to the essence of the individual as such, must, as I explained above, be communicated indirectly. There is no way to communicate directly the experiences of anxiety, guilt, despair, offense, and joy, or what Kierkegaard's pseudonym Johannes Climacus calls "the happy passion" of faith.[39] Kierkegaard's concern is not to write scholarly treatises on the phenomena of subjective experience to impress scholarly audiences. His objective is to help ordinary (albeit literate) people to come to understand what he believes to be the truths of this experience, and this he can do only indirectly.

What Kierkegaard's pseudonym Constantine Constantius says about farce could be extended to cover all humorous communication. Constantius says: "With farce the effect depends largely upon the observer's own energetic contribution."[40] Laughter cannot be compelled.[41] The reader must be open to the comedic dimension of what he reads, which is to say that he must be open more generally to the message the author is trying to communicate. The "reader" to whom Kierkegaard continually refers in the singular is thus very often, if not always, the person who gets the joke.

36. CUPH, 426 / CUP1, 508 / SKS 7, 461.

37. SKS 17, 226. The date of this entry is 1837, a year before Kierkegaard's first book, *From the Papers of One Still Living* and six years before what is generally considered to be the beginning of his mature authorship in 1843. The translation here is my own. The new *Kierkegaard's Journals and Notebooks* (KJN), ed. Niels Jørgen Cappelørn, Alastair Hannay, David Kangas, Bruce H. Kirmmse, George Pattison, Vanessa Rumble, and K. Brian Söderquist (Princeton: Princeton University Press, 2000-present) uses Kierkegaard's confusing abbreviation "χstn" for "Christian" (see "Søren Kierkegaard's Journals and Notebooks [Princeton: Princeton University Press, 2007]," *Scottish Journal of Theology* 63: 2, pp. 246–248) and inexplicably copies the earlier translation by the Hongs of "høiere" as "loftier" rather than as the cognate "higher" (JP 2, 1690). Also, the passage is awkward without the interpolated "because it," which neither the new translation nor the earlier translation has.

38. CUPH, 426 / CUP1, 508 / SKS 7, 461.

39. RPC, 128 / PF, 59 / SKS 4, 261.

40. RPC, 27 / R, 159 / SKS 4, 34.

41. As is evidenced by the failure of many scholars to appreciate the pervasiveness of humor in Kierkegaard's authorship.

Humor in Kierkegaard's Works

Kierkegaard was a jokester from the time he was very small, hence his nickname "Gafflen" (the fork). That is, he delighted in poking fun at people and/or situations he found amusing.[42] Later, as John Updike observes, Kierkegaard's "satirical pen" became "a feared weapon."[43]

References to humor begin to appear in Kierkegaard's journals in the 1830s, long before he published the works for which he is widely known. Kierkegaard observes, for example, in an entry dated 1837, that

> humor is irony taken to its maximum vibration. Even though Christianity [*det Xhristelige*] is the genuine *primus motor*, it is still possible to find peoples in Christian Europe who have come no further than describing irony and who are hence incapable of achieving the absolutely isolated, uniquely personal humor.[44]

Many of Kierkegaard's references to humor in his journals relate to comic writers, and one of the main sources on which he draws for humorous effect is comedic theater. He was a great lover of comedic theater. "As a true son of his

---

42. See "Barndom og Skoleår" in *Erindringer om Søren Kierkegaard*, ed. Steen Johansen (Copenhagen, CA: Reitzel, 1980), pp. 11–22.

43. John Updike, "The Fork," in *Picked Up Pieces: Essays* (New York: Random House, 2012), pp. 99–14.

44. SKS 17, 234 (DD: 36). I have made several changes here to the English translation of this passage in *Kierkegaard's Journals and Notebooks* (KJN 1, 225). KJN has "Although the Xn aspect is the real primus motor, there are still people in a Christian Europe who have not come to describe more than irony." There is nothing in the Danish, however, that corresponds to KJN's "aspect." That's an attempt on the part of the translator, or translators, to make sense of Kierkegaard's "*det Xhristelige*," which translates literally as "the Christian" where "Christian" functions as an adjective. There is no noun, however, that it qualifies, so the translator simply added "aspect" without indicating that it was added. KJN also includes "a" in front of "Christian Europe." This is literally correct, but it's unnecessary. What other kind of Europe was there? Danish, like German, uses articles more often than does English, so to include them all in a translation is not only unnecessary, but it yields a translation that is unidiomatic. The Danish term that I have translated as "peoples" and that KJN translates as "people" is "*Folk.*" "*Folk*" unequivocally refers, however, to "a people," and not to "people." It is a stab at the Danish people as a group. They are the "*Folk*" in "Christian Europe" to which Kierkegaard is snidely referring. If he had meant "people," he'd have written "*mennesker*" (or "*Mennesker*" given that he was writing in the nineteenth century). Finally, where I have "the absolutely isolated, uniquely personal humor," KJN inexplicably has "the absolutely isolated humor that subsists in the person alone." This is not, as one might expect, a literal translation. The Danish is: "*den absolut-isolerede, personlig-ene-bestaaende Humor.*" That translates literally as: "the absolutely isolated, uniquely personal humor."

native land," writes David F. Swenson, Kierkegaard was influenced by the "full wealth" of Danish literature. "But of all Danish writers," continues Swenson,

> He appears to owe most to Holberg, the great pioneer of Danish comedy.[45] Holberg's humor is something which Kierkegaard may almost be said to have absorbed *in succum et sanguinem* [in juice and blood]. The Holberg comedies served for him a veritable language; and the more technical philosophical treatises are replete with references to Holbergian characters and situations, giving substance and mass to the delicate comedy of their fine-spun polemic.[46]

The first literary personage to be gored by Kierkegaard's "satirical pen" was Hans Christian Andersen. Andersen's arguably failed attempt at a novel, *Kun en Spillemand* (Only a Fiddler),[47] was the subject of Kierkegaard's extended review, published in 1838, the title of which, *From the Papers of One Still Living, Published against His Will*, has got to be intended as some kind of a joke. And, indeed, the tone of much of this work is satirical as can be seen in the following passage from the beginning, a passage that represents what would appear to be Kierkegaard's first published allusion to Holberg's comedy *Erasmus Montanus*, a work he would allude to often later in his authorship.

> Andersen loses himself not so much in high-flown [*høittravende*] as in long-winded [*langttravende*] observations, in which the hero is a superb peripatetic who, because he has no essential reason for stopping anywhere and because existence [*Tilværelse*] on the contrary is always a circle, ends up going in a circle, even though Andersen and others who have lived for many years on [a] hill believe he is walking straight ahead because the earth is as flat as a pancake[48]. [49]

45. Although the Danes like to claim Ludvig Holberg as one of their own, he was in fact Norwegian.

46. David F. Swenson, *Something about Kierkegaard*, ed. Lillian Marvin Swenson (Macon, GA: Mercer University Press, 1983), p. 79.

47. H.C. Andersen, *Kun en Spillemand* (Hedehusene, Denmark: Nyt Dansk Literatur Selskab, 1988).

48. Kierkegaard appears to have been particularly fond of the phrase "flat as a pancake" (*flad som en pandekage*). I'm told by professional comedians that the "k" sound is considered to be particularly funny. This could be part of the appeal of the phrase for Kierkegaard. It might also be that Kierkegaard enjoyed the irreverence, or incongruity, of the insertion of the expression "pancake" into a piece of writing that otherwise had pretensions to erudition.

49. FPOSL, 78 / SKS 1, 34. I have taken the liberty of changing Watkin's "the hill" to "a hill." The Danish expression is *"paa Bjerget,"* which, since the definite article in Danish is enclitic, translates literally as "the hill," but which more than likely means "a hill." I say more than likely because the allusion to Holberg's *Erasmus Montanus* is so conspicuous that Kierkegaard may well have assumed his readers would immediately recognize the "hill" in question as the one referred to in this work.

Humor becomes one of the chief means by which Kierkegaard communicates with his readers. We've already seen that Kierkegaard's interest in the concept of humor predates what scholars think of as his mature authorship.[50] He used humor to make clear to his readers how ridiculous it was to seek answers to life's most pressing questions in objective reflection. Objectivity, as Climacus points out in Kierkegaard's *Postscript*, published in 1846, in a passage that again alludes to Holberg's play *Erasmus Montanus*,[51] is not always an indication of what one could call well-ordered thinking. "I shall here permit myself to tell a story," begins Climacus,

> that without any adaptation on my part comes direct from an asylum. A patient in such an institution seeks to escape, and actually succeeds in effecting his purpose by leaping out of a window. [H]e .... prepares to start on the road to freedom, when the thought strikes him (shall I say sanely enough or madly enough?): "When you come to town you will be recognized, and you will at once be brought back here again; hence you need to prepare yourself fully to convince everyone by the objective truth of what you say, that all is in order as far as your sanity is concerned." As he walks along and thinks about this, he sees a [skittle] ball lying on the ground, picks it up, and puts it into the tail pocket of his coat. Every step he takes the ball strikes him, politely speaking, on his hinder parts, and every time it thus strikes him he says: "Bang, the earth is round." He comes to the city, and at once calls on one of his friends; he wants to convince him that he is not crazy, and therefore walks back and forth, saying continually: "Bang, the earth is round!" But is the earth not round? Does the asylum still crave .... another sacrifice for this opinion, as in the time when all men believed it to be flat as a pancake? Or is a man who hopes to prove that he is sane, by uttering a generally accepted and generally respected objective truth, insane? And yet it was clear to the physician that the patient was not yet cured; though it is not to be thought that the cure would consist in getting him to accept the opinion that the earth is flat.[52]

50. Kierkegaard published a few short articles, as well as two books: *From the Papers of One Still Living* and *The Concept of Irony* before 1843. His mature authorship is generally considered to begin in 1843 with the publication of *Either/Or, Fear and Trembling*, and *Repetition*.

51. See Ludvig Holberg, *Erasmus Montanus eller Rasmus Berg*, III, 2, *Den Danske Skue-Plads*, I-VII (Copenhagen: 1788), V, no pagination; III, 3, *Comedies by Holberg*, tr. Oscar James Campbell, Jr., and Frederic Schenck (New York: American-Scandinavian Foundation, 1935), p. 145. The play concerns a conflict between Erasmus, who knows the world is round, and villagers, who think it is flat.

52. CUPSL, 174 / CUP1, 194–195 / SKS, 7, 178–179. I have elected here to use the wording (with a couple of minor modifications) of the Swenson-Lowrie translation of the *Postscript* because I believe it preserves the literary qualities of the original Danish text better than do the two more recent English translations by Howard V. and Edna H. Hong [CUP1] (Princeton: Princeton University Press, 1992) and Alastair Hannay [CUPH] (Cambridge: Cambridge University Press, 2009).

It is not merely what one could call a misguided pursuit of objectivity to which Kierkegaard, or his pseudonym Climacus, objects. One of the main objects of his satirical barbs is the Hegelian phantom of "pure thought,"[53] which Climacus calls "a psychological curiosity, a remarkable piece of ingenious combination and construction in the fantastic medium of pure being."[54]

Pure thought, asserts Climacus,

> for someone existing, is a chimera when the truth is to be existed in. Having to exist under the guidance of pure thought is like traveling in Denmark with [the help of] a small map of Europe on which Denmark shows no larger than [the nib of a pen]—yes, even more impossible.[55]

Climacus, the pseudonym Kierkegaard used when he published *Philosophical Crumbs* and the *Concluding Unscientific Postscript to the Philosophical Crumbs*, is a self-professed humorist, and most Kierkegaard scholars are agreed that the *Postscript* is hilarious; hence it is the focus of John Lippitt's *Humor and Irony in Kierkegaard's Thought*. Less notice has been taken of humor in the *Crumbs*, yet humor pervades this work as well, as can be seen in the following passage that is excerpted from Climacus's discussion in *Crumbs* of what he refers to euphemistically as the "difficulty" of trying to prove the existence of God. "It is generally very difficult to prove that something exists," observes Climacus. "And what is worse for those brave souls who nevertheless dare to undertake such a project, the difficulty is not one that will confer celebrity on those who preoccupy themselves with it."[56]

Climacus's point here, clearly, is not that it is "difficult" to prove the existence of God, or anything else for that matter, but that it is impossible, and that those

---

53. The expression "pure thought" appears more than fifty times in the *Postscript*.

54. CUPH, 254 / CUP1, 304 / SKS 7, 277.

55. CUPH, 260 / CUP1, 310–311 / SKS 7, 283. I have altered the translation in two places here. First, I have followed the lead of Swenson and Lowrie in adding "with the help of" to the phrase "like traveling in Europe with [the help of] a small map of Europe" (see CUPSL, 275). The Danish is: "*at skulle reise i Danmark efter et lille Kort over hele Europe.*" Swenson and Lowrie were correct in that the Danish *efter* means something like "according to" (see *A Danish English Dictionary*, ed. J.S. Ferrall and Thorl. Gudm. Repp, Copenhagen, 1845, s.v., *efter*). Second, I have changed the "steel pen-point" that appears in all three existing English translations of the *Postscript* to "the nib of a pen." The Danish is simply "*Staalpen,*" which means a steel pen rather than a quill pen. The reference is clearly to the nib of the pen, however, rather than to its "point." The nib is the metal end of a pen that touches the paper and from which the ink flows. It is generally about the size of a fingernail. Many, if not most, nineteenth-century pen nibs would have been smaller than are contemporary nibs, so even it is probably best to think of something the size of the nail on a person's little finger.

56. RPC, 113 / PF, 40 / SKS 4, 245.

"brave souls" who do not realize this and "nevertheless dare to undertake such a project" only make themselves look ridiculous in a manner not unlike that of a person who would attempt to fly by vigorously flapping his arms.

And then there is the incongruity between the length of *Philosophical Crumbs* (approximately 100 pages) and its *Postscript* (more than 500 hundred pages), and the obvious contradiction between Climacus's name and his position in both the *Crumbs* and the *Postscript*. That is, the name, Johannes Climacus, originally belonged to Saint John Climacus, or John of the Ladder.[57] While the original Climacus described a metaphorical ladder by means of which one could come closer to God, Kierkegaard's Climacus proclaims repeatedly that he is not Christian[58] and that indeed, according to Christianity, if one is not in the right relation to God, through faith in Christ, then one is absolutely separated from him (or her or it). So there is no ascending nearer to God for Kierkegaard's Climacus, despite his name.

The contradiction that we saw above is associated by Kierkegaard with "the comic" and appears in a number, if not all, of Kierkegaard's pseudonyms. Johannes de silentio, the pseudonymous author of *Fear and Trembling*, is *not* silent, but loquacious, as is Frater Taciturnus, the pseudonym who appears as the author of a part of *Stages on Life's Way*. Constantine Constantius, the pseudonymous author of *Repetition*, is unable to achieve repetition, which is to say, constancy or contentment, as can be seen in the following passage from *Repetition*. "No one is ever granted even as little as a half an hour out of his entire life," writes Constantius,

where he is absolutely content in every conceivable way. ... I was close to achieving it once. I got up one morning in unusually good humour. This positive mood actually expanded as the morning progressed, in a manner I had never before experienced. By one o'clock my mood had climaxed, and I sensed the dizzying heights of complete contentment, a level that appears on no scale designed to measure moods, not even on the poetic thermometer. My body no longer seemed weighed down by gravity. It was as if I had no body, in that every function hummed along perfectly, every nerve rejoiced, the harmony punctuated by each beat of my pulse which served in turn only to remind me of the delightfulness of the moment. I almost floated as I walked, not like the bird that cuts through the air as it leaves the earth, but like the wind over the fields, like the nostalgic rocking of waves, like the dreamy progress of clouds across the sky. My being was transparent as the clear depths of the ocean, as the night's self-satisfied stillness, as the soft soliloquy of midday. Every mood resonated melodically in my soul. Every thought, from the most foolish to the

---

57. See, for example, *John Climacus: The Ladder of Divine Ascent*, trans . Colm Luibheid and Norman Russell (Mahwah, NJ: Paulist Press, 1982).

58. I believe he is lying when he claims this, but that issue is not relevant to the present discussion; hence this is not the place to develop that argument.

most profound, offered itself, and offered itself with the same blissful festiveness. Every impression was anticipated before it came, and thus awoke from within me. It was as if all of existence were in love with me. Everything quivered in deep rapport with my being. Everything in me was portentous; all mysteries explained in my microcosmic bliss that transfigured everything, even the unpleasant, the most annoying remark, the most loathsome sight, the most fatal collision.

As I said, it was exactly at one o'clock that my mood reached its peak, where I sensed the heights of perfect contentment. But then suddenly I got something in my eye. I do not know whether it was an eyelash, an insect, or a piece of dust. I know this though, that my mood immediately plummeted almost into the abyss of despair. This is something that everyone who has ever experienced these heights of contentment, and still speculated to what extent complete contentment was possible, will easily understand. Since that time I have given up any hope of ever being completely contented in every way, given up that hope that I had once nourished, of being, if not always completely content, then at least occasionally completely content.[59]

Scholars sometimes forget that Climacus is not the only one of Kierkegaard's pseudonyms who is a self-professed humorist. Lippitt, in his aforementioned study of humor and irony in Kierkegaard, mentions *Either/Or* (vol. I), *Stages on Life's Way*, and *Prefaces* as explicitly humorous works but fails to mention *Repetition*, which is shot through with humorous passages such as the one above and the following one where Constantius recounts the story of his unexpectedly early return home after his aborted attempt to recreate the joys of an earlier trip to Berlin. "I have always been very suspicious of revolutions," begins Constantius,

to the extent that, for this reason, I hate all forms of cleaning or straightening up, in particular the scrubbing of floors. I had thus left the strictest instructions [with my servant] to ensure that my conservative principles would be maintained even in my absence. But what happened? My faithful servant was of another mind. He supposed that if he initiated a frenzied cleaning immediately after my departure, the whole thing would be completed by the time I returned home again, and he was certainly the man to accomplish this. I return. I ring the doorbell; my servant appears. It was a moment rich with import. My servant became as pale as a corpse. Through the half-opened door to my rooms I glimpsed the horror: everything was in a state of chaos. I was stunned. He was so confused he did not know what to do. His conscience smote him and—he slammed the door again in my face. That was too much. My distress had reached a climax, my principles sank, I feared the worst, to be treated as a ghost in the manner of Grønmeyer the businessman.[60]

59. RPC, 40–41 / R, 173–174 / SKS 4, 46–47.
60. RPC, 38–39 / R, 171 / SKS 4, 45. Grønmeyer the businessman is a character in a comedy, *Kjøge Huuskors*, by J.L. Heiberg. Grønmeyer's old farmhand, Niels, mistakes him for a ghost and tries to shoo him away with a pitchfork. Notice that there are two "k" sounds

Humor, for Kierkegaard, does not exclude seriousness: quite the contrary. Humor is present even in Kierkegaard's edifying or "upbuilding" discourses, as is clear from Kierkegaard's reflections in his journal on the idea of "learning" as it is presented in "What We Learn from the Lilies of the Field and the Birds of the Air," Part Two of his *Upbuilding Discourses in Various Spirits*, published in 1847.

> The dialectic in the concept: to learn means that the learner relates to the teacher as to his ideal genus proximum. As soon as the teacher is merely assigned a lower place within the same genus and is situated beneath the learner, the situation becomes humorous. This is how it is in learning from a child or from a stupid person; because the child or the stupid person can .... be called the teacher [only] in a humorous sense.
>
> But the situation becomes even more humorous when the teacher and the learner do not even have a common genus but relate to [each other] inversely, in qualitative heterogeneity. This is the absolutely humorous situation. The lilies and the birds.
>
> The presentation is edifying, mitigated by humor's touching jest and jesting earnestness. At many points the reader will be moved to smile, never to laugh, never to laugh ironically. The tale of the worried lily, which, however, is also a parable, is absolutely humorous. Thus also with the entire discourse about being clothed. In general, the humorous is present everywhere because the design itself is humorous.[61]

At times, Kierkegaard's humor is very subtle. Less-experienced readers of Kierkegaard often laugh at the description of the self in *The Sickness unto Death*, published in 1849, as "a relation which relates to itself, or that in the relation which is its relating to itself. The self is not the relation but the relation's relating to itself."[62] If, however, one remembers Kierkegaard's assertion that the comical is

in the title of Heiberg's play. Kjøge, now spelled Køge, is a small harbor town to the southwest of Copenhagen. Perhaps it is partly the "k" sound and partly a memory from when I worked as a translator for the translation center at the University of Copenhagen, but I can never hear mention of Køge without wanting to laugh. I had been employed to translate a tourist brochure about Køge in which it was proudly announced that while there were not many poisonous insects, the area boasted an impressive variety of bats, which interested tourists could see taking over the night sky shortly after dusk.

61. KJN 4, 90–91 (NB: 129) / SKS 20, 91. I made a couple of minor grammatical corrections to the text here. First, I moved "only" to the proper position. Second, I changed "one another," which is correct only when there are more than two parties in the relation in question.

62. SUDH, 43 / SUD, 13 / SKS 11, 129. I have chosen Hannay's translation here not merely because I believe it is better than the Hongs's but because the Hongs's translation unintentionally adds a comical dimension that, amusing as the original is, is not present in the original and of which it would be unsporting of me to take advantage.

present wherever there is contradiction and that the elements that make up the "relation" that is the self, according to both Kierkegaard and the pseudonymous author of *The Sickness unto Death*, Anti-Climacus, then one will realize that the description of the self at the beginning of this work was very likely intended by Kierkegaard to be humorous.

The passages above are only a few of the examples of humor one could produce from the texts in question, and those texts, in turn, are only a few of the many works by Kierkegaard that contain humorous passages. Given the extent to which, as it should now be clear, humor pervades many of Kierkegaard's works, one is tempted to conclude that the famous *"hemmelige Note"* (secret note), which Kierkegaard purports in a journal entry from 1843,[63] would explain his entire authorship, but which no one will ever find even the slightest hint of among his papers, is actually a grand joke he is playing on later scholars whom he envisioned searching and searching for this key that would unlock the authorship.

I hope it is clear now that Kierkegaard was, indeed, a great humorist and that this is one of the qualities that has traditionally endeared him to a reading public that extends well beyond the walls of academe. I believe that there is much more humor in Kierkegaard's authorship than anyone has hitherto suspected and that great progress will be made in understanding his thought if we approach his works with a view to discovering the humor they contain.

It is possible, of course, that I am attributing too much significance to humor in Kierkegaard's thought. I would answer such an objection by quoting the following passage from the aphorisms that make up the *Diapsalmata* section of the first volume of Kierkegaard's *Either/Or*:

I was transported to the seventh heaven. There sat all the gods assembled. As a special dispensation, I was granted a favor of making a wish. "What do you want," asked Mercury. "Do you want youth, or beauty, or power, or a long life, or the most beautiful girl, or any one of the other glorious things we have in the treasure chest: Choose—but only one thing." For a moment I was bewildered; then I addressed the gods, saying: My esteemed contemporaries, I choose one thing—that I may always have the laughter on my side. Not one of the gods said a word; instead, all of them began to laugh. From that I concluded that my wish had been granted and decided that the gods knew how to express themselves with good taste, for it would indeed have been inappropriate to reply solemnly: It is granted to you.[64]

My guess is that one of the reasons that Kierkegaard is not more widely appreciated to be a humorist is that he would have thought it in poor taste to point out all the humor in his works. A joke is not nearly so funny, after all, if you have to explain it. Kierkegaard wrote, I believe, for people who got his jokes, for people for whom explanations were unnecessary.

63. KJN 2, 157 (JJ: 95) / SKS 18, 170.
64. EO1, 42–43 / SKS 2, 51–52.

Chapter 6

A DESIRE TO BE UNDERSTOOD: AUTHORSHIP AND AUTHORITY IN KIERKEGAARD'S WORK

Daniel Berthold

Kierkegaard's authorship poses a certain dilemma. I am not speaking of the dilemma Kierkegaard himself poses (and then quickly disposes of) in his *Point of View for My Work as an Author*, written at the age of thirty-five, seven years before his death, but only published posthumously by his brother at Kierkegaard's request.[1] Kierkegaard poses the dilemma of his authorship as being that, on the one hand, his many pseudonymous works are "enigmatic myster[ies]," since they are written from points of view outside what he insists is the "religious totality" of his authorship.[2] On the other hand, *The Point of View* explains away the mystery, showing how the apparently nonreligious works are in fact indirectly religious. The dilemma I am interested in exploring is rather that in removing the mystery of the pseudonymous or "aesthetic" works, Kierkegaard creates another mystery: how are we to read the demystified authorship alongside a lifelong practice of an ethics of authorship that *insists* on mystery by concealing the intentions of the author? The art of Kierkegaard's style of communication requires that the author must "disappear, as it were," as he writes in his journal.[3] Or as Anti-Climacus,

1. In a journal entry of 1849, Kierkegaard refers to the various "Notes" he had written about his authorship as well as to the *Point of View*, writing that "everything of this nature shall be finished as it is until after my death" (referenced in PVL, 160). See also Walter Lowrie, *A Short Life of Kierkegaard* (Princeton: Princeton University Press, 1965), p. 211: "[Kierkegaard] had expected to die soon after [*The Point of View*] was finished, and so to leave it for posthumous publication." And Joakim Garff, *Søren Kierkegaard: A Biography*, trans. Bruce Kirmmse (Princeton: Princeton University Press, 2005), p. 560: "*The Point of View* was consigned [by Kierkegaard] to posthumous publication, which was seen to by Peter Christian Kierkegaard."
2. PVL, 5, 6 / PV, 23, 24 / SKS 16, 11, 12. I have chosen to use translations by Walter Lowrie and David and Lilian Swenson over the more recent editions of Howard and Edna Hong in gratitude for their friendship with my father, Fred Berthold, who introduced me to Kierkegaard through the translations of his friends more than forty years ago.
3. JP 1, 657 / SKS 27, 420–434 (Papir 371: 2).

Kierkegaard's last (and only religious) pseudonym, puts it, this art consists in the author becoming "an absentee."[4]

There is no doubt that Kierkegaard was preoccupied with the theme of religious faith from the very start of his authorship. He published the first of his "upbuilding discourses," the religious works written under his own name, in the same year (1843) as his first three pseudonymous works (*Either/Or*, edited by Victor Eremita; *Fear and Trembling*, by Johannes de Silentio; and *Repetition*, by Constantin Constantius). And he continued to accompany his pseudonymous works with edifying discourses to the end. Furthermore, there is no doubt that Kierkegaard himself came to interpret his work in its entirety as a religious authorship: "I am and was a religious author," he writes in *The Point of View*, and "the whole of my work as an author is related to Christianity, to the problem 'of becoming a Christian.'"[5] But this isn't what's at issue. Rather, the question is one of authority: by what authority does the author determine the meaning of his or her authorship?

Kierkegaard tells us at the outset of *The Point of View* that he has a "strong impulse," so strong that it is even a "duty," "to explain once for all, as directly and frankly as possible, what is what: what I as an author declare myself to be."[6] He "begs" his readers to read *The Point of View* "not curiously, but devoutly, as one would read a religious work" and pleads that all of his works, from the very beginning, should be read in this way, since even the "aesthetic" works "are an incognito and a deceit in the service of Christianity."[7] And in "'The Individual,' Two 'Notes' Concerning My Work as an Author" (published posthumously together with *The Point of View*), he suggests that those who miss the religious unity of the authorship have simply "misunderstood" him, and the time has come "to remove the misunderstanding."[8]

But *why* this desire, this impulse, this duty? It might seem obvious: isn't this a fundamental human desire, to be understood? But again, this isn't the question. Whatever motivated Kierkegaard's "strong impulse," the fact remains that he had devoted his authorship to the idea that "truth is subjectivity"[9] and that between self and other—and hence between author and reader—there is an insurmountable gap: "each individual is isolated and compelled to exist for himself"[10] and thus compelled to determine meaning ("truth") for him- or herself. Notwithstanding the "frank" "public attestation" of *The Point of View*,[11] Kierkegaard had often expressed distaste for direct proclamation: "All direct communication" makes him "uncomfortable," since "what I have to say may not be taught."[12]

---

4. TC, 133 / PC, 133 / SKS 12, 137.
5. PVL, 5–6 / PV, 23 / SKS 16, 11.
6. PVL, 5 / PV, 23 / SKS 16, 11.
7. PVL, 6 / PV, 24 / SKS 16, 12.
8. PVL, 125 / TSI, 114 / SKS 16, 94.
9. CUPSL, 169 / CUP1, 189 / SKS 7, 173.
10. CUPSL, 287 / CUP1, 323 / SKS 7, 294.
11. PVL, 6 / PV, 24 / SKS 16, 12.
12. JP 1, 646 / SKS 20, 321–323 (NB4: 72).

Rather, his own method of "indirect communication" is meant, by leaving the inner, private meanings and intentions of the author in doubt, to authorize the reader's own responsibility (authority) for determining meaning. As he writes in the "First and Last Declaration," which he appends under his own name to Johannes Climacus's *Concluding Unscientific Postscript* (which at the time, in 1846, Kierkegaard thought might be his last work), he himself is "only a reader" of his own works, having "no knowledge of their meaning except as a reader."[13] Johannes had earlier written in the *Postscript* that the writer must be careful not to fall into the conceit that "an author [is] .... the best interpreter of his own words, as if it could help a reader [to know] that an author had intended this or that."[14]

The Latin *auctor*, author, is etymologically the founder, creator, originator, even the father. In this sense, the author might be compared to Lacan's "Father," whose function is to impose Law and regulate desire: "the true function of the Father .... is fundamentally to unite .... a desire and the Law."[15] The author as Father imposes his authority—in Latin, *auctoritas*, the power of command, the assertion of legal validity and rightful ownership over what has been produced—so as to confine the desire of the reader within the boundaries set by the legally valid intentions of the author. When Kierkegaard invokes his authority in *The Point of View*, claiming his rightful ownership over the meaning of his works, he relegates the desire of the reader—the reader's own power of interpretation—to that of "misunderstanding" if it departs from the Law of the originator.

But the Latin *auctor*/author is also (and literally) "the one who causes to grow." And this is the way Kierkegaard presents his authorship, as a maieutic act—the act not of the Lacanian Father but of the Socratic midwife[16]—in the service of allowing the reader to engage in her own labor of bringing meaning and value to birth. To do this, however, Kierkegaard must write without authority, and this is precisely what he says he does. In a "supplement" to "My Activity as a Writer" (1851), Kierkegaard notes that "I myself have from the first clearly asserted, and again and again repeated, that I am 'without authority.'"[17] And in his "Understanding with the Reader," Johannes Climacus writes that the author is "superfluous; let no one therefore take the pains to appeal to it as an authority; for he who thus appeals to it has *eo ipso* misunderstood it. To be an authority is far too burdensome."[18] Indeed, Johannes is not the author of the text at all, "properly speaking," but only a "*souffleur*" or stage manager.[19] The question is not whether there is a director behind the scenes—of course Kierkegaard is the author behind the author—but

---

13. CUPSL, 551 / CUP1, 626 / SKS 7, 570.
14. CUPSL, 225 / CUP1, 252 / SKS 7, 228-229.
15. Jacques Lacan, *Écrits*, trans . Alan Sheridan (London: Tavistock, 1977) p. 321.
16. See PF 10 / SKS 4, 219; CUPSL, 74, 222 / CUP1, 80, 248-249 / SKS 7, 80, 225-226.
17. PVL, 153 / OMWA, 12 / SKS 13, 19. See also BA 27 / Pap. VII 2 B 235 / SKS 15, 114.
18. CUPSL, 546 / CUP1, 618 / SKS 7, 561.
19. CUPSL, 551 / CUP1, 625 / SKS 7, 569.

what authority he claims, and the extent to which he uses his direction to decenter that authority, to write in such a way that ultimately, as Roland Barthes puts it, a text's meaning "lies not in its origin," its author, "but in its destination," its reader.[20]

In what follows, I will develop the argument for a reading of how Kierkegaard *the man's* eventual giving in to the very human impulse to be understood cannot be reconciled with Kierkegaard *the author*. I will look at Kierkegaard's commitment to subjectivism, his notion of the tragic character of language—that speech cannot bring together the interiorities of self and other—and the idea that his works perform the death of the author, before returning to *The Point of View* and its assertion of authority. I will argue that to accept the authoritative role of the author invoked in *The Point of View*, by which Kierkegaard imposes a "legitimate" meaning upon his work, is in fact to delegitimize the ethical practice of the previous authorship.

The Ethics of Subjectivity

The well-known dictum of the *Concluding Unscientific Postscript* that "truth is subjectivity"—a phrase that informs all of Kierkegaard's other works as well—is not simply an epistemological claim that we humans are incapable of "objective" answers to existentially important questions. It also implies an ontology of fundamental aloneness and an ethics of subjectivity. "With respect to every reality external to myself," Johannes Climacus informs the reader of the *Postscript* (who is, ironically, presumably a reality external to himself), "I can get hold of it only through [imagining] it. In order to get hold of it really, I would have to make myself into the other .... and make the foreign reality my own, which is impossible."[21] The other, as a subjectivity, is unreachable by any other subjectivity. In his recognition of the irremediably foreign reality of the other/reader, Kierkegaard tends to let go of the other as an essential component of his own self-identity. The other/reader is finally alone and must find her own way, and for his part, Kierkegaard retains his own aloneness, his foreignness: he is "a stranger and an alien," and as author, he "has become unreal" to the reader.[22]

Kierkegaard's sacrifice of his relation to his fiancée Regine Olsen is only the most glaring biographical sign of this performance of renunciation, this letting go of the other, but it is inscribed thoroughly in the exposition of his ethics, whose principles include these:

There is only one kind of ethical contemplation, namely, self-contemplation. Ethics closes immediately about the individual.

The ethical is concerned with particular human beings, and with each and every one of them by himself.

---

20. Roland Barthes, "The Death of the Author," trans . Stephen Heath, in *Image, Music, Text* (New York: Hill and Wang, 1977), p. 148.

21. CUPSL, 285 / CUP1, 321 / SKS 7, 292.

22. CIC, 263, 276 / CI, 246 / SKS 1, 285.

One human being cannot judge another ethically, because he cannot understand him except as a possibility.

The only question of reality that is ethically pertinent is the question of one's own reality.[23]

It is true that Kierkegaard still retains a place for the other, but as Emmanuel Levinas suggests, he tends to short-circuit his need for the human other by displacing it onto a desire for God.[24] "I perfectly understand myself in being a lonely man," Kierkegaard confides in his journal, "without relation to anything, …. with only one consolation, God who is love."[25] Kierkegaard's relation to the human other is thus always the relation of two foreign selves. But as such, there can only be an indirect and enigmatic relation between the author and reader.

Indirect Communication

Indirect communication is the central ethical principle of Kierkegaard's authorship, and yet ironically, it requires the deployment of strategies generally not associated with ethics: disguise, concealment, and even deception. "I give you advance notice," Kierkegaard confides in his journal to his imagined reader, "that there will come moments …. when I …. must set between ourselves the awakening of misunderstanding."[26] That is, the reader's reliance on the traditional expectation of the authority of the author must be disrupted: to understand the task of reading as the task of uncovering the intentions of the author is a misunderstanding (a misunderstanding, we should remember, that Kierkegaard later seeks to remove in his *Point of View* and "Two Notes"). And lest there be any doubt about the method of this awakening, another journal entry puts it even more bluntly: "To deceive belongs essentially to [my method of] communication; …. and the art consists in …. remaining faithful to …. the deception [throughout]."[27]

Kierkegaard seeks to write in such a way that the inherently deceptive nature of authorship—that it invites the common assumption that to understand the text is to understand the author's inner intentions—is exacerbated to the point of absurdity: the author intentionally becomes unreliable, fantastic, mythological, so that reliance on the author is replaced by a practice of self-reliance. Thus, the

---

23. CUPSL, 284, 286, 287 / CUP1, 320, 322, 323 / SKS 7, 291-292, 294.

24. Emmanuel Levinas, "A propos de *Kierkegaard Vivant*," trans. Jonathan Rée. Included as "Two Notes," in *Kierkegaard: A Critical Reader*, ed. Jonathan Rée and Jane Chamberlain (Oxford: Blackwell, 1998), pp. 33–38. And Levinas, "The Trace of the Other," trans. Alphonso Lingis, in *Deconstruction in Context: Literature and Philosophy*, ed. Mark C. Taylor (Chicago: Chicago University Press, 1986), pp. 345–59.

25. JSK, 738 / KJN 4, 347 (NB4: 119) / SKS 20, 347.

26. JP 1, 662 / SKS 21, 61 (NB6: 80).

27. JP 1, 653 / SKS 27, 411 (Papir 368: 10a).

ethics of indirect communication has its origin in the troubling thought of the impossibility of any direct encounter with the other yet seeks a circuitous path to the other by the movement of self-withdrawal—removing the author's authority as an obstacle to the reader's independence. The author provokes the reader but "then shyly withdraws (for love is always shy)."[28]

In a journal entry where Kierkegaard speaks of the ethics of indirect communication, he writes that the author "must always [recall] that he himself is not a master teacher but an apprentice, ... because ethically the task [of indirect communication] is precisely this, that every man comes to stand alone."[29] Thus it is that Socrates "abandons" the other[30]—confesses his own ignorance, admits to his failure to resolve anything—just as Kierkegaard's pseudonymous authors all vanish. Each of the authors is utterly fantastic. As Stephen Crites says, "they are sheer personae, masks without actors underneath, [mere] voices,"[31] or, in Josiah Thompson's words, they are all "characters whose very essence is to lack flesh," to be "disembodied."[32] The art of indirect communication, as we have seen Anti-Climacus put it, consists in the author becoming "an absentee."[33]

We should not be misled into thinking that Kierkegaard's "upbuilding discourses," which he calls examples of *direct* communication,[34] revoke the ethical center of indirect communication. The upbuilding discourses, like all of Kierkegaard's works, are written for "the individual": "The communicator .... can only be a single individual, and again, the communication .... can only be addressed to the individual," Kierkegaard writes in the "Two Notes."[35] And "the individual" addressed by the discourses is of course still the "foreign" subjectivity addressed by the pseudonymous works, ultimately unreachable by the author, so that in the prefaces to each of the upbuilding discourses, Kierkegaard insists that he writes "without authority."[36]

The "directness" of the edifying discourses is not, therefore, anything like the directness of, say, Hegelian philosophy (or at least Kierkegaard's understanding of it), which Kierkegaard characterizes as a monstrous invocation of authority whose intrusive objectivism—intoning its truths through a giant "speaking trumpet"[37]—forecloses the possibility of respecting the subjectivity of the reader. Rather, the

---

28. PVL, 25-26 / PV, 44 / SKS 16, 26.

29. JP 1, 649 / SKS 27, 396 (Papir 365: 13).

30. CIC, 202-203 / CI, 177-178 / SKS 1, 224-225.

31. Stephen Crites, "Pseudonymous Authorship as Art and as Act," in *Kierkegaard: A Collection of Critical Essays*, ed. Josiah Thompson (Garden City, NY: Doubleday, 1972), p. 216.

32. Josiah Thompson, "The Master of Irony," in *Kierkegaard: A Collection of Critical Essays*, ed. Josiah Thompson (Garden City, NY: Doubleday, 1972), p. 109.

33. TC, 133 / PC, 133 / SKS 12, 137.

34. PVL, 144 / OMWA, 7 / SKS 13, 13–14.

35. PVL, 117 / TSI, 110-111 / SKS 16, 90.

36. BA, 180 / WA, 99 / SKS 11, 103.

37. JP 1, 650 / SKS 27, 400 (Papir 366: 2a).

"direct communication" of the discourses maintains the practice of writing without authority and an insistence on the responsibility of the reader to authorize the meaning of the text. True, Kierkegaard writes the discourses under his own name and in this sense directly affirms that these are "his truths." But *truth is subjectivity*, and without the accompanying indirect, pseudonymous authorship, whose task is to expose the error of mistaking the author's truths for those the reader supplies through his own project of reading and interpreting, the edifying discourses would be deceptive in a pernicious sense (as opposed to the ethically oriented deceptions of the "aesthetic" works): they would deceive the reader into thinking that the author wrote with authority. Indeed, without the movement of withdrawal or self-removal of the author, the edifying discourses would slide into the monstrosity of objectivism and *auctoritas*, just what the entire practice of Kierkegaard's authorship seeks to avoid.

The Tragic Character of Language

Kierkegaard confesses in his journal that "only when I write do I feel well. ... If I stop [writing] for a few days, right away I become ill .... So powerful an urge, so ample, so inexhaustible [is my need to write], ... subsist[ing] day after day for .... years."[38] And yet for Kierkegaard, to write is in a profound sense to lose oneself, since the inwardness of subjectivity is precisely what cannot be expressed in language. Subjective inwardness is for Kierkegaard "reality," yet "reality I cannot express in speech," since "the Word *annuls* it [simply] by talking about it."[39] This is the tragic nature of language that while it is necessary to express the inner and to reach the other, it immediately forsakes inwardness by becoming outer. As Sartre puts it, language is a "*fuite hors de moi*" (a flight outside myself)—and leaves the meaning of what is said in the hands of what is external to us, the other.[40]

For Kierkegaard, then, language exiles us from our true home, the space of existential interiority. "The real *is* inwardness," Johannes Climacus writes,[41] and yet it is precisely language, "the word," that "annuls" this reality. Language makes us homeless, and Kierkegaard longs for a way to protect his "private personality," which is his true home, his "inner sanctum," "just as the entrance to a house is barred by stationing two soldiers with crossed bayonets."[42] What is crucial to see is that the self-protective project of Kierkegaard's authorship, by which he conceals himself from the reader, is also what allows his authorship to be an act of gift-giving to the reader.

---

38. JSK, 674 / KJN 4, 82 (NB: 108) / SKS 20, 83.
39. JCC, 148 / JC, 167-168 / SKS 15, 55.
40. Jean-Paul Sartre, *L'être et le néant* (Paris: Éditions Gallimard, 1943), p. 422.
41. CUPSL, 289 / CUP1, 325 / SKS 7, 296.
42. TA, 99 / SKS 8, 94.

The Death of the Author

This gift to the reader is, to borrow Derrida's phrase that serves as the title for his reading of Kierkegaard's (Johannes de Silentio's) *Fear and Trembling*, a "gift of death." And it is just in this gift of death, this self-imposed alienation of the author from the meaning of his text, that the ethical principle of Kierkegaard's relation to his reader is achieved. Kierkegaard as author effectively "disappears,"[43] opening up the space for "the reader himself to put two and two together, if he so desires," as Johannes Climacus remarks in the *Postscript*.[44]

We may recall Lacan's definition of the function of the "Father" as "fundamentally to unite a desire and the Law." By leaving it to "the reader himself to put two and two together, if he so desires," Kierkegaard seeks to disown the Father by breaking the connection between Law and desire: the reader's desire must be freed from the tether of the Law, the Father/author's *auctoritas*. Kierkegaard performs this severing of Law and desire through a double act of sacrifice: the author sacrifices himself by vanishing beneath his disguises, but the reader is also sacrificed in an important sense—that is, the reader as conventionally understood, the reader as mere apprentice, subservient, and acquiescent. "Nothing is done to minister to [the] reader," Kierkegaard insists, since such ministry would imply an unwarranted binding of the reader to the authority of the author.[45]

Michel Foucault writes in his "What Is an Author?" (1969) that the author "must assume the role of the dead man in the game of writing."[46] A year earlier, Roland Barthes had argued that "writing is the destruction of every voice, of every point of origin":

> As soon as a fact is narrated no longer with a view to acting directly on reality but intransitively, that is to say, finally outside of any function other than that of the very practice of the symbol itself, this disconnection occurs, the voice loses its origin, the author enters into his own death.[47]

Kierkegaard's authorship is precisely about this intransitivity, this practice of the symbol that silences the voice of the speaker in the very instance of its speech, this absence of the author's imprint upon his own work. As William Afham, one of the pseudonymous authors of *Stages on Life's Way*, puts it, "by myself I am capable of nothing at all."[48] The author incapacitates himself so that the reader may exercise her own capacity for signification.

43. JP 1, 657 / SKS 27, 434 (Papir 371: 2).
44. CUPSL, 264-265 / CUP1, 298 / SKS 7, 272.
45. Ibid.
46. Michel Foucault, "What Is an Author?" trans. Donald Bouchard and Sherry Simon, in *The Foucault Reader*, ed. Paul Rabinow (New York: Pantheon, 1984), p. 102f.
47. Barthes, "The Death of the Author," p. 142.
48. SLW, 86 / SKS 6, 84.

Conclusion: From Death to Resurrection

A great irony of Kierkegaard's authorship is that while the act of incapacitation by which he renounces his authority is in part motivated by his desire to protect his "private personality," his "inner sanctum," leaving himself unreachable by the reader,[49] yet in carrying out this authorial project, he constantly risks losing himself in the merely "poetic" excesses of his pseudonymity. Thus, in a late journal entry, he laments:

> For many years my melancholy has had the effect of preventing me from saying "Thou" to myself, from being on intimate terms with myself in the deepest sense. Between my melancholy and my intimate "Thou" there lay a whole world of fantasy. This world it is that I have partly exhausted in my pseudonyms. Just like a person who hasn't a happy home spends as much time away from it as possible and would prefer to be rid of it, so my melancholy has kept me away from my own self while I, making discoveries and poetical experiences, traveled through a world of fantasy.[50]

This haunting sense of being lost to himself is the cost Kierkegaard pays for the ethical practice of his authorship, his commitment to the death of the author by which, as Barthes says, it is not in the origin (author) that the text finds its meaning but its destination (reader).[51]

It is perhaps just this lostness to himself that leads Kierkegaard to the eventual revocation of the authorial death that had been the foundation of his prior authorship and that explains the resurrection of the author as legal authority in *The Point of View*. In April of 1848, Kierkegaard had a profound religious experience in which he received God's forgiveness for his sins and which he interpreted as compelling him to speak of his authorship in a new way: "My whole nature is changed," he writes in his journal; "My concealment and inclosing reserve are broken. I am free to speak."[52] He then writes *The Point of View for My Work as an Author: A Report to History* in which he speaks directly, frankly, and openly, declaring the legitimate meaning of his authorship that had been so misunderstood. But as a result, the ethical program of his authorship becomes undone. Kierkegaard's maieuticism, which he had previously understood as a provocation of the reader to think for himself, now becomes something else: as he writes in the "Two Notes" that accompanied the posthumous publication of *The Point of View*, his "direct communication" answers his desire for the "pure receptivity" of the reader who is "like the empty vessel which is to be filled."[53]

---

49. TA, 99 / SKS 8, 94.
50. JSK, 641 / KJN 4, 96-97 (NB: 141) / SKS 20, 97.
51. Barthes, "The Death of the Author," p. 148.
52. JP 5, 6131 / SKS 20, 357 (NB4: 152).
53. PVL, 145n. / OMWA, 8n. / SKS 13, 14n.

Yet even though he came to feel that God wished him to assume the responsibility of authority over his work, Kierkegaard had his doubts. Just after completing *The Point of View*, he wrote in his journal that "*The Point of View* must not be published, no, no. And this is the deciding factor: …. I cannot tell the full truth about myself."[54] In another entry of the same time, he insists that "there shall not be any direct discussion of myself …. until after my death, because I am …. essentially a poet; but there is always something enigmatical in a poet's personality, and above all he must not confuse himself with an [actual] character."[55] Perhaps even more interesting than that Kierkegaard saw how *The Point of View* would endanger his "poetic," enigmatic existence as author is that he nevertheless seemed to think it would be appropriate to reveal himself in his "actuality" after death, as though this wouldn't equally threaten his carefully constructed persona as unreachable and mythological. While living, he must be authorially dead, but in biographical death, he wishes to be resurrected with an authority he previously denied himself.

After writing *The Point of View*, torn between his urge to reveal himself and his recognition that such revelation would transgress against the ethics of his authorship, he considered publishing the work under the pseudonym Johannes de Silentio, which would have converted the "I" of the text into a fictional character.[56] In another journal entry, he toyed with making this conversion explicit by writing a Foreword in the voice of the pseudonym "A-O," who tells us that the author of *The Point of View* ("Søren Kierkegaard") "speaks in the first person; but one will, I hope, remember that this author is not Magister K but my poetic creation."[57] Finally, Kierkegaard abandoned these subterfuges, leaving himself as the author of his own "Report to History" and thus becoming resurrected at the (near) end of his authorship as himself (i.e., as Magister K, not "Magister K").

There has been some speculation that *The Point of View* is just another—perhaps the ultimate—Kierkegaardian joke, a particularly devilish way of perfecting the fiction of himself. As Henning Fenger puts it, his authorship was "a gigantic play in which [he] acted a profusion of roles, among them that of Søren Kierkegaard in countless versions."[58] But even well before *The Point of View*, Kierkegaard yearned for readers who would be worthy of his gifts, who would understand him in the way that the "imagined reader" introduced in the Appendix to the *Postscript* would—the reader who "understands [him] at once and line by line."[59] This fantasy

---

54. JP 6, 6327 / SKS 21, 248 (NB9: 78).

55. JP 6, 6383 / SKS 21. 340 (NB10: 169).

56. JP 6, 6327 / SKS 21, 250 (NB9: 78).

57. Pap. X 2 A 171 / KJN 6, 351 (NB14: 8) / SKS 22, 347. Also cited in Joakim Garff, "The Eyes of Argus: *The Point of View* and Points of View on Kierkegaard's Work as an Author," trans. Jane Chamberlain and Belinda Ioni Rasmussen, in *Kierkegaard: A Critical Reader*, ed. Jonathan Rée and Jane Chamberlain (Oxford: Blackwell, 1998), p. 98.

58. Henning Fenger, *Kierkegaard, The Myths and Their Origins*, trans. George C. Schoolfield (New Haven, CT: Yale University Press, 1980), p. 26.

59. CUPSL, 548 / CUP1, 621 / SKS 7, 563.

of a relationship to an imagined reader where there would be no gap between the author's intention and the reader's immediate comprehension—precisely the reader who Kierkegaard denies himself by renouncing his authority—culminates in his direct instructions to the reader in *The Point of View* about how to correctly understand him. The author who had given himself over to death finally gives in to a sense of resentment over the idea that it is *not* finally he who constitutes the reader by determining what she should understand but rather the reader who constructs the author, in a sense stealing his soul. However strong Kierkegaard's commitment was to his death as an author, he eventually turns back from his grave and seeks to reappropriate his stolen soul.

Franz Kafka wrote in a letter to his fiancée Felice Bauer that "writing means revealing oneself to excess."[60] Kierkegaard's authorship, as we have seen, is committed to precisely the opposite principle, that the author must remain in concealment. The logic, such as it is, that Kierkegaard presents in *The Point of View* for rescinding his ethics of concealment and revealing himself (and thus asserting his authority) is that since his work is now essentially "complete," it is appropriate to explain what it all really means: "the reason I considered silence my duty was that the authorship was not yet at hand in so complete a form that the understanding of it could be anything but misunderstanding."[61]

But the logic collapses: I'm done, so I can speak, I can reveal myself. This is precisely the logic that Johannes Climacus had ridiculed so mercilessly in his *Postscript* with regard to Hegel's claim that his philosophical "system" was a complete whole:

> I shall be as willing as the next man to fall down in worship before the System, if only I can manage to set eyes on it. Hitherto I have had no success .... Once or twice I have been on the verge of bending the knee. But at the last moment, when I already had my handkerchief spread on the ground, to avoid soiling my trousers, and I made a trusting appeal to one of the initiated who stood by: "Tell me now sincerely, is it entirely finished; for if so I will kneel down before it, even at the risk of ruining a pair of trousers ...."—I always received the same answer: "No, it is not yet quite finished."[62]

Crucially, it is not simply that Hegel was continually adding on to what was supposed to be already complete—as, we may add, Kierkegaard did as well after writing *The Point of View*: he had yet to create his final pseudonym, Anti-Climacus (author of *Training in Christianity* and *The Sickness Unto Death*), and had many more upbuilding discourses to write. Rather, the real absurdity of any claim to a complete authorship is that "an existing individual" can never "conclude," since to

---

60. Franz Kafka in Elias Canetti, *Kafka's Other Trial: The Letters to Felice*, trans. Christopher Middleton (Richmond, UK: Calder and Boyars, 1974), p. 37.

61. PVL, 5 / PV, 23 / SKS 16, 11.

62. CUPSL, 97-98 / CUP1, 107 / SKS 7, 104.

exist is to be a "persistent striving."[63] Until death releases us from the burdens and joys of time, there is always a "postscript" to come, always a future that cannot be determined by the past without contradicting the imperative of existence itself: to become, to strive, to be irredeemably incomplete. Kierkegaard's resurrection as authority over his work—a work predicated on the ethical principle of being "without authority"—is a mark of his own very human vulnerability to the seductive myth of self-completion, the desire to be whole and thus capable of asserting the signification or truth of one's life and work. And yet we are always only incomplete; we are "fragments," and, as Kierkegaard himself insists, a fragment pretending to be a whole "is nonsense."[64]

The Point of View poses an unresolvable dilemma: in asserting his authority over the meaning of his authorship, Kierkegaard makes the ethics of his authorship impossible. Either we reject the authoritarianism of *The Point of View* or we reject the authorship that *The Point of View* is a point of view *about*. The "religious totality" of his work that he proclaims in *The Point of View* is aimed at bringing his true readers closer to faith, which in his view is the only thing that can save us from the meaninglessness of existence. And yet faith demands silence, not proclamation, since faith cuts us off from the world of social, linguistic conventions that regulate our relations to others. We stand alone before God in fear and trembling, shaken loose from the symbolic order, from the entire world of "the finite" in which we are at home in language. Thus, Abraham, the knight of faith, "cannot speak."[65]

Nor should Kierkegaard speak authoritatively about faith. And he knows this. He knows what the Seducer of *Either/Or* knows: that "love loves secrecy; .... it loves silence," and it hates all "revelation," all "public notice," and all "proclamation."[66] This is why Kierkegaard says so often in his journals that he must "remain silent, ... as if I would keep the truth to myself."[67] In another journal entry, he speaks against "the mobs of speakers, teachers, [and] professors" and fantasizes about "ordering them to be silent, saying: 'Shut up, and let us see what your life expresses, for once let this [your life] be the speaker who says who you are.'"[68]

But Kierkegaard finally does speak. He proclaims what cannot be proclaimed; he gives "public attestation"[69] precisely where "public notice" must be foregone. The love he had shown to his reader through his lifelong practice of self-negation as authority turns impatient, irritated, and breaks its silence. He speaks, finally, so as to show how his authorship from beginning to end is an effort to bring others to faith, precisely that which requires silence.

63. CUPSL, 110 / CUP1, 121 / SKS 7, 117.
64. CUPSL, 98 / CUP1, 107 / SKS 7, 104.
65. FTL, 91-129 / FT, 82-120 / SKS 4, 172-207.
66. EOS1, 383 / EO1, 388 / SKS 2, 376.
67. JP 1, 646 / SKS 20, 323 (NB4: 72).
68. JP 3, 2334 / SKS 26, 296 (NB33: 52).
69. PVL, 6 / PV, 24 / SKS 16, 12.

Perhaps the reader of Kierkegaard's works will find in them a particularly moving exploration of human suffering, or of the life of subjectivity and interiority, or perhaps even a cautionary tale of what Albert Camus sees as the "philosophical suicide" entailed by the life of faith, which demands the negation of lucidity and a flight from "the irrational silence of the world."[70] Perhaps the reader will see the work as an exploration of different ways of living and orienting ourselves in the world where, as Victor Eremita, the "editor" of the papers of the aesthete (A) and the ethicist (B) collected in *Either/Or*, says, "when the book is read, then A and B are forgotten; only their views confront one another" such that "no finite decision" between the two can be made by appeal to the "particular personalities" of the authors but must be made by the reader herself.[71]

Is there a religious unity to Kierkegaard's work? Kierkegaard says there is. But it is not up to him to say, at least if we accept the ethical framework that informed his authorship, where the author must be "forgotten." The author is without authority. It is up to the reader to say.

---

70. Albert Camus, *The Myth of Sisyphus and Other Essays*, trans. Justin O'Brien (New York: Vintage, 1955), pp. 28, 37–41.

71. EOS1, 13-14 / EO1, 13-14 / SKS 2, 20-21.

Chapter 7

ILLEGIBLE SALVATION: THE AUTHORITY OF LANGUAGE IN *THE CONCEPT OF ANXIETY*

Sarah Horton

Language is dangerous, as Vigilius Haufniensis, the pseudonymous author of *The Concept of Anxiety*, is well aware. Language makes possible the self-forgetfulness of objective chatter by dividing the self from itself, and even our ability to distinguish good and evil fails when signs vanish into illegibility. Positioning himself as a detached observer, Haufniensis views with suspicion that which thus escapes observation. But although his warnings about the dangers of language are true, I argue that this very illegibility is the condition of possibility for salvation. Language may kill the self by permitting chatter, yet salvation (one might even say *resurrection*) is possible only because language opens the self to alterity and leads us to the atonement that no observations and definitions can access. Haufniensis, the watchman of Copenhagen, thus sets up a guard against the possibility of salvation by resisting the authority of language.

By writing of language indirectly, via a pseudonymous author who distrusts it, Kierkegaard forces us to confront this illegibility that a more direct writing style might have obscured by its very clarity. Directness would risk giving the impression that *this* text, *this* author, had mastered language, but here pseudonymity calls the author's authority into question from the start, which prepares us to realize that the play of language always escapes the bounds that anyone could authorize. Awareness of language's dangers never permits us to control it, and as we discover by considering what Haufniensis does and does not say about language and sin's origin (which prove to be intertwined questions), such grasping for control is precisely sin.

The Inaccessible Origins of Sin and Language

Haufniensis's observations concerning the origin of sin immediately raise a problem that he never adequately addresses: the origin is precisely that which cannot be observed. He acknowledges that if we are to explain sin by its origin, that origin cannot be located outside history: "No matter how the problem is raised, as soon as Adam is placed fantastically on the outside, everything is confused."[1] Thus, on the one hand, Adam cannot be located radically outside the human race, or else any explanation of his sin fails to explain anyone else's. Yet a dilemma emerges straightaway, for on the other hand, Adam cannot be treated as just another human being within history, such that any of us could have chosen (as Adam could have done) to refrain from sin, or else we deny hereditary sin, thereby succumbing to the Pelagian heresy, which claims that man could potentially be good without God's aid. Summing up the dilemma, Haufniensis explains that "man is *individuum* and as such simultaneously himself and the whole race, and in such a way that the whole race participates in the individual and the individual in the whole race. If this is not held fast, one will fall either into the Pelagian, Socinian, and philanthropic singular or into the fantastic."[2] In short, any orthodox analysis of sin must maintain both that each individual is responsible for his or her own sin and that each individual is, because of Adam, born into a sinful race. And because Adam is neither radically outside the human race nor within the human race in the manner of subsequent individuals, the origin of sin cannot be located on either side of the dichotomy between without and within, exterior and interior. More exactly, the origin cannot be located: it haunts history but slips away as soon as one claims to have found it.

Rather than directly considering this haunting absence of the origin, however, Haufniensis reiterates that although sin enters history with Adam and each individual is therefore born into a sin-tainted history, the individual is still responsible for his or her own sinfulness and cannot blame it on Adam. Thus, "the history of the race proceeds quietly on its course, and in this no individual begins at the same place as another, but every individual begins anew."[3] Adam alone came into an innocent world, yet each individual's sin originates in that individual—a statement that simply displaces the problem of sin's origin by focusing on its origin in each individual. And even as Haufniensis continues to seek the origin, he undermines his investigation by insisting that "the transition that is to be made from innocence to guilt" be understood as a "qualitative leap,"[4] thereby locating an innocent original state radically and inaccessibly outside of history. Indeed, as the starting point of the leap is unobservable and nonlocalizable, the claim that there is a leap at all is impossible to confirm. As Sylviane Agacinski points out, "It is the leap that posits sinfulness and not the other way around: sinfulness already presupposes the leap—but the understanding will have none of that. For philosophy (in other words, the faculties of the intellect, the understanding, and reason), the leap is a blank. And philosophy has always worked hard at filling it in."[5] Filling in this blank is, however, precisely what philosophy is unable to do.

1. CA, 28 / SKS 4, 332.
2. CA, 28 / SKS 4, 335.
3. CA, 34–35 / SKS 4, 314.
4. CA, 43 / SKS 4, 349.
5. Sylviane Agacinski, *Aparté: Conceptions and Deaths of Søren Kierkegaard*, trans. Kevin Newmark (Tallahassee: Florida State University Press, 1988), p. 97 (*Aparté: Conceptions et morts de Sören Kierkegaard* [Paris: Aubier-Flammarion, 1977], pp. 77–78).

Able to observe only the endpoint—sinfulness—Haufniensis can never determine that it is in fact the endpoint of a leap. Thus, the observer turns away from the reality of sin to pursue an unobservable state of innocence—which, paradoxically, allows him to remain only an observer by giving him an excuse to not grapple concretely with sin. To truly face one's own sin, one must willingly remain haunted by that blank—that is, one must give up one's need to control the narrative by explaining everything.[6] Disinterestedly explaining sin is an attempt to explain it away by pretending that it has no relevance to life.

Interestingly, Haufniensis implicitly warns against this detached manner of proceeding: "Every man loses innocence in essentially the same way that Adam lost it. It is not in the interest of ethics to make all men except Adam into concerned and interested spectators of guiltiness but who are not guilty, nor is it in the interest of dogmatics to make all men into interested and sympathetic spectators of the Atonement [*Forsoning*] but who are not atoned for."[7] Asking how sin originated with Adam amounts to refusing to acknowledge one's own guilt, as though sin were something foreign that one could consider only from the outside, and refusing to admit guilt is refusing the atonement. Yet Haufniensis remains a psychological observer, not an ethicist or a dogmatist, and he insists on a strict demarcation between these sciences.[8] Thus, even as he considers how sin originates in each individual, and not only in Adam, he still examines the problem from the outside. Readers must keep in mind that his analyses will therefore remain disconnected from the lived experiences of sin and atonement—a point that will become crucial as we examine his approach to language.

Indeed, the investigation into sin's origin demands an inquiry into language, for the command not to eat of the tree of the knowledge of good and evil was spoken. That prohibition puzzles Haufniensis, for an innocent Adam could not have understood it and therefore, on hearing it, experienced no guilt but rather anxiety in the face of "freedom's possibility."[9] According to this account, language

---

6. This point recalls Paul Ricœur's conclusions that "we never have the right to speculate about original sin ... as if it had a proper consistency.... We never have the right to speculate on *the evil already there*, outside the evil that we do.... We never have the right to speculate on either the evil that we inaugurate, or on the evil that we find, without reference to the history of salvation." Ricœur, "'Original Sin': A Study in Meaning," trans. Peter McCormick, in *The Conflict of Interpretations: Essays in Hermeneutics*, ed. Don Ihde (Evanston, IL: Northwestern University Press, 1974), p. 286 ("Le 'péché originel': étude de signification," in *Le Conflit des interprétations: Essais d'herméneutique* [Paris: Seuil, 1969], p. 282). The detached examination of sin, as though it were irrelevant to our lives and certainly not something from which we need to be saved, is itself sin.

7. CA, 36 / SKS 4, 342. Translation modified.

8. See the Introduction (CA, 9–24 / SKS 4, 317–331) in which Haufniensis carefully distinguishes psychology, dogmatics, and ethics.

9. CA, 44 / SKS 3, 350.

precedes even sin: thus, it is not only the origin of language but language itself that escapes the confines of history and cannot be assigned a location. And if the origin of sin is unobservable, how much more the origin of language! Haufniensis in fact leaves that latter origin a mystery and refuses even to attribute the prohibition to God, asserting rather that "the imperfection in the narrative—how could it have occurred to anyone to say to Adam what he essentially could not understand—is eliminated if we bear in mind that the speaker is language, and also that it is Adam himself who speaks."[10] Haufniensis thus isolates Adam, leaving him alone with language—and he does not ask in what sense one who is alone with language is truly alone. It is true that he briefly acknowledges in a footnote that language interrupts man's ipseity:

> If one were to say further that it then becomes a question of how the first man learned how to speak, I would answer that this is very true, but also that the question lies beyond the scope of the present investigation. However, this must not be misunderstood, as though, through evasive replies in the manner of modern philosophy, I wanted to give the impression that I *could* answer the question in another place. But this much is certain, that it will not do to represent man himself as the inventor of language.[11]

He does not, however, pursue the matter further. That man did not invent language entails that by speaking man enters into relation with an other, even if that other is simply language itself, but Haufniensis, the observer, refuses to be the observed and so does not take this opportunity to consider alterity. In particular, there is no room in his version of the Edenic narrative for God, the divine Other.

One might argue that the absence of God from Haufniensis's version of the story is an attempt to defend God by making it impossible for him to bear the slightest responsibility for Adam's sin. Haufniensis does imply that this is his motivation when he explains why the serpent is such an enigma: God does not tempt anyone, yet attributing the temptation to the serpent also fails, "for the serpent's assault on man is also an indirect temptation of God, since it interferes in the relation between God and man, and one is confronted by the third statement [in James 1:13–14], that man is tempted by himself."[12] If temptation comes from the self, then one who sins turns inward on himself, rejecting any relation to alterity. When one considers sin in this light, Haufniensis's choice to write God out of the narrative appears not as a righteous attempt to justify God but as a suspicious refusal to acknowledge alterity. On the one hand, God is absent from this account of the Fall precisely because sin is a turning away from God. On the other hand, however, Haufniensis's attempt to locate sin's origin serves as a distraction from the lived reality of sin and so reenacts that turning away from God. God's absence from Haufniensis's version of the story can thus be read on two levels: first as

10. CA, 47 / SKS 4, 353.
11. Ibid. Translation modified.
12. CA, 48 / SKS 4, 353.

a natural reflection of sinful man's self-absorption and second as an indication of Haufniensis's own reluctance to acknowledge any other who might observe him or call him out of his detached observation. Although writing God out of the narrative may be a reasonable decision when considered from the standpoint of an observer commenting disinterestedly on sin, that very standpoint is itself problematic.

Chatter: The Dangers of Language

Haufniensis's unwillingness to be observed by any other accords with his suspicion of language, for, as indicated above, language is an other that disrupts the self. Here, we must attend to a crucial nuance: it is not that his claims about the dangers of language are wrong per se but rather that they are selectively chosen truths.[13] Warning that people must not forget their responsibility for sin by falling into a detached objectivity, he states,

> How sin came into the world, each man learns solely by himself. …. That the man of science ought to forget himself is entirely true; nevertheless, it is therefore also very fortunate that sin is no scientific problem, and thus no man of science has an obligation (and the project maker just as little) to forget how sin came into the world. If this is what he wants to do, if he magnanimously wants to forget himself, then he will become, in his zeal to explain all of humanity, as comical as that privy councilor who was so conscientious about leaving his calling card with every Tom, Dick, and Harry that in doing so he at last forgot his own name. Or his philosophical enthusiasm will make him so self-forgetful that he needs a good-natured, level-headed wife whom he can ask, as Soldin asked Rebecca when in enthusiastic self-forgetfulness he also lost himself in the objectivity of the chatter, "Rebecca, is it I who is speaking?"[14]

Thus, we see that language can certainly be dangerous, for it might degenerate into objective chatter, a universalizing attempt to explain everyone in which the individual is lost. One who produces universal explanations will end by forgetting herself so entirely that she is no longer even aware of herself as a speaker. This is a legitimate warning, odd as it may be to find it coming from the pen of one who, for all his insistence on the individual, remains a detached observer. Furthermore, the fact that this warning follows closely on the analysis of the prohibition may further incline readers to view language with suspicion: thus far in the text, we have seen that language conditions anxiety and now that it can lead to a dangerous

13. He does later comment more favorably on language and does not simply view it as bad. As I will argue in section four ("The Illegible Sign"), however, even those more favorable passages still reveal an unwillingness to acknowledge alterity.
   14. CA, 51 / SKS 4, 356. Translation modified.

self-forgetfulness. It is thence easy enough to conclude that language primarily leads us astray.

Indeed, commenters have tended to follow Haufniensis in his suspicion of language. Hugh S. Pyper argues, for instance, that "language introduces the possibility of error and therefore of doubt .... Language is inextricably implicated in the genesis of doubt, and therefore of anxiety."[15] Moreover, he proposes that "the serpent *is* the problem of language and its interpretation, the creative potential of counterfactuality, which opens the way to deception and the dizziness of possibility."[16] And Peter Fenves maintains that "the 'problem' of 'original sin' comes down to this: 'chatter,' which is original language, outgrows its origin and corrodes the very language that is determined to bring it to a halt."[17] Yet must we hold language responsible for the possibility of error, and must we accept that chatter is "original language" and ultimately contaminates all language? Let us take the latter question first: it errs by presupposing the quest for the origin that, as I have argued, cannot succeed. If we accept that we cannot find the origin—cannot fill in the blank, to borrow Agacinski's words—and must rather grapple with sin as part of our lived experience, then we can no longer seek an external explanation for error, doubt, deception, and chatter. We ourselves bear the responsibility for them all.

But are we not thereby letting language off too easily? Error, doubt, deception, and chatter are real dangers, and although the self may well be responsible for these failings, it is true that they are possible only because language enables the self to distance itself from itself. One who was perfectly self-identical could never forget herself in chatter, or distance herself from her beliefs to state, deceptively, what she did not accept as true, or waver, divided and doubtful, between two positions, or erroneously call one thing by another's name. If, however, language did not exist, the individual would be unrecognizable. As Steven Shakespeare notes, according to Haufniensis's account, "in the disruptive power of language is the inauguration of the fall. Language cancels our immediate innocence. However, language does not come upon humanity from the outside; it is intrinsic to its very structure."[18] We simply cannot conceive of a nonlinguistic humanity. Language enables the self to enter into relation with the other and also grounds the self's own existence. Moreover, Shakespeare adds that "the text contains no such one-sided equation of language with good or evil. Language is the presupposition of sin, not sin itself."[19] As I will argue, if we read the text attentively, we see that language is also the presupposition of atonement. The self that is interrupted by and conditioned by

---

15. Hugh S. Pyper, "Adam's *Angest:* The Language of Myth and the Myth of Language," *Kierkegaard Studies Yearbook* (2001), p. 93.

16. Ibid., p. 95.

17. Peter Fenves, *"Chatter": Language and History in Kierkegaard* (Stanford: Stanford University Press, 1993), p. 84.

18. Steven Shakespeare, *Kierkegaard, Language, and the Reality of God* (Burlington: Ashgate, 2001), p. 72.

19. Ibid., p. 73.

language may seek to become entirely absorbed in itself in a rejection of alterity (and this Haufniensis will call inclosing reserve)—but language can also lead the self to embrace the relation to the other that constitutes it. Thus, it will turn out that language is certainly dangerous, but the very danger that interrupts and destabilizes the self also saves. In short, Fenves is right to warn against chatter, and Pyper is right to say that language makes error and doubt possible, but what they neglect to consider is that language also makes salvation possible.

Deriving the Self

Before we can properly consider how language makes salvation possible, however, it is necessary to return to the impossibility of locating sin's origin in order to examine in more detail the constitution of the self. Again, Haufniensis insists that the sin of each individual originates with that individual: "To want to deny that every subsequent individual has and must be assumed to have had a state of innocence analogous to that of Adam would be shocking to everyone and would also annul all thought, because then there would be an individual who is not an individual and who relates himself merely as a specimen [*Exemplar*] to his species."[20] The puzzle of the origin of sin in each subsequent individual is, however, no easier to solve than that of its origin in Adam, for innocence has no place in history. Haufniensis himself implicitly acknowledges that it is impossible to speak of the origin:

> While the history of spirit (and it is precisely the secret of spirit that it always has a history) ventures to stamp itself upon the countenance of the man in such a way that everything is forgotten if only the imprint is distinct and noble, the woman on the other hand will make her effect as a totality in another way .... The expression must be that of a totality that has no history. Therefore silence is not only a woman's greatest wisdom but also her highest beauty.[21]

Note the connection between silence and that which cannot be located within a history. One cannot speak of that which has no history—but spirit always does have a history. And that spirit always has a history is its secret, both because spirit wishes to conceal this fact—for spirit longs for an originary time of innocence when it had no history—and also because the absence of an origin must be secret, must be hidden, for an absence cannot be located anywhere. The nowhere of the origin haunts spirit everywhere, for spirit constantly bears within itself the blank space that no attempt to find the origin can fill. Spirit, the uniting of "the psychical and the physical,"[22] is a synthesis with no origin, no moment of innocent prelapsarian self-identity located somewhere outside history. It has always been

---

20. CA, 60–61 / SKS 4, 365.
21. CA, 66 / SKS 4, 370. Translation modified.
22. CA, 43 / SKS 4, 349.

constituted precisely by this blank, this absence of any origin, that renders it other than itself.[23]

Although Haufniensis associates womanly beauty with the absence of history, he also states that "in a sense, [woman] signifies that which is derived,"[24] as she was created after Adam. If the origin is always absent, however, then every individual is derived, and Haufniensis acknowledges that "the difference *in pleno* [common] to all subsequent individuals is derivation."[25] Moreover, as he has already observed, "in order to posit the synthesis [spirit] must first pervade it differentiatingly, and the ultimate point of the sensuous is precisely the sexual."[26] The pre-Eve Adam thus appears as another nonlocalizable origin, for he is truly a self only once Eve exists, only once her difference from him constitutes him as well. As Kevin Newmark aptly notes, "Adam must now be understood as himself and his other, as becoming a self only by passing through his own sexual difference in his relation to Eve."[27] Thus, although Haufniensis, still in pursuit of the origin, implies that only *subsequent* individuals are derived (and has less to say about Eve than about Adam), it turns out that Adam too is derived and that he, like all subsequent individuals, can exist as a self only via difference. Eve does come from Adam, yet he comes from her as well: she "signifies that which is derived" not because she came second but because her creation (her derivation from him) was just as much his creation (his derivation from her). To be a self is precisely *not* to be absolutely self-identical. And because Adam (like everyone else) becomes a self only through derivation, he never experienced the ahistoric origin that spirit desires yet can never reach. "[D]eny[ing] that every subsequent individual has and must be assumed to have had a state of innocence analogous to that of Adam" may well be "shocking to everyone,"[28] but we are here led to a conclusion that is more shocking still: we cannot speak of any state of innocence, neither in the case of subsequent individuals nor in the case of Adam. Innocence is, and always has been, a haunting absence.[29] Moreover, the

23. See also Kevin Newmark's remark that "in Kierkegaard, the hidden event that lies in this way beyond the mastery of any subject, the shadowy secret to which the subject constantly bears witness in its faith, is the rapport between the self and its absolutely other, that is to say, the wound of death conditioning the self in its relation to everything else." Newmark, *Irony on Occasion: From Schlegel and Kierkegaard to Derrida and de Man* (New York: Fordham University Press, 2012), pp. 84–85. At stake in *The Concept of Anxiety* is how language constitutes the self in its relation to the other (or as other than itself) and how the self responds to being thus opened and divided by language.

24. CA, 63 / SKS 4, 368.

25. Ibid.

26. CA, 49 / SKS 4, 354.

27. Newmark, *Irony on Occasion*, p. 80.

28. CA, 60–61 / SKS 4, 365.

29. See also Agacinski's remark that "in this sense, innocence is merely dead and absent ... The fall is neither a passage, nor a beginning, nor an end; it does not designate a limit where innocence would stop and culpability would begin. Rather, it would be a gap or an opening [*ouverture*] ... The fall is the name for the possibility *of* differences." Agacinski,

sexual difference between man and woman appears as a visible reminder that the individual is truly a self only through his or her difference from another, and the impossibility of absolute self-coincidence is thereby inscribed in our very bodies.

The attempt to locate the origin can now appear in its true light: it is an attempt to control one's own identity by filling in this blank, this absence, that constitutes the self by rendering it different from itself. In other words, it is an attempt to erase that difference by tracing the self back to a pure, undifferentiated origin. Furthermore, because it is language that relates the self to its other and constitutes the self as other than itself (as discussed in the preceding sections), this desire to control one's own identity amounts to a desire to control language, to neutralize its differentiating power. Yet as absolute self-identity, independent of language, is impossible to attain, turning away from language destroys the self rather than constituting it as self-identical. Speaking of the genius, who "knows that he is stronger than the whole world,"[30] Haufniensis draws a telling analogy:

> The significance of the genius to himself is *nil*, or as dubiously melancholy as the sympathy with which the inhabitants of the Faroe Islands would rejoice if on this island there lived a native Faroese who astounded all of Europe by his writings in various European languages and transformed the sciences by his immortal contributions, but at the same time never wrote a single line in Faroese, and then at last forgot how to speak it. In the deepest sense, the genius does not become significant to himself.[31]

The genius who is so confident in his own strength ends up losing himself—and it is thereby as if he lost his native language, the language into which he was born and which, having renounced it, he forgot entirely. The analogy is limited insofar as Haufniensis does not suppose that this person abandoned all language, only his native Faroese, but it still stands as a sobering reminder of the intertwining of language and the self.

The Illegible Sign

We now can finally consider how language makes salvation possible. Shortly before introducing the crucial notion of inclosing reserve, Haufniensis remarks in a footnote that "the good cannot be defined at all. The good is freedom."[32] A few

---

Aparté: Conceptions and Deaths of Søren Kierkegaard, p. 99 (*Aparté: Conceptions et morts de Sören Kierkegaard*, pp. 79–80). Translation modified. It does not follow that difference is sin. On the contrary, as will become clear in the following section, sin involves the rejection of difference, and the attempt to identify a pre-Fall originary state of innocence, inasmuch as it is the rejection of difference, is sin.

30. CA, 100 / SKS 4, 402.
31. CA, 101 / SKS 4, 404.
32. CA, 111 / SKS 4, 413.

pages later, he adds that "the good, of course, signifies the restoration of freedom, redemption, salvation, or whatever one would call it."[33] The good is beyond definition: when it comes to the good, language slips away from our grasp and cannot be fixed in place with definitions that we would seek to impose. Thus, we are able only to gesture toward the good with words such as "the restoration of freedom, redemption, salvation" and can never turn it into an object that is simply present to us. As the self can never fully comprehend the good, the good always remains other, irreducible to interiority. Given that the disruption of the self is associated with the Fall, one may be tempted to conclude that such disruption is simply bad and that the absolute self-identity associated with the supposed pre-Fall state of innocence would be good, but it now becomes apparent that the good is a disruptive force. Absolute self-identity would be not good but rather inhuman, and as we can finally come to see, sin is the refusal of alterity, the attempt to force language to serve one's misguided desire for such self-identity. It is language that opens us to alterity, and for this reason, the demonic cannot endure it.

Turning now to inclosing reserve, Haufniensis explains that

> the demonic is *inclosing reserve* [*det Indesluttede*] *and the unfreely disclosed* [*Aabenbare*]. The two definitions indicate, as intended, the same thing, because inclosing reserve is precisely the mute, and when it is to express itself, this must take place contrary to its will, since freedom, which lies in the ground of unfreedom, by entering into communication [*Communication*] with freedom from without, revolts and now betrays unfreedom in such a way that it is the individual who in anxiety betrays himself against his will.[34]

The demonic cannot speak—or, more exactly, the demonic does not speak willingly. Haufniensis notes that the involuntary disclosure need not be in words,[35] but language is still operative in such a wordless disclosure, for (as argued above) it is language that renders the individual other than himself, preventing him from closing in on himself in absolute self-identity, and that thereby compels *dis*closure or, in other words, an opening (however unwilling) to alterity. Involuntary disclosure, precisely because it is involuntary and indeed contrary to the will of the demonic individual, indicates that the demonic individual is still divided, and it is therefore the mark of the failure to attain absolute self-identity. One cannot escape language—cannot truly become inclosed on oneself such that alterity is kept out—but insofar as it is possible to exist in opposition to language, the demonic does so. Haufniensis adds that "freedom is always *communicerende* [communicating] (it does no harm to take into consideration the religious significance of the word); unfreedom becomes more and more inclosed [*indesluttet*] and does not want communication."[36] Note that *communicerende* means not only "communicating"

33. CA, 119 / SKS 4, 421.
34. CA, 123 / SKS 4, 425. Translation modified.
35. CA, 129 / SKS 4, 430.
36. Ibid.

but also "taking communion." By rejecting language, the demonic also refuses any form of community with the other, including God, the divine Other.

By thus connecting language and the religious, Haufniensis here portrays language comparatively positively—but his positive observations are restrained, for they are precisely and only *observations*. He asserts that "inclosing reserve is precisely muteness. Language, the word, is precisely what saves, what saves from the empty abstraction of inclosing reserve."[37] Indeed, this is so, for language and freedom cannot be separated. Furthermore, as Haufniensis also acknowledges, the loss of communication is also the loss of the self: "Communication is in turn the expression for continuity .... It might be thought that inclosing reserve would have an extraordinary continuity; yet the very opposite is the case, although when compared with the vapid, enervating falling away from oneself continually absorbed in the impression, it has an appearance of continuity."[38] The attempt to become inclosed on oneself can only destroy the self, as the self's ground is that very blank that opens it to alterity. Again, the self must be other than itself in order to be truly a self. Thus, although the demonic individual may appear continuous, he is actually disintegrating utterly. Only the embrace of language as that which constitutes the self can prevent this destruction.

The problem here is that Haufniensis remains a psychological observer who is concerned with the origin of the demonic. Near the beginning of his analysis of the demonic, he explains that "in relation to innocence [the demonic] is an actuality posited by the qualitative leap."[39] Discussing the demonic in such terms again conceals the fact that there has never been an originary state of innocence. He states that in the demonic "freedom is lost,"[40] which covers over the extent of the problem by suggesting that freedom at some point was *not yet* lost. Even his remark that "language, the word, is what saves" is phrased in a strikingly detached manner (a point the translation unfortunately obscures by inserting the words "the individual"): whom, exactly, does language save? Who needs to be saved? Certainly, Haufniensis has willingly accused all individuals of sin,[41] yet here, precisely at this moment when he asserts that language saves, he does so in as abstract a manner as possible without referring to anyone or everyone. Is this a mere oversight that we might reasonably overlook on the grounds that he does at least recognize that no one *remains* innocent? One could suppose so—and yet, coming from a figure who positions himself as an observer and who has previously expressed suspicion of language, the abstractness of this remark makes it appear as another attempt to distance himself from the lived reality of the demonic. Furthermore, given that the search for an origin is precisely a turn away from alterity and toward the self,

37. CA, 124 / SKS 4, 425–426. Translation modified.
38. CA, 130 / SKS 4, 431. Translation modified.
39. CA, 123 / SKS 4, 424.
40. Ibid.
41. Recall his statement: "*Every* man loses innocence in essentially the same way that Adam lost it." (CA, 36 / SKS 4, 342.) Emphasis added.

it is not surprising that he hesitates, even momentarily, when considering the individual's need for salvation.

This momentary hesitation is unsurprising for another reason as well: language is dangerous, to the point where one might struggle to see how it could save the individual. Recall also that the good lies beyond definition: how then does language relate us to the good? This question becomes even more pressing when Haufniensis marks both inclosing reserve and the good with an x. Although at first he marks only the demonic with the x, stating, "Let x signify the demonic, the relation of freedom to it something outside x,"[42] he then tears down that distinction: "Let the inclosing reserve be x and its content x, denoting the most terrible, the most insignificant, the horrible, whose presence in life few probably even dream about, but also the trifles to which no one pays attention; what then does the good signify as x? It signifies disclosure."[43] Disclosure, or the good (and so, by implication, freedom), is thus represented with the same symbol that represents inclosing reserve, raising the terrifying possibility that no distinguishing mark allows us to tell the difference between them. If the x may be the mark of the demonic or of salvation, what even is the difference between them? The x becomes a horrifyingly illegible sign, communicating nothing, for behind it the demonic and the salvific blend together beyond all possibility of distinction. As Fenves comments, "No longer is there even the pretense that something—the good ...—stands outside the x. Nothing can stand outside so long as x stands for everything, and the x is, once again, this sheer coming outside itself: ... disclosure 'itself,' ... communication no longer capable of communicating anything, communication as ex-communication."[44] On this reading, there is no escape from ex-communication, from the x that undoes any possibility of salvation. Communication becomes utterly impossible. Fenves thus concludes his analysis of *The Concept of Anxiety* with the warning that "the drift of the x empties every communication" and that "our age" is "an age in which communication again and again crosses itself out."[45] The individual thus cannot look to language for salvation; language simply is this empty, drifting x (insofar as we can even write "is" of the x). Searching for signs, we find only the x blocking our path.

One can, however, read the x in another way, a way that does not cut off the possibility of salvation: namely, the x is the demonic attempt to flee illegibility, and illegibility is necessary for salvation. Haufniensis can say nothing satisfactory about salvation precisely because it emerges beyond the limits of definition, and so no distinguishing sign can mark it for us. Recall that embracing communication and thereby giving up the pursuit of self-identity is giving up the quest for an originary innocence. And giving up the quest for innocence is abandoning any attempt to exculpate ourselves (to however slight a degree) by insisting that *we*

---

42. CA, 124 / SKS 4, 426.
43. CA, 126–127 / SKS 4, 427–428. Translation modified.
44. Fenves, *"Chatter,"* p. 111.
45. Ibid., p. 112.

were good once. In short, embracing communication requires that we give up the desperate fear of being always already caught in sin. It is precisely the demonic that sees a threat in the illegible sign, for if we lose the power to draw distinctions, if guilt and goodness blur together such that we cannot tell them apart, then we have no way to defend ourselves against the charge that we were never innocent. Remember also that the demonic attempts to control language. Here the demonic responds to the inevitable failure of that attempt by concealing with an x that which escapes definition, as if it were a temporarily unknown quantity that could yet be discovered and not an ineradicable illegibility that no algebraic manipulations can ever solve for.[46] It is the demonic that seeks to conceal behind the x the failure of distinctions, of definitions that fix differences firmly in their respective places. It is not that the x is itself an illegible sign; rather, by means of this legible letter, the demonic seeks to cover over the illegibility that it cannot endure. With the x, we sign our own writs of excommunication. To be saved by language, one must abandon the attempt to control it, to resist its authority, to fight its ultimate illegibility by imposing definitions and distinctions on that which we do not have the power to read.

This argument should not be mistaken for a false reassurance that salvation is easy or cheap. On the contrary, it indicates that salvation is beyond our power. Even our capacity to distinguish good and evil, which one might have thought essential to salvation, turns out to be a trap, precisely because we *lack* that capacity and therefore cannot put our trust in it. Nor should we suppose that salvation will grant us the ability to find some realm of pure distinctions and fixed definitions. On the contrary, "whoever lives in daily and festive communion [*Omgang*] with the thought [*Forestilling*] that there is a God could hardly wish to spoil this for himself, or see it spoiled, by himself piecing together a definition of what God is."[47] Note that even here Haufniensis continues to speak abstractly: he refers not to one who lives in communion with God but to one who lives in communion with the *thought* that there is a God. Unwilling to consider the *actuality* of an undefinable God, he stops at the *thought* that such a God exists. One who willingly lets language open her to alterity must face God's actuality, and furthermore she must face it without the aid of definitions that would allow her to abstractly mark out what God is and so reassure her that she really is dealing with God. Thus, error and sin remain, terrifyingly, possibilities, for one might be mistaken about

---

46. Haufniensis uses the analogy of algebra three times: in a footnote to the beginning of his discussion of anxiety about evil, he notes that he "can indicate the particular state only very briefly, almost algebraically" (CA, 113 / SKS 4, 415); in his analysis of inclosing reserve and disclosure, shortly after introducing the x, he asks, "How could I finish even a merely algebraic naming ...?" (CA, 128 / SKS 4, 429); and in his analysis of the somatic-psychic loss of freedom, he states that it is "so difficult to talk about these things *in abstracto*, since speech itself becomes algebraic" (CA, 137 / SKS 4, 437). Although these remarks hint at the limitations of the algebraic, the analogy may lead one to suppose that x could be solved for.

47. CA, 147 / SKS 4, 447. Translation modified.

who God is—but refusing God through fear of error and sin is itself error and sin. Haufniensis, the psychological observer, falls into this latter error: he cannot endure this unobservable, undefinable God. No sooner does he state that "the true autodidact is precisely in the same degree a theodidact .... Therefore he who in relation to guilt is educated by anxiety will rest only in the Atonement"[48] than he must conclude, for psychological observation can go no farther. Indeed, the observer still cannot resist implying that one can be both an autodidact and a theodidact, although his text has revealed that one cannot teach oneself salvation. Language opens the self to alterity, and salvation comes thereby.[49]

Where Does Language Lead?

As noted above, commenters have tended to accept Haufniensis's suspicion of language, and at this point, it is instructive to consider a particularly noteworthy example. George Pattison does not consider language as potentially salvific and argues that it is dangerous because it bears within itself the threat of meaninglessness:

> That there is that which precedes and constrains the free play of language if language is to "work" as a medium of communication, that not everything can be named at will, is not simply a requirement registered, as it were, by the external world, as if language's first obligation was to be true to external appearance: rather, it is a requirement that Spirit, qua Spirit and therefore freely, places upon itself. It is the task not so much of imposing or constraining meaning but of continually claiming, reclaiming, retrieving, and recollecting meaning; the work of truth/*aletheia* as the endless deliverance of meaning from the tide of forgetfulness and dissipation, and of *poiesis* as the "making" and free rendering of the truth thus delivered.
>
> Here, then, is where we encounter the prohibition: the requirement of the limit, that Spirit, precisely as the agent of language must place upon itself. But also the penalty: for the breach of that limit is, by definition, the giving of Spirit

---

48. CA, 162 / SKS 4, 460–461.

49. One might ask how inwardness fits with this insistence on alterity. Inwardness and abstraction are incompatible: "The individuality who wants to make himself into an abstraction precisely lacks inwardness" (CA, 141 / SKS 4, 442). Inwardness thus resists the abstractions of inclosing reserve; it is precisely not an attempt to achieve absolute self-identity. Seeking to lose oneself in pure exteriority is just as much a rejection of the divided self as is inclosing reserve: the former seeks unity outside subjectivity, the latter inside. As any flight into abstraction amounts to a rejection of the ultimate illegibility of language, inwardness may be understood as the self's willing acceptance of its essential relation to language and so to alterity, although Haufniensis certainly does not consider it in those terms.

itself over to meaninglessness, its surrender to a power that leads it where it will not go and, thus, its ceasing to be Spirit, its death.[50]

Spirit, on Pattison's view, falls by giving in to "the free play of language," to meaninglessness. His warning against meaninglessness is all very well so far as it goes, but it tells only half the story. Indeed, communication would be impossible if we simply denied the need for words to have any commonly agreed-upon meanings. But what does it mean to refer to spirit as "the agent of language"? Is spirit the agent who acts on language or the agent who acts in language's service and so is acted on by it? Pattison seems to imply that spirit should act on language, lest it be led to meaninglessness and death. What if, however, "its surrender to a power that leads it where it will not go"—or, at least, where it *cannot, of itself, will to go*—were precisely what is necessary for its *life*? Fearing being led to meaninglessness is itself a grave danger, for that fear leads one to impose abstract definitions on everything and so to resist that alterity which cannot be reduced to abstract definitions. We see the fear of meaninglessness in Haufniensis's attempt to conceal the illegible with an *x*, as though there were a sign we could read provided we could follow the map or solve the equation. Like the fear of sin, the fear of meaninglessness may seem virtuous but all too easily becomes sin, becomes the rejection of language's authority and hence of any hope for meaning. Surrendering to the power of language indeed means, for spirit, being led "where it will not go"—that is, to that which cannot be defined. It is true that in the absence of fixed definitions, we have no comforting assurance that we are being led toward life—little wonder, then, that spirit cannot find God without being led![51] But as horrifying as being thus led may seem, it is the alternative that is death.[52]

In his *The Philosophy of Kierkegaard*, Pattison does not warn against being led astray by language (indeed, he emphasizes that spirit alone is responsible for its fall), but he states that "'grasping at finitude' is, rather, when, having become anxious in the face of its own possibilities and not daring to submit them to the obligation of concrete, responsible communication, spirit flees responsibility for its limitation and projects the responsibility onto another: a forbidding voice, a tempting

---

50. George Pattison, "The Most Dangerous of Gifts or 'What Did Language Say to Adam?'" *Kierkegaard Studies Yearbook* (2001), p. 232.

51. Cf. the passage in *Practice in Christianity* in which, commenting on Christ's call, "Come here to me, all you who labor and are burdened, and I will give you rest," Anti-Climacus states, "All his willingness to help perhaps still would not help if he did not say this word and thereby take the first step, for in the calling out of this word ('Come here to me') he does indeed come to them" (PC, 21 / SKS 12, 32). Translation modified. In other words, we cannot of ourselves go to God; rather, through language, he comes to us and draws us to himself.

52. Pattison's concerns may call to mind Haufniensis's remark that "the purpose of language is to conceal thoughts—namely, to conceal that one has none" (CA, 108 / SKS 4, 410). But using language for concealment is not being unwillingly led by it; rather, one who uses language to conceal a lack of thought is seeking to use language for her own purposes.

serpent."[53] This warning is still incomplete, however, for although we may respond to language's indeterminacy by abandoning any responsibility to convey meaning and simply babbling nonsense, we may also flee that indeterminacy by attempting to establish meanings that are more fixed than is possible. Indeed, these two errors ultimately form but one: we babble nonsense that entirely misses the truth when we seek to establish those impossibly fixed meanings. Our "responsibility to speak the concrete or actual world of truth,"[54] as Pattison puts it, requires that we avoid insisting on definitions where there are none to be had—which is itself a form of objective, abstracting chatter.

In conclusion, it is entirely true that language is dangerous and that indeterminacy makes meaningless chatter possible. Indeed, in an 1854 journal entry, Kierkegaard identifies the dangers of language in a manner that recalls Haufniensis's warning against chatter: "Language, the gift of speech, engulfs the human race in such a cloud of drivel and twaddle that it becomes its ruination. God alone knows how many there are in every generation who have not been ruined by talking, who have not been transformed to prattlers or hypocrites."[55] Yet this warning is not the final word on language, for the very indeterminacy that permits the self to lose itself in "drivel and twaddle" also breaks open inclosing reserve and grounds the self's relation to God.[56] Regretting the gift of language, as though it had cost us some originary goodness, fundamentally misunderstands goodness: the pure self-identity sought by one who insists on investigating the origin of sin would be inhuman, not good. Salvation demands that we give up that attempt to find the origin, which is really a reenactment of the Fall, for it is an attempt to demarcate the boundaries of good and evil.[57] And let us be clear: no legible sign marks salvation, and language is certainly dangerous, even deadly. That

53. George Pattison, *The Philosophy of Kierkegaard* (Montreal: McGill-Queen's University Press, 2005), p. 82.

54. Ibid.

55. JP 3, 2237 / SKS 26, 392–393 (NB35: 33).

56. Here it is worthwhile to note that in *Christian Discourses*, Kierkegaard conceives of the good as communication such that it benefits all people: "Thus the goods of the spirit are in themselves essentially communication [*Meddelelse*]; their acquirement, their possession, in itself a benefaction to all" (CD, 117 / SKS 10, 128). Communication, or the good, is not confined to the self's relation to God; rather, Kierkegaard suggests that the self becomes rightly related to others through right relation to God. We see also that, despite the critical comments on language in the above-cited journal entry, he does elsewhere make positive references to communication and thus implicitly to language.

57. This point recalls Dietrich Bonhoeffer's argument that the Fall was precisely the desire to judge good and evil for oneself. See Dietrich Bonhoeffer, "God's Love and the Disintegration of the World," in *Ethics, Dietrich Bonhoeffer Works*, vol. 6, ed. Clifford J. Green, trans. Reinhard Krauss, Charles G. West, and Douglas W. Stott (Minneapolis: Fortress Press, 2009), pp. 299–339 ("Die Liebe Gottes und der Zerfall der Welt," *Ethik, Werkausgabe*, Band 6 [München: Christian Kaiser Verlag, 1998], pp. 301–342).

it saves (even, perhaps, resurrects) does not lessen the danger. Yet by employing a pseudonym who resists language's authority, Kierkegaard dramatically shows us that such resistance, however reasonable it may seem, is ultimately demonic. It is indeed a risk to be led by language to that which lies beyond all definition, but only through bowing to language's authority and being thus led can we be freed from objective chatter and inclosing reserve.

Chapter 8

THE VERY TANG OF LIFE: LYRICAL JESTING IN
KIERKEGAARD'S *POSTSCRIPT* TITLE

Edward F. Mooney

Philosophy necessarily stands in the radiance of what is beautiful and in the
throes of what is holy.

—Heidegger[1]

[He] is trying to write the drama of life as it is, with all the stage directions,
to express, not only what the actors do, say, think, and feel, but also what
they are expressing. If one could succeed, the result would be life itself,
completely known. We would see why, we would understand—and also we
would feel the very tang of life itself.

—John Herman Randall[2]

We think of Kierkegaard as opinionated and didactic, offering propositions like
"Truth is Subjectivity" and raising questions like "Is there a teleological suspension
of the ethical?" A contrarian and often a skeptic, he teaches that ever-so-many
positions or propositions are untenable. He also gives us, in a positive vein,
brilliant psychology and philosophy. Yet beyond saying or arguing one thing or
another, his words stir the soul in special ways, in ways that are paradoxically both
elusive and vividly present. They are present and elusive in the way the beautiful
or the sacred are both radiantly present and strangely elusive. Of course much
philosophical writing is straightforwardly propositional and argumentative. But

---

1. Martin Heidegger, *Hegel's Phenomenology of Spirit*, trans. Kevin Maly et al.
(Bloomington: Indiana University Press, 1988), p. 42.
    2. John Hermann Randall, "F. H. Bradley and the Working-Out of Absolute Idealism,"
Journal of the History of Philosophy 5: 3 (July 1967), p. 264, describing Bradley's *Appearance
and Reality*. See Kelly Jolley, "Quantum est in Rebus Inane" (blog), March 22, 2016. <https://
kellydeanjolley.com/2016/03/22/john-herman-randall-jr-on-bradleys-book-of-life/>
(accessed: March 20, 2018).

as our first epigram makes clear, Heidegger, for one, frames philosophy quite differently. He sees it—and I'd think Kierkegaard is with him on this—as standing, at its best, "in the radiance of what is beautiful and in the throes of what is holy." Kierkegaard's *Postscript* philosophy, or para-philosophy, can carry us to the cusp of coming-to-be, to the radiance and presence of an ever-unfolding world both holy and beautiful. This is a thorough rejection of an abstract, objectified, disenchanted world.[3] It's a rejection, too, of an abstract, objectified, disenchanted sense of selves and words.

I

Much of Kierkegaard's writing is a kind of drama or theater. The words of the second epigram were written with F. H. Bradley in mind, but they serve as a good launch into Kierkegaard's terrain. In his dramas, Kierkegaard is trying "to express, not only what [his] actors do, say, think, and feel, but also what they are expressing [*in* that doing, saying, thinking, and feeling]."[4] Two sorts of expression address the depths of the self or the soul.

First, I can be stirred by what actors "do, say, think, and feel"—what they straightforwardly express, as if from a script. Straightforward words in a script can be eloquent. Second, I can be stirred by a *presence* in saying, doing, thinking, or feeling. This is more elusive.

I can speak words of love (a first sort of expression) while my tone of voice, its rhythm and timbre, and my bodily rigidity or slackness express (sometimes elusively) fear or hesitation. Words can be expressive just as words: a stenographer takes down the speech of a tearful witness—but neglects the tears, and a bodily and vocal radiance. She can't record in any detail the face of the witness, the tone, volume, and emotive modulations of the voice, the tightness in the limbs, betraying fear, excitement, awkwardness. Being attuned to such presence is like hearing (or missing) subtleties in musical phrasing.

Similarly, words from a text can stir the soul in two ways. As I read, I can focus on taking notes for a quiz or for an expository essay; the words unspoken, not dramatically enacted, can be quite expressive. They can also project a presence. Although not delivered by an embodied, vocalizing person, they nevertheless have weight, impact, pitch, rhythm, overtones, bite, softness, or volume. Not all writers

---

3. Because much of Kierkegaard's writing is suspicious of philosophy, we might speak of his "para-philosophy." His desire to bypass objectivist philosophy in restoring a sense of the presence of words, selves, and the world is part of the broader project of romantic re-enchantment of the world. For a wonderfully illuminating discussion, see Anthony Rudd, "Wittgenstein and Heidegger as Romantic Modernists," in *Wittgenstein and Heidegger*, ed. David Egan, Stephen Reynolds, and Aaron James Wendland (London: Routledge, 2013), pp. 228–244.

4. Randall, "F. H. Bradley and the Working-Out of Absolute Idealism," p. 264.

of philosophy want to make their words come alive. They disavow any interest in what Wittgenstein calls the inexplicit "spirit" of their writing.[5]

Texts like Kierkegaard's *Postscript* can express opinions and raise questions, and launch a debate. They can also *hum* like a chorister treading home from church, or *crackle* like the punch lines of a comic, or *shout* like an insecure Sunday preacher. Sometimes, as in the *Postscript*'s full title, the presence of unfolding words can seem like the *crash*—and then gently recessing *purr*—of waves at the beach. The rhythmic hum and crackle, crash and purr give me a world itself in its presence, in its elusive and mysterious coming-to-be.

I make an unusual request. I ask you to set Kierkegaard's opinions and arguments to one side. Don't discard them, but let them be teleologically suspended, as it were. Suspending a focus on opinion and argument lets the *presence* of words take center stage. With that, we access a neglected dimension of their "tang of life." Presence is not *more* important than opinions, questions, or arguments, but it's nevertheless *strikingly* important; it conveys the spirit of inquiry. Like a whisper or a cry, Kierkegaard's words can suspend the dominance of my exclusively cognitive tracking of sentences—a good thing, for then there's space and time for the revelation of new if elusive vistas.

II

Kierkegaard's aims are exorbitant. Like Bradley, he wants "to write the drama of life" and to convey "the very *tang* of life itself." It can arrive in "bare words." She says, "I love you!"—and means it. The "tang of life" can also arrive in a subtle (or not so subtle) *presence* that delivers, in addition to her words of love, an enchanting naïveté. Or perhaps an alarming insecurity. Kierkegaard's words can deliver bare fact or opinion: "the world is full of wonder and terror." I record this opinion in my notebook. His words can also deliver the *presence*—even the *music*—of the wonder and terror that unfolds as part of "the tang of life." I'm stirred at this point to read aloud some of my favorite lyrical passages from the early parts of *Fear and Trembling*.

Bradley tries to write "the drama of life as it is" and to convey "the tang of life itself." So far, so good. But he also wants to understand the drama and make it "*completely known*." Heidegger and Kierkegaard will demur. Aiming for unruffled understanding and complete knowledge is aiming for a mirage. As important, to even try to render life as a finished block of knowledge is *unbecoming*. The attempt aims to erase access to "the radiance of what is beautiful and ... the throes of what

---

5. Wittgenstein writes that "[the] spirit of a book has to be evident in the book itself, and can't be described ... It is a great temptation to try to make the spirit explicit." By the book's "spirit," he means the book's presence (I suspect). Talking about the crash or hum or cackle of words is trying to evoke their presence, and to evoke something elusive is the opposite of "making it explicit." See Ludwig Wittgenstein, *Culture and Value*, trans. Peter Winch (Chicago: University of Chicago Press, 1980), pp. 6–7.

is holy." It will erase any instance of being swept up in wonder, terror, or exaltation. These give me "the tang of life itself" even as, for the moment, a full focus on knowledge and comprehension is sidelined.

Kierkegaard is aligned with Kant in holding that complete knowledge escapes us. But he has a deeper point to make: fixating on the quest for complete knowledge drains our sense of being alive—alive in more than a medical sense. To be vibrantly alive is to be animated by the unknown. Think of the intense animation of sports fans and players for whom the outcome of a close match is and must be radically unknown. Or consider Kierkegaard's young man in *Repetition* yearning for love, awaiting, as he puts it, his "thunderstorm." He is alive and awaiting something beyond his ken. Or consider Abraham's surprise and shock at the Lord's demand for Isaac in *Fear and Trembling*. Who knew the future held that summons?[6]

No one can give us life "completely known" because life is always unfinished, full of happy and fearsome surprises, poised always on the cusp of the new. Kierkegaard rejects the dominance of the all-too-human drive toward detached summations and frozen theory. He offers words that convey stirring, vibrant presence at the cusp of the new.[7]

I pause with an instance of the lyrical "feel and tang" of *coming-into-being*, with the unexpected, comic, even *monstrous* title of what we know, in shorthand, as "*Postscript*." Letting the full title unfold gives us "a tang of life." Propositions and opinions in *Postscript* are passed over, as are facts from his life. In a museum, a landscape painting catches my eye. To take in *more* of it, I won't rush forward to determine the painter and her dates or read up on her technique. I'll let my amazement or puzzlement before the canvas continue its ebb and flow.

III

For the sake of efficiency or cognitive mastery, we disable moments when the presence of wonder or jest is viscerally apparent. Disabling the fear and trembling of *Fear and Trembling* lets me get closer to the argument. Paring down the enormity and bravado of the full *Postscript* title—*Concluding Unscientific Postscript to Philosophical Crumbs: A Mimic, Pathetic, Dialectical Compilation, an Existential Contribution*—lets me get closer to dispassionate analysis.[8] Yet I

6. Subjectivity includes our susceptibility to the surprise of personal address.

7. "Kierkegaard created [his novel] position by merging Hegel's insistence that we must have some kind of contact with anything we can call real (thus rejecting the noumenal), with Kant's belief that reality fundamentally exceeds our understanding; human reason should not be the criterion of the real. The result is the idea that our most vivid encounters with reality come in experiences that shatter our categories." Lee Braver, "A Brief History of Continental Realism," *Continental Philosophy Review* 45 (2012), p. 275.

8. Neither the Wikipedia article on Kierkegaard nor the Amazon.com listings give the full title. Robert L. Perkins (*International Kierkegaard Commentary, Volume 12: Concluding*

thereby lose an immediate resonance. The fourteen-word title to this 600-page tome gets stripped down to "*CUP*" or "*Postscript*," and the foreshortening buries its presence. Gradually elongating the minimal title allows a crescendo of what I call genesis-unfolding. Expanding *Postscript* through successive surprises opens moments of laughter and wonder. If the experiment fails, only annoyance at its flamboyant chutzpah will be left.

The expansion proceeds stepwise like this:

- **CUP** or ***Postscript*** becomes
- ***Concluding Unscientific*** Postscript *(or we might say* "Unscholarly Addendum").[9] That, in turn, stretches out to become
- *Concluding Unscientific Postscript* **to Philosophical Crumbs** *(or we might say* Philosophical "Fragments," "Trifles," "Tidbits," or "Scraps"). An already long title now grows once again. We have
- *Concluding Unscientific Postscript to Philosophical Crumbs:* **A Mimic- Pathetic-Dialectical Compilation** *(where mime, tragedy, and philosophy are mixed).* And then, at long last, the full title emerges. *Concluding Unscientific Postscript to Philosophical Crumbs: A Mimic, Pathetic, Dialectical Compilation,* in full resonance and enormity, becomes
- ***Concluding Unscientific Postscript to Philosophical Crumbs: A Mimic-Pathetic-Dialectical Compilation: An Existential Contribution***.[10]

Unfolding the title replicates a musician's strategy in attempting to master a difficult passage. She had at first breezed through it carelessly. Recognizing she has missed something, she slows to move forward one measure at a time, starting with the first problematic measures. She works on them, then adds the next set, then expands again to take three sets in a row, etc., until the whole passage comes easily: its presence flows.

Each of these elongations, if we reflect a moment, raises the question of what we hold in our hands. It's a book to file under the letter "K," and it then morphs to a shockingly funny, annoying, mischievous, lively unknown.

Unscientific Postscript to Philosophical Fragments [Macon, GA: Mercer University Press, 1997]) and Rick Anthony Furtak (*Kierkegaard's Concluding Unscientific Postscript: A Critical Guide* [Cambridge: Cambridge University Press, 2010]), settle for the shorter, manageable title. See my discussion pp. 179 and 221 in *On Søren Kierkegaard: Dialogue, Polemics, Lost Intimacy, and Time* (Farnham, UK: Ashgate, 2007).

9. This rendering is suggested by Alastair Hannay, in *Kierkegaard, A Biography* (Cambridge: Cambridge University Press, 2002), p. 315.

10. Read it rhythmically, musically in 4/4 time, with "—" marking rests, **bold** marking accents, and " / " marking measures. "*Concluding Unscientific* **Postscript**—/ to **Philo-sophical Crumbs**—:/ A **Mimic**-Pathetic-Dialectical Compilation,/ an **Existential** Contribution—."

What's so shocking?

- Why take seriously something avowedly *unscientific or unscholarly*?
- Why pick up a book frankly advertising itself as a follow-up to *crumbs* of philosophy? Can wisdom be delivered in a scattering of crumbs?
- How can a text combine both *the mimicry of comedy* and *the pathos of tragedy*?
- How can *dialectical philosophy* be combined with *comedy and tragedy*?
- How can a *compilation* escape being a hodgepodge or unruly stack?
- What in the world is *an existential contribution* ("existential" is not yet a commonplace term)?

The title goes against nature and is monstrous, or burlesque, perhaps the work of a court jester. Its humor takes away the possibility that *Postscript* primarily addresses non-ironic analytical minds with technical distinctions between religiousness A and B, or between history and faith.

The impulse to reduce the title to a single word rests on convenience. It also buffers anxiety: how can the full title possibly be held in mind? To avoid vertigo, I fix on something stable: it's just a book with a faded yellow cover and a manageable title, "*Postscript.*" The presence of even part of the full title offers a swirling slice of thought, a cognitive-affective swerve, an ontological jest. Nothing could *possibly* be a "*Concluding Unscientific Postscript to Philosophical Crumbs: A Mimic-Pathetic-Dialectical Compilation: An Existential Contribution.*" Nothing could *possibly* be as convoluted and enticing as this lyrical title, just as nothing could *possibly* be as alluring as this child's lyrical smile. We tame the allure of a kid's smile by saying "all kids are cute." We tame the sparkle of a book's extravagant title by thinking, "it's just '*Postscript.*'" Or we brush it aide: "*All philosophy is weird, a bad joke.*"

Minus the subtitle, Alastair Hannay's translation is *Concluding Unscholarly Addendum to Philosophical Crumbs*—a spoof of academic titles.[11] "*Unscholarly Addendum*" suggests "inconsequential afterthoughts." "*Crumbs*" (or "trifles") are inconsequential, too. Picture crumbs as remains falling from the table of a royal magician. With dramatic flourish, he turns them into fodder for an acquisitive mind. Alternatively, what we *took* to be the promise of a full-table treatise turns out to be mere trifles or scraps.

A *Mimic-Pathetic-Dialectical* work is at least two-thirds theater. Mimicry, miming, and jesting are theatrical. Pathos and tragic passion are, too. Dialectic might seem squarely "philosophical," and so, offstage—but perhaps not. Johannes Climacus can be the impresario directing the "mimic-pathetic" theater, assembling it contrapuntally, dialectically, as comedy, tragedy, satire, or farce.

Postscript is a compilation of theatrical scripts and scenarios, and also *An Existential Contribution.* As onlookers, even as deeply affected spectators, I might come to an "existential" realization that I am *more* than an onlooker and that there are demands, calls, and invitations there that challenge me. *Postscript*

---

11. Hannay, *Kierkegaard, A Biography*, p. 315.

aims at existential provocation while remaining ridiculously funny, the work of a court jester. The title can be tweaked even more: *An Unsystematic Appendix to Philosophical Smidgeons.* The targets of this slapstick are academia and professors in general and perhaps Hegel's "Scientific System," if not the vanity of philosophy generally. Climacus might be a Shakespearean fool, uniquely wise, performing to a half-deaf philosopher-king, or throwing crumbs to swine.

The mockery might go inward. Self-administered parody and jest can both hide and reveal a jester's unwillingness to swim the currents of a Christian life. Climacus exhibits the difference between *seeing* the truth and acting *in* the truth. He's a dithering figure advancing toward the brink of Christian commitment, then hesitating. We recognize *ourselves* in his mirror. It's no jesting matter to live truly on the cusp of coming-to-be.

IV

Kierkegaard the author and citizen is out of the picture. In my attention to the presence or radiance of words, I suspend biography and history. Yet what can it mean to identify Kierkegaard as an author while turning away from biography?

We appreciate many folktales, ancient epics, pieces of architecture, snatches of tunes, while knowing nothing, or next to nothing, about the material conditions of their genesis. The powers of creation are evident despite knowing next to nothing about individuals bringing them into life. The mysteries of creation lie on the surface of the words. To read Homer, I don't need an historical poet or his diaries. I *do* need ahistorical musical inspiration. "Sing in me muse, Sing of the man of twists and turns driven time and again off course." So opens *The Odyssey*.[12] Or think of the Grimms's fairy tales. Surely they're inspired by muses, but no single author is blessed. We need muses even for cases where authors *can* be historically identified: consider Beethoven or J. D. Salinger. The spirits of creation sing through Kierkegaard's dramas, too.

Say a bottle holding an unsigned manuscript washes up on a beach. I can ask who wrote it. Say I have a Renaissance painting of dubious provenance. Was it actually produced in Raphael's studio? How much of the brush work is his and how much, the work of his assistants? Yet the genesis-unfolding and presence of a work doesn't raise questions of provenance—as if the mystery and radiance is only the puzzle of *who* laid brush to canvas, or put pen to paper, or wrote under pseudonyms, or plagiarized. Citizen-Kierkegaard disappears while I'm immersed in genesis-unfolding. Unsigned bundles of words washed up on the beach, even if subsequently shown to be Kierkegaard's, and are as radiant *before* being linked to a Danish author as they are afterward.

---

12. Homer, *The Odyssey*, trans. Robert Fagles (New York: Penguin, 1997), p. 77. Slightly amended.

The mystery of creation-underway, of unfolding amazement or radiance, among words or among tidal flats, is a presence to linger with, not a problem to solve. Taking up a problem is often optional—whether to bother to analyze a tidal surge—and sometimes non-optional—whether to check the map when I'm lost. But being taken by a thrilling musical phrase, or seduced by the jest of a title, is not a matter of choice. The abstractions of the mind–body problem, or the challenges of a detective mystery, can be taken up or put down. The thrill of a Bach cadence *hits us* or *doesn't*. When we're struck by the wondrous surface of Kierkegaard's words, the urge to explain or take academic notes is suspended.[13]

As scholars, we ask who authors Kierkegaard's pseudonymous *Postscript*. Is it Citizen-Kierkegaard? Or is it Johannes Climacus, erstwhile resident of an imaginary landscape populated by assistant professors, cemetery visitors, and Socratic stand-ins? We can't check with *Climacus* to see if he admits to being Kierkegaard in disguise. We can't check with Kierkegaard to see if *he* admits to being Climacus in disguise. Why trust what a master of disguises says about which disguises aren't *really* disguises? Climacus signs off as S. Kierkegaard in *Postscript*.[14] But why take that avowal as determinative? Can we distinguish true identity papers from forgeries or true faces from disguises? Happily, we can respond to the text's liveliness without a clue as to the text's "real" author. We can hear music without knowing the musician. If signed texts *and* pseudonymous ones are revelatory, we can stop with the revelations.

Kierkegaard refused to become academic. He wrote an *unscholarly*, unacademic *Postscript*. He didn't spend years on how Hegel or Luther matured. To enjoy Homer, I'm not required to show how oral tradition shaped *The Odyssey*. Yet I still refer to Homer or Hegel or Kierkegaard. I speak nonhistorically, nonempirically about them. "Hegel" or "Homer" can refer to an *experiential presence*. The proper names evoke a unified angle of vision, a kind of Kantian "transcendental unity of apperception." They are conveniences that stand for an elusive center of narrative power and imaginative brilliance that leaps from the pages at hand.

V

There are moments that elicit a gasp or exclamation, a silent or vocalized "*Wonderful! Wow!*" These words don't corral anything in a category. They are less a cogitation than a reflex, a mimicking almost musical reflex or moment of applause. People vary in susceptibility to such reflex. Dullards fail to register on any scale of

---

13. We periodically set *Postscript* aside for other matters. But we don't do this with the finality or closure that marks finishing a puzzle or solving a problem. *Postscript* is *never* finished in that sense!

14. In the final pages of *Postscript*, Climacus *revokes* all he has written. Taking something back can be slapstick and cruel. I give you a sparkling invitation. Then, to your chagrin (and my audience's callous delight), I grab it back, revoke it. April fool! Revocation can be part of

exuberance. Extroverts can rise over the top. This is not a trivial matter. As one writer puts it, "our most vivid encounters with reality come in experiences that shatter our categories."[15]

There is no single sort of "event" that evokes a reflex of wonder, terror, amazement, or surprise. It might be a poetic image, a surprising title by a Danish philosopher (or para-philosopher), a heart-stopping sunset.[16] Salman Rushdie names five sorts of mysteries that trigger a silent or voiced gasp of recognition:

> Five mysteries hold the keys to the unseen: the act of love, and the birth of a baby, and the contemplation of great art, and being in the presence of death or disaster, and hearing the human voice lifted in song. These are the occasions when the bolts of the universe fly open and we are given a glimpse of what is hidden; an eff of the ineffable. Glory bursts upon us in such hours: the dark glory of earthquakes, the slippery wonder of new life, the radiance of Vina's singing.[17]

What Rushdie calls "keys to the unseen," "effs of the ineffable," are a kind of presence that instills "a tang of life." "*These are the occasions when the bolts of the universe fly open and we are given a glimpse of what is hidden.*" For a friend unmoved by what stuns me, descriptions or explanations are no substitute for direct access. I put her in the path of the ineffable rather than try a tedious speech.

Rushdie's five mysteries are only a start, though an excellent one. There are many local, less-universal sites of alluring mysteries. A child's smile, a sweet portrait, a view of Back Cove as it shifts from drab tidal mud fields to expansive watery mirrors that reflect the city: each day, each night, declaring glory. Whether or not there is agreement about how to elaborate Rushdie's five mysteries—birth, acts of love, great art, the presence of death and disaster, heart-shattering song—here are some themes they embody.

Presence Counts: The mysteries Rushdie names are moments we overlook if we adopt only a dispassionate, objective outlook on things. Curiosity can overtake wonder. How do we know we're in love? What is so attractive about this

---

an insider's joke, showing who's in and who's out, a kind of one-upmanship made to tickle a subgroup of philosophers—those who get the joke on Hegel. Hegel thought dialectic was always progressive and forward moving (in this parody). Revocation is backward moving. See my "*Postscript*: Humor takes it back," in *On Søren Kierkegaard* (Chapter 12).

15. Braver, "A Brief History of Continental Realism," pp. 261–289.

16. The mystery here is not simple ignorance—not knowing where Kenya is on the map. If you say the incarnation is a mystery, an atheist can think that's a dodge, a confession of ignorance *and* an attempt to shut down questioning. I seek out mystery that makes us hold our breath in wonder or awe or fear. It's not "solved by better knowledge."

17. Salman Rushdie, *The Ground Beneath Her Feet* (London: Picador, 2000), p. 19. See my discussion in "Saving Intimate Voice in the Humanities," in *Lost Intimacy in American Thought: Recovering Personal Philosophy from Thoreau to Cavell* (New York: Continuum, 2009), p. 163.

performer's rendering of Beethoven? Is the brain wired to have moments of awe? This inquisitive and analytical frame of mind comes on the scene secondarily, *after* being stirred or stunned. Detached explanation is not our only value. I cherish the genius or genesis of love or song as I access it moment by moment.

Mystery delivers infinite value. Its value is inexhaustible in the way a child's smile can be inexhaustible. It's a presence, not a simple fact to record in a ledger. Fact-seeking or analytic frames of mind are only part of life underway. I don't need explanations for *why* we fall in love (though they might be available). When reduced to abstract objects of inquiry, wonder, dread, or love are lost. It's not easy to convey the glisten of genius unfolding. Its marvels are seemingly "pulled from thin air." They are unfurled on every other page in Kierkegaard's writing.

Dark Matter: Rushdie mentions a dark mystery: being in the presence of death and disaster. If pure wonder marks a moment of light and celebration, terror, despair, or horror (Goya's riveting "The Horrors of War") marks a nadir of darkness. Kierkegaard's complacent churchgoers need the dark awakening of Abraham climbing Moriah. At impact, death and disaster rule out affirmation or celebration. Yet disaster leaves a striking potentially affirmative imprint, not only a traumatic one. It leaves an aching for what is lost—precious things, precious people, things worth holding, valuing, even in their loss. It leaves an imprint of our vulnerability— which is a thing of wonder (and fear). Finally, a terrible onset of darkness need not indefinitely suffocate onsets of light. Mysteriously, the sun also rises.

Explanation and Shimmering: Explaining a sunset's reflection on snow is a digression from the experiential impact of the now glancing light. Letting one's absorption amplify is staying with the phenomena. Moving too quickly to explain breaks the spell and risks explaining away. Love or sunsets live on despite an urge to invoke brain states or loneliness as causes. Such explanatory invocations change the subject. The prose on the wall beside a museum painting focuses on facts that can work *at the expense* of experiential impacts. A passage from Dostoevsky or Beethoven, or a child's smile or falling in love, can confound us as a mystery that defies explanation—not that explanations *can't* be offered but that radiant impacts survive *without* explanation or interpretation.

Kierkegaard's authorship, or parts of it, can confound us as a mystery that defies explanation. It's not that explanations *can't* be offered, but that a mysterious impact can survive *without* explanation or interpretation. The onset of unfolding radiant creativity survives, when it does, autonomously. Explaining a cellist's captivating phrasing is disastrous if the moment of wonder disappears in the process. I want to know what unhappy facts led to Hitler's rise and what happy facts allow a child to smile. As important, I don't want to erase my terror thinking of Hitler, nor my wonder seeing a child's smile.

Ordinary and Extraordinary: The mysteries Rushdie names can appear as both commonplace and miraculous. What's so special about childbirth? It's part of daily routine for nurses and clerks in maternity wards. What's so special about song? It's all around us, like the sound of mid-town traffic. For morgue workers, there's nothing special about death. Yet I trust we know there's also something hauntingly wondrous or terrible on occasions of death, song, or birth.

These mysteries—love, birth, great art, death or disaster, and singing—involve visceral encounters. When they strike, the humdrum disappears. A mystery clings to a particular painting, in some respects quite ordinary. That sense of uncanny coming-to-be may reappear a week later, as I recall my first encounter. But even this later thought about genius and genesis depends on immediate eruptions from this painting or that. Mystery offers visceral escape from the humdrum.

Double and Multiple: Artists, writers, congregants, mothers, citizens, sons must have double vision, letting both facts and *presences*, both explanations and *stunned silence*, have a place at the table. But double vision is just the start. We need multiple vision. *What* we encounter—straight facts and shimmering presences—activates double vision. That we are *there* for the encounter activates another perspective. Being present to *it* opens toward triple vision. That I am here available to the radiance of a cellist's phrasing is a wonder added to the wonder of her playing.

We can expand our purview. To transition from one kind of phrasing to another (and yet another) requires fluidity of focus. It's not focusing on a static object. So triple vision gets augmented indefinitely. We need to face the wonder and terror— or the brute fact—of needing multiple angles of vision distributed temporally to take in the truths, the realities, of all that's available.

VI

The dynamic, unstable *Postscript* title stands in for the array of Kierkegaard's recurrent exemplifications of the mystery of creation. A book is two pounds—and also packed with genius. A child's smile is a recordable event—and bursting with visceral mystery that "shatters our conventional categories." It's also a moment of flux. The phrasing of the cello emerges about *here* in the musical line and completes its appearance a few seconds later, about *here*, and then has passed. The *Postscript* title's expansions and contractions are like the emergence and retreat of a cellist's phrase. Try reading it as a single word; let it swell into a twelve- or fourteen-word mini-aria that then disappears, except in memory—the way a phrase from the cello or a child's smile emerges and disappears into a memory trace. The emergence can seem like a genie that rises from a bottle, then becomes vapor; we're not sure how to call the phrase or smile back into existence. I can no more force the unfolding title into a bottle for repetition or distribution than I can get a genie back into its bottle.

I can arrest the title long enough to ponder whether the English should read "*unscholarly*" rather than "*unscientific*," should read "Philosophical *Fragments*" rather than "Philosophical *Crumbs or Trifles*." I can ask whether the "crumbs" at issue are the Biblical crumbs from the table of a rich man and whether philosophy *ought* to be crumbs or fragments rather than explanations, systems, and arguments. I can arrest emerging flow to ask how philosophy can be *comic mimicry* or how it can be *tragic pathos* or whether this is the spot where "*existential philosophy*" is born. I can ask whether this title is the work of Kierkegaard or the work of

Johannes Climacus, whether Climacus is a genie climbing out of the earth up toward heaven, John the Climber. But "Kierkegaard" may be as much a *nom de plume* as "Climacus."

Kierkegaard's acerbic disdain, in *Postscript*, for "assistant professors" is disdain for all who restrict their interest to analysis and explanation. He wanted more from a thinker. Here is Heidegger asking us to go deeper than the "outer" sense of philosophical sentences. Referring to Hegel's *Phenomenology*, he writes, "here as everywhere else in genuine philosophy—[the inner form] is not an addition which is meant for the literary connoisseur. Nor is the question that of literary decoration or of stylistic talent. Rather, its inner form is the inner necessity of the issue itself."[18] Of *Postscript*, we could say that its inner form (satire, jest, irony) is not an accidental or merely literary addendum to the proposition that truth is subjectivity. The inner form, presence delivered through jest, exemplifies the necessity of subjectivity. Heidegger goes on:

> For philosophy is, like art and religion, a human-superhuman affair of primary and ultimate significance. Clearly separated from both art and religion and yet *equally primary* with both of them, philosophy necessarily stands in the radiance of what is beautiful and in the throes of what is holy.[19]

Kierkegaard's writing has an "inner form" that is more than literary; it brings me the wonder of coming-to-be, and next to the wonder of the beautiful and holy, art, and religion. Hearing the *presence* of creation brings us to "a human-superhuman affair of primary and ultimate significance."

Assistant Professors are bemired in single vision, content to limit their lectures to argument, analysis, or exposition. They have no ear for Blake's "double vision" (presence and facts) or for the allure of a child's smile or the terror of a tsunami. They hold up *Postscript* and assign study passages. There's no time to be stunned by a *Final Unscholarly Afterthought in 600 Pages, a Sequel to Scraps of Philosophy: A Mimicking, Pathos-filled, Dialectical Compendium and Existential Provocation.*

I've tried to *evoke* an onset of wonder as it occurs in the full unfolding of *Postscript*'s title or in the wonder of a cello's phrasing or a child's smile. But I've also tried to draw pictures of how that moment of wonder can be followed by the contrasting desire for elaborations. Delicately pursued, they don't utterly destroy that moment but lay out possible second or third angles of vision. I lay out prospects, vantage points, and appeal to your sense that these are intelligible and alluring. I give what Wittgenstein calls "perspicuous representations," persuasive images or pictures that render satisfying angles of vision.[20] I think Wittgenstein learned much

---

18. Martin Heidegger, *Hegel's Phenomenology of Spirit*, trans. Parvis Emad and Kevin Maly (Bloomington: Indiana University Press, 1988), p. 42.

19. Ibid.

20. Ludwig Wittgenstein, *Philosophical Investigations* (Oxford: Blackwell, 1973), section 122.

from Kierkegaard—among other things, how one could give multiple pictures of the lay of the land, shuffling many of them rather than fixating on a single picture. This is an alternative to either submitting to a general skepticism (there are just too many angles for us to have knowledge) or reverting to a search for airtight argument or systematic derivation (we can *show* this angle to be correct).

VII

Afterthought: Creativity, Egoism, Self-abnegation

I have ducked questions of the psychology of an actual author—Kierkegaard, say. Nevertheless, I can't resist this afterthought that focuses on the psychology of actual authors. It is thinking about self-centeredness and self-abnegation that interests me. They have a tangential connection to understanding unfolding creation.

Undergoing the immediate experiential impact of creation-underway may seem to displace my importance; my identity as a reader defers to the majesty of something other, something that's underway independent of my will. I might gasp, under my breath, that I am but dust and ashes. On the other hand, looking back in retrospect on a work I have written, I might be in awe of it seeing it not just as a creation but as *my* creation. I might gasp, under my breath, that I've created a world, I'm a world-creator, I'm everything. The phase of seeing only the majesty of a world can feed into the idea that makes actual historical authors for the moment inessential. Disappearing acts in Kierkegaard's use of pseudonyms, or Climacus's revocation of authorship in *Postscript*, can seem to be a self-sacrifice or self-abnegation.[21] Authorial disappearance, however, is the mirror opposite of the vaunted self-assertion of the author, the writer as hero, as godlike in world-creation.

Martin Buber relays a pertinent piece of wisdom. A Hassidic story recommends that we carry two notes in our pockets. On the first will be written "The world was made for me." On the second will be written "I am dust and ashes."[22] Artists and writers are obviously at the center of the world as they create. The world is made for them because they make it. It takes extreme egotism and self-assertion

21. See "*Postscript*: Humor Takes It Back," in my *On Søren Kierkegaard*.
22. Attributed to Rabbi Simcha Bunim of Peschischa, the story goes like this: Everyone must have two pockets, with a note in each pocket, so that he or she can reach into the one or the other, depending on the need. When feeling lowly and depressed, discouraged or disconsolate, one should reach into the right pocket and, there, find the words: "For my sake was the world created." But when feeling high and mighty, one should reach into the left pocket and find the words: "I am but dust and ashes." See Martin Buber, *Tales of the Hasidim: Later Masters* (New York: Schocken Books, 1948), pp. 249–250. And see my discussion, "Chutzpah, Self-Abnegation, Creation," on Zeteo (blog) <http://zeteojournal.com/2016/04/24/9162/#sthash.YbGOqdl5.dpuf>.

to do what Kierkegaard does—shape worlds with the tip of his pen. And it takes egotism and self-assertion to say of *Fear and Trembling* that it will make his name immortal—or to create an off-hand throwaway title like *Philosophical Crumbs*. Yet Kierkegaard is not just writing advertisements for his wit, invention, and surpassing intelligence. He also writes in extreme self-abnegation. He keeps walking offstage to let his figures and pseudonyms speak on their own.[23] He wants to be famous and wants simultaneously only *anonymous* words to have presence. One note says, "The world was made for me," and the other says, "I am dust and ashes." The latter is what allows us to suspend history and biography and matters of his style. He is both present and absent, both the epitome of self-assertion and the epitome of self-emptying and self-sacrifice. He is a world maker (like Bach) and yet acknowledges his nothingness before the worlds he creates.

The Odyssey, Lascaux cave paintings or Acadian fiddle tunes are more or less anonymous. We *submit to the allure* of these words, paintings, or tunes. But once we have discrete creators on the historical stage, we find them exemplifying both self-assertion and self-emptying. And scholars vacillate between listening only to the text and listening to the hero who creates it.

Another afterthought. Just as the full *Postscript* title resonates magnificently, so I, or any other writer or reader, can take our existence as resonating wondrously. We are the center of our worlds. Or we might be humbled by magnificence, and we find ourselves dust and ashes. We're humbled when too much is going on and too many wonders compete for our attention. Think of Bakhtin's notion of the carnivalesque.[24] To follow the mimicking tragic carnival of *Postscript* requires multi-vision. We look to this sideshow and then to that. The actual author (if there is one) gets out of the way and lets words or acts speak for themselves.

These are miracles and mysteries not in the sense that they contravene laws of nature or show gaps in explanatory schemes but in the sense that laws of nature or explanatory schemes become, under the impact of wonder or terror, beside the point—not for all time but for the instant of allure or repulsion. And for any full life, these moments are essential: sometimes miraculous, always mysterious, not to be denied or scorned. "Our most vivid encounters with reality come in experiences that shatter our categories."[25]

In a sense it's a miracle that you, or I, or your uncle and my neighbor are here at all—that we exist at all. We matter, and that puts us one by one at the center of the universe. We know simultaneously that our angle of perception can change and that each of us *also* can seem as nothing. And everything in between. So with the neglected music of *Postscript*'s full title. It presents a full "tang of life"—and can disappear, as vaporous as dust.

23. See "On Style and Pseudonymity," in my *Excursions with Kierkegaard: Others, Goods, Death, and Final Faith* (London: Bloomsbury, 2013), pp. 57–82.

24. See discussion of what I call, after Bakhtin, "the carnivalesque sublime," in *Excursions with Kierkegaard*, pp. 61 and 81, note 23.

25. Braver, "A Brief History of Continental Realism," pp. 261–289.

Chapter 9

"I CAME TO CARTHAGE"; "SO I ARRIVED IN BERLIN": FLEEING, ESCAPE, AND AUTOBIOGRAPHICAL MEMORY IN AUGUSTINE'S *CONFESSIONS* AND KIERKEGAARD'S *REPETITION*

Eric Ziolkowski

Religion, Fleeing, and Escape

Acts of fleeing (or flight) and escape are a well-known topos in the lives of numerous religious leaders. On at least one occasion, Confucius was reportedly forced to flee precarious political circumstances,[1] and, according to legend, Laozi fled westward from China near the end of his life. Prince Siddhartha Gautama, the Buddha-to-be, fled his pampered, worldly life in the palace—including his wife, his newborn son, and his concubines—imposed upon him by his father. In the Bible,[2] Jacob fled from Laban and, later, from Esau; Joseph fled from Potiphar's wife; Moses fled from Pharaoh; Mary and Joseph, with their newborn, fled from Herod into Egypt[3]; the adult Jesus fled from the Pharisees reportedly more than once, but according to two of the canonic gospels, at his crucifixion, he was taunted for his apparent inability to escape from the cross.[4] This point is exploited in the medieval Jewish, anti-Christian, pseudo-account of Jesus's life, *Toledot Yeshu* (The Generations of Jesus), which alleges that the "three hundred and ten disciples" who helped Jesus earlier to escape from Jerusalem to Antioch

---

1. One of the paintings in the 105-picture series, *The Acts of the Master*, by the Ming painter Qiu Ying depicts *Confucius's Fleeing from a State*. According to Donfeng Xu, who called my attention to this painting, there are variations about the story to which this picture corresponds. The *Analects* (15.2) offer a brief record and make no mention of Confucius's fleeing. The fleeing is mentioned only in essays allegedly by the Daoist philosopher Zhuangzi.

2. See also *Encyclopedia of the Bible and Its Reception*, co-ed. Hans-Josef Klauck, et al. (Berlin: De Gruyter, 2009–; hereafter *EBR*), 9:168–74, s.v. "Fleeing, Flight."

3. See also *EBR* 9:200–213, s.v. "Flight into Egypt."

4. Matt. 27:40, 42; Mark 15:30, 32.

from a mob of disapproving elders "could not save him" from being killed in Jerusalem.[5] The Qur'ān[6] suggests that Jesus did not need to escape the crucifixion because he was never crucified; rather, another man was substituted and crucified in his place.

Also, whole religious peoples or groups have fled from adverse circumstances. Just as the Israelites fled Egypt, so Muḥammad and his followers fled Mecca on their Hijra (migration, withdrawal) to Medina. The early history of the Church of Jesus Christ of Latter-day Saints (LDS, the Mormons) in the United States, a saga of persecutions of LDS faithful, entailed their flight with their prophet Joseph Smith, Jr., from Palmyra, New York, to Kirkland, Ohio; from Kirkland to Independence, Missouri; from Missouri to Nauvoo, Illinois—all of which culminated, after Smith's assassination, with the Mormons' westward migration or "exodus," led by Brigham Young, from Ohio to the Great Salt Lake, Utah.

An impulse to escape seems inherent in much of what is commonly construed as "religious." The English term "religion" and its cognates in other European languages derive from "one of two Latin verbs, *religare* (to bind or fasten) or *relegere* (to collect again, to go over again [as in reading])."[7] Neither of these terms evokes an image of fleeing or escape; if anything, they conjure a sense of being restrained or bound. Yet few religions lack an aspiration to some form of *transcendence*, a word whose root in the Latin verb *transcendere*, "to climb over or beyond, surmount" (*trans*, across + *scandere*, to climb), suggests escape. In Karl Jaspers's view, from the eighth to the second-century BCE in East Asia, South Asia, West Asia, and the northeastern Mediterranean, the simultaneous discoveries of the "transcendent," those pivotal spiritual, moral, and intellectual "breakthroughs" (*Durchbrüche*) that made humans conscious of "Being" as a whole, of themselves, and of their limitations, defined the "axial age" (*die Achsenzeit*)—those six centuries of unprecedented human creativity that determined the philosophical and spiritual directions of the world's major civilizations and religious traditions.[8] Related to transcendence, there is also *mysticism* in which William James said "personal religious experience has its root and centre,"[9] and whose relation to "transcendental matters"[10] has led it to be associated with *escapism* in a pejorative

---

5. *Toledot Yeshu: The Life Story of Jesus*, 2 vols., ed. and trans. Michael Meerson, et al. (Tübingen: Mohr Siebeck, 2014), 1:175, 177 [=2:90, 91]. Cf. New York JTS 2221, 41r.20–23, 41v.11–15 in *Toledot Yeshu*, 1:197, 199 [=2:105, 107].

6. Qur'an 4:157.

7. Gregory D. Alles, "Religion [Further Considerations]," in *Encyclopedia of Religion*, 15 vols., 2nd ed., gen.-ed. Lindsay Jones (Detroit: Macmillan Reference USA, 2005), 11:7702.

8. See Eric Ziolkowski, "Axial Age Theorising and the Comparative Study of Religion and Literature," *Literature and Theology* 28: 2 (June 2014), pp. 129–150.

9. William James, *The Varieties of Religious Experience* (Cambridge, MA: Harvard University Press, 1985), p. 301 [lec. 16].

10. *OED*, s.v. "mystic [adj., def. 5]."

sense. Thus, Max Weber, lecturing to a Munich audience during the German Revolution, warned against trying to escape the harsh political realities of the day through a "mystic flight from the world" (*mystische Weltflucht*).[11]

Why have I broached fleeing and escape in religious myth, legend, and history, as well as in the religious dimensions of mysticism and transcendence? This chapter compares the ways this theme figures in the accounts of two sojourns in a pair of classic writings by two dominant religious thinkers and writers from very different times and places in the Western Christian tradition: the *Confessions* written 397–401 by Augustine of Hippo and Søren Kierkegaard's *Repetition*, which appeared in Copenhagen under the pseudonym Constantin Constantius in 1843. I consider the young Augustine's move from his North African hometown of Thagaste to Carthage, and later, his flight from Carthage to Rome, in juxtaposition with Constantius's trip from Copenhagen to, and brief sojourn in, Berlin—a barely disguised retelling of Kierkegaard's own second trip from Copenhagen to Berlin in 1843, with echoes of his earlier flight to that city in 1841 after he abandoned his fiancée Regine Olsen. Through a comparison of several occurrences of the flight-escape topos in the *Confessions* and *Repetition*, as well as in Augustine's and Kierkegaard's lives, I aim to reveal a striking commonality between the two authors—though one qualified by a crucial difference. The chapter is concerned with the narrative techniques and strategies by which they construe their fleeing and escapes within the contexts of the existential workings of what Augustine conceptualized as *providence* and Kierkegaard/Constantius as *repetition*.

For the record, Kierkegaard owned a complete set of Augustine's works in Latin,[12] a separate Latin edition of Augustine's *On Christian Doctrine* (*De doctrina christiana*),[13] and close to sixty works by some forty-four thinkers and scholars who discuss Augustine.[14] Yet it is unknown how widely or often he consulted Augustine. From the beginning of the delayed, "serious reception"[15] of Kierkegaard's writings

---

11. Max Weber, "Politik als Beruf" (1919), in Weber, *Gesammelte politische Schriften*, 5th ed., ed. Johannes Winckelmann (Tübingen: J. C. B. Mohr, 1988), pp. 559, 560. Translation mine.

12. *Sancti Aurelii Augustini Hipponensis episcopi Operum. Opera et studio monachorum Ordinis S. Benedicti e Congregatione S. Mauri*, 18 vols., 3rd ed. (Bassano: Ex typographia Remondiniana, 1797–1804). ASKB 117–134.

13. *S. Aurelii Augusutini, de doctrina christiana*, ed. Carl Hermann Bruder (Leipzig: Tauchnitz, 1838). ASKB 135.

14. See the list of such authors, based on ASKB, in Robert Puchniak, "Augustine: Kierkegaard's Tempered Admiration of Augustine," in *Kierkegaard and the Patristic and Medieval Traditions*, ed. Jon Stewart, *Kierkegaard Research: Sources, Reception and Resources*, vol. 4 (Hampshire, UK: Ashgate, 2008), pp. 17–21.

15. Habib C. Malik, *Receiving Søren Kierkegaard: The Early Impact and Transmission of His Thought* (Washington, DC: Catholic University of America Press, 1997), p. xvii.

in the 1920s to today, the extent of Augustine's influence on Kierkegaard's thinking has been subject to widely differing views.[16]

Ideas of Fleeing and Escape in Augustine and Kierkegaard

As Augustine may have been consumed by aspirations of escape, his theological understanding of the human condition is epitomized by a figurative reading of the divine injunctions of Jeremiah 51:6a (Vulg.: *Fugite de medio Babylonis*; "Flee ye from the midst of Babylon") and Isaiah 48:20a (*egredimini de Babylone fugite a Chaldeis*; "Come forth out of Babylon, flee ye from the Chaldeans"), which he paraphrases in *The City of God* (*De civitate Dei*):

> And what do we warn, but to flee from the midst of Babylon [*de medio Babylonis esse fugiendum*]? Because this prophetic injunction is to be spiritually [*spiritualiter*] understood thus: that, advancing in the living God, by the steps of faith, which works through love, we must flee [*fugiamus*] out of the worldly city, which is assuredly a society of impious angels and men.[17]

In the *Confessions*, Augustine presents himself as a child walking the streets of this "Babylon" with his companions, floundering in its filth [*volutabar in caeno eius*], while his mother "had fled out of the midst of Babylon [*de medio Babylonis fugerat*]" (an echoing of Jeremiah 51:6a),[18] though she still "tarried in its outskirts [*ibat in ceteris eius tardior*]."[19] This imagery alludes to the opening of Psalm 136

---

16. Lee C. Barrett considers Augustine "responsible for much of the framework in which Kierkegaard thought" and finds the saint's writings to be "the source of theological tendencies that blossomed in Kierkegaard's writings." Barrett, *Eros and Self-Emptying: The Intersections of Augustine and Kierkegaard* (Grand Rapids, MI: William B. Eerdmans, 2013), p. 3. Cf. JP 1, p. 504, s.v. "Augustine" by Gregor Malantschuk. In contrast George Pattison avers that "Augustine was not a foundational thinker for Kierkegaard in the sense of determining the intellectual context of his work." Pattison, "*Johannes Climacus* and *Aurelius Augustinus* on Recollecting the Truth," in *International Kierkegaard Commentary, Volume 7: "Philosophical Fragments" and "Johannes Climacus"*, ed. Robert L. Perkins (Macon, GA: Mercer University Press, 1994), p. 255. The spaces in Kierkegaard's published writings devoted to Augustine's ideas are, in Puchniak's view, "minimal"; see "Augustine: Kierkegaard's Tempered Admiration," p. 13.

17. Augustine, *De civitate Dei contra paganos* 18.18.1, PL 41:574. Hereafter PL = Patrologiae cursus completes, series latina, 222 vols. (Paris: Jacques-Paul Migne, 1844–55; indexes, 1862–65).

18. As noted by James J. O'Donnell, editor of Augustine, *Confessions*, 3 vols., Latin text and English commentary (Oxford: Clarendon Press, 1992), 2:125. All translations of Augustine are mine.

19. *Conf.* 2.3.8. See also O'Donnell in Augustine, *Confessions*, 2:125's annotation.

in the Vulgate [= 137 in most English translations], where, in his later *Exposition* (*enarratio*) of that psalm, Augustine figuratively casts morally corrupt people as those dwelling "in the middle of Babylon [*in medio Babylonis*]."[20] Still appealing to the psalm's imagery, he distinguishes between the center and the outskirts or suburbs of "Babylon"—that is, the city (*medium Babylonis, et exteriora Babyloniae*):

> There are those who are not in its center [*in medio eius*], that is, who are not overwhelmed by such worldly concupiscence and pleasures. Those who, truly, ... are very wicked, dwell in the center of Babylon [*in medio Babylonis*], and are barren woods, just as the willows of Babylon [*ligna sterilia, tamquam salices Babylonis*[21]].[22]

Cicero's *Hortensius*, which Augustine read at age eighteen, filled him with a philosophical yearning to "fly back [*revolare*] from earthly things to [God],"[23] and the idea of escape in a theological sense crops up in the *Confessions*, which states that his mother's soul, at death, "was freed [*soluta*: literally, unbound] from the body."[24] This assumption that life entails the entrapment of the soul in an innately corrupt material body and worldly environs, from which it must seek release—or escape—through death, retains more than a hint of Augustine's earlier Manicheanism. However, in two of his *Expositions of Psalms* (*Enarrationes in psalmos*), he interprets biblical images of escape in ways consistent with the "spiritual," symbolic, typological method of scriptural exegesis he espoused in *On Christian Doctrine*, whereby Old Testament scriptures are read as foreshadowing the New Testament. For Augustine, Psalm 3's image of King David as he "fled [*fugisse*] from the face of his own son [Absalom] warring against him"[25] may refer not only "historically" (*historice*) to Jesus's withdrawal to the Mount of Olives after Judas's departure from the Last Supper but also "spiritually" (*spiritualiter*) to when "the Son of God, that is, the virtue and wisdom of God, deserted [*descruit*] the mind of Judas, when the tailed devil lay hold of him."[26] "We customarily speak in this manner," adds Augustine. "We say: 'It escapes me [*Fugit me*]', because it does not come to mind; and of a very learned man we say: 'Nothing escapes

20. *Enarrat. Ps. 136*, §6, CCSL 40:1967, lines 14–15. (CCSL = Corpus Christianorum, series latina [Turnhout: Brepols, 1953-].) All translations of the *Enarrationes* are mine, though I have consulted renderings in the series, *The Works of Saint Augustine: A Translation for the 21st Century*, ed. John E. Rotelle (Brooklyn/Hyde Park, New York: New City Press, 1990-); hereafter WSA.

21. Cf. Ps. 136:2, Vg.

22. *Enarrat. Ps. 136*, §6, CCSL 40:1967, lines 15–20.

23. *Conf.* 3.4.8. See also Robin Lane Fox, *Augustine: Conversions to Confessions* (New York: Basic Books, 2015), p. 84.

24. *Conf.* 9.11.28.

25. *Enarrat. Ps. 3*, §1, CCSL 38:7, lines 6–7; cf. Psalm 3:1, referencing 2 Samuel [2 Kings, Vulg.] 15:13–18.

26. *Enarrat. Ps. 3*, §1, CCSL 38:7 lines 11–14; referencing John 13:27.

him [*Nihil eum fugit*]'. Therefore truth escaped [*fugit*] the mind of Judas when it ceased illuminating him."[27] At the same time, Augustine reads Psalm 123/124, a jubilant expression of gratitude by the Israelites for God's deliverance of them from enemies, as referring to Christian martyrs who, from the afterlife, exult because they "escaped [*euaserunt*]" from worldly torments. "While we," in contrast,

> are here [in this world] and wandering about, we have not yet escaped [*perigrinamur, nondum euasimus*]. Certain members of this body, of which we also are, have gone before us .... And this the holy martyrs sing: for they have already escaped [*iam enim euaserunt*], and are in exultation with Christ, to receive at last the incorruptible body, the same that had first been corruptible, in which they suffered pains ....
> This psalm gives attention to the escapers [*evadentes*], that is, those who have already escaped [*evaserunt*].[28]

This suggestion that as humans "wandering about" in this world, "we have not escaped," hearkens back to the *Confessions*, Books 1–9, which chart the gradual "turning back" (*conversio*) by Augustine from his early spiritual "wanderings" (*errores*) away from God, from whose presence he, like all humans, had been alienated from birth onward as a "fallen" son of Adam.[29] Augustine ties this theme to the notion of fleeing and escape when, addressing God, he pictures himself as a youth, like the prodigal son,[30] "loving my ways and not yours, loving the freedom of a runaway [*fugitivam libertatem*]."[31] In this disparaging, retrospective, allegorical self-portrait as a young "runaway" or "fugitive" (*fugitivus*), Augustine approximates the existential evocations of fleeing (*flygte*) and escape (*undgå*) found throughout Kierkegaard's writings, journals, and notebooks.

To my knowledge, no major Western religious writer touches more often than Kierkegaard does on these two notions. Typically, he observes, the world regards fleeing as cowardly (*feigt*),[32] even though Jesus himself hoped once to escape his divinely ordained suffering and death,[33] and Kierkegaard acknowledged very early his own need "to go out for a walk to escape [*undgaae*] misunderstanding."[34] In

---

27. *Enarrat. Ps. 3*, §1, CCSL 38:7, lines 20–24.
28. *Enarrat. Ps. 123*[124], §§3–4, CCSL 40:1827, lines 11–18, 32–33.
29. On the *Confessions*' Christianization of the hero's physical wanderings in Virgil's *Aeneid*, see Eric Ziolkowski, "St. Augustine: Monica's Boy, Antitype of Aeneas," *Journal of Literature and Theology* 9: 1 (March 1995), pp. 1–23.
30. Luke 15:11–32. See O'Donnell in Augustine, *Confessions*, 2:160's annotation to the phrase *fugitivam libertatem*.
31. *Conf.* 3.3.5.
32. JP 3, 2921 / SKS 27, 663 (Papir 560).
33. KJN 4, 225 (NB2: 222) / SKS 20, 226; see Matt. 26:39; Mark 14:36; Luke 22:42.
34. JP 5, 5413 / SKS 27, 225 (Papir 261: 3).

different places, to cite but a few examples, Kierkegaard writes of the propensity of human beings to flee from themselves,[35] from dangers,[36] from severe trials (unlike Abraham),[37] from suffering (unlike martyrs),[38] from the devil (thereby reversing James 4:7's instruction, "Resist the devil and he will flee from you"),[39] from evil,[40] from heavy thoughts,[41] and from sinful thoughts.[42]

Certain historical cultures devised what Kierkegaard regards as distinctive ways of escape, which he subjects to scrutiny and criticism. For example, Greek Stoicism permits suicide not "to avoid great dangers"[43] but rather "as the ultimate escape route [*sidste Udvei*]."[44] However, Kierkegaard views this as self-contradictory, "ridiculous," and a "union of pride and cowardice"[45] because if Stoics are true to their conviction that sufferings do not exist for them, then it is ridiculous to kill oneself for no reason; or, if suicide is a sensible measure to take, then this proves that sufferings do exist for Stoics. Also cowardly in Kierkegaard's view is the avenue the medieval Catholic monastery afforded the person for fleeing the world.[46] Yet, even if Protestant Christians, unlike Catholics, "did not flee [*flygte ikke feigt*] from life in cowardly fashion, nor did Christ,"[47] the Protestant engages in "an even greater flight [*flygte*] from actuality" by conforming to a secular mentality all week and then, on Sunday, spending "a quiet hour" in church, having his or her imagination stirred by a priest's sermon, whose content stems from the priest's own stirred imagination.[48]

In Kierkegaard's view, the rigor of Christianity lies in the fact that every divine call is addressed to *one* person, "the single individual" (*den Enkelte*), and so any religious approach "that takes numerical form" amounts to "deceit that wants to escape [*slippe*] the rigor."[49] Thus, the modern societal process by which persons' individualities are "leveled" by the "crowd" is condemned by Kierkegaard for making possible "the most corrupt of all escapes [*Udflugter*],"[50] that of "every

35. KJN 1, 18 n.1 (AA: 12.1) / SKS 17, 23.
36. KJN 4, 303 (NB4: 30) / SKS 20, 303; and KJN 4, 346 (NB4: 118) / SKS 20, 346.
37. KJN 2, 121 (HH: 8) / SKS 18, 129.
38. KJN 8, 288 (NB23: 74) / SKS 24, 245.
39. KJN 8, 253 (NB23: 93) / SKS 24, 254.
40. KJN 8, 277 (NB23: 145) / SKS 24, 277; see also KJN 5, 120 (NB7: 75) / SKS 21, 115.
41. JP 3, 3408 / SKS 27, 353 (Papir 340: 8).
42. KJN 5, 118 (NB7: 74) / SKS 21, 113.
43. KJN 9, 177 (NB27: 62) / SKS 25, 176.
44. KJN 7, 234 (NB17: 83) / SKS 23, 231.
45. KJN 7, 234–235 (NB17: 83) / SKS 23, 231.
46. KJN 9, 322 (NB29: 36) / SKS 25, 319.
47. KJN 9, 458 (NB30: 82) / SKS 25, 452.
48. KJN 7, 493 (NB20: 172) / SKS 23, 485.
49. KJN 8, 209 (NB23: 11) / SKS 24, 211.
50. JP 2, 1996 / Pap. VII 1 B 158: 3. In the margin, Kierkegaard compares the individual hiding in the crowd to Adam's "hid[ing] among the trees—but still he did not escape [*undgik*] God."

individual who flees [*flygter*] into the crowd—and thus flees in cowardly fashion from being a single individual."[51]

Kierkegaard suggests that if an utterly unspiritual individual were to recognize the rigor of true Christianity's demands (sin-consciousness, self-denial, suffering, etc.), that person "would have to shun [*flye*, i.e., flee] Xnty [*sic*] as the greatest plague."[52] In critiquing the complacent bourgeois Christianity of contemporary Denmark, Kierkegaard charges that the self-styled, ungenuine "Christians" who inhabit "Christendom"—a term that bears strictly negative connotations for him—flee (*flygte*) from Christ as did Jesus's own disciples,[53] despite Jesus's earlier invitation in the Gospel, "Come to me ..., and I will give you rest."[54] Inhabitants of Christendom try "to shirk [*skulke ... fra*]" or "escape from 'imitation' [*slippe ... for »Efterfølgelsen«*]" of Christ,[55] and "everyone flees [*flye*] from [any rare, true Christian],"[56] and from everything "essentially Christian."[57] Kierkegaard points to any number of ways used to escape true Christianity: freethinkers escape Christianity by equating it with bitterness[58], human mediocrity devises "countless fads ... to escape [*unddrage sig*, evade] the Christian requirement"[59], Christian pastors who marry and have children are guaranteed an excuse or escape (*Udflugt*) through the need to support them[60], and state Christianity makes possible "all

---

51. KJN 4, 126 (NB: 215) / SKS 20, 126; see also JP 3, 3405 / SKS 27, 351 (Papir 340: 3). Related to the idea of escaping "into the crowd" is the idea that the individual can "escape [*slippe*] the strain of solitude" (KJN 5, 44 [NB6: 62] / SKS 21, 46) or "take shelter [*flye*, i.e., escape] in sociality" (KJN 5, 133 [NB7: 97] / SKS 21, 128). With respect to "the public," "there is only one way out [*Udvei*], that of shrewdness: to take care that one's personal life is as secluded as possible...—but Xnty does not rlly [*sic*] permit a person to live in that way" (KJN 7, 238 [NB17: 90] / SKS 23, 235). Related to the notions of the crowd, sociality, and the public into which the individual escapes is the idea of "anonymity," which offers "a way out [*en Udvei*, a way of escape]" (KJN 7, 438 [NB20: 68] / SKS 23, 430).

52. KJN 8, 80 (NB21: 135) / SKS 24, 84.

53. KJN 9, 304 (NB29: 10) / SKS 25, 302.

54. Matthew 11:28; quoted in KJN 7, 462 (NB20: 116) / SKS 23, 454; see also KJN 8, 473 (NB25: 44) / SKS 24, 466. The first three words of Matt. 11:28 appear beneath, and the entire verse appears above, Bertel Thorvaldsen's marble sculpture of Christ (modeled in plaster, in Rome, 1821) at the east end of Copenhagen's Vor Frue Kirke, where it was installed in 1833. As discussed by Roger Poole, *Kierkegaard: The Indirect Communication* (Charlottesville: University Press of Virginia, 1993), p. 245, two of Kierkegaard's 1847–50 *Discourses at the Communion on Fridays* (delivered in that church) reference this verse, which is the text for *Practice in Christianity*.

55. KJN 8, 516 (NB25: 89) / SKS 24, 506–507.

56. KJN 7, 328 (NB18: 99) / SKS 23, 322.

57. JP 3, 2455 / SKS 27, 676 (Papir 578).

58. JP 6, 6912 / SKS 26, 157 (NB32: 55).

59. JP 3, 2917 / SKS 27, 626 (Papir 501).

60. KJN 8, 40 (NB21: 60) / SKS 24, 44.

sorts of escapes [*Udflugt*]" for Christian teachers—for example, arranging that they remain personally uninvolved so that what they teach remains a function of their office.[61] Ultimately, Kierkegaard characterizes "doctrine," the Church, and the state all alike as "quibbles [*Udflugter*, escapes] and caprices" that distract or prevent people from following the "existential way" of genuine Christianity.[62] Near the end of his life, he pronounces "Christendom's escape [*Xsthedens Udvei*]" a "high treason"[63] and predicts that his country "shall not escape punishment [*ikke gaae Straf forbi*]"[64] for its moral corruption.

For all his criticisms of people's cowardly compulsion to flee and escape from Christ and everything essentially Christian, Kierkegaard remains fond of quoting and alluding to Psalm 139:7's suggestion that nowhere in the universe can the human being flee and hide from God's presence[65] or avoid the divinely imposed consequences of trying to avoid or escape (*undgaae*) or shirk (*skulke*) God's imperatives.[66] Just as in the *Confessions*, the pervasive imagery of Augustine's wandering away from God is counterbalanced by constant recognitions of moments when God's providence, often characterized as a "hand" or "hands" (*manus*),[67] worked secretly to guide Augustine back to the divine source, so in Kierkegaard, the countless exposures of the ways humans try to flee and escape *from* true Christianity are balanced out by his persistent reflections on the need— in his words—to "flee to" or "take refuge in" (*flye til*) God,[68] "[divine] grace [*Naaden*],"[69] or "the exemplar [or prototype, *Forbilledet*; i.e., Christ]."[70]

Also, like Augustine in the *Confessions*, Kierkegaard in his journal persistently questions and critically probes his own past and present escapes and his motivations behind them. From 1846 onward, he often comments upon significant escapes he has made or not made in the course of his life. For

---

61. JP 3, 3228 / SKS 27, 662 (Papir 559).
62. KJN 8, 217 (NB23: 30) / SKS 24, 219.
63. JP 2, 1766 / SKS 26, 352 (NB34: 40).
64. KJN 9, 416 (NB30: 37) / SKS 25, 411.
65. KJN 3, 197 (Not6: 29) / SKS 19, 201. See also TDIO, 24 / SKS 5, 404; EUD, 350 / SKS 5, 338; *Two Discourses on the Communion on Fridays* in WA, 172 / SKS 12, 288; CD, 272 / SKS 10, 291.
66. KJN 4, 217–218 (NB2: 198) / SKS 20, 218–219.
67. *Conf.* 3.11.19; 5.7.13; 6.4.6; etc.
68. KJN 5, 24 (NB6: 28) / SKS 21, 27; JP 4, 4486 / SKS 26, 159 (NB32: 60); see also KJN 9, 196 (NB27: 80) / SKS 25, 194.
69. KJN 7, 173 (NB17: 11) / SKS 23, 11; KJN 5, 9 (NB6: 3) / SKS 21, 13. More often than not, Kierkegaard, in speaking of "fleeing to" or "taking refuge in" grace, favors the verb *henflye* over *flye*: e.g., KJN 5, 52 (NB6: 70) / SKS 21, 53; KJN 7, 408 (NB20: 15) / SKS 23, 399; KJN 7, 172 (NB17: 8) / SKS 23, 170; KJN 8, 231 (NB23: 51) / SKS 24, 232; KJN 9, 156 (NB27: 44) / SKS 25, 157; KJN 9, 205 (NB27: 87) / SKS 25, 203. Consider also KJN 8, 493 (NB25: 67) / SKS 24, 485: "taking refuge in his love, concealed beneath 'grace' [*henflye til hans Kjerlighed, skjult under »Naaden«*]."
70. KJN 5, 9 (NB6: 3) / SKS 21, 13; KJN 6, 335 (NB13: 88) / SKS 22, 332.

example, in 1846, contemplating the breakage of his marital engagement with Regine Olsen five years earlier, he reflects that she "with girlish overconfidence reveals her enormous strength and lets me sense a way out [*Udvei*] of something that had been begun through a grievous error—a way out, to end an engagement, because she let me surmise that she was strong."[71] Later, in 1848, he confesses: "The minute I catch myself cowardly fleeing [*flygtet*] a danger into which [God] has willed to lead me, well, then the danger would be evaded—but to my own destruction."[72] In the following year, he asserts: "I do not escape [*slipper*] the rigor [of Christianity]."[73] In other instances that year, acknowledging that he originally thought of being an author as "a temporary escape [*Udflugt*] from moving to the country as a priest,"[74] Kierkegaard fervently thanks God "that he has not let me escape [*slippe*] but has held me to one single idea."[75] If he had not endured the "consequences" of his public "action" against the Copenhagen tabloid *The Corsair* several years earlier (i.e., public ridicule and humiliation), he "would have completely escaped the *double* danger [*Dobbelt-Fare*] with respect to Xnty [*sic*]."[76] Here he is alluding to the danger the Christian faces in contending *both* with the internal challenges of belief and religious self-transformation, *and* with the outer opposition the world mounts against anyone who pursues the Christian ideal of loving others.[77]

The confessional air of some of these later allusions might call to mind Augustine's *Confessions*. This is not only because of the formal, literary-generic kinship between those allusions and the latter work, as each one of them exemplifies *confessio* in the original Latin sense of acknowledgment, admission, confession. The *Confessions* is also recalled because, as I already suggested, the dialectic of fleeing and escape *from* genuine Christianity, versus fleeing and escape *to* faith, grace, and Christ, in Kierkegaard corresponds somewhat with that of sinfully wandering away from, versus being providentially drawn back to, the divine source in Augustine's *Confessions*.

Let us turn to consider the similar bearing of the fleeing-escape motif upon the account of Augustine's eleven years in Carthage in the *Confessions*, and the depiction of the second, return trip to Berlin by Constantius in *Repetition*.

---

71. KJN 4, 34 (NB: 34) / SKS 20, 36. JP 5, 5913 renders "*Udvei*" here as "way of escape."
72. KJN 4, 346 (NB4: 118) / SKS 20, 346.
73. KJN 6, 250 (NB12: 174) / SKS 22, 248.
74. KJN 5, 300 (NB10: 60) / SKS 21, 290.
75. KJN 6, 55 (NB11: 105) / SKS 22, 59.
76. KJN 6, 394 (NB14: 77) / SKS 22, 390.
77. On the "double danger," see also WL, 76, 81–82, 192, 194–204 / SKS 9, 82, 87–88, 191, 193–203. See also JP 1, 653 / WL, 446 / SKS 27, 410 (Papir 368: 7.b); KJN 5, 169–170 (NB8: 39) / SKS 21, 39; and PC, 222 / SKS 12, 217. For discussion, see Sylvia Walsh, *Living Christianly: Kierkegaard's Dialectic of Christian Existence* (University Park: Pennsylvania State University Press, 2005), pp. 101–102.

Augustine's Escape from Carthage; Constantius's Arrival in Berlin

Let us start with two textual markers: "I came to Carthage" (*Veni Karthaginem*); "So I arrived in Berlin" (*Til Berlin ankom jeg da*). The first of these quotations opens Book 3 of Augustine's *Confessions* and remains one of that work's most notorious sentences. The second quotation occurs a little less than halfway through Part 1 of Kierkegaard's *Repetition*. The statement by Augustine marks one of the most providentially determinative turning points of his life prior to his conversion; the statement by *Repetition*'s Constantius marks a critical juncture in what he calls his "Venture in Experimenting Psychology," which recalls Kierkegaard's pivotal abandonment of Regine.

The notoriety of Augustine's statement, "I came to Carthage," stems from the irony in its timing. The *Confessions*' first two books were largely devoted to depicting the condition of inherited, Adamic sin into which Augustine, like all humans, was born, and the consequent pattern of his compulsive "turning" and "wandering" away from God, from infancy through late teens. Augustine's spiritual condition then was one Kierkegaard would undoubtedly perceive as *fleeing from God*: "In my youth, I flowed away from [*defluxi abs*] you and wandered, my God, too far off from your steadfastness."[78]

In following this closing statement of Book 2, Book 3's opening recollection, "I came to Carthage," is ironic, perhaps even sarcastic, because there could not have been a worse place than that particular metropolis for a hot-blooded, "fallen" seventeen-year-old like Augustine to be. In Carthage, he found himself in "a frying pan of dissolute lusts [*sartago flagitiosorum amorum*]," where, desiring "to love and to be loved," he "therefore polluted the stream of friendship with the filth of concupiscence and beclouded its luster with the hell of lust."[79] As chronicled from Book 3 through Book 5, Chapter 8, over the next dozen years (371–383 CE), except for one year back in Thagaste (375–376 CE), Augustine remained in Carthage—as a student of rhetoric, then as a teacher, and all the while "wandering" farther from God through his association with the Manichaeans, his carnal relationship with his mistress, and so forth.

If *coming to Carthage* thus represented the descent of Augustine to his moral, spiritual nadir, the only way he could convert and be saved would be by *escaping Carthage*, though he did not realize this at the time. As he now confesses, his main reason for leaving Carthage for Rome was that he had heard that the students there were better, quieter, and more disciplined than the unruly Carthaginian students. Only in retrospect does he realize that it was God's guidance that persuaded him to go to Rome: "But you [i.e., God], my hope and portion in the land of the living, moved me to pull away from Carthage, changing my worldly location [to Rome] for the salvation of my soul."[80] Here, Augustine paraphrases Psalm 141:6/142:5,

78. *Conf.* 2.10.18.
79. *Conf.* 3.1.1.
80. *Conf.* 5.8.14.

a prayer for God to help the psalmist to *escape* persecution. However, there was a big problem connected with his mother Monnica: "Why I departed from this place [Carthage] and went to that place [Rome], you knew, God, but you did not indicate it to me or to my mother."[81]

The big problem confronting Augustine was, simply, that his clinging mother did not want her son to leave. How did Augustine solve this problem? He lied to her, deceiving her with the excuse that he was going to the docks to see off a friend whose ship was departing: "She bewailed horribly my setting out, and followed me all the way to the sea. But I deceived [*fefelli*] her, as she violently held me fast, that she might either retain me or proceed with me."[82]

The *Confessions'* account of Augustine's abandonment of, and escape from, Monnica at Carthage has been compared to Aeneas's abandonment of, and flight from, his lover, the widowed Carthaginian Queen Dido.[83] Required as a schoolboy to memorize the text of Virgil's epic, Augustine—as he now regrets—had learned to bemoan Dido's suicide out of love for Aeneas, while Augustine himself "died" from his failure to love God.[84] The parallels between that renowned scene of flight (*fuga*)[85] in the *Aeneid* and Augustine's own later departure from Monnica are patent. Both scenes are set in Carthage. In both, the hero abandons the woman he most loves in order to proceed to Rome—or, in Aeneas's case, to its future site. Both heroes' departures are divinely sanctioned: Aeneas is driven by fate, as the gods remind him; Augustine is compelled by divine providence of which he is unaware at the time. In both actions, stealth is employed: Aeneas's surreptitious departure is found out by Dido, who begs him to stay before admonishing him to his face; Augustine lies to Monnica, who likewise begs him to stay, and then he secretly flees and later learns that she upbraided him in absentia when she realized

---

81. *Conf.* 5.8.15.

82. Ibid.

83. *Aen.* 4.279–705. See, for example, Charles Kligerman, "A Psychoanalytic Study of the Confessions of St. Augustine," *Journal of the American Psychoanalytic Association* 5: 1–4 (1957), pp. 469–484; John J. O'Meara, "Augustine the Artist and the *Aeneid*," in *Mélanges offerts à Mademoiselle Christine Mohrmann*, ed. Lodewijk Joseph (Utrecht/Antwerp: Spectrum, 1963), pp. 252–261; Camille Bennett, "The Conversion of Vergil: The *Aeneid* in Augustine's *Confessions*," *Revue des Études Augustiniennes* 34 (1988), pp. 47–69 (see p. 61); Ziolkowski, "St. Augustine: Monica's Boy, Antitype of Aeneas," pp. 8–12; O'Donnell, *Augustine: A New Biography*, p. 55. For O'Donnell in Augustine, *Confessions*, 2, pp. 307–308, Dido also resembles the mother of Euryalus, whose words at *Aen.* 9.287–89 "are echoed in characterizing M[onnica] at [*Conf.*] 6.1.1." Fox, *Augustine: Conversions to Confessions*, p. 160, dismisses the Monnica/Dido analogy: "the comparison is not one which Augustine's language evokes and the details of the two occasions differed." However, this dismissal ignores the workings of Christian typological thinking, which never based itself on absolute equations between Old Testament types and their New Testament antitypes.

84. *Conf.* 1.13.20–21.

85. *Aen.* 4.282.

his deceit. Both women are chaste North African widows who grieve and weep over the heroes' escapes.

The two escapes differ in that the woman Augustine leaves behind is his mother, not his lover, and while the forsaken Dido curses Aeneas and his descendants and then kills herself in a spectacular manner, the abandoned Monnica not only will recompose herself but will later pursue Augustine to Italy and win him over to her faith before dying naturally and quietly. Moreover, when encountered once more, as a posthumous "shade" in the world *below*,[86] Dido sullenly refuses to speak with Aeneas, whereas Monnica, before her own death, will achieve through her conversation with Augustine at Ostia an ecstatic vision of divine Wisdom *above*.[87] Moreover, Dido's shade, when last seen, retreats to join that of her first husband, Sychaeus,[88] leaving Aeneas to be the one now shedding "tears afar" (*lacrimae longe*) in her regard,[89] whereas the moribund Monnica seems indifferent that her own body will be buried far from the grave of *her* husband, Patricius.[90] The *Confessions'* last mention of Monnica is when Augustine asks God to let her rest "in peace with her husband [*in pace cum viro*]."[91] If this image seems reminiscent of the reunited shades of Dido and Sychaeus, any notion that Augustine might be alienated from his parents' reunited souls in the Christian afterlife as Aeneas was from Dido and Sychaeus's shades in the pagan underworld is promptly corrected. Augustine explains that Monnica and Patricius, though they were his "parents" in this transitory world, are also his "siblings" (*fratres*) under the authority of God and within the Catholic Church, and hence Augustine's "fellow citizens in the eternal Jerusalem [*civium meorum in aeterna Hierusalem*]."[92]

In Book 5, the analogization of Augustine's deceitful escape from Monnica, to Aeneas's abandonment of Dido, brings us back to Kierkegaard. Not only was he familiar with the Dido–Aeneas story (to which he twice alludes in his writings, including once in *Repetition*),[93] but he also once deceitfully (and notoriously!) fled from a woman—not his mother or lover (*pace* Freud) but rather his former fiancée, Regine Olsen. On October 25, 1840, two weeks after formally terminating his engagement to her (October 11), Kierkegaard left Copenhagen, on his first trip to Berlin, to attend lectures by Schelling. From his journals, we know that he loved

---

86. *Aen.* 6.6.450–476.
87. *Conf.* 9.10.25.
88. *Aen.* 6.472–474.
89. *Aen.* 6.476; see also vv. 455, 468.
90. *Conf.* 9.11.28.
91. *Conf.* 9.13.37.
92. Ibid.
93. ASKB does not list Virgil's *Aeneid*, but *Either/Or*'s "A" likens Elvira in Mozart's *Don Giovanni* to Dido's wrathful shade in the underworld (EO1, 197 / SKS 2, 193). In *Repetition*, as noted by the Hongs (R, 368 n. 75), Constantius's claim that, in a Berlin restaurant, "Like Proserpine, I plucked a hair from every hair" (R, 170 / SKS 4, 44), seems to allude to *Aen.* 4:698–699, where it is said that Dido cannot die before the queen of the underworld, Proserpine, takes a hair from Dido's head.

Regine for the rest of his life, even after she became engaged to another man and married him. Yet Kierkegaard deemed himself unfit for marriage,[94] and as already quoted, believed that he had escaped "a grievous error" by breaking his engagement. His journals and other evidence suggest that he tried to lead Regine to believe that he was a "deceiver,"[95] like the "Seducer" whose "diary" constitutes the bulk of the *Either/Or* I, which Kierkegaard composed in Berlin during his first stay there.

This story of a deceptive escape from engagement also informs *Repetition*, which Kierkegaard drafted during his second Berlin visit. The book's pseudonym, Constantius, becomes the "confidant" of an anonymous melancholy "young man" in a predicament similar to Kierkegaard's: he was in love with a "young girl," the only one he had ever loved or ever would love,[96] but "a few days later he was able to recollect his love" and "was essentially through with the entire relationship,"[97] even though the relationship had awakened in him "a poetic creativity."[98] As he proved incapable of confessing this to her, "His depression entrapped [*hildede*] him more and more,"[99] and the young man continues to charm and enthrall his beloved. In turn, she loves him even more to the point that Constantius compares him to the prototypical Greek mythic captive, Prometheus: "bolted to the rock while the vulture pecked his liver, [he] enthralled the gods with his prophesying .... He bit the chain that bound him, but the more his passion seethed, ... the tighter the chain."[100] That this analogy casts the beloved in the role of the tyrannical gods who enchained Prometheus is confirmed when Constantius confides that he himself (unjustly) blames the girl for the young man's sufferings and for having "made no attempt to save him with that which he needed and which she could give him—namely, freedom [*Friheden*]."[101] Noteworthily, Kierkegaard's library lists a complete edition of Percy Bysshe Shelley's poetic works translated to German, including the lyrical drama *Prometheus Unbound*,[102] which depicts both the agonized captivity of the Miltonic, Lucifer-like titular hero (Act 1) and his subsequent release (Act 3). Yet this edition was published in 1844, the year after *Repetition* appeared, and Kierkegaard's sole, brief reference to Shelley's play is in an undated journal entry from that same year, 1844.[103]

94. For example, KJN 3, 226 (Not8: 20) / SKS 19, 230–231.
95. See, for example, the Hongs, "Historical Introduction," R, pp. xiv–xv.
96. R, 137 / SKS 4, 15.
97. R, 136 / SKS 4, 14.
98. R, 137 / SKS 4, 15; cf. Kierkegaard's self-description as a "kind of poet."
99. R, 138 / SKS 4, 16.
100. R, 141 / SKS 4, 18.
101. R, 143 / SKS 4, 20; see also R, 187 / SKS 4, 57.
102. Percy Bysshe Shelley, *Der entsesselte Prometheus: Lyrisches Drama in vier Akten*, in *Percy Bysshe Shelley's Poetische Werke in einem Bande*, trans. Julius Seybt (Leipzig: W. Engelmann, 1844), pp. 55–92. ASKB, 1898.
103. KJN 2, 280 (JJ: 280) / SKS 18, 228; referencing Shelley, *Der entsesselte Prometheus*, p. 57. The Prometheus myth is recounted in Wilhelm Vollmer, *Vollständiges Wörterbuch der Mythologie aller Nationen: Eine gedrängte Zusammenstellung des Wissenswürdigsten aus der*

In *Repetition*, mirroring Kierkegaard's relationship with Regine, Constantius now proposes to the young man that he transform himself into a trickster and deceiver, making himself "unpleasing to her," as well as "inconstant, nonsensical."[104] Yet the narrative soon shifts, as the young man simply disappears—rather than committing suicide, as he did in Kierkegaard's original manuscript.[105] Constantius embarks on what he describes as an "investigative journey" to Berlin, a city he (like Kierkegaard) visited once before, to investigate now whether it is possible to experience repetition of his past experiences there. If this idea seems farcical, it *is* farcical, as Kierkegaard remarks in his journal that Constantius "generates" through this journey "the mood for farce [*Possen*] and here reaches the peak of the humorous."[106] Furthermore, while in the original draft it was the failure to experience repetition of his first love that led the young man to kill himself, the role of Kierkegaard's own implicit literary alter ego now shifts onto the pseudonym with a doubled, repetitive name, Constantin Constantius.[107] From the moment Constantius records, "So I arrived in Berlin," he follows so closely in his actual author's footsteps that the apartment next to the Gendarmenmarkt where he stayed on his first visit to Berlin, and to which he now returns in quest of repetition, is presumably the same Jägerstrasse apartment in which Kierkegaard lodged on his Berlin visits and in which he composed the book *Repetition* of which Constantius is the pseudonym.

For Kierkegaard, repetition epitomizes a mode of escape we touched upon at the beginning of this chapter. His drafts of 1843–1844 associate this category in contrast to the Greek notion of recollection and to Hegelian "mediation," with "transcendence" (*Transcendents*) and hence the "sphere of freedom" (*Frihedens Sphære*).[108] However, on his second Berlin visit, Constantius fails to experience repetition, no matter how or where he seeks it. He finally realizes that "the only repetition was the impossibility of a repetition,"[109] because in the temporal world, "only repetition of the spirit is possible, even though it is never so perfect in time as in eternity, which is the true repetition."[110]

The same proves true of the young man. He rejected Constantius's advice to turn himself into a deceiver and instead fled his beloved in a manner comparable

---

Fabel- und Götter-Lehre aller Völker der alten und neuen Welt (Stuttgart: Hoffmann, 1836), pp. 1363–1364, which Kierkegaard also owned (*ASKB* 1942–43).

104. R, 142 / SKS 4, 19.

105. Compare R, 276–277 / Pap. IV B 97, 5–6 with R, 145 / SKS 4, 22. See the Hongs, "Historical Introduction," R, xx; Garff, *Søren Kierkegaard*, pp. 245–246. Garff sees the revision as reflecting Kierkegaard's "[loss of] faith in *Repetition* as an indirect communication to Regine" (Garff, *Søren Kierkegaard*, 246) after she became engaged to Schlegel.

106. KJN 2, 183 (JJ: 181) / SKS 18, 198.

107. Cf. the Hongs, "Historical Introduction," R, xx.

108. R, 308 / Pap. IV B 117, 289; see also R, 318 / Pap. IV B 117, 298; R, 321 / Pap. IV B 118.7, 302; R, 324 / Pap. IV B 120, 308–309.

109. R, 170 / SKS 4, 44.

110. R, 221 / SKS 4, 88.

(though not identical) to Aeneas's flight from Dido, Augustine's flight from Monnica, and Kierkegaard's from Regine: without saying a word to her, he snuck off by ship from Copenhagen to Stockholm.[111]

Blocked from the possibility of transcendent escape through repetition, Constantius, like the young man he unsuccessfully advised, and like the pre-converted Augustine, never escapes what Kierkegaard calls aesthetic existence—the first of the three Kierkegaardian stages of existence, twice removed from the third, religious stage, with the ethical stage in between. Symptomatic of this shared existential predicament is a remarkable kinship between the pre-converted Augustine in Carthage and Constantius in Berlin: their mutual attraction to the theater, which epitomizes the aesthetic because what it presents is not reality but only an imaginary imitation of reality.

"Everything Is Transformed into a Stage Setting"

As Gerardus van der Leeuw points out, the enmity of the Christian church to theater is historically grounded in an antagonism not between theater and religion but rather between two religions: the ancient, pre-Christian fertility religion of the *sacer ludus* (holy play), with its frankness and sexual symbols, and the new ascetic religion, which disdained "not only the ancient forms of the fertility play, but also … the lighthearted way of life of the actors, and, above all, of the actresses."[112] Augustine wrote of the honor in which actors in Greece had been held for their religious function as propitiators of the gods,[113] and, like him, Kierkegaard in his youth was an ardent devotee to the theater, and only later, with his deepening religiosity, grew skeptical of, and often critical toward, the art of drama.

In Augustine's time, Carthage was known for its theaters, a cultural importation to North Africa from Greece and Rome,[114] though tragedy and comedy had lost the eminence they had enjoyed in Greece and were displaced by such "lower" forms of dramatic art as Atelan farce and mime.[115] Allusions to the allure of the shows in the Carthaginian theaters later crop up in several of Augustine's sermons expounding the Psalms—for example, where he speaks of "the bustle of a city [i.e., Carthage] where shows are numerous" (*quid faciat ciuitas ubi abundant*

---

111. R, 192, 193 / SKS 4, 61, 63.

112. Gerardus Van Der Leeuw, *Sacred and Profane Beauty: The Holy in Art*, trans. David E. Greene (Oxford: Oxford University Press, 2006), p. 98. See also Hermann Reich, *Der Mimus: ein litterar- entwickelungsgeschichtlicher Versuch* (Berlin: Weidmann, 1903).

113. Augustine, *De civitate Dei* 2.11, PL 41:55–56.

114. See Auguste Audollene, *Carthage romaine, 146 avant Jésus-Christ–698 après Jésus-Christ* (Paris: Ancienne Librairie Thorin et Fils, 1901), p. 683.

115. Augustine, *De civitate Dei* 2.12–13, PL 41:56–58. See also van der Leeuw, *Sacred and Profane Beauty*, p. 98.

spectacular)[116] or observes of churchgoing Christians: "from these, if there is a public show, [many] will hurry to the amphitheater; these are above number."[117] In another *Exposition*, interpreting the symbolism of the olive presses at the head of Psalm 80 in the Vulgate,[118] he harks back to the years before his conversion, when his own weakness for the theater had mirrored his friend Alypius's passion for the gladiatorial matches in the arena.[119] Think of the "great spectacle" of oil being strained into the vessel, he urges: "truly, can the madness of the circus [*circi insania*] be compared with this spectacle [*spectaculo*]?"[120]; "Not insufficiently have divine shows [*diuina spectacula*] in the name of Christ held your thoughts, and kept you in suspense, not only about craving something, but also about fleeing [*fugienda*] something."[121] Elsewhere, he chides "many" among his Christian listeners for knowing of Aeneas's descent to the underworld more from stage productions of the scene in the theater than from the text of Virgil's *Aeneid*.[122]

All such passages betray the lasting impression left on Augustine by the Carthaginian theater scene. In his *Confessions*, just after his announcement, "I came to Carthage," he confesses, "Theater shows [*spectacula theatrica*] drew me away, full of images of my own miseries and kindling my fire."[123] Then occurs the passage quoted and endorsed by Kierkegaard in his earlier-mentioned journal entry of 1851 against the theater. In that passage, which falls in a preestablished North African patristic tradition of harsh, often vitriolic polemics against the theater,[124] Augustine questions why the audience at a theater play (*spectaculum theatricum*) is encouraged to take aesthetic pleasure in observing the sufferings of

116. *Ennarat. Ps. 103*, CCSL 40:1486, line 22. Here I adopt Maria Boulding's rendering in WSA, pt. 3, vol. 19 (2003), p. 123. Literally, the passage translates as: "what the city does where spectacles abound."

117. *Enarrat. Ps. 39*, §10, CCSL 38:433, lines 11–12; cf. Ps 39:6, Vulg. = NRSV 40:5.

118. The referenced phrase, *pro torcularibus* (for the winepresses), has no counterpart at the head of the corresponding psalm in the KJV and most other English versions, Psalm 81, with the exception of Douay-Rheims (the Vulgate's English rendering), where this psalm retains the number 80.

119. Compare *Conf.* 3.2.2–4 with 6.8.13. And see Boulding's annotation to her translation of this *Enarratio*, WSA, pt. 3, vol. 18 (2002), p. 152n. 3.

120. *Enarrat. Ps. 80*, §1, CCSL 39:1120, line 20.

121. *Enarrat. Ps. 80*, §23, CCSL 39:1134, lines 1–3.

122. Sermon 241; preached 411 CE.

123. *Conf.* 3.2.2.

124. See Tertullian, *De spectaculis*, PL 1:630A–662B; Cyprian, *Epistles* 1.8, PL 4:207A–212A; 61, PL 4:362A-364A; and *Liber de spectaculis*, PL 4:779–788A; and Lactantius, *Divinae Institutiones* 6.20, PL 6:710A–711A. Likewise the Roman emperor Julian, the Apostate pronounced the theater "the most noxious activity, the most reprehensible manner of spending time" (quoted by van der Leeuw, *Sacred and Profane Beauty*, p. 98; see also Gaston Boissier, *La fin du paganisme: étude sur les dernières luttes religieuses en occident au quatrième siècle* [Paris: Hachette, 1891]).

characters onstage without feeling any inclination to assist them. For Kierkegaard, this passage shows "what a self-contradiction aesthetic sorrow is, because a person involuntarily breaks off right at the point where it should lead one to action."[125] Several years earlier, in a similarly Augustinian, anti-theatrical vein, he stated:

> To want to observe [*betragte*: literally, to look at, to spectate] and observe, to be uplifted by what is highest by observing—observing suffering for a good cause instead of going forth into the true tension of actuality—instead of going forth into the true tension of actuality—instead of suffering, etc. …. This lust for observing [*Betragtningens Vellyst*] is just as sinful as when a debauched person is fearful of having children: in observing [*Betragtningen*] one wants to have pleasure and take leave of earnestness.[126]

Quite likely Kierkegaard was familiar—and sympathetic—with the formulation of the corruptive "danger" of dramatic art, specifically the danger of losing one's own self through the adoption of another's in "playacting" (*Verstellung*) by a character in an early comic masquerade by Goethe.[127]

As for Augustine, it was long after his Carthage years, during his mystic vision with Monnica at Ostia, that he experienced a full, albeit fleeting, extrication from the aesthetic perspective. In order to "touch" (*attingo*) eternal Wisdom by means of thought, he and she had to progress through the successive silencing of the flesh, the soul, and "all dreams and imaginary revelations."[128]

Constantius, in contrast, never flees from his own "dreams and imaginary revelations." Like young Augustine in Carthage, he is drawn to theatrical shows, albeit not tragedy but rather the farces (*Posse*) at the Königstädter Theater.[129] Yet, as Constantius indicates, Berlin had three theaters,[130] and another of those theaters

---

125. KJN 8, 282 (NB23: 156) / SKS 24, 282. Here Kierkegaard quotes *Conf.* 3.2.2 from Friedrich Böhringer, *Die Kirche Christi und ihre Zeugen*, 9 vols. [in 7] (Zurich: Meyer und Zeller, 1852–58), Band 1, Abt. 3, p. 110 (ASKB 173–77). See also Howard Pickett, "Beyond the Mask: Kierkegaard's *Postscript* as Anti-theatrical, Anti-Hegelian Drama," in *Kierkegaard, Literature, and the Arts*, ed. Eric Ziolkowski, (Evanston, IL: Northwestern University Press, 2018), p. 102.

126. KJN 5, 9 (NB6: 4) / SKS 21, 13. JP 1, 1051, in its own translation of this passage, renders "*betragte*" as "to spectate"; "*Betragtningens Vellyst*" and "*Betragtningen*" as "lasciviousness of spectatorship" and "*Betragtningen*" as "spectating." For Pickett, "Beyond the Mask," p. 113 n. 11, "*JP*'s 'spectate' better captures *betragte*'s connotations than *KJN*'s 'observe' (*KJN* 5:9)."

127. Johann Wolfgang von Goethe, *Das Jahrmarktfest zu Plundersweilern: ein Schönbartspiel*, in *Goethes sämmtliche Werke*, 3 vols. (Stuttgart: J. G. Cotta, 1869), vol. 1, p. 428; see also van der Leeuw, *Sacred and Profane Beauty*, p. 102.

128. *Conf.* 9.10.25.

129. Cf. van der Leeuw's point that early Christianity, in conquering the ancient world, found there "not … tragedy or comedy, but only the least elevated dramatic forms … mime and pantomime. Today we would call it vaudeville" (*Sacred and Profane Beauty*, p. 98).

130. R, 154 / SKS 4, 29.

stood—and still stands today—between the two churches on Gendarmenmarkt, right outside his apartment window. I conclude by quoting his subsequent account, suffused with "dreams and imaginary revelations" through which the moonlit Gendarmenmarkt, viewed from Constantius'/Kierkegaard's apartment, metamorphoses into a theatrical realm of dream:

A candelabra stands on a writing table; a gracefully designed armchair upholstered in red velvet stands before the desk. The first room is not illuminated. Here the pale light of the moon blends with the strong light from the inner room. Sitting in a chair by the window, one looks out on the great square, sees the shadows of passersby hurrying along the walls; everything is transformed into a stage setting [*Alt forvandler sig til en scenisk Decoration*]. A dream world glimmers in the background of the soul. One feels a desire to toss on a cape, to steal softly along the wall with a searching gaze, aware of every sound. One does not do this but merely sees a rejuvenated self doing it. Having smoked a cigar, one goes back to the inner room and begins to work. [131] *

131. R, 151–152 / SKS 4, 27–28.
* Earlier versions of this essay were presented in several different forums: Text, Religion and Literature: International Conference on Chinese and Western Traditions in Honor of Anthony C. Yu, at Fudan University, Shanghai, June 20, 2016; the conference, Kierkegaard, Augustine, and the Catholic Tradition, at Villanova University, Philadelphia, October 28, 2016; and at Renmin University, Beijing, June 16, 2017. A Chinese translation of the Fudan conference version will appear in the proceedings from that gathering.

Chapter 10

KIERKEGAARD ON ANDERSEN AND THE ART OF STORYTELLING

Eleanor Helms

Introduction: Hans Christian Andersen as Storyteller

In this chapter, I will consider Søren Kierkegaard as a literary critic—that is, as the author of a review of a novel by Hans Christian Andersen, *Only a Fiddler*. The review reads as a litany of complaints, targeting the novel's moralizing "maxims,"[1] descriptions of places,[2] use of epigraphs,[3] and unjustified representation of its hero as a genius.[4] Kierkegaard furthermore includes criticisms that appear to be directed at Andersen's education and personal development,[5] including a charge that he is "superstitious,"[6] though admitting he "as good as does not know Andersen personally."[7] These seemingly petty attacks have led readers to look for some deeper meaning in the review while at the same time acknowledging its failings. For example, Joseph Westfall has proposed that Kierkegaard oversteps his bounds as a reviewer but that the review nevertheless does the performative work of "poetizing" Andersen as a character, thus "alleviating the consequences of his [Andersen's] literary failure."[8] Joakim Garff has claimed that Kierkegaard does not himself accept the standards he puts forward in the review and that the review instead works mainly through contradictions between the text and its author: "My only (but unquestionably also my best) argument is that his text does the reader the favor of boisterously contradicting its author again and again—just as Kierkegaard's review brought the review itself into contradiction

---

1. FPOSL, 77, 82 / SKS 1, 32, 37.
2. FPOSL, 86 / SKS 1, 42.
3. FPOSL, 92–93 / SKS 1, 48.
4. FPOSL, 95 / SKS 1, 50.
5. FPOSL, 72–75 / SKS 1, 28–30.
6. FPOSL, 88 / SKS 1, 43.
7. FPOSL, 83 / SKS 1, 38.
8. Joseph Westfall, "A Very Poetic Person in a Poem," in *Kierkegaard Studies Yearbook* (2006), p. 41.

when he argued for a life-view he didn't possess."[9] The strength of the review, for Garff, is the philosophical problems it raises rather than any special insight into Andersen's novel. Bruce Kirmmse similarly shifts attention from the review to its author, proposing that the review is most importantly a self-critique, pointing out similarities with Kierkegaard's own life and authorship.[10] These interpretations share a reluctance to read Kierkegaard's review *as* a literary review, reclassifying it instead as some other kind of text: a creative work in its own right (Westfall), a deconstructive work with a performative element (Garff), or an effort at self-assessment (Kirmmse). On these interpretations, it would be unproductive to treat this work as Kierkegaard's presentation of the characteristics of a good novel or a critical analysis of whether *Only a Fiddler* is one.[11]

I will show, however, that Kierkegaard's apparently arbitrary critiques together compose a strong literary review in the traditional sense. That is, *From the Papers of One Still Living* assesses the extent to which Andersen's novel lives up to ideal standards of what a good novel ought to be—namely, a synthetic unity of form and content, of universal and particular. Moreover, the standards underlying Kierkegaard's critique of Andersen—including those that reference Andersen's development and interior life—are not as out of place as readers like Westfall and Kirmmse suggest. In fact, they are as old as aesthetics itself: they are consistent with Aristotle's standards set forward in *Poetics* and—unsurprisingly—show influences of the German Idealism pervasive in Kierkegaard's Denmark.

At the same time, the criticisms are representative of Kierkegaard's own philosophy, especially the need for a "synthesis" between ideality and reality that occurs in existence and for each individual. In this vein, Karl Verstrynge has claimed that Andersen's novel principally fails because it does not synthesize ideality and reality,[12] where "reality" must here be understood within the limits of the fictional work. I agree with Verstrynge and will further argue that this task of synthesis unifies the seemingly disparate criticisms of Kierkegaard's review, including the references to Andersen's individual life development. I

9. Joakim Garff, "Andersen, Kierkegaard—and the Deconstructed *Bildungsroman*," trans. K. Brian Söderquist, in *Kierkegaard Studies Yearbook* (2006), p. 99.

10. Bruce H. Kirmmse, "'Sympathetic Ink'—The Sniveler and the Snail: Andersen and Kierkegaard in Golden Age Denmark," in *Kierkegaard Studies Yearbook* (2006), p. 16; and Garff, "Andersen, Kierkegaard—and the Deconstructed *Bildungsroman*," pp. 94–95.

11. One reader who does treat *From the Papers* more directly as a literary review is Nina Christensen, who considers it—along with other writings, including Kierkegaard's journals, and books on stories that he owned—as suggestive of Kierkegaard's overall attitude toward stories and fantasy. See Christensen, "What Is a Child? Childhood and Literature for Children in Selected Texts by Søren Kierkegaard, Hans Christian Andersen, and Their Contemporaries," in *Kierkegaard Studies Yearbook* (2006), pp. 148–164.

12. See Karl Verstrynge, "'The Art in All Communication': Kierkegaard's View of 'Essential Authorship,' 'Essential Knowing' and Hans Christian Andersen's Skills as a Novelist," in *Kierkegaard Studies Yearbook* (2006), pp. 54–67.

will also propose J. R. R. Tolkien's *The Lord of the Rings* as a work that does meet Kierkegaard's standards and show similarities between Tolkien's own reflections on storytelling and Kierkegaard's. Tolkien discusses the role of a reader's belief or disbelief in a fictional world, offering new ways of situating Kierkegaard's *From the Papers* in the context of his wider philosophical concerns.

A Work of Art as One Thing: Aristotle and German Idealism

As Verstrynge has proposed, the most important issue in *From the Papers* is the synthetic unity or disunity of Andersen's novel. Does it enact a synthesis between the universal and the particular?[13] The insistence that a work of art must be unified, and that moreover such unity is a function of universality, is at least as old as Aristotle. In *Poetics*, Aristotle emphasizes that the characters' happiness or downfall ought to be logically connected to the earlier events rather than occurring by mere chance, as historical events do. The relationship of necessity guarantees that events are internally, not just externally, related:

> We have laid it down that a tragedy is an imitation of an action that is complete in itself, as a whole of some magnitude .... Now a whole is that which has beginning, middle, and end. A beginning is that which is not itself necessarily after anything else, and which has naturally something else after it; an end is that which is naturally after something itself, either as its necessary or usual consequent, and with nothing else after it; and a middle, that which is by nature after one thing and has another after it. A well-constructed plot, therefore, cannot either begin or end at any point one likes; beginning and end in it must be of the forms just described.[14]

By contrast, Aristotle expresses strong distaste for works whose events are only incidentally related: "Of simple plots and actions the episodic are the worst. I call a Plot 'episodic' when there is neither probability nor necessity in the sequence of

13. See Verstrynge, "The Art in All Communication," pp. 59 and 64. I disagree with Verstrynge's interpretation of ideality and reality as the "distant" (ideality) and the "proximate" (reality). Verstrynge focuses on the level of engagement with one's time and place, where both the poet and speculative thinker are characterized by withdrawal (p. 60). If we instead keep the focus on *From the Papers* as a *literary* review, Kierkegaard's claim will have to be limited to the relationship of the parts of the work to the idea of its whole—as both Aristotle and Kant emphasize—rather than the individual (author) to society. Verstrynge moreover treats ideality as equivalent to imagination (the poetic), which I would not wish to do. It is also important to clarify in what sense a fictional work expresses "reality" except as a correlate to the reader's belief in the way that I am proposing.

14. Aristotle, *Poetics*, in *The Basic Works of Aristotle*, trans. Richard McKeon (New York: Random House, 1941), 7.1450b23–34.

its episodes."[15] A whole should at all times be evident in the work as a logical (i.e., necessary) relationship of all its events. This logical relationship leads Aristotle to describe poetry as having "the nature rather of universals, whereas those of history are singular."[16] Complexity is desirable, but only as long as unity is not sacrificed, or as Aristotle puts it, "consistently with its being comprehensible as a whole."[17]

I will argue that Kierkegaard is holding Andersen's novel to a standard of logical necessity much like the one Aristotle puts forward. But Kierkegaard's idea of what it means to be a complete whole is further influenced by German Idealism. For Immanuel Kant and G. W. F. Hegel, enacting a whole means actualizing a unity in different kinds of elements, namely, producing a synthesis of ideality and reality, as Verstrynge has emphasized.[18] For the German Idealists, such a unity is put forward as a task, rather than a simple fact at a given moment, because the universal must be understood together with singularity. This is the case with beauty for Kant, where the universality of a judgment of taste must reconcile with the individuality of the feeling:

> The object is an object of liking *for me;* the same may not apply to others: Everyone has his own taste. And yet there can be no doubt that in a judgment of taste the presentation of the object (and at the same time of the subject as well) is referred more broadly [i.e., beyond ourselves], and this broader reference is our basis for extending such judgments [and treating them] as necessary for everyone.[19]

That is to say, our idea of the work as a unified thing organizes our experience of it without being directly "in" (that is, constitutive of) our experience.[20] German Idealism adds the expectation that this ideal will be (at least initially) manifested as a "maxim" or "principle"—that is, as a propositional statement that frames and guides the concrete. But in judgments of taste (beauty) for Kant, the universal

---

15. Ibid., 9.1451b33–35. It tends to happen, Aristotle finds, when the poet is swayed by the wishes of the audience and includes a happy ending that is not justified by the characters' personalities or the arc of the plot (13.1453a34–39).

16. Ibid., 9.1451b7–8.

17. Ibid., 7.1451a10–11.

18. See Verstrynge, "The Art in All Communication," p. 64.

19. Immanuel Kant, *Critique of Judgment,* trans. Werner S. Pluhar (Indianapolis: Hackett, 1987), §57, Ak. 339, p. 212.

20. Kant calls this unity "purposiveness," and it organizes our experience of beautiful things in both art and nature as well as our presumption that living organisms are wholes (rather than collections of parts). "Judgment's concept of a purposiveness of nature still belongs to the concepts of nature, but only as a regulative principle of the cognitive power, even though the aesthetic judgment about certain objects (of nature or of art) that prompts this concept of purposiveness is a constitutive principle with regard to the feeling of pleasure or displeasure" (Kant, *Critique of Judgment,* Ak. 197, p. 37).

principle must maintain its relation to contingent, concrete elements, especially a feeling of pleasure in the beautiful object, and so remains "subjective" (a feeling) *without sacrificing universality.*[21] Kant finds this combination puzzling and that it can even result in antinomies,[22] but he does insist in the end that aesthetic judgments of taste "can be based a priori on a principle that is subjective and yet universally valid."[23] For the purposes of this essay, I will take Kant and Hegel to agree on this point, with Hegel offering additional emphasis on this unity as a task:

> The True is the whole. But the whole is nothing other than the essence consummating itself through its development. Of the Absolute it must be said that it is essentially a *result*, that only in the *end* is it what it truly is; and that precisely in this consists its nature, viz. to be actual, subject, the spontaneous becoming of itself. Though it may seem contradictory that the Absolute should be conceived essentially as a result, it needs little pondering to set this show of contradiction in its true light.[24]

While it is odd to situate a universal historically (as something that comes about in time), Hegel argues it is not contradictory if we understand an end as essentially related to its beginning, as Aristotle does in the concept of purpose (*telos*), to which Hegel then turns.[25] Andersen, by contrast, skips over the task and challenge of unity. Kant and Hegel begin with the presumption that universals and singulars are dissimilar and then work to show how they can (or must) nevertheless be unified. Andersen helps himself to the universal and pronounces it concrete without taking the trouble to make it so. Yet an enacted, embodied synthesis is essential for a novel, whose material is concrete characters, events, and places who yet belong to a wider whole—that is, to the novel.

   A "life-view" ordinarily does the work of giving particular events their universal significance. Kierkegaard describes a life-view in a novel as that which "frees it from being arbitrary or purposeless."[26] The lack of a life-view in Andersen's novel is easy to diagnose because, like many novels of its time, it makes several obvious efforts to compensate for the lack. Kierkegaard recognizes the usual symptoms in *Only a Fiddler*: "But when such a life-view is lacking, the novel either

----

21. See especially Kant, *Critique of Judgment*, §38 Ak. 290, p. 155: "If it is granted that in a pure judgment of taste our liking for the object is connected with our mere judging of the form of the object, then this liking is nothing but our consciousness of the form's subjective purposiveness for the power of judgment, which we feel as connected in the mind with the presentation of the object."

22. Ibid., §56, Ak. 338, pp. 210–211.

23. Ibid., §57, "Comment I," Ak. 344, p. 217.

24. G. W. F. Hegel, *Phenomenology of Spirit*, trans. A. V. Miller (Oxford: Oxford University Press, 1977), 20, p. 11.

25. See Ibid., 22, p. 12.

26. FPOSL, 81 / SKS 1, 36.

seeks to insinuate some theory (dogmatic, doctrinaire short novels) at the expense of poetry or it makes a finite and incidental contact with the author's flesh and blood."[27] Andersen's novel in fact relies on *both* of these strategies. That is, instead of engaging in the task of bringing about synthetic unity, Andersen attempts to obviate the need for it in two main ways, just as Kierkegaard describes: that is, (1) he *pronounces universal "maxims"* as a way of simulating the relevance of the narrated events for the novel as a whole, producing an artificial generality that fails to satisfy the Aristotelian-Idealist notion of a universal made concrete, and (2) he *offers his personal guarantee* as author in order to motivate the reader's belief in the events of the story. In the next two sections, I discuss examples of these two compensating tactics Kierkegaard exposes in *Only a Fiddler*. Both strategies point to Andersen's recognition on some level of the importance of synthetic unity, but at the same time, they make his failure to realize this unity even more conspicuous.

Strategy 1: Epigraphs and Platitudes

Andersen's first compensating strategy is the repetition of universal statements or what Kierkegaard calls "maxims" and "propositions." Kierkegaard notes generally that it is easy for authors of his day to "rest satisfied with propositions that they have not yet sufficiently experienced,"[28] such that even talking about the importance of living life fully can take the place of actually doing it. Describing the "bourgeois mentality" infecting his time, Kierkegaard writes, "The error is not that it rejoices like a child at little things but that despite a contrast existing in its consciousness it clings to the little things and claims that they are just as good as the great, clings to this proposition and thereby forgets to enjoy the little things— and this latter feature is precisely the error."[29] Even when the repeated proposition attests to the importance of "the little things," which Kierkegaard does not doubt, the proposition becomes untrue when it takes the place of the enjoyment it purports to celebrate. Rather than sending the speaker or listener on a quest to enjoy these "little things," attention lingers on the proposition and, ironically, a deep satisfaction in how true it is, while at each moment the proposition is becoming *un*true by making it impossible to actually enjoy the "little things."

The discussion of maxims and propositions would have brought German Idealism to mind for Kierkegaard's contemporary readers. A "maxim," as a principle of action that may or may not be universalizable, is a central component in Kant's ethics. In that context, a "maxim" suggests something that has the potential for generality and ideality and so *could* be a way of linking a particular action in the present to an ideal concept of that action. But it might also turn out *not* to be universalizable but rather conditioned by particular interests (i.e., a maxim that is

27. FPOSL, 81 / SKS 1, 36–37.
28. FPOSL, 82 / SKS 1, 37.
29. FPOSL, 86 / SKS 1, 41.

merely hypothetical rather than categorical).[30] Even a *mere* (hypothetical) maxim regulates action in the sense of guiding and framing it but "could still be opposed to the objective principles of a practical reason."[31] Only rational principles achieve universality.

Some of Hegel's comments on "propositions" also shed light on Kierkegaard's charge against Andersen. Hegel writes in the *Phenomenology of Spirit* that in dealing with non-actual things (objects of mathematics) "there is only a truth of the same sort, i.e. rigid, dead propositions. We can stop at any one of them; the next one starts afresh on its own account, without the first having moved itself on to the next, and without any necessary connection arising through the nature of the thing itself."[32] For Hegel, even more than for Kant, universality is less a matter of consistency than of totality. That is, a universal is a whole with parts, where even logical necessity depends on this relation to a whole: "It is in this nature of what is to be in its being its own Notion, that *logical necessity* in general consists. This alone is the rational element and the rhythm of the organic whole."[33] For Hegel, to reconcile the concrete world of sense experience with the ideal world of concepts means to understand each singular object or event contextually, as belonging to a geographical and historical whole. At the same time, every (apparently) contingent particular thing must be recognized as part of the *necessary* development of Absolute Spirit.[34]

The "propositions" Andersen scatters throughout *Only a Fiddler* show that Andersen acknowledges the importance of universality, but these remain "mere maxims," as Kant would put it. On the other hand, in the context of such apparently universal statements, Christian's life is not presented as something that *might* happen to someone (possibility), or that *did* happen to an individual (actuality) but rather as essentially indicative of the fate of a true genius (necessity). Andersen directs the reader's attention toward such universal significance through interpolated observations about genius and geniuses in general. For example, after a character comments that Christian is "after all, a kind of genius," the narrator goes on to observe: "He placed, in truth, as much faith in this consolation as many another true genius who lays his fate in the hands of a wealthy man or woman."[35]

---

30. Immanuel Kant, *Groundwork of the Metaphysics of Morals*, trans. Mary J. Gregor (New York: Cambridge University Press, 1996), 4: 414, p. 68.

31. Ibid.

32. Hegel, *Phenomenology*, 26, p. 45.

33. Ibid., 34, p. 56.

34. In pseudo-sciences, by contrast, such as "astrology, palmistry, and similar sciences, what seems to be related is only an outer to an outer, something or other to an element alien to it" (Hegel, *Phenomenology*, 188, p. 314). These sciences can never discover any necessary laws because their elements are essentially unrelated to one another as parts of a whole. "Being externalities, they are indifferent towards each other, and lack the necessity for one another that ought to lie in the relation of an outer to an inner" (Ibid., 188, p. 314).

35. Hans Christian Andersen, *Only a Fiddler*, in *Andersen's Works* (Boston: Houghton Mifflin, trans. Mary Howitt, 1895), p. 106.

This commentary belongs in the work to the extent that it contextualizes the action, like a chorus in a Greek play[36]; Andersen's commentaries are more like "an exclamation mark saying nothing or a figure like those the physicians usually write above their prescriptions" or even just a customary "clearing one's throat."[37] The propositions are part of the novel in the sense of being found in it alongside other sentences, but they are not related to the novel's events in any *necessary* way. Kierkegaard here follows Kant and Hegel, as well as Aristotle, as discussed above, in taking the standard of universality to be necessity. While the events of Christian's life *could* happen to someone, they *need* not happen to Christian; that is, unlike in a Greek tragedy, they do not follow from some personality flaw nor do they serve to remind us of unstoppable forces in the universe, such as Fate. According to Kierkegaard, the events "may well be true in the subjunctive"[38] but "at the same moment as it ends up as a final decision on life's questions it contains an untruth."[39] And in fact, Kierkegaard goes so far as to say some events of Christian's life would be logically ruled out if he is a true genius. Of the events of Christian's life, "it is quite certain that not one of them, nor the whole lot together, would have been able to crush even a moderate genius."[40]

Kierkegaard observes that a work can lack an integrated life-view even if statements about life appear in the work: "For a life-view is more than a quintessence or a sum of propositions maintained in its abstract neutrality."[41] On the other hand, it does require a universal reach beyond the personal experiences of one individual. Particular experiences must be given context as belonging to a whole. A life-view, Kierkegaard emphasizes, "is more than experience [*Erfaring*], which as such is always fragmentary. It is, namely, the transubstantiation of experience; it is an unshakeable certainty in oneself won from all experience [*Empirie*]."[42] "Transubstantiation" is one mode of what I have here been calling "synthesis," where concrete (contingent) particulars take on universality and necessity in light of a whole.[43] It appears, however, that Andersen's novel is arrested at an early stage of a Hegelian development, in disconnected sensory experience that does not yet belong to a whole, though Andersen recognizes the need for it.

Kierkegaard takes acquiring a life-view to be a difficult task. Andersen's shortcuts are prevalent among their contemporaries, which is why Kierkegaard opens his review with a discussion of the times, complaining that members of the present

---

36. FPOSL, 70 / SKS 1, 25.

37. FPOSL, 93 / SKS 1, 48.

38. FPOSL, 88 / SKS 1, 43.

39. FPOSL, 80 / SKS 1, 35.

40. FPOSL, 100 / SKS 1, 55.

41. FPOSL, 76 / SKS 1, 32.

42. Ibid.

43. See my discussions of "transfiguration" in Helms, "The End in the Beginning: Eschatology in Kierkegaard's Literary Criticism," in *Narrative, Identity and the Kierkegaardian Self*, ed. John Lippitt and Patrick Stokes (Edinburgh: Edinburgh University Press, 2015), pp. 113–125.

generation understand the importance of a life-view but not how to acquire one. Rather than taking life as a task, Kierkegaard complains, his contemporaries focus on acquiring a life-view as an end in itself. They try to impose a life-view from the top down, through abstract reflection, rather than developing it up from the events of their lives. Kierkegaard's diagnosis is that his generation has read literature in which this happens successfully and then mimics the external form: "in short, this generation comes to make what that author has by virtue of having lived through it its task and to dwell too much upon the consideration of it as such."[44] A product or sign of a life well lived comes to take the place of the well-lived life. In order to allow a more natural progression, Kierkegaard recommends that a novel "ought as much as possible to be kept free of self-reflection."[45]

Joakim Garff, among others, has taken such warnings against self-reflection to contradict the goal of having an overarching life-view at all. In his discussion of Kierkegaard's own *The Point of View for My Work as an Author*, for example, Garff argues that Kierkegaard fails in his attempt to assert himself as a meta-voice that gives meaning to all the pseudonyms.[46] But Kierkegaard does celebrate such an overarching life-view in the novels he praises, whether it is expressed through a deep poetic mood, in the case of Steen Blicher, or through a harmonious interplay of the novel's events, in Thomasine Gyllembourg's work. "In any case," Kierkegaard writes of these novels, "there is also a unity here, which in its spontaneity significantly points to the future and which inevitably must grip the present age much more than it has done."[47] I have argued that the praises here are directed toward each work's completeness in a Hegelian sense: each part belongs essentially and necessarily to the whole, a totality. In this discussion of Andersen, as set forward above, Kierkegaard never questions the goal of synthesis between the universal and the particular but rather the artificial way Andersen sets out to achieve it.

Epigraphs point to the challenging task of synthesis while enabling Andersen to bypass the challenging part. An epigraph is a difficult way to begin a chapter, because "it ought to relate piquantly to the whole section and not form a pun on one particular expression occurring once in the chapter or be an insipid general statement about the contents of the chapter."[48] It "requires a good deal of taste, a high degree of inwardness in one's subject and in the temperature of the mood," he continues, before baldly concluding: "Now, Andersen does not possess these qualities." Kierkegaard gives Andersen credit for not presuming the epigraphs "have much to say," but he observes that each phrase, through repetition, has "developed such a great love of itself that it is continually seeking to fulfil its destiny,

---

44. FPOSL, 68 / SKS 1, 24.

45. Ibid.

46. See Joakim Garff, "The Eyes of Argus: *The Point of View* and Points of View on Kierkegaard's Work as an Author," in *Kierkegaard: A Critical Reader*, ed. Jonathan Rée and Jane Camberlain (Oxford: Blackwell Publishers, 1998), pp. 82 and 97.

47. FPOSL, 69 / SKS 1, 25.

48. FPOSL, 93 / SKS 1, 48.

to be applied."[49] The directedness of the epigraph toward application in real life is a worthy goal, but the goal belongs to the propositions themselves, which have taken on a life of their own, just like the "isolated historical, geographical, and statistical data, the isolated fragments of exhaustive knowledge," which have become a "*Selbstzwek* [goal in itself]."[50] Kierkegaard views the dominance of these unruly elements as weakness of will on Andersen's part, where his weak personality ("as one who has no power over his thoughts") is overshadowed by the comparative strength of the propositions ("as that which governs the character in a rebellious manner").[51]

Without synthetic integration, the elements of the novel are left more or less on their own. Kierkegaard goes so far as to suggest that Andersen so little understands the workings of such a synthesis that he actively interrupts this natural process— that is, the aim of application that the propositions have of themselves. He even speculates that Andersen must be blind or deaf to such organic trajectories, failing to appreciate them in other novels that have them, such as Gyllembourg or Blicher. These novels would inspire a "certain degree of reflection, which, however, is in no way carried through to any significant degree."[52] Rather than "carrying through his reflection, he on the contrary encloses himself in a very small space of it."[53] In a musical analogy, Kierkegaard writes that Andersen's heroes are "wrapped up in such a web of arbitrary moods and moving through an elegiac duo-decimo-scale of almost echoless, dying tones just as easily roused as subdued."[54] These musical tones are without resonance or reverberation: they reach out to nothing else but fall flat, not enduring beyond the instant of their creation. An epic chorus, by contrast, has a "deep-feeling sensibility for a larger totality."[55] When a reader attempts to find these strains in Andersen's novels, however, she discovers that the elements of the novel exist only in an isolated way, "without one's therefore being rightly able, as long as these remain in their bachelor state, to draw any further conclusions from them."[56] Without the guidance of a universal, the concrete details of the work are likewise isolated, as I discuss below. Instead of being situated as part of a "life-view," the relationship of one detail to another must be accepted on Andersen's authority.

49. Ibid.
50. FPOSL, 94 / SKS 1, 49–50.
51. FPOSL, 92 / SKS 1, 48.
52. FPOSL, 74 / SKS 1, 29.
53. FPOSL, 74 / SKS 1, 30. Kierkegaard expands this thought in *The Sickness unto Death*, describing a purely "sensate" individual as living only in the basement of his own, two-story house (SUD, 43 / SKS 11, 158). For a discussion of the damage this does to one's development as an individual, see Melissa Fitzpatrick, "The Recollection of Anxiety: Kierkegaard as Our Socratic Occasion to Transcend Unfreedom," *The Heythrop Journal* 55: 5 (2013), p. 873.
54. FPOSL, 70 / SKS 1, 25–26.
55. FPOSL, 70 / SKS 1, 25.
56. FPOSL, 77 / SKS 1, 32.

Strategy 2: Author's Guarantee

With the guidance of a universal, a single line in a novel can call a whole character vividly to mind: "The really talented novelist is able by one single oblique remark in the course of the narrative to remind the reader, as it were, so strongly of some character in the novel that he now suddenly appears once again as large as life before him and perhaps more clearly than at any time before—in short, from a single rib he is able to create the whole individual for us." But, as we might expect, "Andersen is far from doing this."[57] Rather than evoking an image, the novel's descriptions of places, for example, merely assert a relationship between one place and another, even though "without describing them in more detail, I have not thereby become the least bit wiser, except insofar as, prompted by the author's naming them, I now find myself, perhaps on the basis of my knowledge of them and with the help of my own poetic talent, in a position to take over the poet's role and poetically paint for myself a picture of their characteristics."[58] At best, the images provide raw material for the reader's own free fantasy. The same is true for the novel's characters and plot. Its main character, Christian, is represented as a genius, but Kierkegaard argues he is really a "sniveler who is declared to be a genius."[59] Kierkegaard seems offended by the plot most of all, where the characters' fates are so little connected to their personalities or choices (whether by "probability" or "necessity," as Aristotle put it). Rather than a "great sequence of appalling consequences, all pointing to the hero's final downfall"—as we find in Greek tragedy, for example—Andersen merely reports a series of events: "On the contrary, Andersen skips over the actual development, sets an appropriate interval of time between, first shows as well as he can the great forces and natural capacities, and then shows their loss."[60] The ending is essentially unrelated to the characters' choices or personalities, as we would find in Greek tragedy. Instead, "Andersen suddenly breaks off their undaunted wandering, sentences them to an arbitrary punishment, cuts off their noses and ears, and sends them to Siberia, and then our Lord, or whoever else wants to, must take care of them."[61]

In place of a necessary relationship among events, Andersen offers his personal guarantee as author.[62] Kierkegaard facetiously refers to this "guarantee" as the "absolute power entrusted to Andersen as poet (to do what he likes)."[63] In addition to a kind of dictatorial abuse of authority (i.e., arbitrary laws for characters' behavior with arbitrary consequences), the problem with this strategy is that it avoids the interesting *artistic* task of producing an object whose material elements

57. FPOSL, 90 / SKS 1, 45.
58. FPOSL, 87 / SKS 1, 42.
59. FPOSL, 88 / SKS 1, 43.
60. FPOSL, 80 / SKS 1, 35–36.
61. FPOSL, 79 / SKS 1, 34.
62. FPOSL, 85 / SKS 1, 40.
63. FPOSL, 91 / SKS 1, 47.

(here, the plot, characters, and themes) are internally related to one another as belonging to a self-standing whole.[64] In Andersen's novel, the elements "stand in so physical a relation to him that their genesis is to be regarded more as an amputation than a production from himself."[65] That is, they remain purely sensible and unmediated—a set of raw impressions. So what makes this a "novel"—a unified work of literature—at all? The reader depends on Andersen's say-so—that is, on his explicit declarations that these are features of one place or a character that endures through time and that the consequences do indeed follow from the characters' actions and personalities.

Kierkegaard focuses much of his review on Christian, Andersen's protagonist, who dies alone, ostensibly as a solitary genius. But Kierkegaard claims that Christian's life should not be taken as paradigmatic of the fate of a genius in the modern world because none of the details of Christian's life identify him as a genius, and therefore nothing follows from what happens to him that applies to a "genius" in general. Kierkegaard writes, "But it is quite certain that there is absolutely nothing in him to suggest an erstwhile genius. One does not even learn anything about his playing."[66] If the reader accepts that Christian is or represents a genius, then, it can only be on Andersen's authority. The reader's reliance on Andersen's authority as narrator becomes even more obvious when we read that he is a "pietist" and has "become 'religious'," about which Kierkegaard remarks, "To make him one of these is not difficult; for this Andersen needs only pen and paper."[67] With the same pen and paper, Andersen could as easily declare him to be a downhill skier or an arsonist, and from Kierkegaard's perspective, he might as well have done so, since none of these traits belong necessarily to or flow essentially from Christian's personality. The reader associates them with Christian's character, again, only on Andersen's authority.

Of course, we can readily distinguish between Andersen as a person in history and his narrator, as Westfall insists we must.[68] We make the best sense of Kierkegaard's accusations here if we interpret them as aimed at the narrator, who has no name other than "Andersen," rather than at Andersen as an empirical individual. On the other hand, Andersen is a well-known storyteller and has signed his novel by name. While Kierkegaard "as good as does not know Andersen personally,"[69] the voice of such a well-known storyteller is likely to be associated

---

64. This description is again rooted in German Idealism. See Kant's *Critique of Judgment* as well as Rachel Zuckert, "Purposiveness and Form: A Reading of Kant's Aesthetic Formalism," *Journal of the History of Philosophy* 44: 4 (October 2006), pp. 599–622.

65. FPOSL, 84 / SKS 1, 39–40.

66. FPOSL, 100 / SKS 1, 55.

67. Ibid.

68. Westfall examines a variety of such possible distinctions regarding Kierkegaard himself in "Who Is the Author of *The Point of View*? Issues of Authorship in the Posthumous Kierkegaard," *Philosophy and Social Criticism* 38: 6 (2012), pp. 569–589.

69. FPOSL, 83 / SKS 1, 38.

in the minds of readers with the novel's narrator, even if we—as philosophers or literary critics—recognize a distinction. This means that the ordinary reader's trust in Andersen's narrator is amplified by her trust in Andersen as a successful author. Likewise, Kierkegaard's experience as reader with the narrator of *Only a Fiddler* is shaped by other things he knows about Andersen—for example, that he likely considers himself a genius, perhaps misunderstood. While there is nothing wrong with writing from one's own experience (Kierkegaard certainly does), and an average reader makes an imperfect distinction between narrator and writer, a reader should not *need* to appeal to the author's empirical experience to explain the novel's literary features: the details should instead take their meaning from other details within the work.

Since Andersen's novel lacks the unity of a life-view, however, the reader is motivated to look elsewhere for their significance, that is, to Andersen's historical life. But this does not mean that Kierkegaard's criticisms are directed to failings in that historical life. Instead, what irritates Kierkegaard as a critic is that Andersen fails in the task of a poet. Kierkegaard here seems to invoke Aristotle's distinction, where poetry is closer to truth than history, asking whether the events of *Only a Fiddler* are "poetically true" or "historically true,"[70] where poetic truth would be determined "by the indeed invisible, yet therefore all the more real, one given in the concept"[71]—here, the concept of a genius Christian is supposed to embody. As with Aristotle, Kierkegaard treats the poetic truth as "more real" for the reasons above: poetic truth is necessary and nonarbitrary. The elements interjected from Andersen's own life, without undergoing poetic transformation, lack this necessity (i.e., are not required by the work itself), and for that reason, lack universality. While they might *not* be failings in the empirical world (historical), they become failings when they intrude in the universal (poetic).

This interpretation makes sense of what might otherwise be Kierkegaard's oddest charge, namely, that Andersen is superstitious. A superstitious person takes a single experience to have universal significance even when there is no logical or causal relation between them. Andersen is too quick in "ascribing to a single chance occurrence, pregnant with foreboding, [significance] for the whole of life."[72] The events of Christian's life are not unbelievable or impossible in themselves (there may even be a real person whose history matches Christian's), but the events do not have the universal implications Andersen accords them as narrator. The result is that the novel never gains any momentum. Rather than a full plot, there are mere "incidents," where time has no "deeper organic relation" to the characters[73] and which Kierkegaard describes as "merely marching on the spot" and "a fixed staring at a single object."[74] The result is that even small

70. FPOSL, 95 / SKS 1, 50.
71. FPOSL, 94 / SKS 1, 50.
72. FPOSL, 88 / SKS 1, 43.
73. FPOSL, 89 / SKS 1, 44.
74. FPOSL, 87 / SKS 1, 42.

occurrences, "some depressing circumstance, a single little humiliation," have a disproportionate effect "in the power he attributes to this to be able to crush even the true genius."[75] A true genius, Kierkegaard protests, should be able to weather such humiliations, "for a genius is not a rush candle that goes out in a puff of air but a conflagration that the storm only incites."[76] Only a superstitious person, who attributes significant effects to insignificant causes, could allow his genius to be toppled by such minor events.

The motivation to find meaning in small details has a legitimate basis. Reading a story always requires seeing its details in light of the work as a whole. In this case, however, the wider awareness of context should prevent fixation on any one part. We can accept this failing in an individual character: "It is something that may well happen to this or that really gifted individual in his development as he, with a morbid irritability and without a survey of his course, is tempted to ascribe too much to a chance occurrence."[77] But it is unacceptable at the level of the novel as a whole, as the perspective of the narrator. If a reader recognizes it as a flaw or blindness in the character, the failing "lets itself be brought into harmony with the presentiment properly rectified poetically," much as an Aristotelian audience member can pity a tragic hero and so acknowledge implicitly that their fate is in fact tragic rather than deserved. Such a "presentiment, precisely in the certainty of having a whole, can never become hypnotized by details."[78] Yet even at the narrative level, such chance occurrence has the last word, offering no opportunity for higher-level reflection. The work as a "whole" is no more mature and attains no more insight than the character. "In a novel there must be an immortal spirit that survives the whole. In Andersen, however, there is absolutely no grip on things: when the hero dies, Andersen dies, too."[79]

So does a novel require a stronger narrator or a weaker one? While Andersen has "full authority [over the characters] to let them go out of their minds," the third-person narrator must offer perspective on the madness without going mad himself[80] or letting any single event have undue consequences. Andersen must disappear from each particular part of the work in order to be "omnipresent" in it as a guide.[81] Kierkegaard's complaints appear contradictory but make sense in context: Andersen must become less of an individual *person*, a character *in* the work, in order to become a *personality*, the narrator *of* the work.

75. FPOSL, 87 / SKS 1, 43.

76. FPOSL, 88 / SKS 1, 43.

77. Ibid.

78. Ibid.

79. FPOSL, 83 / SKS 1, 38.

80. Ibid.

81. See CI, 324 / SKS 1, 353.

Authorship, Interpretation, and Teleology: Kierkegaard and Contemporary Debates

What implications do Kierkegaard's criticisms have for contemporary discussions of authorship and interpretation? Kierkegaard's view at least rules out strong actual intentionalism, even variations such as Noël Carroll's that restrict legitimate interpretations to those born out by the text.[82] In this case, Kierkegaard is confident from evidence in the text that Andersen intends Christian to embody a modern genius (because the narrator directly refers to him in this way). But what interests Kierkegaard philosophically is that Andersen's declarations fail to make Christian *actually* a genius (within the limits of the novel) because he is not *believably* a genius (again, within the limits of the novel). That is, the content of the novel does not support the narrator's treatment of Christian as a genius, even though this treatment occurs in the work itself (by Andersen as narrator). I will further examine the relationship between actuality and believability below.

It does not follow from the rejection of strong author intentionalism, however, that Kierkegaard accepts Michel Foucault's or Roland Barthes's "death of the author" thesis, where the author's absence is importantly *felt* (e.g., as Daniel Berthold suggests, as an encounter with uncanniness).[83] Kierkegaard is not advocating for authorial absence so much as pointing out—as critic—that a particular work fails to have the right authorial presence. We can read *From the Papers* coherently as a call for a mature, holistic authorial presence rather than a celebration of a work that must be composed into a novel by its readers (or by Kierkegaard, as Westfall has proposed).[84] I have also shown one way in which Kierkegaard's criticisms, even those apparently directed at Andersen as a person, instead point to a problem with the novel (that is, its lack of higher-level reflection on the characters' fates). So a defense of Andersen as a person (e.g., as someone who may himself have a life-view but has not incorporated it into the novel) would be misplaced.[85]

I have argued that Kierkegaard's critiques of Andersen's "compensating strategies" instead confirm the traditional importance of unity in a work as the standard for its goodness, as found in Aristotle and Hegel. I suggested that this kind of unity would appropriately be experienced by the reader as acceptance of the actions and events of the novel without requiring Andersen's stop-gap strategies. In the last section, I will show that such acceptance is its own kind of belief, or what I will call "literary belief," that is similar in structure to ordinary belief in the

---

82. Noël Carroll, "Interpretation and Intention: The Debate between Hypothetical and Actual Intentionalism," *Metaphilosophy* 31: 1/2 (January 2000), pp. 75–95.

83. Daniel Berthold, "A Question of Style: Hegel and Kierkegaard on Language, Communication, and the Ethics of Authorship," *Clio: A Journal of Literature, History, and the Philosophy of History* 35: 2 (2006), p. 189.

84. Westfall, "A Very Poetic Person in a Poem," pp. 50, 53.

85. Ibid., p. 48.

physical world or what I will here call "perceptual belief." I will briefly suggest in closing that both types of belief are closely related to religious belief as well.

Literary Belief and Perceptual Belief

Kierkegaard claims that Andersen's Christian is not really a genius (or religious) even though Andersen as narrator says that he is. But what does a storyteller do other than declare that a character is tall, a skilled archer, or frightened of storms? What does a reader ever have to go on other than the author's say-so—that is, the author's designation of a trait as belonging to the fictional character? As developed above, Kierkegaard's view is that each element "could have significance only insofar as it is understood as a situation,"[86] which can only happen when the novel's elements are internally related in necessary ways. For Kierkegaard, I will now show, necessary relations matter because they are the ones that motivate belief.

We understand what they mean when someone says they do not find a character's actions "believable," and we ordinarily take this to mean "in the context of the story." Most of us have experienced this kind of disappointment, whether in movies or books, when characters behave in arbitrary ways (relative to their fictional personalities) or when an ending does not integrate well with the rest of the story. A reader's belief in a fictional world is remarkably similar to belief in the real, perceptual world or what I am calling "perceptual belief": we accept things we perceive through our senses because (1) they are continuous with other things we sense and (2) we anticipate that this continuity extends beyond what we have directly sensed. In other words, a believable fictional world simulates the depth and determinability of the real world.[87] A reader must believe there "is" more to the story than the narrator directly tells.

J. R. R. Tolkien reflected extensively on the importance of a reader's belief and its relation to the depth of the fictional world. Tolkien is somewhat unusual, however, because the depth is not merely simulated: much of the prehistory and geographical horizons of Middle Earth are actually described in *The Silmarilion*. Verlyn Flieger emphasizes that Tolkien considered this temporal and spatial background so essential that he at first refused to have *The Lord of the Rings* published without *The Silmarilion*.[88] He considered the epic history to be the "vast

---

86. FPOSL, 81 / SKS 1, 37.

87. I have discussed the importance of fictional worlds in "Closed Drawers and Hidden Faces: Arendt's Kantian Defense of Fictional Worlds," *Philosophy and Literature* 39: 1A (September 2015), pp. 16–31.

88. See Verlyn Flieger, *Splintered Light: Logos and Language in Tolkien's World* (Kent, OH: Kent State University Press, 2002), p. xv, referencing an exchange with Milton Waltman in 1951, collected in *The Letters of J. R. R. Tolkien*, ed. Humphrey Carpenter, with Christopher Tolkien (New York: Houghton Mifflin, 1981), pp. 136–7.

backcloths" that were essential to making that happy ending believable. Tolkien's goal was to:

> make a more or less connected legend, ranging from the large and cosmogonic, to the level of romantic fairy-story—the larger founded on the lesser in contact with the earth, the lesser drawing splendour from the vast backcloths—which I could dedicate simply to: to England; to my country. ... I would draw some of the great tales in fullness, and leave many only placed in the scheme and sketched. The cycles would be linked to a majestic whole, and yet leave scope for other minds and hands, wielding paint and music and drama. Absurd.[89]

The events in *The Lord of the Rings* provide background for additional literature, including *The Hobbit* but also more obscure additions such as "The Seabell," a poem purportedly "found on loose leaves" or "written carelessly in margins and blank spaces" in the "Red Book," which is "Bilbo's memoir continued by Frodo and others."[90] Verlyn Flieger explains, "Their larger function, of course, is to add to the sub-creative reality of Middle-earth."[91] Such "found" fragments, coupled with Tolkien's efforts to develop the prehistory of Middle Earth and the language of Elvish, further the illusion of a complete world, one that—like the real world—could be infinitely further determined. When *The Silmarilion* was finally published twenty years later (in 1977), it offered an "immensely greater perspective, a suddenly increased depth of field ..., that same illusion of depth that he found and praised in *Beowulf*, the illusion of 'surveying a past ... noble and fraught with a deep significance—a past which itself had a depth and reached backward into a dark antiquity of sorrow' (*MC* 27)."[92] Flieger writes that before its publication: "Critics lauding the richness of Tolkien's world and the detail and dense texture of its background did not altogether appreciate that what they had was only one enlarged corner of a vast canvas, a corner meaningful in itself but with much greater meaning as part of the whole and an extension of it."[93]

In language familiar to both German Idealism and Kierkegaard, Flieger notes that what is explicit in *The Silmarilion* (such as the ongoing history of Middle Earth) is merely implicit in *The Lord of the Rings*. It would of course be impossible and undesirable to make all events in the history of Middle Earth explicit. But the suggestion is not that the reader can fill it in as she chooses. Instead, the uncertainty adds to the character of reality of the stories taken together. As in real life, there is always a horizon that limits our vision, no matter how much we fill in.[94]

John Davenport has developed a relationship between Tolkien and Kierkegaard through the concept of *eucatastrophe*, laying a groundwork for further connections

---

89. Tolkien, *Silmarilion*, p. xii, quoted in Verlyn Flieger, "Introduction," p. xiv.
90. Flieger, *Splintered Light*, p. 161.
91. Ibid.
92. Ibid., p. xvi.
93. Ibid.
94. Ibid., p. 165.

such as the one I am proposing between "literary belief" and religious belief. Tolkien describes literary belief (i.e., "secondary belief") as the reader's motivation to accept an event or detail as real within the fictional work. Tolkien emphasizes that the "depth" of the fictional world is essential for such acceptance. For Tolkien, the art of cultivating such belief happens through careful laying of backcloths that prefigure but do not guarantee the happy ending.[95] Davenport has made good use of Tolkien's explicit definition of *eucatastrophe* as a "sudden and miraculous grace, never to be counted on to recur."[96] But he does not fully develop the importance of the "backcloths" that create such anticipations and, in this case, a history of prior disappointments (many of the characters in *The Silmarilion* do *not* get happy endings). Such disappointments add gravity and significance to the happy ending of *The Lord of the Rings*. Backcloths color and qualify the way a reader encounters *eucatastrophes* as "sudden and miraculous" and yet accepts them as real within the story.[97]

Andersen's novels fail to create such meaningful expectations, and even when created, they are then interrupted or forgotten. Rather than a rich, continuous context, Andersen offers a series of explicit interruptions in the form of universal reflections on the characters' struggles:

> But scarcely are these [adversities] shipped to that world and incorporated there in new individuals before the nisse already loudly proclaims his arrival there, in other words, before the whole mob of depressing reflections about life—either in the form of a blind fate or in the form of the evil in the world (i.e., the actual world) that chokes the good—grow up, with a luxuriance like the thistles in the Gospel, while Andersen sleeps.[98]

The result is the opposite of the expansiveness and depth cultivated by Tolkien, where "instead of carrying through his reflection, he on the contrary encloses himself in a very small space of it."[99] In stark contrast with Tolkien's novels, *Only a Fiddler* offers no unoccupied spaces that might be used playfully, that seem to exist beyond what the author explicitly describes.

Implied background space is essential for belief in the real world of perceptual experience as well—that is, for what I am calling "perceptual belief." Sebastian

---

95. As another example, see Jorge Luis Borges, "Narrative Art and Magic," discussed in my "Closed Drawers and Hidden Faces," pp. 16–31.

96. J. R. R. Tolkien, "On Fairy-Stories," in *The Monsters and the Critics and Other Essays*, ed. C. Tolkien (London, 1983), p. 153, quoted in Davenport, "Faith as Eschatological Trust in *Fear and Trembling*," in *Ethics, Love, and Faith in Kierkegaard: Philosophical Engagements*, ed. Edward F. Mooney (Bloomington: Indiana University Press, 2008), p. 204.

97. For an in-depth discussion of the importance of "backcloths" for Tolkien's work, see Flieger, *Splintered Light*, pp. xv–xvi.

98. FPOSL, 75 / SKS 1, 30.

99. FPOSL, 74 / SKS 1, 30.

Luft describes this basic belief in a world that underlies all particular doubts and beliefs. Even in doubt, he writes,

> If I am doubting a certain thing, if my perception is disappointed, even completely annulled—if I, say, believe over there in the distance there is something and it turns out to be a mere shadow cast by something else—I still believe that the surrounding world "around" this annulment exists. Even disappointments in certain things will not cross out the belief that the world itself will continue to exist.[100]

I can doubt or negate specific beliefs without calling into doubt my underlying belief in reality. That is, basic perceptual belief (i.e., belief in the reality of the physical world one perceives) endures through the experience of many errors and illusions. Similarly, a good storyteller creates a world in which a reader tolerates surprises and disappointments while maintaining her underlying belief in the fictional world. Both perceptual (primary) belief and literary (secondary) belief take place in a context, and this background sustains belief in their respective (primary or secondary) reality.

This background, understood as a whole in which particular events and details take place, clarifies how Kierkegaard's review draws on existing ideas of what makes a novel good (from Aristotle and Hegel) to evaluate *Only a Fiddler*. At the same time, Kierkegaard is laying foundations for his own later work. Elsewhere I have emphasized the importance of "transfiguration" [*forklarelse*] of everyday life in a novel as a model for mature selfhood.[101] Kierkegaard is already using similar language ("transubstantiation of experience"[102]) here at the beginning of his authorship—even prior to its official beginning, as he claims in *The Point of View*.[103] Even in this aesthetic work, at the margin of Kierkegaard's own authorship, we begin to see indirectly what Kierkegaard means by faith. Religious belief is a task for a lifetime; even literary belief is not so easy to achieve.

---

100. Sebastian Luft, "Husserl's Phenomenological Discovery of the Natural Attitude," *Continental Philosophy Review* 31 (1998), pp. 162–163.

101. See "The End in the Beginning," pp. 114–117, as well as John Davenport's response and discussion of the importance of the term in "The Virtue of Ambivalence: Wholeheartedness as Existential *Telos* and the Unwillable Completion of Narratives," in *Narrative, Identity and the Kierkegaardian Self*, pp. 158–160.

102. FPOSL, 76 / SKS 1, 32.

103. Garff discusses this omission in "The Eyes of Argus," p. 80.

Chapter 11

ON "S.K.": DECONSTRUCTING SIGNATURE(S) IN KIERKEGAARD AND SARAH KOFMAN

Joseph Westfall

Of the ironic elements within Kierkegaard's corpus, few are more obviously and importantly ironic than his odd practice of bifurcated authorship, of eliding or evading authorial responsibility through the use of pseudonyms and anonyms, while also employing in a somewhat constrained manner his own name as author. The signed works are only apparently less problematic for readers of Kierkegaard than are the pseudonymous ones, however, as I have noted elsewhere.[1] While the history of world literature offers many examples of authors who write pseudonymously and authors who write only ever in their own names, Kierkegaard stands nearly alone in his combination of these two ascriptive strategies—not to mention his unique use of multiple, interrelated, and semi-self-aware anonyms and pseudonyms. Kierkegaardian pseudonymity is frequently remarked upon and often studied, as is its difference from the "signed" works, but the precise nature of Kierkegaardian signature itself—of what it means for Kierkegaard to sign "his own" name to a work, of what a signature does or can do for Kierkegaard—is not.[2]

---

1. See my "Kierkegaard and the Ingenious Creature: Authorial Unity and Co-Authorship in *On My Work as an Author*," *Kierkegaard Studies Yearbook* (2010), pp. 267–287; and "Who Is the Author of *The Point of View*?: Issues of Authorship in the Posthumous Kierkegaard," *Philosophy and Social Criticism* 38: 6 (2012), pp. 569–589.

2. Two intriguing exceptions to this general absence of interest in the nuances of Kierkegaardian signature are Louis Mackey, "Points of View for His Work as an Author: A Report from History," in *Points of View: Readings of Kierkegaard* (Tallahassee: Florida State University Press, 1986), pp. 160–192, and Lee C. Barrett, "Authorial Voices and the Limits of Communication in Kierkegaard's 'Signed' Literature: A Comparison of *Works of Love* to *For Self-Examination* and *Judge for Yourself!*" in *International Kierkegaard* Commentary, *Volume 21: For Self-Examination and Judge for Yourself!*, ed. Robert L. Perkins (Macon, GA: Mercer University Press, 2002), pp. 13–35.

Signature is retroactively complicated by Kierkegaard's sometime avoidance of it, and a robust theory of Kierkegaardian signature is no less necessary for a reading of Kierkegaard than is a theory of Kierkegaardian pseudonymity. While rather fewer examinations of signature exist in the Kierkegaardian literature, signature has risen to the level of serious interest in contemporary French (and otherwise Continental European) thought, in works by thinkers such as Jacques Derrida (*Glas*, "Signature Event Context," and *Copy, Archive, Signature*),[3] among others. Derrida's conception (and practice) of signature is as something other than, or in addition to, the mere affixing of one's own name to the product of one's own labors, or even the use of a non-nominal signifying mark to testify to and claim responsibility for whatever it is one signs. For Derrida and some other French thinkers of the late twentieth and early twenty-first centuries, signature is less a matter of marking a text with one's name than a practice of infusing a work with oneself.

For Kierkegaard, however, whatever signature is or might be, it must also always be related to the inscription of his own name as the author (and authorized purveyor) of a work. Thus, when looking to find some insight into Kierkegaardian signature in the relatively recent French literature, one may begin with Derrida but one must end, I think, with Sarah Kofman. Kofman does not conduct the rigorous analysis of signature as such that we find in Derrida, but she does take the Derridean insights into signature as a starting point for her own intensive examination of selfhood and self-identity in relation to the name. Thus, we find in Kofman—as in Kierkegaard—a deeply reflective signer or signatory operating according to a latent, and somewhat deconstructive, theory of signature. We see this to some extent in Kofman's writings on her own name and its significance, as well as her thoughts on Derrida's thoughts on signature itself, and we also see this in Kofman's signature contribution to the study of Socrates, that philosopher who more than any other in the history of the West made his contribution in the absence of a signature. Kofman's thoughts on Socrates and the depiction of Socrates throughout the history of philosophy include a thoughtful consideration of Kierkegaard's own treatment of Socrates, and thus, this chapter will culminate in a consideration of the relevance of the Socrates-Kofman-Kierkegaard overlap for questions of signature.

Signature in General

In general, a signature is the written inscription of the name of the author or creator of a work, either at the beginning or end of that work (as in the case of written or cinematic works), or upon the surface of the work (as in the case of

---

3. Jacques Derrida, *Glas*, trans. John P. Leavey, Jr., and Richard Rand (Lincoln: University of Nebraska Press, 1986); Jacques Derrida, "Signature Event Context," in *Margins of Philosophy*, trans. Alan Bass (Chicago: University of Chicago Press, 1982), pp. 307–330; Jacques Derrida, *Copy, Archive, Signature: A Conversation on Photography*, ed. Gerhard Richter, trans. Jeff Fort (Stanford, CA: Stanford University Press, 2010).

paintings, photographs, or other works within the visual arts). In some cases—but not all—a signature is produced in the author's own hand, and in some cases—but not all—the name signed is the signatory's own proper name, as opposed to a pen name or pseudonym. By and large, signatures serve the twofold function of binding an author to a work, such that the signature is simultaneously (a) the authorizing of the signed work as an authentic production of the signatory and (b) the identification of the signatory as (legally and literarily) responsible for the signed work and, if relevant, its socio-politico-legal consequences.

The Danish word for signature is *Underskrift* (a cognate of the German *Unterschriften*), which is literally translated into English as "underwriting"—and, like the English term "underwrite," *Underskrift* has the primary sense of an authorization, authentication, and guarantee of responsibility for the writing.[4] Signature in this sense communicates authority, as in the second function, (b), noted above. The English term "signature," on the other hand, derived from the French *signature* (itself derived from the Latin *signātūra*), has its origins in the Latin verb *signāre*, referring directly to the act of signing and less directly to the process of signification (another sense of "signing"): which is to say that, in the Franco-Latin sense (as opposed to the Dano-German), a signature gives evidence of the singular authorial origin of the signed work (as in the first function, [a], noted above).

Although signatures are signs, and thus stand in for something other than themselves (namely, the signatory), they are nevertheless not meaningful words, exactly: that is, they do not refer to concepts. To sign is not to *conceive*. There is no idea *expressed* by the signature, despite the fact that an idea might be occasioned by the signature's presence. We might say that the signatory can be *identified* or *described* to those unfamiliar with either the signatory or his or her signature, but the signature itself—whatever its indicative power—remains empty, opaque, a cipher. Strictly speaking, signatures—like names—are non-sense.

To the extent that a signature communicates anything, it communicates like a gesture: it points toward that which it designates, rather than articulating anything. One cannot explain or expound upon a name; likewise, then, one cannot explain a signature: there is nothing there to explain. In gesturing toward rather than articulating the thing (that is, the person) it indicates, a signature neither opens nor closes an inquiry or a dialogue. Instead, a signature creates a (personal) context, providing both an affirmation of the authorized historical origin of the signed work and a framework within which one might relate the signed work to other works signed by the same author. The signature is thus, then, a seemingly

---

4. In Kierkegaard's usage, it seems *Underskrift* sometimes takes on the sense of "inscription," such that when Kierkegaard uses the term—and it is relatively rare given the significance of signature to Kierkegaard's project overall—he often specifies *Navns Underskrift* ("name's signature" or "signature of name") to set this sense of the term apart from other possible uses. One might compare the use of "*Navns Underskrift*" in the *Concluding Unscientific Postscript* (SKS 7, 224–225) or in *Three Discourses on Imagined Occasions* (SKS 5, 413) with the use of *Underskrift* plain and simple in *Journal AA* (SKS 17, 13 [AA 5]).

necessary prerequisite for the possibility of a corpus—the *sine qua non* of an authorship as such. In this, signature opens up for the very first time anticipations of authorial style, by way of creating the very possibility of a stylistic unity across multiple works by the same author.

Finally, the notion of style raised here also has some significance for the question of signatures, as one might take the "signature style" (here, "signature" in the sense of "characteristic") of an otherwise unnamed author to be indicative enough of authorial responsibility to constitute a signature. Situated squarely between a more literary practice of signature and the age-old Doctrine of Signatures, style-as-signature seems like it ought to be more useful a notion than it actually is: in the end, unsigned written works, like unsigned (or "signed" but previously unknown) works in the visual arts, are treated as if of suspicious provenance until their authorial origins can be authenticated. No matter how closely a painting approximates Raphael's style, it is not an authentic Raphael until some acceptably conclusive sign or mark (intentional or otherwise) can be expertly identified—which is not to say that the question of style is an uninteresting or authorially (or even signatorially) useless one. Once rightful authorship can be established—whether this is by signature or some other means—then we can, and should, speak seriously about the ways in which the author's authorial self is present throughout the work. Raphael's style is only superficially a question of the technical differences between how Raphael and other Italian Renaissance painters use their brushes. Considerations of style can lead us to ask more profoundly what it is about any painting by Raphael that is *Raphael's*, particularly and personally, the image of the creator in his work, as it were. Kierkegaard is especially concerned with this notion of authorship and this understanding (or ramification) of signature in a work. We can see this concern both philosophically in Kierkegaard's attempts at explaining the authorship of his own works, as well as performatively in his efforts to explain the changing character of Socrates across the works of Xenophon, Plato, and Aristophanes, for example.

Signature in Kierkegaard

It is customary among Kierkegaard scholars to make a distinction between those works Kierkegaard published under one of his many pseudonyms and those works that were published non-pseudonymously; it is similarly customary to refer to those non-pseudonymous works in terms of their veronymity, or "true-namedness," and designate them as "the signed works."[5] Much is made of the differences between the signed and the pseudonymous works to the extent that it seems unreasonable

---

5. On "veronymity" (a term coined by Michael Strawser) in Kierkegaard, see Strawser, *Both/And: Reading Kierkegaard from Irony to Edification* (New York: Fordham University Press, 1999), p. 85 n. 28; and Joseph Westfall, *The Kierkegaard Author: Authorship and Performance in Kierkegaard's Literary and Dramatic Criticism* (Berlin: Walter de Gruyter, 2007), p. 3 n. 4, pp. 75–118.

to believe that the difference is merely designatory or nomenclatural. Rather, the custom among scholars of Kierkegaard is to associate the signed works with Kierkegaard's "own views"—typically religious, typically Christian—and, whatever the pseudonyms say, to relegate the pseudonymous books and their authors in large part to the aesthetic realm. This difference, between religious and aesthetic works, originates of course with Kierkegaard in "A First and Last Explanation" (appended to *Concluding Unscientific Postscript* but signed by Kierkegaard rather than the pseudonym, Johannes Climacus), *On My Work as an Author, The Point of View for My Work as an Author*, and other places, as does the tendency to ascribe a different sort of significance to the pseudonymous works than to those naming "S. Kierkegaard" as the author.

Kierkegaard makes plain in "A First and Last Explanation" that, while he is only in the remotest sense possible authorially related to the pseudonymous works, he is directly responsible for the authorship of the *Upbuilding Discourses*, published under his own name. Kierkegaard explains this difference in terms of "life-views," noting with regard to his pseudonyms:

> What has been written then, is mine, but only insofar as I, by means of audible lines, have placed the life-view of the crea*ting*, poetically actual individuality in his mouth, for my relation is even more remote than that of a poet, who *poetizes* characters and yet in the preface is *himself* the *author*. That is, I am impersonally or personally in the third person a *souffleur* who has poetically produced the *authors*, whose *prefaces* in turn are their productions, as their *names* are also. Thus in the pseudonymous books there is not a single word by me.[6]

In contrast to the distance he instantiates between himself and the pseudonymous writings, however, Kierkegaard insists that "on the other hand I am very literally and directly the author of, for example, the upbuilding discourses and every word in them."[7] The *Upbuilding Discourses*, of course, appeared occasionally over the course of Kierkegaard's pseudonymous authorship, published separately and always under Kierkegaard's own name.

Despite the fact that he does not say as much directly, it seems reasonable to believe that Kierkegaard, too, as the named author of the signed works, has a life-view and that this life-view differs in some substantial (if as yet undefined) ways from those of the pseudonyms—which is to say that Kierkegaard, qua author, differs essentially from (each of) the pseudonymous authors qua author(s). The connection between an authorial identity and a life-view is further bolstered by what Kierkegaard has to say about Hans Christian Andersen in *From the Papers of One Still Living*, and Thomasine Gyllembourg in *A Literary Review*, eviscerating the former for lacking a life-view (in both his art and his life), while praising the latter above nearly all other contemporary novelists for the consistency of her life-view

6. CUP1, 625–626 / SKS 7, 569–570.
7. CUP1, 627 / SKS 7, 571.

across her many works.[8] This would seem to establish the signed authorship—all those works by Kierkegaard that are signed in Kierkegaard's name—as exemplary of not only possibly different ideas but of a different point of view altogether.

To be sure, Kierkegaard never refers to any portion of his authorship as "the signed works," nor does he claim explicitly that it is by virtue of the presence of his own name on the title pages of those works that we should believe that they possess a life-view or understand the nature of the life-view they possess. In fact, in *The Point of View*, Kierkegaard famously insists that his word ought not to be good enough for any reader to trust that his written works possess the religious life-view he claims they do.[9] Reading the words "S. Kierkegaard" on the title page of the book (or as the very last line of an essay or article) teaches us nothing essential about the work.[10] Despite this fact, there *is* a necessary relationship between Kierkegaard's name and the signed works, if only by virtue of the fact that, when we say they are "signed," we only ever mean that they are signed *in Kierkegaard's name* and *by Kierkegaard*. Presuming Kierkegaard would encourage us to hold him to the same high authorial standard to which he holds Andersen, Gyllembourg, and other authors, it follows that, although knowing Kierkegaard's name teaches us nothing about the signed works themselves, the signed works can teach us some important lessons about Kierkegaard.

Kierkegaard tries to set forth his best understanding of the nature of the signed authorship, as well as the relationship between the signed and pseudonymous works, in a little book he published in 1851, *On My Work as an Author*. There, he emphatically notes, "It began **maieutically** with esthetic production, and all the pseudonymous writings are *maieutic* in nature. Therefore this writing was also pseudonymous, whereas the directly religious—which from the beginning was present in the gleam of an indication—carried my name."[11] Importantly, of course, Kierkegaard isn't arguing that the signed works are directly religious *because* he signed them with his own name; rather, he is offering his signature simply as a mark of their direct religiousness. Whereas he will argue that all pseudonymous works are necessarily indirect (and thus maieutic at best), signing a work with one's own name does not mean that the work is thereby not an indirect communication. At least, Kierkegaard never says so.

---

8. For a discussion of the notion of a life-view as it pertains to Kierkegaard's thoughts on authorship, with specific reference to Andersen (in *From the Papers of One Still Living*) and Gyllembourg (in *A Literary Review*), see Lee C. Barrett, "Life-View," in *Kierkegaard's Concepts, Tome IV: Individual to Novel*, ed. Steven M. Emmanuel, William McDonald, and Jon Stewart (London: Routledge, 2016), pp. 89–96; and Westfall, *The Kierkegaardian Author*, pp. 31–74.

9. PV, 33 / SKS 16, 18–19.

10. This seems to be a large part of the point of the entire structure of *Either/Or*, as well as the brief rebuttal of claims that Kierkegaard was that book's "real" author. See "Who Is the Author of *Either/Or*" (COR, 13–16 / SKS 14, 49–51).

11. OMWA, 7 / SKS 13, 13–14.

At the beginning of his posthumously published *The Point of View*, Kierkegaard expands upon his claim to religiousness as an author:

> The content, then, of this little book is: what I in truth am as an author, that I am and was a religious author, that my whole authorship pertains to Christianity, to the issue: becoming a Christian, with direct and indirect polemical aim at that enormous illusion, Christendom, or the illusion that in such a country all are Christians of sorts.[12]

This might seem to resolve the question, at least to a certain extent, of the nature and purpose of Kierkegaardian signature: Kierkegaard signs a work simultaneously to make the work an instance of direct communication and to designate the work as religious, thus the association in Kierkegaard's account in *On My Work as an Author* of his signature with direct religiousness. Yet Kierkegaard himself resists this easy explanation, denying not the content of the claim (that he is a religious author) but his authority to make the claim conclusively, even about his own writings.

We see this in at least three ways in two of the major self-explanatory works in the Kierkegaardian authorship, "A First and Last Explanation" and *The Point of View*. In "A First and Last Explanation," following upon the passages discussed above, Kierkegaard tries to explain his own personal (and authorial) relationship to the pseudonymous works. He writes,

> I have no opinion about them except as a third party, no knowledge of their meaning except as a reader, not the remotest private relation to them, since it is impossible to have that to a doubly reflected communication. A single word by me personally in my own name would be an arrogating self-forgetfulness that, regarded dialectically, would be guilty of having essentially annihilated the pseudonymous authors by this one word.[13]

Something of what he means by the dialectical understanding of the author's relationship to the pseudonymous writings is captured, in a different context, in a footnote in *On My Work as an Author*. There, he notes that he cannot make direct claims about what is said in *Practice in Christianity* (a book ascribed to the pseudonym, Anti-Climacus), "since the communication is doubly reflected: it can also be just the opposite or be understood as such." He concludes the footnote observing, "all doubly reflected communication makes contrary understandings equally possible; then the one who passes judgment is disclosed by the way he judges."[14] Again and again, Kierkegaard returns to this idea in works written under his own name: that the pseudonymous authorship cannot be explained once and for all by Kierkegaard, even though he is in some sense its author; in fact, it is

12. PV, 23 / SKS 16, 11.
13. CUP1, 626 / SKS 7, 570.
14. OMWA, 18n / SKS 13, 25n.

precisely because he is in some sense its author that he cannot explain it once and for all. He explains it as he thinks *we* could understand it: on the reader's behalf and in the name of a reader, not—despite his signature—his own.

More famous, perhaps, is the passage in *The Point of View* to which I alluded above. There, at the beginning of Section B of Part I (titled "The Explanation"), Kierkegaard writes:

> It might seem that a simple declaration by the author himself in this regard is more than adequate; after all, he must know best what is what. I do not, however, think much of declarations in connection with literary productions and am accustomed to take a completely objective attitude to my own. If in the capacity of a third party, as a reader, I cannot substantiate from the writings that what I am saying is the case, that it cannot be otherwise, it could never occur to me to want to win what I thus consider as lost. If I *qua* author must first make declarations, I easily alter all the writing, which from first to last is dialectical.[15]

Kierkegaard seems to resist the simple explanatory power of signature here in two ways: first of all, by suggesting that it's "unfair" for him to offer a declaration of his subjective intent instead of an objective accounting. Since he would find such declarations unconvincing in the cases of other authors, he refuses to offer one in his own case. In addition, however, Kierkegaard here notes that there is an aspect of the authorship itself that prevents a direct declaration on the author's part from being possible: that is, that the writing is "from first to last ... dialectical." He has made reference to this dialectical problem before, in the passage from "A First and Last Explanation" quoted above—and the consequence of forgetting the dialectical nature of the authorship there is repeated here: a fundamental alteration of the entire authorship. Getting into what Kierkegaard means here, precisely, by the term "dialectical" is less important than seeing that, whatever he means, he is saying that there are some things he thinks he cannot communicate directly even in the context of a direct communication, such as *The Point of View* claims to be (in its subtitle, to begin with).[16] To make a direct subjective declaration as to the nature and purpose of the authorship would alter the authorship itself; in other words, something about the authorship requires of its author either silence or indirectness.

This admission of a necessary indirectness, silence, or hiddenness on his part within even the most direct elements of the authorship comes out again, earlier in *The Point of View*, when Kierkegaard addresses the question of explaining his authorship as religious and thus as related in some way to Kierkegaard's own subjective religiousness. There, he writes:

---

15. PV, 33 / SKS 16, 18.
16. "*The Point of View for My Work as an Author: A Direct Communication, Report to History*" (PV, 21 / SKS 16, 7).

It is self-evident that I cannot present completely an explanation of my work as an author, that is, with the purely personal inwardness in which I possess the explanation. In part it is because I cannot make my God-relationship public in this way …. In part it is because I cannot wish (and no one, I am sure, could desire that I do so) to press upon anyone something that pertains solely to my private character, which of course for me contains much of the explanation of my author-character.[17]

Again, here, we find many interesting things at work in Kierkegaard's self-explanation (or lack thereof), but what is of central importance to an inquiry into signature in Kierkegaard is the fact that Kierkegaard admits regularly that there are things he believes, things that are relevant to and explanatory of his work as an author, which he cannot express directly in his own name. In many places, Kierkegaard seems to argue that he understands his own work as an author as the product of a religious—a divine—calling. And yet that could only be evident *to him*, subjectively, as the one called by God to produce such an authorship. As such, Kierkegaard tries to provide an explanation that could make sense objectively to his readers, which is to say from a point of view other than his own. The point of view presented as Kierkegaard's own in *The Point of View* is thus but one possible point of view, the point of view of one possible reader. Anyone *but* Kierkegaard could have stated their actual point of view on the authorship and meaning of this work directly in their own name. It is precisely insofar as it is a signed work—a work signed with the name "S. Kierkegaard" and by Kierkegaard—that it is an instance of a necessary silence or a necessarily concealed and indirect communication.

Kofman (and Derrida) Signing "Sarah Kofman"

No French deconstructionist—perhaps no French thinker or writer of the late twentieth century—comes as close to emulating the Kierkegaardian effects of signature, and certainly only one other has as much to say specifically about Kierkegaard, as Sarah Kofman.[18] Few thinkers in any tradition are as aware as Kofman, I think, of the simultaneous undecidability of the central terms in defining and determining a self, on the one hand, and the subjective (existential) urgency of choosing a self for oneself, two poles held in taut and tense but productive opposition also by Kierkegaard. And so it is not just that Kofman is the most Kierkegaardian of the Derrideans, or that of the Derrideans she has the most to say

---

17. PV, 25–26 / SKS 16, 13–14.
18. Derrida, naturally, is the other.

about Kierkegaard.[19] No, ultimately it is that there is a deeper resonance between Kierkegaard and Kofman than there is between Kierkegaard and some other of these thinkers, including—perhaps especially—Derrida, and this comes out rather clearly in their (Derrida's and Kofman's) different approaches to, understandings, and practices of signature. This results in the fact that, far more than Derrida ever does, Kofman helps us to read, return to, and reread Kierkegaard with a better understanding of what it means for *Kierkegaard* to be the one to whom we return.

Kofman's treatment of the question of signature, however, comes only indirectly by way of her treatment of Derrida's treatment of signature in his formidable tome, *Glas*. Obviously, no simple or summary treatment of *Glas* is possible here, and in at least one sense, the whole work deals with the question of signature. That said, Kofman's response is primarily to a single section of the Genet column in *Glas*,[20] and so, to understand Kofman's take on this nuanced question, we must start with a substantial quotation from that work. Derrida situates the following comments on signature in the context of a discussion of what it means for him to cut various passages from Genet's work and include them, independent of their original context, within his own writing—such that their provenance remains unclear: are the quotations Derrida's, insofar as he is the one who selects and includes them? Or are they—do they remain—Genet's, despite the loss of their original (con)text and purpose? Who is the author of the text when Derrida quotes Genet? Or, to put a somewhat finer point on it, what remains of Genet in the passages Derrida cuts from his work—and, when excised from their origin in this way, can we continue to say that they are *Genet's*?

Raising these and a host of other issues, Derrida writes:

> Even if we could reconstitute, morsel by morsel, a proper name's emblem or signature, that would only be to disengage, as from a tomb someone buried alive, just what neither Genet nor I would ever have succeeded in signing, in reattaching to the lines of a paraph, and what talks (because) of this. We do not comprehend here the text denominated Genet's, it is not exhausted in the pocket I cut [*coupe*], sew [*couds*], and refasten. That text is what makes a hole in the pocket, harpoons it beforehand, regards it; but also sees it escape the

---

19. It is close, but the section of Kofman's *Socrate(s)* that deals with Kierkegaard is perhaps twenty or so pages shorter than Derrida's book on *Fear and Trembling*, *The Gift of Death*. Somewhat surprisingly, when addressing Kierkegaard directly, Derrida has nothing significant to say about irony, pseudonymity, signature, or authorship. In this regard, Kofman's treatment is much more "Derridean" (and certainly more Kierkegaardian) than Derrida's own. See Jacques Derrida, *The Gift of Death*, trans. David Wills (Chicago: University of Chicago Press, 1996).

20. *Glas* is written in two concurrent columns, the left-hand column being a response to Hegel, the right-hand column to the work of Jean Genet. Derrida intersperses various quotations throughout his two simultaneous analyses, but the passage with which we are primarily concerned here is Derrida's own.

text, bear its arrow away to unknown parts. This text here (or *glas*) no more reduces to a reading of Genet—that forms neither its example nor its essence, neither its case nor its truth—than this text here allows itself to be reassembled or arrowed, with others, by my paraph. And everything in it that would tend to the singular form of the signature, of one signature or the other, guards an altogether abnormal value. It comes under [*relève d'*] no rule, nor does it procure one. The operation must be singular each time, and must run [*courir*] its risk [*chance*] uniquely.[21]

Much here depends upon Derrida's identification of the paraph—originally, the flourish at the end of a person's signature that prevents it from being easily copied, which is to say, the *signature* element of the signature—as the point of connection between a signed name and the signatory. What is authored by Genet is Genet's when it is signed by Genet, that is, when it is an original and singular production of the writerly activity of Jean Genet. The signature takes its significance, then, for Derrida, from its singularity, unrepeatability, and thus asystematicity: signatures cannot be systematized, linguistically or otherwise. They cannot be repeated. And their meaning, if they mean anything, cannot be known in advance.

Derrida goes on to suggest that a signature could only convey meaning if, in fact, it were simply a sign within a coherent system of meaningful names/nouns (in French, *noms*). He writes, "It would be otherwise if the signature were only a *glas*-effect, otherwise stated a classification, the network of (no) more than a name. At that point, this operation would somewhere be exemplary and normative, even scientific, if, but so timidly, preliminary: a conception hardly announced."[22] Knowledge (*savoir*) of the signature would only be possible under such conditions—but, as Derrida notes, these conditions do not hold when it comes to signature, and so we are left only with knowledge (*connaissance*) of the signature: as it cannot be known objectively, systematically, it can only ever be witnessed. The witness bears (subjective) witness only to the unrepeatable, to the singular, that which can only ever have occurred once.

Following on the singularity and essential meaninglessness of the signature, Peggy Kamuf notes that what is witnessed in the text is "what one might call the signature *effect*." She continues:

Coursing through all possible sense connections in a common language, an effect of signature can be felt to register, like tremblings set off by nearby explosions. It is an effect, a resonance, an impression, which is to say, it is nothing itself and in itself but rather the trace left behind by some event of signature that was itself never simply present. Under this effect, one can never be sure that the signature is not false, an illusion, a simulacrum, a phantasm. Counterfeit or contraband.

21. Derrida, *Glas*, pp. 169–170.
22. Ibid., p. 170.

"Does it take place? where? how? why? for whom?" These are Derrida's questions and they resonate from then on in everything he writes.[23]

In the case of signature, then, one is called to account not only as the signatory but also as a reader of the signature as a signature: to know the writing as Genet's—to bear witness to Genet's signature—requires that one answer these questions for oneself, subjectively, in one's own name. Genet's signature, then, requires yet another signature, singular testimony to the singularity of the signature that was/is Genet's. Again following Kamuf, we see that this second signature predicated upon the first—what Derrida calls a "countersignature"—is a necessary condition for identifying a signature as anything more than a name. Kamuf, reading Derrida's *Signéponge/Signsponge*,[24] writes that countersignature is "the act of affirming the other work by taking responsibility for it. Countersignature is a response to the other's writing, the other's signing. Which is to say another name for it is reading, but one that figures an act of responsible response, signed and countersigned."[25] Among other things, this means that every signature able to be noted as such is always already in the process of being read—and that this process, and this reading, are themselves both signed and awaiting a (counter)signature. Signature, as a singular event, always calls upon another event, a future singularity, absolutely unique but of the same kind. And that future signature, that countersignature, is itself a signature, which, to be read as a signature, must itself first become read in the event of a further countersignature—and so on, and on, presumably infinitely: signing without end.

Which brings us, somewhat circuitously but absolutely necessarily, to Sarah Kofman, who, like most deconstructionists, reads as a writer and writes as a reader and, in reading Derrida, (counter)signs her own name—a name that is, in turn, as we will see, (counter)signed itself by Derrida. For Kofman, it is thus by way of this notion and practice of signature, evinced in *Glas*, that Derrida opens the very possibility of all writing. She asks, "What end is Derrida pursuing? (Is "Derrida" really the "author" who signs *Glas* with this name? *Glas*, which tolls the death knell [*glas*] for the "author," for the "proper name," for the "signature"?)[26] And then she goes on, in the second person, to challenge:

> Without a doubt, this is the origin of your generalized fetishism, your undecidable oscillation, your necessarily double liaisons. But who is "you"? Derrida? The one

23. Peggy Kamuf, "I See Your Meaning and Raise the Stakes by a Signature: The Invention of Derrida's Work," in *A Companion to Derrida*, ed. Zeynep Direk and Leonard Lawlor (Somerset, NJ: Wiley, 2014), p. 196.

24. Jacques Derrida, *Signéponge/Signsponge*, trans. Richard Rand (New York: Columbia University Press, 1985).

25. Kamuf, "I See Your Meaning and Raise the Stakes by a Signature," p. 197.

26. Sarah Kofman, "Ça cloche," trans. Thomas Albrecht, in Sarah Kofman, *Selected Writings*, ed. Thomas Albrecht, with Georgia Albert and Elizabeth Rottenberg (Stanford, CA: Stanford University Press, 2007), p. 87.

who signs *Glas* with his name? *Glas*, which puts into play the proper name, the signature as the mark of an identity, of a particular author? If the signature is "the network of (no) more than a name" (*Glas*, 170), then *Glas* tolls the death knell for autobiography, for a psychoanalysis of the author; it would not be possible to analyze the clapper of a bell [*cloche*].[27]

"*Glas*," of course, in French, is translated into English as "knell" and refers to the solemn sound of the ringing of a bell—as if to mark a death, or at a funeral, where one is necessarily simultaneously in the presence and the absence of the one dead.

For Kofman, a large part of the significance of *Glas* is in the applicability of its practice of textuality—double columned, two-handed, undermining of traditional distinctions between text and author—to sex: "Everything that has been said of the text can be said of sex."[28] The necessity of some future countersignature for any present signature to be a signature, which binds texts to texts and texts upon texts, forward and backward through history, presents itself in the relationship between sexes as well.

The writing of the double column is the writing of a double, diabolical sex that in its duplicity breaks with all oppositions and all hierarchies. Like each text agglutinated to another text, each sex becomes undecidable, speaks the language, and in the language of the other, penetrates the other: neither feminine nor masculine, neither castrated nor noncastrated, not because it is bisexual, but because it strikes between the sexes, because it is always already a double sex.[29]

Kofman notes that this bisexuality, this double-sexedness, has a precedent in *Glas*, in a passage of Genet's Derrida quotes in *Glas*, which itself references the "double nature" of Tiresias, blind seer of Thebes, "patron of actors," who wore women's clothing and plucked out his beard to live as a woman among women, only then to return to his life as a man in old age. Kofman reads Derrida reading Genet reading Tiresias as never having had "any rest, I mean any fixed point where he could rest."[30] In this, "the power of *jouissance* and its play are not antinomies," and Tiresias is identified (in part) with Dionysus.[31] The absence of firmness and fixity in the text mirrors the absence of firmness and fixity between the sexes, between the one and the other, between opposites (or supposed opposites): between the author and the text authored, between the interpreter and the interpretation, between Derrida and Genet, Derrida and "himself," Derrida and the proper name—the signature, "Derrida."

27. Ibid., p. 89.
28. Ibid., p. 90.
29. Ibid., p. 91.
30. Genet in Derrida in Kofman, "Ça cloche," p. 91.
31. Kofman, "Ça cloche," p. 91.

This bisexual irony recurs in Kofman's work in a brief autobiographical text from 1986 with the title "Tomb for a Proper Name." There, Kofman recounts having dreamt herself a translator of Kafka, but having been troubled by the fact that, in the dream, her name on the cover of the book was written, "Sar ... Ko(a)f ... " She notes of her surname, Kofman, "The error of a city hall employee, which always delighted me, had distinguished *Kofman* from *Kaufman*, more common; and from Kaufmann, which can't help but suggest commerce, money, shit [*caca*], the Jew."[32] She continues,

> *Kof* makes me think of *Ko(p)f*, the head: the "incorrect" spelling dissimulates what is low and dirty; it allows me to bear a quite proper name, my head held high. But why were the last syllables cut off?
>
> • ah, in Hebrew, designates the feminine.
> • Man, Mann designates the masculine.
>
> Isn't the cutting "elision" the equivalent of a double castration, punishment for the one who meant to deny her blood, to erase her lowly origins, to hold her head high?
>
> Sar ... Kof ... Sarkof?
> Both sexes wounded, cat-rat [*chat-rat*], I devour my own flesh: sarcophagus.[33]

From Sarah Kofman to Sarkof to sarcophagus [*sarcophage*], Kofman aligns writing, signature, death, and sexual difference along these post-Derridean lines. She "signs" the fragment, "Sar ... Ko(a)f ..., " as in the dream, retaining the undecidability in the relationship between herself and her name, between waking and dreaming, between masculine and feminine, secular and Jewish, German and Hebrew, dead and alive.

Which makes even more interesting the fact that Derrida, after Kofman's death, when writing an introduction to her (posthumously) selected writings, countersigns her countersignature, further blurring the line dividing the reader and the author, the living and the dead. He writes:

> At first I did not know—and in fact still do not know—what title to give to these words.
>
> What is the gift of a title?
> I even had the fleeting suspicion that such a gift would be somewhat indecent: it would imply the violent selection of a perspective, an abusive interpretative framing or narcissistic reappropriation, a conspicuous signature there where it

---

32. Sarah Kofman, "Tomb for a Proper Name," trans. Frances Bartkowski, in Kofman, *Selected Writings*, pp. 248–249.
    33. Ibid., p. 249.

is Sarah Kofman, Sarah Kofman alone, Sarah Kofman herself, *over there [là-bas]*, beyond here, well beyond me or us here and now, Sarah Kofman who should be spoken about and whom I hear speaking.[34]

For Derrida, it is Kofman—Kofman *herself*—who speaks, even after death, always ever in the present tense if never (again) in the present. Signature, of course, like all writing, presents itself only ever truly in the absence of its author—and yet, of course, nevertheless presents the author somehow by way of the medium of that author's absence. Like a funeral or a tomb.[35]

And so we come full circle, as it were, from Kofman to Derrida and then back again to Kofman. Kofman addresses Derrida directly in "Ça cloche," calling him by name in *her* own name. Derrida countersigns Kofman's signature in the very text in which she countersigns Derrida's signature in *Glas*—of all Derrida's works, the one in which he most thoroughly threatens the very notion of signature. They sign and countersign each other, countersign and sign themselves, thoroughly imbuing each of their writings with a sense of the other—just as Derrida presents not Genet but *Derrida's* Genet, not Hegel but *Derrida's* Hegel. Derrida himself, in his reticent introduction, seems content, however, to cede the shifting floor to Kofman herself—and to be ever more, at least in this text, at least under this signature, *Kofman's* Derrida.

Socratic Signature(s) in Kofman's Kierkegaard

We have now, however, yet another sense of signature at work—and signature in this sense overlaps a great deal with something we might call "style."[36] Signature serves less as a simple ascription of authorial origin, in this practice, than as the pervasive presence of an authorial identity in or throughout the work, the "spirit" (or "ghost") of the (absent) author. Certainly, that Derrida haunts the writings of Kofman, as Kofman haunts at least some of those of Derrida, is without question. Derrida addresses this signatorial phenomenon more or less directly in his notion of countersignature and his discussion of Kofman. Kofman, for her part, does so by way of her magisterial analysis of the figure of Socrates.

In *Socrate(s)*, published in French in 1989 and translated into English in 1998 as *Socrates: Fictions of a Philosopher*,[37] Kofman examines the figure of Socrates from a variety of perspectives and as he is presented by a variety of philosophers, chiefly

34. Jacques Derrida, "Introduction," in Kofman, *Selected Writings*, p. 1.
35. See Derrida, *Glas*, p. 169 ("as from a tomb someone buried alive"); and Kofman, "Tomb for a Proper Name."
36. See Jacques Derrida, *Spurs: Nietzsche's Styles / Éperons: Les Styles de Nietzsche*, trans. Barbara Harlow (Chicago: University of Chicago Press, 1979).
37. Sarah Kofman, *Socrates: Fictions of a Philosopher*, trans. Catherine Porter (Ithaca, NY: Cornell University Press, 1998).

Hegel, Kierkegaard, and Nietzsche. Although Kofman's approach can seem more Nietzschean than Kierkegaardian, she concludes that, of the three nineteenth-century philosophical depictions of Socrates she discusses, Kierkegaard's is the most aware of the potential of the Socratic for thought.

The general approach of *Socrate(s)* is to find in each philosopher's presentation of Socrates the signature of that philosopher, rather than a trace of the historical Socrates, which Kofman takes for granted would be impossible to find. Kierkegaard's Socrates is tellingly Kierkegaard's, not only because Kierkegaard's name appears as author on the title page of *On the Concept of Irony* but more importantly because the Socrates presented in *On the Concept of Irony* (not to mention other works by Kierkegaard or his pseudonyms) is imbued with the spirit of Kierkegaard. While this notion of signature may have its most overt (and most discussed) usefulness in considerations of the authorship of works of photography or architecture—where the writerly or painterly tradition of literally signing the work with one's own name is less common—it is no less useful in considerations of the authorship of personalities (such as Hegel's, Nietzsche's, and Kierkegaard's Socrates[es]) and personae (such as the Socrates of Plato's and Xenophon's dialogues and Aristophanes's *The Clouds*, or the pseudonyms and anonyms of Kierkegaard). In light of the complex of authors and attitudes Kofman examines, it is not difficult to see how, for her, the figure of Socrates is an essentially irresolvable enigma. The significance of the parenthetical "s" at the end of the title of her book in French indicates this much, that when writing of Socrates one has on one's hands simultaneously a plurality and a singularity: there was and can only ever have been one Socrates, unique to history, yet there is no discourse of Socrates so much as there is a discursive succession of highly individualized "Socrateses."

It is this fact of Socrates that Kofman sees as the most fascinating and enchanting thing about him—his unknowability, his unmasterability. And it is what leads her to conclude that all philosophical treatments of Socrates are themselves fictionalizations, what she calls "novels of Socrates." Thus, she notes,

> what matters to us in all these interpretations is not the possibility that we might cut through their diversity to find a single interpretation, the "true" one, that would finally give us a "real Socrates", bound over hand and foot; what is important to us is that these interpretations make manifest the impossibility of any reading that is not, no matter what approach it takes, a reappropriating fiction.[38]

Although it is probably the case—and I think Kofman would agree—that all reading and interpretation is a sort of novelization or fictionalization of that which is read or interpreted, we should not confuse the case of Socrates with more ordinary cases. To be sure, every reader has their own Hegel or Nietzsche, and to that extent every reading of either philosopher is a new interpretation. Yet in both

---

38. Ibid., p. 8.

cases, despite Nietzsche's elusive ambiguity and Hegel's occasional impenetrability, a faithful reader must always relate his or her reading back to the unchanging source texts, the writings of Hegel or Nietzsche. This is, however, impossible in the case of Socrates—and perhaps why so many purported interpretations of the Socratic are in fact readings of Plato. To "read" a philosopher who wrote nothing is to engage necessarily in a kind of literary or at least fictive creativity. It is to bear witness to something one has not witnessed, to stand at the graveside but never alongside the living man.

Kofman, however, following Kierkegaard, thinks the unmasterability of Socrates was a problem even for his contemporaries—and thus that it has as much to do with who Socrates was as it does with what Socrates did or did not write. She notes,

> The Socratic novel thus begins in Socrates' own lifetime: each of the "disciples" heard Socrates' "lesson" in his own way, from his own perspective (Nietzsche unmasks Plato's fictions in particular; he is less sensitive than Kierkegaard is to Xenophon's). As Kierkegaard put it, each one saw him through his own *stereoscope*: Xenophon, with the mentality of a shopkeeper, was able to create only the fiction of a down-to-earth Socrates, a flat, realistic, insignificant figure, so harmless and boring that one could legitimately ask why the Athenian nobility condemned him to death, unless it was precisely because of the unbearable boredom he exuded. Plato, on the other hand, tended to idealize Socrates, to make him an ally by transfiguring him—especially after his death.[39]

The most ancient and original exposures to Socrates are already fictionalizations, texts interpreting the Socratic along the lines of the interpreters' own points of view. Thus, whether one willfully creates a Socrates to be used for one's own ends—as Hegel, Nietzsche, and Aristophanes seem to Kofman to do—or one makes a more genuine effort to uncover the truth of the historical Socrates, an effort Kofman sees in Xenophon and Kierkegaard, the result is the same: each interpreter is really a creator, a novelist, inventing Socrates anew—or, perhaps better, inventing a new Socrates, inventing a Socrates of their own.

As readers of Kierkegaard are aware, the Socrates of Kierkegaard's dissertation is an ironic figure—the ironic figure, or the figure of irony, *par excellence*. "Among the interpreters," Kofman writes, "Kierkegaard spends the most time trying to sort things out; he does so in order to conceive of a 'quite real' Socrates (a Socrates seen in fact through Kierkegaard's own stereoscope), an ironic Socrates who has nothing of his own to affirm, properly speaking, except nothingness."[40] Kofman goes on: "Kierkegaard, finally, imagining Socrates as an ironist, a figure of nothing, of nothingness, removes him from all stable positions. In Socrates and in the irony he emblematizes, Kierkegaard makes manifest a space of resistance to dialectics: Socrates is irreducible to all definitions and specifications: he is and is not."[41] This

39. Ibid., p. 4.
40. Ibid., p. 5.
41. Ibid., pp. 7–8.

is Kofman's take on Kierkegaard's famous—perhaps infamous—preference of Aristophanes over Plato and Xenophon as purveyor of the "real" Socrates, something Aristophanes of course fails to accomplish (and likely never intends), but which *The Clouds* achieves nonetheless by way of an approximation. Ultimately, Kofman favors Kierkegaard's Socrates for much the same reason that Kierkegaard favors Aristophanes's: in rejecting both Plato's überideal and Xenophon's überreal Socrateses, Aristophanes substitutes *nothing* to replace them—the Aristophanic Socrates is Socrates as pure irony, as nothing but irony, as Kierkegaard puts it, and is for that reason, if not a true depiction, certainly not a false one, either. He "is and is not," as Kofman says. Similarly, for Kofman, Kierkegaard simultaneously rejects Hegel's world-historical Socrates and (as she notes, "by anticipation") Nietzsche's life-negating anti-Greek Socrates yet provides no positive, affirmative Socrates in their stead. Kierkegaard's Socrates says nothing, really, in contrast to Hegel's declarative and Nietzsche's over-garrulous Socrateses. This relative silence is what enables Kierkegaard to privilege the maieutic in Socrates over all other traits—the maieutic *as* ironic[42]—and thus severs Socrates from his time, as Kofman reads Kierkegaard having been severed from his. This untimeliness is, for Kofman, the single most identifiable trait Kierkegaard possesses as an author, and he cannot help but imbue his writings—at least his signed writings—with it.

This is true, naturally, of anyone who writes about Socrates, according to Kofman. In her own inimitably Socratic way, she closes her book with the question:

> If the problem of Socrates has caused so much ink to flow, in the final analysis, is it not because behind the "case" of this atopical and atypical monster, each interpreter is trying as best he can to "settle" his own "case," to carry out his reading in such a way that all of his own certitudes will not collapse with Socrates, that his own equilibrium and that of his "system"—even if there is nothing obviously systematic about it—will not be too seriously threatened?[43]

Ultimately, in depicting Socrates in the way he does, Kierkegaard—on Kofman's reading—is attempting to secure what it means for *Kierkegaard* to write, to be himself in his writing, to write as Kierkegaard, or to write the word, "Kierkegaard": to sign a work with (the Aristophanically empty sign that is) his own name. This strange dialectic—Kierkegaard writing Socrates to write, or make it possible to write, "Kierkegaard"—is a problem for Kierkegaard, according to Kofman. Inheriting a specific concern for the role of "conception" in Kierkegaard from Sylviane Agacinski,[44] Kofman writes,

---

42. See, by way of comparison, my "Ironic Midwives: Socrates Maieutics in Nietzsche and Kierkegaard," *Philosophy and Social Criticism* 35: 6 (2009), pp. 627–648.

43. Kofman, *Socrates*, pp. 247–248.

44. See Sylviane Agacinski, *Aparté: Conceptions and Deaths of Søren Kierkegaard*, trans. Kevin Newmark (Tallahassee: Florida State University Press, 1988).

It is awkward for Kierkegaard, as a Christian, to accept being saved by writing. Later, identifying himself both with Socrates (who, as an authentic ironist, "left nothing by which a later age can judge him" [p. 12], nothing in writing) and with Christ ("who did not get mixed up with writing" except for some traces in the sand), Kierkegaard refuses to "conceive"—for conception would make him, a sinner, a rival of women and of God (who alone creates). He will write only under pseudonyms; only his religious work will appear under his own name (his father's name), because there he is speaking in the name of God.[45]

But of course Kierkegaard *does* conceive, later pseudonymously a "concept of anxiety," but early on, too, and in his own name, a "concept of irony." Kofman reads Kierkegaard as a conceiver, as a (reticent) "rival of women and of God," creator as well as creature. The categorical fluidity Kofman uncovers in the dream signature of her own name—the simultaneity of presence and absence that is the tomb for her proper name—is apparent also in Kierkegaard and especially in Kierkegaard's efforts to determine once and for all what writing "Kierkegaard" means.

Following on a reference of Kierkegaard's to Hegel as trying to be a "commander-in-chief of world history,"[46] Kofman focuses her depiction of Kierkegaard in *On the Concept of Irony* in startling contrast to Hegel.

By comparing Hegel to an officer, a more able one, to be sure, but still an officer, a commander, a commander-in-chief, Kierkegaard displaces the problem from the ground of "truth" to the ground of the "will to power," as one might call it anticipatorily. He reveals the will to power that governs the search for truth: Hegel's will to be the great master of world history, its great conqueror, Caesar's equal, or Alexander's, at the very least, triumphant over Athens and Socrates.[47]

Hegel's very traditional, relatively conservative presentation as powerful, commanding, conquering, martial, masterful, and ever striving for triumph aligns him, for Kofman and, according to Kofman, for Kierkegaard, with a certain rigid concept of masculinity: Hegel has, or seeks, an identity (able to be) set in stone. Kierkegaard, on the other hand, is no commander-in-chief—nor does he pretend to be. He anticipates no statues being carved in his honor; he sits for no daguerreotypes or portraits. Even in his final attack on the Danish church, he does not depict himself as the conquering hero: the only comparison for his own work that he can find is *Socrates*, but even then, he does not present himself as having mastered the Socratic. On the contrary, rather than attempting to hunt, kill, and mount irony, Socratic irony, and Socrates on the wood-paneled wall of world history, Kierkegaard sees irony—says Kofman—as a phenomenon only mastered when left alone.

---

45. Kofman, *Socrates*, p. 145.
46. CI, 222 / SKS 1, 266.
47. Kofman, *Socrates*, p. 138.

Having discussed the significance of Kierkegaard's breaking of his engagement to Regine Olsen, Kofman makes her point of view on the relationship between Kierkegaard's Socratic irony, masculinity, and ultimate ambiguity plain:

> If, in order to possess a woman, in order to arouse or keep her love, one must be able to remain at a distance from her and give her nothing, Kierkegaard demonstrates more masculinity in breaking with Regina [*sic*] than by staying with her. He shows that he is more powerful than Hegel, that noisy, spur-wearing knight, by overcoming irony *incognito*, as it were, from a distance, and in silence, ironically: he does so, in other words, by identifying with irony (with the woman), by becoming a woman himself. If masculinity consists, then, not in warlike activity and power but in the feminine science of distance, respect, and silence, and if the conquering activity of philosophy makes up its mind to learn how to conceive correctly, it is obvious that the comparison that inaugurates the Thesis [*On the Concept of Irony*] blurs the traditional distinction between the sexes to a considerable extent. The knight who goes off to conquer a woman and/ or irony can only proceed in disguise, so far as his sex is concerned; he may not know himself which of the two will impregnate the other.[48]

On Kofman's reading, and in a way comparable only to Kofman—to the Kofman of Kofman's dream, Ko(a)f-Man(n) both feminine and masculine, Sarkof of the sarcophagus—Kierkegaard's masculine triumph over Hegel can result only from the choice to abandon traditional masculinity for a femininity of his own; Kierkegaard's masculinity is thus enacted by the enactment of his femininity. He becomes a greater man than Hegel by becoming, ironically, a woman.

What does this mean—and what does it mean for signature? For Kofman, the point here is not (entirely) a Freudian one; it is not that Kierkegaard was masculine or feminine but that he embraced—in embracing irony and Socrates—an ambiguity or, at least, an ambivalence within himself. Kierkegaard, for Kofman, is a *Janus bifrons*, always his own self-differentiating double, man and woman, earnest and ironic, apostle and poet, Christian and apostate, proximate and distant, known and unknowable at the same time. In this, Kofman sees Kierkegaard's Socrates in Kierkegaard, ironic as a midwife, modeled not on Sophroniscus, his father, but on his mother, Phaenarete, ironic in her own right as the infertile mother described in Plato's *Theaetetus*.[49] This makes, or would make, writing pseudonymously profoundly attractive, not as an ironic complication of authorship but, instead, as the most direct route to directness available to a writer like Kierkegaard—not "direct communication," per se, but the direct expression of a simpler soul, a purely fictional creature who can be unproblematically the author of his own works and his own words, as he is of his own name, also. Kierkegaard is not his own author, nor the author of his own name, and so he cannot claim (full) responsibility even

---

48. Ibid., p. 140.
49. Plato, *Theaetetus*, 149a.

for those words that issue from his own pen, even—especially!—when those words are not pseudonymous. When he writes his name at the top or the bottom of the page—when he has the audacity to sign it, to use it as his own—he is and is not the one responsible for what he writes. In this way, we might say that, of all the words Kierkegaard wrote, the least his own were those first (or last) two: "Søren Kierkegaard."

Chapter 12

KIERKEGAARD—WHAT "KIND OF" WRITER?
A DIALOGUE

George Pattison

Those familiar with the world of Kierkegaard studies will realize that this dialogue took place some time in the past, before Copenhagen University finally moved away from its historic location at the heart of the old town, in the square mile in which Kierkegaard spent nearly his entire life, to its new site on Amager. Conferences now take place in luminous glass and steel palaces that bear no memory of the university's historic past. They are, in their way, beautiful, but, coinciding with an epochal change in the nature of university studies, we no longer imagine that we might just have missed a certain skinny figure with a crab-like gait and ironic smile disappearing round a corner.

Some time in the past, then, four Kierkegaard scholars are attending a conference on "Kierkegaard Then and Now" in Copenhagen. After the final session of the day finishes at 5 o'clock, they stroll to Kultorvet, a square in the old town, where they order four beers from a bar in a building in which Kierkegaard himself briefly lived during his student years. The square is thronged with people going in all directions home from work. A mime artist moves among them, picking on one individual after another and aping their movements, sometimes behind their backs, sometimes to their faces. Usually his victims take it in good part, but occasionally they show irritation and, once or twice, respond with overt hostility. He gets a lot of laughs and, when he takes the hat round, gets a good collection.

The four scholars work in diverse fields. One is a literary critic, another a poet, the third is an analytic theologian, and the fourth a German philosopher. For the first part of the conversation, the theologian and philosopher are silent; perhaps they are listening, perhaps just thinking; maybe they feel that both the critic and the poet are getting at them—or maybe they are just enjoying the beer and the late summer sun.

THE CRITIC [*addressing himself to the poet*]: What did you think of the conference today? Didn't you find it a bit frustrating?

THE POET: I always find academic conferences frustrating—but what didn't you like about it?

THE CRITIC: Something I hope we can agree on, namely, that most academics simply ignore the way in which everything Kierkegaard said—or, more precisely, wrote—is conditioned by the way in which he said it, the way in which he wrote it.

THE POET: Of course—as I've always said, he's essentially a poet or, in his own words, a poet of the religious.

THE CRITIC: Hmmm. I sense disagreement in the midst of agreement. But you do agree with me that the question of, shall we say, "style," the "how" of his writing, has to be taken into account before we can really get to grips with what his work means for us today?

THE POET: As I said, he's a poet—and though I don't accept the view that poetry is a purely self-referential practice without further reference to the reality in which we live and move and have our being, I certainly do accept that you can't understand poetry without attending to the language in which it is articulated, that is, to each nuance of vocabulary, construction, and rhythm. In fact, I don't just "accept" it. I positively insist on it. You can't reduce Kierkegaard to a string of abstract propositions as some of us seem to do. [*The analytic theologian raises an eyebrow and coughs but says nothing.*] Why do you sense "disagreement"?

THE CRITIC: Simply because I'm not sure that if we do indeed begin by looking at Kierkegaard's style what we see is a "poet."

THE POET: No? That's what I see—what do you see?

THE CRITIC: Something much simpler: a writer.

THE POET: We can both agree that Kierkegaard was a writer, I suppose. But surely the question then is: what kind of writer—and, it seems to me, we have to conclude that he was, after all and despite everything, a poet or, if you must, "a kind of poet."

THE CRITIC: I'm interested that you say "after all and despite everything." What do you mean by that?

THE POET: Obviously I've read enough Kierkegaard to be aware of everything he says about the poet or the poetic personality being the supreme instantiation of the aesthetic and, as such, as far removed from religious truth as possible. But, for a start, I don't think this question would have concerned him as much as it did if it wasn't a real existential issue in his own life. If Kierkegaard was "a kind of poet," then what we see in the confrontation with the aesthetic is precisely Kierkegaard's struggle with his own poetic vocation.

THE CRITIC: You say "for a start." What else?

THE POET: Simply that Kierkegaard was sufficiently inside the world of poetics to know that there are several fundamentally different "kinds" of poet. Whether he was right or whether he was wrong, what he saw in the early Romantics was a kind of poetic practice that was, if you like, purely literary, an elaborate pose shaped by egoism. The other kind of poetry is poetry as essentially a form of service, responsive to a call or vocation over which the ego has no control. *Respondeo ergo sum!* And it's just at this point that poetic vocation and religious vocation converge. It's not for nothing that poets have always (at least until very recently) spoken of this vocation as "divine," and when there's a genuine vocation in play, this isn't just a matter of self-deification but of recognizing the presence of something at work that's beyond and greater than the self. As a matter of fact, I think he was probably right about Schlegel, but the same argument wouldn't apply to Novalis, and I don't think it would apply to Hölderlin either, but that's a whole other set of questions.

THE GERMAN PHILOSOPHER: Ach! Hölderlin—now if Kierkegaard had read Hölderlin instead of Hegel!

THE CRITIC: Yes! But that would be a whole new set of questions. Kierkegaard himself is already enough to be thinking about.

THE GERMAN PHILOSOPHER: Yes, of course. I don't mean to interrupt. Do carry on.

There is a pause. Both critic and poet seem absorbed in their thoughts. Then both start to speak, almost simultaneously.

THE CRITIC: But what do you mean when you say …

THE POET: So what's your problem …

THE CRITIC: Sorry, please …

THE POET: No, you … please …

THE CRITIC: Alright. Let's try to get clear about what's at issue here, and let me start with something very elementary. When we say poetry, we're obviously not talking specifically about verse but [*looking at the German philosopher*] what the Germans call *Dichtung*. [*The German philosopher indicates assent.*] Are we agreed?

THE POET: Of course.

THE CRITIC: So a writer who writes only prose can also be a poet, while someone who writes verse is not necessarily a poet for that reason.

THE POET: Exactly.

THE CRITIC: It's essentially a matter of motivation or, as you say, vocation.

THE POET: Yes.

THE CRITIC: But this is then palpable in the writing itself, what we referred to as the "how" or perhaps the quality of the writing.

THE POET: Exactly.

THE CRITIC: And that's where my problem begins because I don't see anything poetic about Kierkegaard's style.

THE POET [*surprised*]: Really?

THE CRITIC: Really.

THE POET: So what do you see?

THE CRITIC: Writing.

   Pause.

THE POET: Is that all? Just "writing"? And here's me thinking that literary critics were people who weren't satisfied with vague generalities about "writing" but knew how to classify, categorize, and analyze "writing" into its genres, epochs, styles, aims, and all the rest of it, people who could make judgments about literature instead of just waffling about it. Sorry, I don't mean that personally—but am I wrong?

THE CRITIC: Not at all. I mean "writing" in a quite specific sense.

THE POET: Say more.

THE CRITIC: Very well—you asked for it! But I'll have to have another beer before I do. You?

   The poet responds affirmatively. The critic calls the waiter and orders two more beers. The theologian and philosopher are only halfway through theirs and pass.

THE CRITIC: When I say "a writer," I'm pointing to a kind of literature that has a very distinctive time and place and a very distinctive style, namely, the nineteenth century—to which the Marxist in me would add that this is a style that quite precisely reflects the emerging conditions of an urban, industrialized capitalist society. Up until this time, very few people actually made a living out of writing, unless they had the benefit of an aristocratic patron. Only from the early modern period onward do you start to see men (and, in the first instance, almost exclusively men) aspiring to become "men of letters," men whose life and livelihood was, literally, in "letters," writing for publication and sale and living by their pen. And Kierkegaard is just such a man of letters. Notice how, when he writes about his aesthetic or poetic writings in *The Point of View*, he writes about himself as an "author" and about what he has written as his "authorship." A poet wouldn't use these terms about his work. And this is why I'm entirely unfazed by his obsession with his relation to the public and the poor financial return he gets on this authorship. The problem for Kierkegaard is not that he, as an author, has to have dealings with the market. It's simply that his dealings, as he sees it, are unsuccessful and that he merits a greater financial reward than he has, in fact, had. In any other country, he says, he *would* have been able to live by his writing, and that, he thinks, is just as it should be. In Denmark, however, it needed a special divine providence to provide him with the private income he needed to devote himself to his literary work.

THE POET: So you're saying Kierkegaard wrote for money?

THE CRITIC: No, of course not. What I am saying is that Kierkegaard regarded literature as a bona fide profession in its own right. Money isn't the motivation, but it is a condition, a necessary condition of literary practice—and that means developing a relation with the public, dealing with publishers, printers, and booksellers and the real economics of the production, distribution, and consumption of literature.

THE POET: That sounds almost cynical.

THE CRITIC: I don't mean it like that at all. On the contrary. I'm simply saying that the modern writer, the kind of writer I think Kierkegaard was, isn't about dreaming Romantic dreams but about engaging with the world as it actually is. Literature becomes a form of action and, like any worldly action, has to get to grips with the world as it finds it. Of course, it's a different kind of action from that of the politician, the industrialist, the soldier, and so on, but it's no less "real" in its own way. Maybe it has a certain distance from the world, and that distance is necessary if it's to hold a mirror to life as it's lived, but, when we do, what we see in it is, exactly, life as it is lived. And, the great writers would claim, life as it's really lived and not just as it seems to those who get their view of the world from a daily diet of news, gossip, and, in a word, "idle talk." A small point but a telling one: we know that Kierkegaard took great pains about choosing the font and print layout for his works. That's typical of a writer in my sense, but not of a poet.

THE POET: I'm not sure about the last point—think of Blake. But I start to see what you're getting at. [*Brief pause. He sips his beer.*] However, particularly in the quasi-Marxist terms in which you explain it, the writer seems merely to be an epiphenomenon, a reflection, of the age, an expression of its essential spirit— perhaps even "what the age demands." So how does that square with Kierkegaard's insistence on resisting or rising above the day-to-day reality of the modern world. Isn't the kind of writer you describe just toadying to the capitalist system?

THE CRITIC: Not at all. He's simply paying his dues to reality—and a lot of what I've said could be illustrated from what Kierkegaard himself wrote about Mme. Gyllembourg's novels of everyday life: they take reality as it is but also transform it by virtue of the ethical framework in which they approach it.[1] Just think of some of the great writers of the nineteenth century: Emerson, Carlyle, Hugo, Arnold, Dickens, Dostoevsky, and one could even add Nietzsche (also often claimed for the poets). These were people who engaged with the world in its own contemporary terms but who also challenged and contested the accepted discourses of politics, social life, and religion—not to mention challenging the conventions of literature itself.

---

1. See TA / SKS 8, 7–106.

THE POET: That's a fairly diverse group you've got there—essayists, novelists, historians, politicians, and Emerson and Arnold, at least, were also poets (not very good in Emerson's case, but that's another matter).

THE CRITIC: Yes, and that's part of my point. "Writing" or being a writer in this nineteenth-century sense is a genre-busting business. It's not just that each of them writes in a distinct genre—Emerson essays, Carlyle history, Hugo, Dickens and Dostoevsky novels, Arnold poetry and criticism, Dickens travelogue or whatever. The point is that each of them is internally differentiated with regard to genre. Emerson's works, as you've pointed out, include essays and poetry; Carlyle is an historian and an essayist; Dostoevsky produced his *Diary of a Writer* commenting on current affairs alongside his novels, while *Les Misérables* includes a detailed analysis of the Battle of Waterloo as well as an essay on the difference between insurrection and revolution. Bakhtin has a comment on the nature of the Dostoievskian novel that I think applies more generally to the new kind of professional writer emerging in the nineteenth century. It's a comment that relates to another new phenomenon of the nineteenth century, the mass-circulation newspaper (something that, as we know, also concerned Kierkegaard). The Dostoievskian novel, he said, is like a page from a newspaper on which we see articles dealing with the most diverse subjects—great matters of state, scandals, prices, in short, anything and everything. And that's just what we see when we look at Kierkegaard's authorship as a whole: from the aphorisms of *Either/Or*, through essays on theater and literature, passages of philosophy, religious meditations, polemical analyses of the present age, and much more—especially if we also take the journals and papers into account. Like every true nineteenth-century man of letters, Kierkegaard was essentially a chameleon or, if you like, a thoroughbred mongrel: his own person, to be sure, but only by virtue of being a bit of everything! In these terms, we can take the subtitle of his student play on the old and new soap-cellars as epitomizing his work as a whole: the war of all against all.

THE POET: Very eloquent—but aren't you remaking Kierkegaard in the image of the press he so despised?

THE CRITIC: Did he despise it? Didn't he actually write at least one volume's worth of writings specifically for newspapers and journals?[2] Wasn't it in a newspaper that he launched his most direct piece of communication, his "attack on Christendom"?[3]

THE POET: Just because he published in newspapers doesn't mean that his writing as a whole has the character of journalism, though—does it?

THE CRITIC: No, of course not. And, obviously, I'm not saying that Kierkegaard's writing (any more than Dostoevsky's or Hugo's) was on the same level as the rest of the journalism of his time. When he complains about being a genius in a

---

2. These are collected in SKS 14 but are distributed across a number of volumes of *Kierkegaard's Writings*.
3. See TM, 3–86 / SKS 14, 123–221.

market town, history has essentially vindicated him. What other Danish writers of the 1840s have the kind of international readership that Kierkegaard has acquired? Andersen, of course—but we can't say that Andersen has influenced modern sensibility as a whole in the way that Kierkegaard has. I'm only a "quasi"-Marxist, and I'm not attempting to *reduce* Kierkegaard to a mere manifestation of his age. As I said before, if the writer is to hold a critical mirror to his age, he has not only to represent the age as it is but also to take a certain step back from it or, if you like, beyond it. He reveals the war of all against all, but in doing so, he invites reflection as to how we might seek a peace that transcends our present conflicts. But—NB!—only by acknowledging them for what and as they are. This doesn't mean that Kierkegaard has to give us a catalog of every last detail of what was going on in Copenhagen in his lifetime—and this is where we come back to the question of style. To change metaphors, Kierkegaard's chameleon, mongrel style is a very precise instrument with which to dissect and reveal the essential tendencies of his time in their ethical and, some would say, religious significance. It's diamond-sharp and, like the many facets of a cut diamond, a single Kierkegaardian sentence can take those who know how to read it right to the heart of what is going on not just in his nineteenth century but, I'd say, in modernity as a whole.

THE POET: I wouldn't deny for a moment that there are a lot of different things going on across the whole range of Kierkegaard's writings and, often, a lot of different things going on within the compass of a single work. But what I would want to say is that there are passages that rise above what you call the chameleon or mongrel world of modernity, passages attuned to a different kind of temporality, a different kind of relation to reality. In this regard, I'm happy to borrow your image of the diamond cutter. Or, in one of Kierkegaard's own images, they provide the Archimedean point from which we get to see the whole. These are moments of vision, atoms of eternity in time, bringing unity and coherence to what is otherwise, as you put it, a chameleon reality. This is where we find Kierkegaard's poetry. And it's here that we see Kierkegaard doing something more than taking up a position among others in a multisided debate, as your man of letters does. Here we see Kierkegaard pointing—who can do more?—to something that comes from outwith present-day reality and calls us, as the poet himself is called, to see that this reality itself can never be the sole measure of what should count as real.

THE CRITIC: Isn't that describing the poet in terms that Christianity reserves for prophets and apostles? Isn't that rather counterintuitive in the light of Kierkegaard's own distinction between the poetic genius and the apostle?

THE POET: Not at all because what Kierkegaard objects to in the poetic genius is his egoism, as when Goethe prays to his own genius rather than to God. The poet privileged by early Romanticism is the kind of poet who finds his inspiration and, if you like, his poetic sustenance in himself. The Kierkegaardian poet of the religious is one who is basically attempting to translate the Word of divine calling into the language of his own time and place.

THE CRITIC: So give me an example.

THE POET: How do you mean?

THE CRITIC: An example. Give me an example of one of these moments of vision. Give me a bit of Kierkegaardian poetry.

THE POET: Goodness! Where to begin? What about the Diapsalmata? Or how he evokes the overture to *Don Giovanni* in the essay on Mozart? Or the opening of the Eulogy on Abraham where he ponders the possibility that a wild, fermenting power lies at the heart of everything and "there is no eternal consciousness in man,"[4] or the wonderful evocation of silence in one of the discourses on the lilies and birds—"Out there it is silent: when all things fall silent in the silence of night, yet no less when the day is stirring and its thousand chords create an ocean of sound—even then it is silent."[5] Give me half an hour, and I could think of many more. In fact, the British art critic Herbert Read even wrote out a passage about angels from the Journals in verse, comparing it to Rilke:

They have followed me in the bright moonlit nights
and to the solitary forests by the sea;
They have walked by my side in the dark streets
at midnight and at the break of day;
they have raced by my side on horseback,
they have accompanied me in their carriage,
they have filled my house with their presence,
they have penetrated into my own room.
Their voices have sounded in my ear
and sounded in my soul:
the tissue of my soul is spun from their delicate strains.[6]

As he recites this, the poet's voice moves from the discursive tone of the preceding conversation and takes on a ritual, incantatory force.

THE GERMAN PHILOSOPHER [*clapping*]: Very good! Very good indeed.

THE CRITIC: Indeed. But how does it serve your argument?

THE POET [*disappointed*]: You mean you don't hear it? Don't you hear how the rhythm of the language gradually takes over the explanatory tone of the prose discourse and creates a kind of musical effect, a song of the soul, if you like, a song

---

4. FT, 15 / SKS 4, 112.
5. WA, 13 / SKS 11, 18–19.
6. H. Read, *Annals of Innocence and Experience* (London: Faber and Faber, 1946), pp. 116–123.

that, like all music, dances with silence, with the silent interval that makes the separation and structuring of notes and chords possible?

THE CRITIC: So where Hegel puts poetry above music, you'd put music above poetry? And doesn't that mean we have to transcend language in order to become religious? So what does religion then *mean*?

THE POET: I'm definitely not thinking in Hegelian terms, not least because I'm not thinking of higher or lower or of there being some kind of competition between different art forms. What I'm talking about is the musicality of language itself, the music that's in language, and the silence that's in that music in language. And as the discourse on silence makes clear, it's attending to that silence that makes us ready to hear the Word of God.

THE CRITIC: Maybe I'm just tone-deaf, then, but I don't hear anything like that in Kierkegaard. In several of the passages you mention, I see only a carefully constructed pastiche of early nineteenth-century nature writing, a pastiche that engages the reader's familiarity with a set of literary conventions in order to set up an argument about the relationship between man, nature, and God. But that argument has a very specific field of signification *in* language, not above it. And call me cynical, but I can't help making the comment that the passage on *Don Giovanni* is actually plagiarized from Wagner (or so I've heard), while, if I'm right, Read admits to having paraphrased Kierkegaard, rather than quoting him directly! I'm happy to concede that there's great literary intelligence at work here, but I see only the literary craftsman, not the breath of divine inspiration. And I don't feel that I need to see more. Can you help me?

THE POET: I'm not sure. At one level, it probably is a case of either you see it or you don't, either you hear it or you don't, either you feel it or you don't—as Kierkegaard and his contemporaries always said, poetry is a kind of "immediacy." Often, of course, that is to do with how poetry expresses the immediacy of our experience of nature, of human emotion, and of human love, but Kierkegaard also related it to a higher immediacy, an immediacy after reflection that is also, in a fundamental sense, before reflection. I've spoken about this in terms of calling, and I do think that is the pivot on which all of this turns (the poet can only be a poet because he is called to be a poet), but I suppose we could also gloss this moment, this event, this encounter with immediacy, or whatever we call it in more specifically Christian terms as the sudden realization that we are standing before God and looked on by God with his infinite, eternal look of love.

THE CRITIC: That seems to be several steps further down the road, and I haven't even made the first step. Persuade me that Kierkegaard's literary style isn't like that mime artist, mimicking the passers-by for our entertainment?

THE POET [*surprised*]: You really think that's what's happening here?

THE CRITIC: I insist (again) I'm not saying it's *just* parody, *just* quotation, *just* text feeding on text. Even the mime artist is doing something that changes our relation to the reality he mimics, and much more so in the case of Kierkegaard. To be sure, he's wanting to get his readers to think about God and about the possibility of Christian faith, but he's neither a poet nor a preacher. As a writer, he is, perhaps like all writers, essentially indirect: he gives us the materials, but we have to do the job ourselves.

THE POET: This seems to me to make words too external. Surely we are the beings that we are by virtue of being shaped in and through our words. Another Kierkegaardian quote: "Speak that I may see you!"[7] Kierkegaard had never read *I and Thou*, of course, but I think he understood intuitively (as all poets understand) that the word is a living bond between human beings. When I speak to you, I don't just tell you about something that happened to me. I communicate something of myself, my experience, my life to you so that you too are able to feel in yourself the power that makes me as I am. At least, that's what happens when language is working as it should, and it's that optimal function of language that poetry sets in motion—often having to do so, as in Kierkegaard's time, in a context in which (I quote again) "men speak only to conceal the mind."[8]

THE CRITIC: To my mind, this is making Kierkegaard sound too much like his contemporary Grundtvig, the preacher-poet whose "living word" galvanized his congregation. But Kierkegaard never aimed at that and, apart from the fact that he loathed Grundtvig, he sought readers, not a congregation. Surely the whole message of his edifying writings is that, as he says somewhere, the author is essentially absent and the reader is left to work it all out in solitary fear and trembling?

THE POET: Of course, if we're going to be literal, Kierkegaard was a writer, not a speaker. But what attracted you to Kierkegaard in the first place? Wasn't it because you heard in his writing a voice like no other voice, a voice that spoke words you'd never heard before, a word revealing facets of the world, of yourself, that you'd never otherwise have known existed?

THE CRITIC: I don't deny I've learned a lot from Kierkegaard. He's always given me a lot to think about. But what excites me about his writing is its complex, multi-referential polyphony, a polyphony that enables him both to reflect and to critique his time in extraordinary detail, so that the study of text and context become inseparable.

THE POET: But what about what it's about?

For the last few minutes, the analytic theologian and the German philosopher, who for much of the conversation both seemed to be absorbed in watching the passing crowd, have been listening intently.

---

7. CI, 14n. / SKS 1, 76; SLW, 398 / SKS 6, 369.
8. SLW, 339 / SKS 6, 315.

THE ANALYTIC THEOLOGIAN: Exactly! "What it's about"! That's what it's about, not the words, not the style, not the context, but *what's* being said, the content, the meaning! But I'm afraid, poet, that you're a very poor defender of Christian faith. I can't see any future for a faith that has to rely on the kind of silent feelings and intuitions of love that you were talking about. You spoke of the logos, but logos means both word and reason. Speech has to be about something. It has to have a *content*, something definite, something clear and distinct. In the case of Christian faith, this means a definite teaching and definite doctrinal propositions that can be understood and defended or opposed. In this respect, I'm with you, critic: we have to be much more definite than all this poetic hand-waving, though, unlike you, I don't see this just in terms of literary history. When Kierkegaard speaks about the love of God and about forgiveness, he's saying something that is as comprehensible and real today as it was in the nineteenth century and, I may add, in the first century. You don't need literary history to believe in forgiveness!

THE CRITIC: I don't think that what I do or what I'm proposing is *just* "history." History is a part of it since we can only fully understand any linguistic product in terms of its context, but then we also have to understand its internal dynamics— its rhetorical moves, its prosody, its tropes, its genres, and so on. But I've never claimed that that is *all* we have to do or that there's nothing outside the text. I concede that we also need to see what Kierkegaard is about, but that means first undertaking the kind of work I've just mentioned. And, I might add, it's also in this regard that we make our decisions for privileging one writer over another. You can doubtless explain to me the precise theological differences between Kierkegaard and his contemporary Martensen, but the reason why we still go on reading Kierkegaard and have left Martensen to the theologians (and not very many of them, at that) is that Kierkegaard simply is a more satisfying and complex writer and that is also why his work is still able to hold up a critical mirror to the age in a way that Martensen is not. And while theology isn't my thing, I think that Kierkegaard's literary superiority is also connected with why he is qualified to serve as a spokesman for Christianity in ways that Martensen is not. Martensen may have excelled in spelling out a string of clear and distinct concepts in a good old-fashioned school-masterly way, but because his work fails to capture the thick, complex, interactive, and multi-aspected style of modernity, he cannot really tell me what a modern Christian faith might look like—which is what I need if I'm to make a decision for or against it.

THE ANALYTIC THEOLOGIAN: I don't have a view on the respective literary merits of Kierkegaard and Martensen—in fact, I've never read the latter and insofar as he seems to have been a Hegelian, I don't think I'd find him very congenial. But what I do know is what Kierkegaard himself clearly teaches: that the decision of faith is not relative to historical location and that whether we are contemporaries of Jesus, like Peter or the sinful woman, or whether we are what Kierkegaard called disciples at secondhand, everyone who confesses that Jesus is the Christ in whom all sins are forgiven is saying exactly the same thing. Furthermore, we can't be got to believe anything like this on the basis of literary style, and if we think that's what's happened, then we're deluding ourselves. I admit that sometimes a beautifully formed phrase may provide the occasion for us getting insight, perhaps by attracting our attention to what is at issue, but whether we can believe it to be true or not demands a different kind of persuasion. And as I understand it, this is precisely what Kierkegaard means when he says again and again that he doesn't have authority to teach and is only preparing the way for a full-blooded declaration of Christian faith. But once we get to the point of being presented with that faith, its teaching, its demands, and its promises, we need arguments and we need to test the witness offered by scripture and tradition in the light of reason.

THE POET: But surely we must be moved to want to believe. Let's say you have established your compendium of propositions that someone must believe if they are to call themselves a Christian. Let me take an example. Experts rate Poussin as one of the great painters of the Western tradition. I myself don't like his work. It doesn't do anything for me, and I can't really see what makes it different from that of many of his contemporaries. But even if someone could persuade me that I was wrong, and that he was a great painter, it wouldn't follow that, speaking personally, I would *like* his work any more than I do now. If the work itself doesn't move me, explanations and arguments don't help: I have to see for myself. And that, I'm saying, is what true poetry does: it opens our eyes or, better, ears. It helps us hear the movement of the love that moves the sun and other stars. That's what Kierkegaard does for us, and that's why he remains great.

THE GERMAN PHILOSOPHER: Yes! That's right—and philosophy *must* listen to poetry if it is not to collapse into abstraction. But philosophy is still needed. As you say, poetry awakens us to a certain mood, a certain feeling. I might even call it the feeling of holiness. Here is a simple object, the glass on the table. I am not a poet but if I were, then I could set out the way in which the glass is present to us so as to open our eyes to the interplay of glass, liquid, light, and refreshment that transforms the everyday into a manifestation of the holy. But what is said in the poem can be said only in the manner of poetry, and if the poem is truly to impact on our lives, then we must translate it into a language that makes that truth manifest in such a way that we can hold fast to it. And that is the language of philosophy, although [*he raises his finger and looks pointedly at the analytic theologian*] this need not be the language of propositions. The philosopher will never supplant the poet, and the work of the poet will always precede the labor of the philosopher, as Homer, Pindar, and the tragedians preceded the birth of philosophy. But then, as now, the poets' words required interpretation; they call for thinking.

THE ANALYTIC THEOLOGIAN [*irritatedly*]: But why do you reject formal propositions? How can you even talk about truth if there is not a proposition of which we can say that it is true or false?

THE GERMAN PHILOSOPHER: Because the essence of language is not that simple. Truth that is more than tautologous cannot be unqualifiedly identical with itself. If we are to escape tautology, then there must be difference, time, and dialogue.

Nothing will ever be simply what it is. Meaning cannot be separated from the entire hermeneutical context.

THE ANALYTIC THEOLOGIAN: But then anything can mean anything, and in that case, we'd be better off sticking with poetry. At least it sounds nice—whereas the sort of philosophy you're talking about ends up producing strings of barbaric neologisms!

The German philosopher raises his eyebrows but says nothing.

THE POET [*after an embarrassed pause*]: I'd be very worried if poetry was valued only because it sounds nice. That's reducing it to entertainment. It's not "nice"; it can be very challenging, as in Rilke's "Torso of Apollo": "You must change your life."[9] The poet speaks because speech is demanded and what he says demands a lot from the listener in return. In poetry as in religion, it's a matter of "not less than everything." In the case of Kierkegaard, for example (and let's not forget him), it demands that we become nothing, pure attention to the silent word of God that holds everything there is in being!

THE ANALYTIC THEOLOGIAN: I'm sorry but I just don't see anywhere in the Bible where it says God's Word is silent. A silent word is no word at all. This is precisely the kind of error into which Schleiermacher led romantic theology.

THE CRITIC: Actually, I'm not unsympathetic to our theological friend. In the end, I can't claim to be a person of faith, but I do want to be sure that what we're talking about in any given conversation really is something real and tangible, something for which there is evidence for and against, something about which we can make a judgment. That reality for me is the concrete literary and social world in which Kierkegaard was the writer that he was: out of which he developed and to which he spoke and through which he can, if you like, speak to us today—but always under the condition of patient and cautious critical interpretation.

THE GERMAN PHILOSOPHER: I have no objection to patience, caution, criticism, or interpretation, but yet—I insist—it is the thought and not the surface of the text that most calls for thinking.

THE POET: I can accept that thinking as you describe it may have a certain proximity to poetry. But I come back to what I said at the beginning. What everything hinges on is that the poet is a poet as responsive to a word of calling. His is not a bourgeois social role, like the man of letters. He lives in the present age, but his true life is beyond it.

9. Rainer Maria Rilke, "Archaic Torso of Apollo," in *Ahead of All Parting: The Selected Poetry and Prose of Rainer Maria Rilke*, trans. Stephen Mitchell (New York: Modern Library, 1995), p. 67.

THE CRITIC: Goodness! I've just noticed the time. We have to reconvene for dinner in ten minutes. We'd better be drinking up and making our way.

THE GERMAN PHILOSOPHER: Ah! That's so typical of the modern world. We never give ourselves time to think anything through to the end because we always have to be somewhere else! Plato and Kierkegaard had their symposiasts talk philosophy after dinner and all night.

THE ANALYTIC THEOLOGIAN: But then they didn't have to produce research reports and quantified outcomes.

THE CRITIC: True, but perhaps it'll leave us free to enjoy the dinner!

When they arrive at the restaurant, our group splits up and is absorbed into the larger gathering of twenty or thirty conference attendees. Here, as often on such occasions, the talk is about people, about "who's in, who's out," about friends and memories, and, occasionally, plans. As they walk back to their hotel later in the evening, they are mostly silent. It has been a good day and a pleasant evening with good food, good wine, and good company. Yet each in their own way senses that neither in the conference itself, nor in their conversation, nor at dinner had an essential word been said or, to say the same thing another way, each felt that their own words had somehow, inexplicably and unintentionally, blunted or distorted and that the conversation had somehow obscured the truth they were each struggling to articulate. Each therefore resolved to work harder at making themselves understood the next day.

INDEX

abandonment, 24, 112, 163–5, 212

Abraham (Biblical patriarch), 19, 118, 142, 148, 159, 222

absence/absentee, 104, 108, 112, 114, 122, 124, 127–9, 152, 187, 194, 205, 207, 211, 224

absurdity, 7, 65, 85, 111, 117, 189

accountability, 3

acting/actor/actress, 77–8, 82, 84, 86–8, 112, 139–40, 168, 205

action, 44–9, 51, 54–5, 59, 63, 75, 79, 85, 145, 153, 170, 175, 178–80, 184, 187–8, 219

Adam (Biblical first man), 122–4, 127–8, 131, 158–9, 163

Adorno, Theodor, 7

aesthetics, 16, 20, 22, 30, 63, 169–70, 174, 177, 191, 198, 218

Agacinski, Sylviane, 122, 126, 128, 210

Alexander III of Macedon (the Great), 211

Alles, Gregory D., 154

alterity. See otherness

Alypius of Thagaste (Saint), 169

ambiguity, 2, 4, 25, 47, 69, 89, 209, 212

Amir, Lydia B., 91–2, 95

Andersen, Hans Christian, 5, 25, 28, 100, 173–88, 190, 197–8, 221

anonymity, 1, 7, 15, 62–3, 73, 152, 160, 166, 193, 196, 208

anthropology, 78

anxiety, 2, 37, 94, 98, 123, 125–6, 130, 133–5, 144, 148, 211

apostle/apostolic, 49, 51–2, 55–6, 212, 221

Archimedes, 221

Aristophanes, 65, 196, 208–10

Aristotle, 25, 42, 45, 47–9, 51, 93, 174–8, 180, 183, 185–7, 191

Arnold, Matthew, 219–20

art/artist/arts, the, 16, 18, 22–3, 38, 62, 88, 107, 147, 149–51, 168, 170, 175–6, 183, 195–7, 223

atonement, 33, 36–7, 121, 123, 126, 134

Auden, W. H., 92

audience. See spectator

Audollene, Auguste, 168

Augustine of Hippo (Saint), 24, 155–8, 161, 163–5, 168–70

author of the authors. See pseudonym/ pseudonymity

authority, 3–6, 9, 15, 22, 24, 35–6, 41, 67, 76, 108–19, 121, 133, 135, 137, 165, 182–4, 186, 195, 199, 226

autonomy, 10

awakening, 22, 27–8, 31, 35, 61, 111, 148, 166

Babylon, 156–7

Bach, Johann Sebastian, 146, 152

Bakhtin, Mikhail, 17, 152, 220

Barrett, Lee C., 156, 193, 198

Barthes, Roland, 24, 110, 114–15, 187

Bauer, Felice, 117

beauty, 54, 88, 127–8, 139–41, 150, 176–7, 215, 226

Beethoven, Ludwig van, 145, 148

belief, 5, 25, 41–3, 45–6, 77, 85, 87, 126, 162, 175, 178, 187–8, 190–1, 201, 225

Bennett, Camille, 164

Berlin (Germany), 24, 104, 155, 162–3, 165–8, 170

Berthold, Daniel, 187

Bible, 19, 92, 149, 153, 157, 164, 169, 190, 226–7

Bigelow, Pat, 60, 65–6, 71

biography, 7, 14, 21, 44, 110, 116, 145, 152
auto-, 25, 205–6

Blake, William, 150, 219
Blicher, Steen Steensen, 181–2
body, 64–7, 69, 96–7, 112, 127, 140, 146, 157–8, 165, 170, 178
Boesen, Emil, 81–2, 93
Böhringer, Friedrich, 170
Boissier, Gaston, 169
boldness (*parrhesia*), 51–2
Bonhoeffer, Dietrich, 136
boredom, 81, 209
Borge, Victor, 91
Borges, Jorge Luis, 76, 190
Boulding, Maria, 169
Bradley, F. H., 139–41
Braver, Lee, 142, 147, 152
Buber, Martin, 7–8, 151, 224
Buddha (Siddhartha Gautama), 153
Bunim, Simcha, 151

Cain, David, 28
calling. *See* vocation
Camus, Albert, 7, 119
Cappelørn, Niels Jørgen, 1, 11–13, 21, 36
Carlyle, Thomas, 219–20
Carnivalesque, 17, 152
Carroll, Noël, 187
Carthage, 24, 155, 162–4, 168–70
Cervantes, Miguel de, 76
character, 42, 45, 47, 49, 51, 55, 57, 201
chatter, 24, 121, 125–7, 136–7, 219
Christendom, 23, 32–3, 47, 53, 57, 93, 160–1, 199, 220
Christensen, Nina, 174
Christian/Christianity, 5, 12–13, 16, 19, 23–4, 30–9, 41–2, 47–9, 51–4, 57, 59, 92–5, 97–9, 103, 108, 145, 153, 158–62, 164–5, 168–70, 197, 199, 211–12, 221, 223–6
Cicero, Marcus Tullius, 157
comedy/comic, 52, 85, 91–2, 94–100, 103, 105, 125, 141–2, 144, 149, 168, 170
communication, 10, 23, 30, 41–2, 59–60, 64–5, 67, 69–71, 83, 94, 98, 101, 107, 111–12, 130–6, 195, 199, 224
    direct, 38, 51, 66, 71, 73, 94, 98, 108, 112–13, 115, 199–201, 212, 220
    indirect, 29, 39, 61, 65, 71, 77, 82, 85, 94, 98, 109, 111–13, 167, 198–201
communion, 36–7, 131, 133

Conant, James, 10, 18–19, 21
concealment, 23, 38, 88, 94, 111, 113, 115, 117, 127, 133, 135, 161, 201, 224
confession, 36–7, 39, 50, 52–3, 56, 162–3, 166, 225
confidence, bold (*Frimodighed*), 47, 50–6
Confucius, 153
conscientiousness, 47
consciousness. *See* mind
contentment, 93, 103–4. *See also* happiness
continuity, 25, 131, 188, 190
contradiction, 2, 92, 95–7, 103, 106, 159, 170, 173, 177, 186
contrition, 47
Copenhagen (Denmark), 2, 15–16, 25, 105, 121, 155, 160, 162, 165, 168, 215, 221
copy, 76, 203
corrective, 93–4
courage, 47, 51, 77, 80
cowardice, 158–60, 162
Crites, Stephen, 112
critic/criticism, 25, 48, 85, 173–5, 185, 187, 189, 215, 218, 220, 222, 224, 227
crowd, 51, 68, 70, 159–60. *See also* public
culture, 11, 53
Cyprian (Saint), 169

Daab, Annelise, 91
Daise, Benjamin, 16
Davenport, John, 189–91
David (Biblical monarch), 44–5, 47, 157
death, 34, 36–7, 56, 82, 89, 93, 107, 114, 116, 118, 128, 135–6, 147–9, 157–8, 164–5, 186, 205–7, 209
    of the author, 24, 110, 114–15, 117, 187, 204
deception, 9, 18–20, 71, 77, 85–8, 103, 111, 113, 126, 159, 164–7
deconstruction, 1, 8–9, 12–13, 15, 19–22, 25, 174, 194, 201, 204
Deleuze, Gilles, 23, 75–6
demonic, 32, 130–3, 137
Denmark, 6, 16–17, 23, 52, 102, 160–1, 174, 218
Derrida, Jacques, 7–8, 19–20, 25, 114, 194, 201–7

desire, 17–18, 60–3, 65, 71, 108, 111, 114–15, 129–30, 136, 163, 171, 201
despair, 93, 98, 104, 148
detachment. *See* distance
dialectic/dialectical, 23, 29, 31, 37–8, 48–9, 52–3, 57, 65, 70, 72, 75, 79, 105, 144, 147, 162, 199–200, 209–10
dialogue, 23, 80, 85, 195, 208, 215, 226
diaries, 1, 80, 82, 145, 166
Dickens, Charles, 219–20
difference, 3, 128–9, 206, 226
discourse, 1, 31, 35–6, 42–3, 49, 51, 56, 71–2, 105, 113, 208, 219, 222–3
disguise. *See* mask
distance, 3, 10, 12, 19, 62, 73, 123, 125–6, 131, 142, 148, 175, 197, 212, 219
dogma/dogmatics, 42, 49, 73, 123, 178
Dostoevsky, Fyodor, 148, 219–20
doubt, 83, 87, 116, 126–7, 178, 191
drama/dramatic. *See* theater/theatrical
dramaturgy. *See* theater/theatrical
dread. *See* anxiety
duplication, 75–6, 78, 212

earnestness, 1–2, 8–10, 12, 20, 29, 32–3, 47, 50–1, 56, 105, 144, 170, 212
edification/edifying, 12, 17, 19, 31–3, 35–6, 45, 47, 49, 51, 57, 60–1, 68, 70, 72, 105, 224
editor (*Udgiver*), 32, 35, 61, 81, 83, 119
Emerson, Ralph Waldo, 219–20
emotion, 44–5, 47–51, 223
epistemology, 43, 45, 57, 110
eros/erotic. *See* love
error, 7, 113, 126–7, 133–4, 136, 227
Esau (Hebrew Bible figure), 153
escape. *See* fleeing/flight
eternality, 32, 86, 97, 167, 170, 221–3
ethical/ethics, 10, 19, 23–4, 33, 39, 44–8, 50, 54, 79, 81, 88, 96–7, 110–14, 118–19, 123, 154, 157, 161, 163, 219, 221
  of authorship, 24, 107, 110, 115–16
  -religious, 29, 31–2
  teleological suspension of the, 139
eucatastrophe, 189–90
Eve (Biblical first woman), 128
existentialism, 16
experiment, 77, 82–4, 143

faith, 2, 6–7, 10, 23–4, 33, 41–2, 47, 50, 52, 65, 70, 97–8, 103, 108, 118–19, 128, 144, 156, 162, 165, 167, 191, 209, 224–7
fantasy, 33, 79, 88, 115, 174, 183
farce, 16, 85, 98, 144, 167–8, 170
femininity, 205–6, 212
Fenger, Henning, 18–19, 21, 27, 116
Fenves, Peter, 126–7, 132
fiction, 1, 6, 21, 25, 76, 83–4, 116, 174–5, 188, 190, 208–9, 212
finitude, 64, 97, 178
Fischer-Lichte, Erika, 78
Fitzpatrick, Melissa, 182
fleeing/flight, 24, 101, 113, 119, 121, 124, 130, 132–4, 149, 153–70
flesh. *See* body
Flieger, Verlyn, 188–90
footnote, 96, 199
forgiveness, 37, 39, 47, 115, 225
Foucault, Michel, 114, 187
Fox, Robin Lane, 157, 164
fragmentation, 12, 20–1, 62, 118, 180, 182, 189, 206
freedom, 51, 60–1, 67, 69, 88, 101, 114, 123, 129–32, 134, 137, 166–7
Freud, Sigmund, 165, 212
friendship, 49, 67, 69–70, 147, 163, 169
Furtak, Rick Anthony, 143

Garff, Joakim, 5, 12, 14, 17, 19, 21–2, 28, 107, 116, 167, 173–4, 181, 191
genesis. *See* origin/original/originary
Genet, Jean, 202–5, 207
genius, 63, 129, 148–9, 173, 179–80, 183–8, 220–1
genre, 1, 7–9, 22, 218, 220, 225
gentleness, 47
Gettier, Edmund, 42
God, 4, 6, 17, 31–4, 36–9, 41, 48, 51, 53–6, 62, 67–8, 70–1, 73, 98, 102–3, 111, 115–16, 118, 122, 124–5, 131, 133–6, 142, 156–8, 161–5, 183, 201, 211, 221, 223–5, 227
Goethe, Johann Wolfgang von, 170, 221
Gorgias, 86–8
Gospel. *See* Bible
gossip. *See* chatter
Governance, 4–5, 11. *See also* God

Goya, Francisco, 148
grace, 34, 37, 39, 55, 93, 161–2, 190
grammar, 9, 44, 49
grave. *See* tomb
Greve, Wilfried, 11
Grimm, Jacob and Wilhelm, 145
Grundtvig, N. F. S., 224
Guadalquibir River, 22, 27–30, 32–5, 39
guilt, 35, 94, 97–8, 122–3
Gyllembourg, Thomasine, 5, 181–2,
    197–8, 219

Hamann, Johann Georg, 95
Hannay, Alastair, 96, 101, 105, 143–4
happiness, 50, 76, 93, 142, 148, 175,
    189–90
Hartshorne, M. Holmes, 19
Hegel, Georg Wilhelm Friedrich, 49, 75,
    79, 97, 102, 112, 117, 142, 145–7,
    150, 167, 176–7, 179–81, 187, 191,
    202, 207–12, 217, 223, 225
Heiberg, Johan Ludvig, 104–5
Heiberg, Johanne Luise, 86
Heidegger, Martin, 139–41, 150
Helms, Eleanor D., 11–12, 22, 28, 180,
    188, 190–1
hermeneutic/hermeneutics, 9, 64, 227
    of suspicion, 12, 18
Herod Antipater, 153
hiddenness, 24, 29, 60–3, 65, 70–1, 80, 88,
    127–8, 147, 200
history, 7, 11, 15, 29–30, 61, 121–4, 127,
    144–6, 151–2, 155, 159, 175–7, 179,
    182, 184–5, 188, 190, 194–5, 205,
    208–11, 215, 220–1, 225
Hitler, Adolf, 148
Holberg, Ludvig, 100–1
Hölderlin, J. C. Friedrich, 217
holiness, 55, 139–40, 142, 150, 158, 226
Holy Spirit, 33
Homer, 145–6, 226
honesty, 47
Hong, Howard V. and Edna H., 30, 83, 98,
    101, 105, 107, 165–7
hope, 33, 41, 47, 69, 104, 135, 163
Howland, Jacob, 15
Hughes, Carl S., 17–18, 28, 30
Hugo, Victor, 219–20
Hultberg, Helge, 91–2, 96

humility, 47, 50–1, 152
humor, 23, 81, 91–2, 94–5, 97–9, 101–2,
    104–6, 144, 167
    incongruity theory of, 95, 100, 103
husband. *See* marriage

Idealism, German, 174, 176, 178, 184, 189
ideality, 16, 29, 31, 38–9, 49, 84, 86–8,
    174–6, 178, 209–10
identity, 4, 8, 21, 24, 88, 110, 126–30, 132,
    134, 136, 146, 151, 194, 197, 205,
    207, 211, 226
idle talk. *See* chatter
imaginary/imagination, 17, 38, 48–9, 54,
    56–7, 76, 79, 83, 110–11, 116–17,
    146, 159, 168, 170–1, 175
    construction (*see* experiment)
immediacy, 29, 44, 60–5, 75, 77, 84–6, 88,
    97, 110, 126, 143, 149, 151, 184, 223
inclosing reserve, 115, 127, 129–34, 136–7
infinitude, 17, 29, 64, 97, 148, 223
innocence, 97, 122–3, 126–31, 133
intent/intention (authorial), 1, 6, 8, 12,
    18–20, 76, 107, 109, 111, 117, 196,
    200, 228
intentionalism, 1, 187
interesting, 32
interiority. *See* inwardness
interpretation, 2, 5–9, 11–13, 15, 20–1,
    60, 76, 83, 92, 108–9, 113, 126, 148,
    174–5, 185, 187, 205–6, 208–10,
    226–7
inwardness, 29, 61–2, 69, 73, 97, 110–11,
    113, 119, 122, 124, 130, 134, 145,
    174, 181, 201
irony, 7, 13, 18–19, 25, 29–30, 32, 55–6,
    59–60, 62, 65, 72, 85, 97, 99, 104–5,
    110–11, 115, 144, 150, 163, 178,
    193, 202, 206, 209, 211–12, 215
Isaac (Biblical patriarch), 19, 142

Jacob (Biblical patriarch), 153
James, William, 154
Jaspers, Karl, 154
Jesus (Christ), 33–4, 36–7, 39, 41–2, 50,
    52–6, 103, 135, 153–4, 157–62, 169,
    211, 225
John (Apostle), 52
John Climacus (Saint), 103

Jolley, Kelly, 139
Joseph (Hebrew Bible figure), 153
Joseph (New Testament figure), 153
journalism, 1, 3, 15, 219–20
joy, 41, 47, 56, 69, 94, 98, 118
Judaism, 153, 206
Judas Iscariot (Apostle), 157–8
Julian (Roman emperor), 169
Julius Caesar, Gaius (Roman emperor), 211
justice, 47
justification, 8–9, 21, 30, 42–3, 45–6

Kabell, Aage, 94
Kafka, Franz, 117, 206
Kamuf, Peggy, 203–4
Kant, Immanuel, 25, 59, 95, 142, 146,
    175–80, 184
Kierkegaard, Peter Christian, 6, 107
Kierkegaard, Søren (anonyms and
    pseudonyms):
  A, 7, 60, 63, 81, 84–5, 89, 119, 165
  A. F. . . . ., 3
  Anti-Climacus, 5–6, 30, 33–4, 38, 106,
    107, 112, 117, 135, 199
  A-O, 4, 38, 116
  B/Judge William, 60, 79, 86, 119
  Constantin Constantius, 16, 24, 78–9,
    82, 86, 98, 103–4, 108, 155, 162–3,
    165–8, 170–1
  Frater Taciturnus, 80, 82–3, 103
  Hilarius Bookbinder, 80
  Inter et Inter, 86
  Johannes (the seducer), 60, 73, 118, 166
  Johannes Climacus, 5, 10, 15–16, 18,
    24, 73, 76, 79, 83, 95–8, 101–4, 109–
    10, 113–14, 117, 144–6, 150–1, 197
  Johannes de silentio, 3–4, 6–7, 10, 70,
    103, 108, 114, 116
  Jutland pastor, 60–1
  A Married Man, 86–7
  S. Kjerkegaard, 62
  Victor Eremita, 3, 16, 61, 108, 119
  Vigilius Haufniensis, 24, 121–36
  William Afham, 114
  young man (*Repetition*), 142, 166–8
  young man (*Stages on Life's Way*), 80, 84
Kierkegaard, Søren (writings):
  newspaper articles, 3, 6, 34, 101, 198,
    220

  published, 1–2, 14–15, 23, 81, 92, 94,
    99, 108, 196
    Christian Discourses, 12, 31, 34, 45,
      136
    The Concept of Anxiety, 24, 121–37
    On the Concept of Irony, 15–16, 25,
      27, 30, 59, 101, 208, 211–12
    *Concluding Unscientific Postscript
      to Philosophical Fragments*,
      2–3, 10, 15, 24, 35–6, 76, 83, 95,
      101–3, 109–10, 114, 116–17,
      140–4, 146, 149–52, 195, 197
    "The Crisis and a Crisis in the Life
      of an Actress," 86
    *Discourses at the Communion on
      Fridays*, 22, 28, 33–5, 38, 160–1
    Either/Or, 2–3, 7, 16, 35, 47, 59–62,
      70, 73, 79, 81, 101, 104, 106, 108,
      118–19, 165–6, 198, 220, 222
    "An Explanation and a Little More,"
      3–4
    Fear and Trembling, 3, 6, 10, 19, 93,
      101, 103, 108, 114, 141–2, 152,
      202
    "A First and Last Explanation," 2–3,
      5–6, 10, 109, 197, 199–200
    For Self-Examination, 33
    From the Papers of One Still Living,
      28, 62, 98, 100–1, 174–5, 187,
      197–8
    A Literary Review, 197 8
    "A Little Explanation," 3
    The Moment, 6, 16, 33–4
    On My Work as an Author, 2, 4–6,
      11–12, 32, 35, 70, 197–9
    Philosophical Fragments, 15–16, 95,
      102–3, 152
    Practice in Christianity, 31–6, 117,
      135, 160, 199
    Prefaces, 104
    "Public Confession," 3
    Repetition, 16, 78, 82, 101, 103–4,
      108, 155, 162–3, 165–7
    The Sickness unto Death, 31–3, 93,
      105–6, 117, 182
    Stages on Life's Way, 80, 82, 86,
      103–4, 114
    *Three Discourses on Imagined
      Occasions*, 195

Upbuilding Discourses, 3, 6, 12, 31,
  33, 68, 105, 108, 112–13, 117, 197
*Upbuilding Discourses in Various
  Spirits*, 31, 50, 105
"Who is the Author of *Either/Or*,"
  3, 198
Works of Love, 31, 47, 60–1, 67,
  69–73
signed, 3–4, 8, 14–15, 18, 20–1, 25,
  27, 34, 36, 60, 73, 146, 193, 196–8,
  201, 210
unpublished, 1, 4, 14–15, 23, 83
  The Book on Adler, 83
  journals, 2, 4–5, 18, 27, 30, 32,
    35–6, 38, 42, 81, 87–8, 94, 98–9,
    105–6, 107, 111–13, 115–16,
    118, 136, 158, 161, 165–7, 169,
    174, 195, 220, 222
  Judge for Yourself!, 33
  letters, 81–2
  notebooks, 2, 4, 81, 158
  papers, 4, 11, 94, 97, 106, 220
  *The Point of View for My Work as
    an Author*, 2, 4–6, 8, 11–13, 15,
    17, 21, 23, 25, 32, 59, 65, 68–70,
    107–11, 115–18, 181, 191,
    197–200, 218
  "The Single Individual," 68, 108,
    111–12, 115
Kirkconnell, W. Glen, 28
Kirmmse, Bruce H., 28, 174
Kligerman, Charles, 164
knowledge, 22, 42–3, 45–50, 53–4, 57, 63,
  123, 141–2, 147, 151, 182–3, 199,
  203, 208, 212
Kofman, Sarah, 25, 194, 201–2, 204–12

Laban (Hebrew Bible figure), 153
Lacan, Jacques, 109, 114
Lactantius, Lucius Caecilius Firmianus,
  169
language, 8, 10, 24, 62–8, 75–6, 81, 94,
  96–7, 100, 110, 113, 118, 121,
  123–37, 189, 191, 203, 205, 216,
  221–4, 226
Laozi, 153
Law, David R., 11, 28
leap, 7, 122–3, 131. *See also* faith
Lehmann, Edvard, 92

Lehmann, Orla, 5
Lessing, Gotthold Ephraim, 77
leveling, 51, 159
Levinas, Emmanuel, 111
lie/lying. *See* deception
life-view, 62, 174, 177, 180–2, 185, 187,
  197–8
linguistics. *See* language
Lippitt, John, 30, 92, 102, 104
listener/listening, 63, 169, 178, 215, 226–7
literalism, 7, 14, 21
literary theory, 8, 12, 14, 19–20, 75
literature, 1–2, 7, 11, 14–15, 17–18, 20, 22,
  25, 48, 61–2, 71, 76, 80, 82, 84, 93,
  100–1, 150, 162, 167, 173–6, 178,
  180–91, 193, 197, 200, 208–9, 216,
  218–20, 223, 225, 227
logic, 44, 48–9, 75, 175–6, 179–80, 185
love, 2, 17, 23, 31, 33, 41, 47, 49, 53, 59,
  60–73, 81–2, 84, 86–7, 94, 111–12,
  118, 140–2, 147–9, 156, 158, 161–6,
  181, 212, 223, 225–6
  first, 84–5, 167
  preferential, 69
Lowrie, Walter, 101–2, 107
Luft, Sebastian, 190–1
Luther, Martin, 146
Lutheranism, 6, 37, 93–4
lyric. *See* music

MacIntyre, Alasdair, 7–8
Mackey, Louis, 1, 6, 13, 20–1, 193
maieutics, 9, 13, 15–17, 29, 38, 60, 70–1,
  109, 115, 198, 210, 212
Malantschuk, Gregor, 97, 156
Malik, Habib C., 155
Manicheanism, 157, 163
manliness. *See* masculinity
Marion, Jean-Luc, 23, 60, 64–9
marriage, 60–1, 77, 79–82, 84, 86–8, 95,
  160, 162, 165–6
Martensen, Hans Lassen, 225
Martin, H. V., 92
Marxism, 218–19, 221
Mary (Mother of Jesus), 153
masculinity, 80, 205–6, 211–12
mask, 6, 12, 21, 88, 111–12, 114, 146, 212
Matuštík, Martin Beck, 17–18
mediation, 75, 167

meekness, 47

melancholia/melancholy, 33, 92, 94, 115, 129, 166

memory, 25, 64, 149, 215

metamorphosis, 86, 171

metaphysics, 4, 75

method/methodology, 1, 7–9, 12–14, 20–1, 61, 72, 109, 111, 157

midwife/midwifery. *See* maieutics

Milton, John, 166

mime/mimicry, 76, 142–4, 146, 149–50, 152, 168, 170, 181, 215, 223–4

mind, 2, 42, 48, 75, 94, 127, 146, 177–8, 185, 222, 224

mission/missionary, 23, 41–2, 53, 57

Møller, Poul Martin, 77–8, 87

Monnica (Saint), 164–5, 168, 170

mood, 7, 9–10, 49–51, 103–4, 167, 181, 226

Mooney, Edward F., 143, 147, 151–2

morality. *See* ethics

Moravscik, Julius, 46

Morreall, John, 94–5

Moses (Biblical prophet), 153

motion. *See* movement

movement, 35, 75–6, 81, 83, 86, 89, 113, 179, 216, 224, 226

Mozart, Wolfgang Amadeus, 7, 62, 165, 222

Muench, Paul, 15

Muhammad, 154

Müller-Wille, Klaus, 76–7

music, 7, 24, 44, 62–3, 140–1, 143–9, 152, 182, 189, 222–3

Mynster, Jacob Peter, 34, 39

mysticism, 68, 154–5, 170

name, 15, 30–4, 38, 54, 67, 96, 103, 108–9, 113, 126, 134, 146, 152, 184, 193–5, 197–208, 210–13

narrative, 25, 44–5, 47, 51, 57, 123–5, 146, 155, 167, 186

Nathan (Biblical prophet), 44–7

necessity, 77–8, 97, 150, 175–6, 179–81, 183, 185, 188, 196, 200–1, 204–5, 209, 219

neighbor, 17, 31, 60, 69–70, 72

Newmark, Kevin, 128

newspaper. *See* journalism

New Testament. *See* Bible

Nietzsche, Friedrich, 75, 208–10, 219

Nissen, Lowell Allen, 91

nonsense, 8, 10, 18, 21, 118, 136, 167, 195

Norris, Christopher, 20–1

nothingness, 34, 64–5, 85, 152, 180, 195, 203, 209

Novalis (Georg Philipp Friedrich Freiherr von Hardenburg), 217

novel. *See* literature

obedience, 47

objectivity, 10, 12, 24, 66–8, 79, 101–2, 110, 112–13, 121, 125, 136–7, 140, 147, 179, 200–1, 203

Oden, Thomas C., 91

O'Donnell, James J., 156, 164

offense, 98

Old Testament. *See* Bible

Olesen, Tonny Aalgaard, 92, 95

Olsen, Regine, 81, 88–9, 110, 155, 162–3, 165–8, 212

O'Meara, John J., 164

ontology, 110, 144

origin/original/originary, 29, 35, 60–1, 63, 71, 76, 86, 110, 112, 114, 122–4, 126–9, 131–2, 136, 145, 148–9, 184, 195–6, 202–4, 206–7

other/otherness, 62, 64–9, 110–13, 125–31, 133–5, 151, 162, 204–5, 207

pantomime. *See* mime/mimicry

parable, 51–3, 56, 105

paradox, 23, 46–7, 62, 88, 123, 139

Parrill, Lloyd Ellison, 91

passion, 10, 49, 57, 81, 92, 144, 166, 169 happy (*see* faith)

patience, 47

Patricius, 165

Pattison, George, 16–18, 79–80, 134–6, 156

Paul (Apostle), 51

Pelagius, 122

penitence/penitent, 22, 28, 37–9

pen name (*nom de plume*). *See* pseudonym/pseudonymity

performance/performative, 17, 66–7, 75–7, 82–3, 86, 110, 145, 148, 173–4, 196

Perkins, Robert L., 22, 28, 142

persona, 4, 9–10, 12, 15, 21, 32, 112, 116
personality, 23, 30, 61, 88, 113, 115–16,
      119, 176, 180, 182–4, 186, 188, 208,
      216
perspective, 5, 7–9, 12, 14, 22, 63, 73, 81,
      149, 170, 184, 186, 207, 209
Peter (Apostle), 52, 225
Phaenarete, 212
phenomenology, 12, 59–60, 62–4, 68–9, 93
philology, 15
philosophy, 1, 7, 9–11, 13–15, 19–20,
      22–5, 35, 44–5, 48, 59–60, 62, 64–5,
      69–70, 72–3, 75–7, 92, 94–6, 100,
      112, 117, 119, 122, 124–5, 139–41,
      143–5, 147, 149–50, 153–4, 157,
      174–5, 185, 187, 194, 196, 207–9,
      212, 215, 217, 220, 226–8
physical. *See* body
Pickett, Howard, 17, 170
Pindar, 226
Plato/Platonic, 16, 22, 48–9, 80, 196,
      208–10, 212, 228
play/playfulness, 76, 79, 81, 134–5, 190,
      205
playwright. *See* theater/theatrical
Plessner, Helmut, 78
Plutarch, 86
poet/poetics/poetry, 9, 12–14, 20, 22–3,
      25, 28, 32, 35, 38–9, 48–9, 51, 57,
      68, 70, 81, 84, 88, 103, 115–16, 145,
      147, 166, 173, 175–6, 178, 181,
      183, 185–6, 189, 197, 212, 215–18,
      220–7
point of view, 2, 4–7, 18, 20, 36, 70, 72,
      79, 118, 198, 201, 212. *See also*
      perspective
polemics, 25, 35, 100, 169, 199, 220
polyphony/polyvocality, 7, 224
Poole, Roger, 1, 10–12, 15, 18–21, 160
Possen, David D., 34
possibility, 24, 78–9, 97, 111, 121, 123,
      126, 179, 196, 204
postmodernism/poststructuralism, 12, 20
Potiphar (Hebrew Bible figure), 153
Poussin, Nicolas, 226
praise, 52–3, 55, 72–3, 181
presence, 37, 61, 96–7, 105, 130, 132,
      139–50, 152, 158, 161, 187, 195–6,
      198, 203, 205, 207, 211, 217, 222,
      226

pride, 50–1, 54–5, 69, 72, 159
Protestantism, 159. *See also* Lutheranism
providence, 20, 25, 155, 161–4, 218
pseudonym/pseudonymity, 1–10, 12–25,
      27–8, 30–6, 38–9, 48, 60–1, 68, 70,
      76, 81–2, 95, 98, 102–4, 106, 107–8,
      112, 114–17, 121, 137, 145–6,
      150–2, 166–7, 181, 193–9, 202, 208,
      211–13
psyche. *See* mind
psychoanalysis/psychology, 9, 21, 24, 45,
      47–9, 54, 77, 82, 95, 102, 123, 131,
      134, 139, 151, 205
public, 3–4, 38, 68, 70, 91–2, 106, 108, 118,
      160, 162, 169, 201, 218–19
publication/publishing, 2–4, 6, 20, 28,
      30–3, 38, 116, 189, 218–19
      posthumous, 2, 6, 33, 65, 70, 77, 107–8,
      115, 199, 206
publisher. *See* editor (*Udgiver*)
Puchniak, Richard, 155–6
punctuation, 9
purity (of heart), 47
Pyper, Hugh S., 126–7

Qiu Ying, 153
Qur'ān, 154

Randall, John Herman, 139
Raphael (Raffaello Sanzio da Urbino), 145,
      196
Read, Herbert, 222–3
reader/readership/reading, 2–3, 5–10, 13,
      17–23, 25, 27, 31–2, 36–7, 47–51,
      55–7, 59–60, 62–3, 68–9, 72, 76–7,
      82–4, 89, 92, 94, 98, 100–1, 105–6,
      108–15, 117–19, 125, 149, 151–2,
      174–5, 178–9, 181–3, 185–8, 190–1,
      193–4, 198–204, 208–10, 221,
      223–4
reality, 3, 21, 30, 37, 62, 67, 76, 79–80, 88,
      110–11, 113–14, 123–4, 131, 142,
      146–7, 149, 152, 155, 168, 174–6,
      185, 188–91, 198, 208–10, 216, 219,
      221, 224–5, 227
recollection, 134, 163, 166–7
redemption, 31, 130
reflection, 2, 39, 78, 85–6, 89, 101, 161,
      181–2, 186–7, 190, 194, 219, 221,
      223–4

Reich, Hermann, 168
religion/religious, 1, 19–20, 22, 24, 27–8, 38, 73, 86, 92, 94–6, 98, 107–8, 115, 118–19, 130–1, 144, 150, 153–5, 159, 162, 168, 184, 188, 190–1, 197–201, 211, 216–17, 219–21, 223, 227
renunciation, 24, 60, 110, 115, 117, 129
repetition, 25, 64, 75–6, 81, 84, 86, 89, 103, 149, 155, 167–8, 178, 181, 203
representation, 23, 75, 81, 88, 150, 221
responsibility, 4, 8, 32, 37, 67, 70, 88, 109, 113, 116, 122, 124–5, 135–6, 193–7, 204, 212
resurrection, 115–16, 118, 121, 137
review. *See* critic/criticism
revocation, 10, 112, 115, 146–7, 151
rhetoric, 7, 42, 44–5, 49–50, 163, 225
Ricoeur, Paul, 123
Rilke, Rainer Maria, 222, 227
Robinson, Marcia C., 17
role-playing, 18, 23, 77, 82, 84, 116, 183
Roman Catholicism, 159, 165
Romanticism, 140, 216, 219, 221, 227
Rötscher, Heinrich Theodor, 87–8
Rudd, Anthony, 140
Rushdie, Salman, 147–8

sacred. *See* holiness
sacrifice, 19, 36, 72, 88, 92, 110, 114, 151–2
Salinger, J. D., 145
salvation/savior, 24, 33–4, 41–2, 55, 93, 121, 123, 127, 129–34, 136–7, 163, 211
Sartre, Jean-Paul, 113
satire, 38, 99, 102, 144, 150
scene/scenery/scenography, 77–82, 85, 89, 109, 169
Schelling, Friedrich Wilhelm Joseph, 165
Schlegel, Johan Frederik, 167
Schlegel, K. Friedrich von, 217
Schleiermacher, Friedrich, 227
Schönbaumsfeld, Genia, 8, 14–15
Schopenhauer, Arthur, 95
Schousboe, Julius, 91
Scribe, Eugène, 84–5
scripture. *See* Bible
secrecy/secret, 61, 71, 77, 87, 118, 127–8
seducer/seduction, 60, 73, 118, 146

self, 12, 24, 47–8, 60, 62, 76–9, 105–6, 108, 110–11, 115, 121, 125–6, 128–31, 134, 136, 140, 170, 191, 194, 196, 201, 217
-abnegation, 151–2
-contradiction (*see* contradiction)
-deception (*see* deception)
-denial, 34, 69, 72, 88, 160
-doubling (*see* duplication)
-examination, 32–3
-forgetfulness, 24, 121, 125–6, 199
-identity (*see* identity)
-interpretation, 5, 7–9, 11
-knowledge, 34
-reflection (*see* reflection)
-sacrifice (*see* sacrifice)
-transformation (*see* transformation)
sense, 10, 44
seriousness. *See* earnestness
sermon, 36, 61, 159, 168
sex, 31, 66–7, 69, 128–9, 168, 205–6, 212
Shakespeare, Steven, 126
Shakespeare, William, 86, 145
shame, 33, 37, 54–5, 94
Shelley, Percy Bysshe, 166
signature, 6, 25, 184, 193–6, 198–208, 211–12
silence, 10, 29, 32–4, 64–5, 103, 114, 117–19, 127, 147, 149, 170, 200–1, 210, 212, 215, 222–3, 225, 227
simulacrum. *See* copy
sin, 24, 31, 33, 36–7, 92–3, 115, 122–7, 129–31, 133–6, 159–60, 162, 170, 211, 225
hereditary or original, 122, 126, 163
single individual, 29, 31, 37, 51, 66, 68, 70, 112, 159–60
Smith, Jr., Joseph, 154
Socinianism, 122
Socrates/Socratic, 9, 13, 15–17, 19, 22, 25, 27, 29–30, 32, 38, 46–8, 50, 53–4, 57, 59, 96, 109, 112, 146, 194, 196, 207–12
Söderquist, K. Brian, 30
Søltoft, Pia, 63
song. *See* music
Sontag, Frederick, 93
Sophroniscus, 212
soul, 36, 48–9, 54, 62, 97, 139–40, 157, 163, 165, 170–1, 212, 222

speaking/speech, 10, 38, 42, 65–7, 72, 76, 80, 97, 110, 113, 118, 123–5, 136, 140, 147, 152, 178, 207, 211, 224–5, 227

spectator, 18, 37, 77–8, 84, 86–8, 98, 144, 146, 169–70, 176, 186

spheres. *See* stages (of existence)

Spinoza, Baruch, 69

stage (theatrical), 9, 17–18, 78, 80–2, 84, 109, 139, 141, 152, 171

stages (of existence), 60, 97, 168
    aesthetic, 2, 7, 12–14, 23, 27, 32, 35, 47, 49, 60, 72–3, 79–80, 97, 107–8, 113, 168, 197, 216
    ethical, 2, 47–8, 79, 97, 168
    religious, 2, 5, 12–14, 23, 25, 27, 32, 39, 72–3, 80, 97, 168, 198

Stewart, Jon, 15

story/storytelling, 17, 25, 44–6, 48, 78, 151, 174–5, 178, 184, 186, 188–91

Strawser, Michael, 13–15, 60, 63, 70, 72–3, 196

style, 7–9, 22, 75, 91, 107, 121, 150, 152, 196, 207, 216–18, 221, 223, 225

subjectivity, 10, 12, 29, 67–8, 94, 98, 108, 110, 112–13, 119, 134, 139, 142, 148, 150, 176–7, 181, 200–1, 203–4

suffering, 33–4, 44, 50, 55–6, 65, 80, 87, 92–3, 119, 158–60, 166, 169–70

Swenson, David F., 100–2
    and Lilian Swenson, 107

synthesis, 97, 127–8, 174–8, 180–2

Taylor, Mark C., 16

temperance, 47

temporality/time, 28, 50, 80, 97, 118, 167, 177, 184, 188, 221, 226

terror, 141, 147–50, 152

Tertullian (Quintus Septimius Florens Tertullianus), 169

Thales, 96

theater/theatrical, 1, 9, 16–18, 23, 75, 77–80, 83–8, 99, 116, 139–41, 144–5, 168–71, 180, 189, 220

theology, 1, 6–7, 11, 17, 23, 42, 49, 59, 68, 94, 156–7, 215–16, 225, 227

Theunissen, Michael, 11

Thompson, Josiah, 112

Thomte, Reidar, 51

Thorvaldsen, Bertel, 160

Tietjen, Mark, 1, 11–12, 22, 28, 73

title, 10, 24, 80, 92–3, 95, 100, 105, 114, 141–7, 149–50, 152, 198, 200, 206, 208

Tolkien, J. R. R., 25, 175, 188–90

tomb, 117, 165, 202, 206–7, 211

tone, 9, 51, 100, 140, 182, 222–3

tragedy, 82, 88, 92, 110, 113, 143–4, 149, 152, 168, 170, 175, 180, 183, 186, 226

transcendence, 93, 154–5, 167–8

transfiguration, 86, 104, 180, 191, 209

transformation, 12, 37, 41–2, 62, 68, 75, 79, 86, 88, 162, 167, 185, 226

transubstantiation, 62, 180, 191

truth, 7, 18–20, 29, 39, 41–3, 45, 47, 54, 68, 70, 87–8, 93, 95, 98, 101–2, 108, 110, 112–13, 116, 118, 134, 136, 139, 145, 149–50, 158, 177–80, 185, 199, 203, 208–11, 216, 226, 228

typesetting, 9, 219

undecidability, 13–14, 25, 70, 72–3, 201, 204–5

understanding, 22, 41–51, 53–4, 56–7, 59, 77, 83–4, 87, 97, 106, 108, 110–11, 117, 122, 124, 139, 141, 151, 179, 196, 198–202, 216, 225, 228
    mis-, 12–13, 42, 85, 108, 136, 158, 185

union, 68–9

unity, 23, 25, 75, 108, 119, 134, 174–8, 181, 185, 187, 196, 221

universality, 31, 49, 79, 174–80, 182–3, 185, 190

upbuilding. *See* edification/edifying

Updike, John, 99

Van der Leeuw, Gerardus, 168–70

veronymity/veronymous, 4, 60, 196

Verstrynge, Karl, 174–6

vice, 50–1

Virgil (Publius Vergilius Maro), 158, 164–5, 169

virtue, 47–57, 135, 157
    epistemology, 45
    ethics, 12, 49

vocation, 23, 25, 49, 57, 201, 216–17, 221, 223, 227

voice, 7, 15, 23, 37, 52, 73, 112, 114, 140, 147, 222, 224
void. *See* nothingness
Vollmer, Wilhelm, 166
Vor Frue Kirke, 17, 35–6, 160
Vulgate. *See* Bible

Wagner, Richard, 223
Walsh, Sylvia, 28, 30–1, 35, 39, 162
Waltman, Milton, 188
Watkin, Julia, 100
Weber, Max, 155
Westfall, Joseph, 6, 16, 28, 173–4, 184, 187, 193, 196, 210
Whitmire, Jr., John E., 28
will, 130, 134–5, 151, 162
 -power, 80
 to power, 211
 weakness of (*akrasia*), 46, 182
Williams, Robin, 94
wisdom, 87, 127, 144–5, 151, 157, 165, 170
 practical (*phronesis*), 47–8
Wittgenstein, Ludwig, 10, 14, 48–9, 141, 150

woman, 37, 82, 84, 127–8, 164–5, 211–12, 225
wonder, 52, 55, 87, 142–3, 147–50, 152
Wong, Joe, 95
word(s), 3, 7, 9–10, 33, 44, 47–9, 51–2, 64–6, 71, 85, 94, 96–7, 101, 109, 113, 130–1, 135, 139–41, 145–6, 149, 152, 195, 197–9, 210, 213, 221, 223–5, 227–8
writer/writing, 2–5, 8–9, 18, 21, 23, 33, 59–60, 62–7, 71, 73, 76, 83, 99–100, 109–10, 113–14, 117, 121, 139–41, 146, 149, 151–2, 155, 185, 194–200, 202–4, 206–7, 209–13, 216–21, 223–5, 227

Xenophon, 196, 208–10
Xu, Donfeng, 153

Young, Brigham, 154

Zhuangzi, 153
Ziolkowski, Eric, 22, 27, 71, 154, 158, 164
Zuckert, Rachel, 184

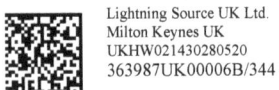

9 781350 163812